Praise for **See What You Made Me Do**

"A landmark work by one of our finest journalists."

—Nick Feik, editor, *The Monthly*

"*See What You Made Me Do* is a thorough, thoughtful, solutions-oriented examination that demands to be taken seriously... The most important work of Australian nonfiction this year."

—Zora Simic, *Australian Book Review*

"Jess Hill is a brave woman. Her book, *See What You Made Me Do*, gives us a chance—just a slim one—to shift our thinking on domestic violence past the stalemate we are in."

—Gay Alcorn, *The Guardian*

"Sometimes you begin reading a book and everything else you need to do or think about instantly recedes. *See What You Made Me Do* by Jess Hill is one such book... To call it courageous is a gross understatement."

—Elke Power, *Readings Monthly*

"Walkley Award–winning journalist Jess Hill's experience as a Middle East correspondent is evident in her coverage of another battleground closer to home: the horror of domestic abuse... *See What You Made Me Do* is an outstanding piece of investigative journalism."

—Kirsten Krauth, *The Saturday Paper*

"[*See What You Made Me Do*] is startling. I couldn't stop reading it and it made me understand the issue in a very different way than it's ever been explained to me."

—Ellen Fanning, host, *The Drum*

"Essential reading... Should be thrust into the hands of every Australian—man, woman, medical professional, police officer, social worker, politician, teacher, writer."

—*Good Reading*

"In all my long acquaintance with the subject, I've never come across such a thorough examination... It's my bet that *See What You Made Me Do* will be the definitive text on domestic abuse for some time."

—Sara Dowse, *The Canberra Times*

"Comprehensive, well-researched, and exquisitely written...a unique and powerful contribution... If *See What You Made Me Do* is a call for action, then it is unlike any that has yet been written in Australia in its accessibility, depth of research, and in its capacity, unlike government or academic reports, to capture the visceral feeling of domestic terror."

—Alecia Simmonds, *Sydney Review of Books*

"Anyone who wants to understand the pattern, cause, and effect of domestic abuse should read this book... It might be the one thing that takes someone from thinking domestic abuse only happens to 'other people' to understanding it as a pervasive, pernicious, deadly behavior that they might have the power to change."

—Jane Gilmore, *The Sydney Morning Herald*

"This book represents a new way of thinking about and acting on domestic abuse...and is an example of exceptional research and the power of storytelling in nonfiction."

—*The Garret Podcast*

"Confronting in its honesty, this book challenges you to keep reading no matter how uncomfortable it is to face the profound rawness of people's stories. Such a well-written book and so well researched, *See What You Made Me Do* sheds new light on this complex issue that affects so many of us."

—Rosie Batty, survivor advocate and Australian of the Year

"Hill is an investigative journalist who has been writing about domestic violence for a large portion of her career, and her experience shows... [She] sets out her argument in a measured, factual but highly engaging way that covers every side of the argument. Refreshingly, there is no rant... She is relentless in her search for facts.

—Jen Bowden, *Westerly Magazine*

"With gut-wrenchingly confronting stories and deep, primary-sourced research, Hill's book provides a deep exploration of historical, institutional, and political failures, but what stuck with me was her analysis of where men fit in all of this—our sense of entitlement, our rage at our own shame, at our failed performance of manhood."

—Phil Barker, advocate, No to Violence

see
what
YOU
made
me
do

see what YOU made me do

The Dangers of Domestic Abuse That We
Ignore, Explain Away, or Refuse to See

JESS HILL

sourcebooks

Published by Sourcebooks
P.O. Box 4410, Naperville, Illinois 60567-4410
(630) 961-3900
sourcebooks.com

Originally published as *See What You Made Me Do* in 2019 in Australia by Black Inc., an imprint of Schwartz Publishing.

Library of Congress Cataloging-in-Publication Data is on file with the publisher.

Printed and bound in the United States of America.
SB 10 9 8 7 6 5 4 3 2 1

Contents

Notes on My Methods

In this book, wherever possible, I have replaced the term "domestic violence" with "domestic abuse." I did this because in some of the most dangerous cases of domestic abuse, physical violence is rare, minor, or barely present. As victim advocate Yasmin Khan writes in an article for *Women's Agenda*, "Many women that we support assure me there has been no domestic violence—'he's never laid a hand on me'—but on deeper questioning and reflection, realize they have been abused for many years, in ways that have been more subtle but [are] just as damaging and potent."[1] Khan has made it her mission to replace "domestic violence" with "domestic abuse," as police have done in the UK. "Let's change the language," she writes, "and stop sending a message…that it's only a serious issue when there has been physical violence." When I read Khan's article, it stopped me in my tracks. I knew immediately: We need to make this change. The entire book was reedited to reflect it, where appropriate, and the subtitle was changed on the cover. As my wonderful editor Kirstie Innes-Will assured me, the gain is worth the effort.

On the subject of language, I understand that terms like "victim" and "survivor" are loaded, and many who have lived through domestic abuse prefer one or the other (or neither). Even when someone has left an abusive person, the abuse may continue; they may alternate between feeling like a victim and survivor; or they may occupy both roles simultaneously. The term "perpetrator" is also vexed, particularly because it conveys a two-dimensional picture that is essentially dehumanizing. It's a far from perfect term, but I use it for two reasons. Firstly, there is no other efficient term to replace it. Secondly, it can actually be liberating for victims/survivors—and an important step in their recovery—to see their abuser in two-dimensional terms. It gives them permission to stop trying to help the perpetrator and to reconsider the abusive process with some objectivity; and it gives them the space to start the process of deprogramming themselves from the perpetrator's influence.

There is a distinct power imbalance built into the journalist–source relationship, because the journalist usually has ultimate power over what gets published. For the survivors featured in this book, I wanted to flip that and give the power back to them. If this process was not a positive experience for them, there was no point in doing it. Every survivor I interviewed was reassured that this was *their* story, not mine. This meant giving them the chance to review their stories, suggest revisions, or ask for things to be deleted—especially if there were safety concerns. The process was sometimes laborious but always worthwhile. It has been an honor to work with every one of them.

Where necessary, I have also omitted the cultural backgrounds of several people in this book. I did so either for the survivor's protection or because I have identified them as parties to a family law case (and it's therefore illegal, under Australian legislation, to say more).

Much of the analysis in this book is also applicable to same-sex relationships. It was a difficult decision to write in the male/female binary, but I did so because men's violence against women is by far the most serious. Men's violence must be named. I do, however, deeply regret any pain that causes to survivors of same-sex abuse. This book is written for you, too.

As I am both Australian and Australia-based, that's where much of my investigation on the ground has taken place (though several accounts included here are from the United States and the UK). However, the relevance of such stories extends far beyond Australia. I have drawn on research, news stories, policies/laws, and interviews with experts from across the

Western world. As this book strives to show, this is a crisis of human nature, connected inextricably to the history of Western society and culture. The words of Australian survivors quoted in these pages have a universal resonance; the details of their stories are not specific to one nation, even when they concern the justice and family law system. It's actually astounding just how many commonalities appear in domestic abuse stories from across the Western world, even in how victims/survivors and perpetrators are responded to by different criminal justice and family law systems.

Although this book was originally published in Australia, it now reads as though it were written for an American audience, because I spent many months updating this edition with new statistics and stories from across North America. Where I've retained original Australian sources, I say so explicitly, so there will be no confusion.

The stories in the chapter on family law are those of adult and child survivors. It was considered unsafe to contact the alleged abusers in each case. I did, however, look carefully at their affidavits, and strove to be as fair as possible.

Some of the ideas in this book are heavily contested, as I have made clear throughout. Although I've been fortunate enough to have some of the best minds review many of the following chapters, the responsibility for errors and inaccuracies is entirely mine. If you notice something of concern, please contact me, and I will do my best to correct future editions.

Introduction

At the office of Safe Steps, a 24-7 family violence helpline, the phones have gone quiet. "I get nervous when they stop ringing," says one worker. It's a rare occurrence. At its busiest, Safe Steps receives a call every three minutes. Many women are repeat callers: on average, they will return to an abusive partner seven times before leaving for good.

"You must get so frustrated when you think a woman's ready to leave and then she decides to go back," I say.

"No," replies one phone counselor pointedly. "I'm frustrated that even though he promised to stop, he chose to abuse her again."

———————

A year into my reporting on domestic abuse, I had a terrible realization. It was 2015, and I was hanging clothes out to dry on a stunning summer night. The air was cool on my skin. I felt content, peaceful, safe. As I walked toward our back steps, washing basket in hand, a cascade of thoughts swept through me with such force it made my eyes sting. To feel safe in the dark—even in my own backyard—was a *privilege*. How many women would never feel safe in their backyard? How many would be approaching their back steps with a sense of dread? How many would be steeling themselves for what might happen to them in bed that night? How many would feel their breath quicken at every rustle of leaves, terrified that somewhere in the dark, the man they once loved was waiting for them?

We talk a lot about the danger of dark alleys, but the truth is that in every country around the world the home is the most dangerous place for a woman. Of the eighty-seven thousand women killed globally in 2017, more than a third (thirty thousand) were killed by an intimate partner, and another twenty thousand by a family member.[1] Every day in the United States, four women are killed by a man they've been intimate with.[2] These statistics tell us something that's almost impossible to grapple with: it's not the monster lurking in the dark women should fear, but the men they fall in love with.

———————

This is a book about love, abuse, and power. It's about a phenomenon that flourishes in private and in public, perpetrated mostly by men who evade scrutiny. It's about all the questions we don't ask, such as: "Why does *he* do it?" It's about turning our stubborn beliefs and assumptions inside out and confronting one of the most complex—and urgent—issues of our time.

For the first time in history we have summoned the courage to confront domestic abuse. This has been a radical shift, and in years to come, 2014 will likely stand as the year when the Western world finally started taking men's violence against women seriously. But nowhere did an entire population wake up to it like Australia did on the 12th of February that year. For me, the events of that day would also change the direction of my life and my work.

On that day, Australians watched a solitary woman, raw with grief, look downward and skyward and out across a clutch of reporters who'd barely hoped for a statement. An ordinary woman standing in a middle-class Australian street talking about the public murder of her eleven-year-old son at the hands of his father. An ordinary woman who for eleven years had struggled to keep her son safe and protect the love he had for his father. After all, wasn't that what she was supposed to do? Bury her own fear and manage the risk, so her child could have a dad?

"No one loved Luke more than Greg, his father. No one loved him more than me," Rosie Batty insisted, defending the love of a father who had just beaten and stabbed her son to death. After surviving and leaving Greg's violence, she had warned for years that he was dangerous, unpredictable, and a risk to her son. In courts and police stations her warnings had been minimized, dismissed, believed, acted on, and then lost in the system, just like those of countless victims before her. Now her predictions had come true. Not behind closed doors, where such horrors are usually carried out, but in front of children and parents on a public cricket ground. "If anything comes out of this, I want it to be a lesson to everybody," said Rosie Batty on the street that day. "Family violence happens to everybody, no matter how nice your house is, how intelligent you are. It happens to everyone and anyone."

In the eyes of mainstream Australia, Batty *was* everyone—not from the stigmatized poor or the privileged rich, but from the demilitarized zone of the white middle class. When she refused to go away and mourn quietly, her urgent pleas for action—backed by the force of her colossal loss—breached the barrier of indifference and compelled people to take notice. Her grief was pure and blameless, and everybody was invited to share it. As a nation, the scales fell from our eyes the day Luke Batty was murdered. Forty years after the first women's refuge opened in Australia, we were finally ready to believe in domestic abuse. Survivors—once exiled from respectable society—were invited to tell their stories. We were ready to listen. We *needed* to understand. Their stories made headline news—not just for a few weeks, but for months on end. I personally set aside every other issue I was writing about and have focused exclusively—and obsessively—on domestic abuse ever since. By the end of that year, the Premier of Victoria, the state Luke lived and died in, would announce the formation of a royal commission to investigate family abuse and violence. To this day, each of the more than two hundred recommendations from that commission are being acted on. Victoria's response has been utterly transformed; that state now has what is arguably the most well-funded and comprehensive response to domestic abuse in the world.

It's hard to pinpoint why, after so many tragedies and decades of advocacy, one murder became such a decisive tipping point, but Luke's murder occurred at a critical time. All over the world, survivors were casting off their shame and demanding to be heard. By April 2014, the White House had been persuaded to intervene on American campuses, where sexual assaults were common, and the perpetrators largely unpunished.[3] "We all know that many of our schools just aren't safe," said Vice President Joe Biden, "[and] colleges and universities can no longer turn a blind eye." A month later, in May, the misogynistic ravings of Elliot Rodger turned to murderous rage near the University of California, where he killed six and injured fourteen. Rodger murdered more men than he did women, and he was probably mentally ill, but the animating force of his misogyny was undeniable. In a chilling 137-page manifesto, he railed against the "sluts" who denied him the sex he saw as his birthright and the men who were taking his rightful due. "The girls don't flock to the gentlemen. They flock to the alpha male," Rodger wrote. "Who's the alpha male now, bitches?"[4]

Rodger's worldview wasn't that of a lone madman; it was echoed and encouraged in the online forums he frequented and the men's rights groups he joined. It was forced on women online by trolls who threatened them (and often their children) with rape and violence. For women all over the world, seeing this familiar brand of hate turn to murder was the final straw. A hashtag, #YesAllWomen, became a rallying point, eliciting more than a million vignettes of fear, harassment, threats, and violence. Later that year, the public assault on Janay Palmer by her NFL-star fiancé, Ray Rice, triggered another tidal wave of online truth-telling, this time about domestic abuse, with the hashtag #WhyIStayed. "I have been waiting all my life for what 2014 has brought," commented the American writer Rebecca Solnit. "It was a watershed year for women, and for feminism, as we refused to accept the pandemic of violence against women—the rape, the murder, the beatings, the harassment on the streets, and the threats online."[5] Survivors— once exiled from respectable society—were finally being invited to tell their stories. We were ready to listen. We *needed* to understand.

With these stories came shocking statistics. Across America, more than twelve million people are subjected to rape, physical violence, or stalking by an intimate partner every year.[6] Nearly one million women have survived being shot or shot at by an intimate partner.[7] Nearly twenty people are assaulted every minute.[8] More than 80 percent of mothers homeless with their children have experienced domestic abuse.[9] American police are called to a domestic incident every forty seconds.[10]

The media, obsessed with Islamic terrorism, had let a gigantic crime wave go virtually unreported. The public was reeling. How could this be true? What was causing it? How could violence against women still be so widespread?

———

Domestic abuse cuts a deep wound into our society. It has been experienced by one in three American women.[11] It drives up to one in five female suicide attempts.[12] Of the escalating population of women in prison, 77 percent— primarily women of color, incarcerated for nonviolent offenses—have been subjected to intimate partner violence.[13] From this yawning chasm comes a never-ending exodus of women and children, fleeing their homes: in a single day in the United States in 2015, more than 31,500 adults and children sought refuge in an emergency shelter or transitional housing program— and almost eight thousand more could not be accommodated, because there were simply no beds for them.[14] We see the impact of domestic abuse every- where, but rarely do we trace the breadcrumbs back to where the destruc- tion begins. We see only the ruinous aftermath—rising homelessness, more and more women in prison—and wonder how things got so bad.[15]

We may be able to grasp *intellectually* that domestic abuse can happen to anyone, but many of us still can't imagine it affecting anyone we know— even when the evidence is right in front of us. This is what the Australian national chair of The Women's Services Network (WESNET), Julie Oberin, hears routinely from the aspiring social workers she teaches. "[In the beginning] they say things like, 'I don't know anybody who's been a victim of domestic violence,'" she says. "By week three, we get disclosures. They say, 'I realize my childhood was a family violence childhood, but no one's ever named it.' One woman said, 'I rang my sister, and I said, you're in a domestic violence relationship—he's controlling everything you do and everywhere you go, you need to get some help.' There's a big barrier [to seeing domestic violence], because there is all that focus on *some* people, rather than an understanding of it being entrenched throughout the society."

That focus on *some* people leads us to believe that domestic abuse only happens to certain types of women: the poor, the vulnerable, the mentally ill, or those with "victim" mentalities. Some women *are* overrepresented: those who are Indigenous, disabled, or on insecure visas; those who grew up with domestic abuse; the young; and women who live in rural communities. In regional and remote areas, reported incidents of physical violence are higher than in the cities—and women there are even more trapped than their urban counterparts.[16] But when police and victim advocates say that domestic abuse can affect *anyone*, they're not making it up. In all reputable studies of domestic abuse survivors—and there have been thousands—not one researcher has been able to find a victim "type." As one review concludes, "there is no evidence that the status a woman occupies, the role she performs, the behavior she engages in, her demographic profile or her personality characteristics consistently influence her chance of intimate victimization."[17] In the hands of a sophisticated abuser, even the most secure and strong-minded woman can be reduced to someone utterly unrecognizable, even to herself.

Well-meaning people often say we should stop using terms like "domestic abuse" or "domestic violence," insisting that such language hides a brutal reality and that we should instead call it what it is: assault, or terrorism, or just "violence." But this misses the point. Domestic abuse is not *just* violence. It's worse. It is a unique phenomenon, in which the perpetrator takes advantage of the partner's love and trust and uses that person's most intimate details—deepest desires, shames, and secrets—as a blueprint for the abuse.

We also say domestic abuse is a crime, but that's not quite right, either. Crimes are incidents: if you get assaulted, you can call the police and report an assault. Criminal offenses are committed *within* domestic abuse, but the worst of it cannot be captured on a charge sheet. A victim's most frightening experiences may never be recorded by police or understood by a judge. That's because domestic abuse is a horrifying language that develops slowly and is spoken only by the people involved. Victims may be terrified by a sideways look, a sarcastic tone, or a stony silence, because these are the signals to which they have become hyperattuned, the same way animals can sense an oncoming storm. These are the signals that tell them danger is close, or that it has already surrounded them.

For many victims, the physical violence is actually what hurts the least. Almost uniformly, victims who haven't been physically assaulted say they wish their abuser would just hit them...anything to make the abuse "real."

After all, it's not a crime to demand that your girlfriend no longer see her family. It's not a crime to tell her what to wear, how to clean the house, and what she's allowed to buy at the supermarket. It's not a crime to convince your wife she's worthless, or to make her feel that she shouldn't leave the children alone with you. It's not a crime to say something happened when it didn't, or to say it so many times that you break her sense of what's real. You can't be charged for turning someone's entire family against them. And yet these are the kinds of controlling behaviors that show up as red flags for domestic homicide. By the time that "real" crime occurs, it's too late.

––––––––––

For decades now, experts have recognized that the repetitive infliction of traumas like these can produce a form of mental captivity in which victims struggle to define their own reality. In this abusive environment, minor assaults and humiliations can occur so regularly that they become as unremarkable as breathing. Even if we could find a reliable way to criminalize this behavior, how might survivors prove that in so many ways they were trapped—even though it looked to the world like they could have just left? For friends and family, especially those who've never experienced domestic abuse, none of this makes sense. It doesn't make sense that women who are smart and independent will stay with a man who treats them like dirt. It doesn't make sense that even after fleeing, a woman will often return to her abuser, and even plead for him to take her back. It doesn't make sense that someone known as a good bloke could be going home to hold a knife to his wife's throat. If we were to think about *his* actions as much as we think about hers, it would make even less sense that a man who inflicts abuse on his partner would want to stay—or even kill her after she leaves. Why does *he* stay?

None of it makes sense. What's even more confusing is that the perpetrator commonly believes with all his heart that *he* is the victim, and will plead his case to police even as his partner stands bloody and bruised behind him. These perpetrators' victimhood is what makes them feel their abuse is justified. They're not like those other men, because they're just defending themselves.

This is the kind of doublethink that enables an abuser to say—and believe—that violence against women is wrong. Four months before convicted murderer Steven Peet was arrested for the murder of Adeline

Wilson-Rigney and her two young children, Amber Rose and Korey Lee Mitchell, he shared a Facebook post that said, "The day you raise your hand to a woman. That day you're officially not a man!"[18] When he posted that, he probably meant it. If we are to confront domestic abuse, we need to make sense of these baffling contradictions.

It is now common to hear male politicians and business leaders say things like "real men don't hit women," but they are still sidestepping the root of domestic abuse. Men don't abuse women because society tells them it's okay. Men abuse women because society tells them they are entitled to be in control. In fact, society says that if they are *not* in control, they won't succeed: they won't get the girl, they won't get the money, and they will be vulnerable to the violence and control of other men. Men who internalize these beliefs won't necessarily become abusers. Many will enjoy remarkable success, some will spend a lifetime wrestling with these beliefs, and a shocking number of them will end up committing suicide, believing they have failed. But for some of these men—those with a pathological sense of entitlement—getting their way at home is a birthright. "Addressing control," writes sociologist Evan Stark, "is far more difficult than stopping men from being violent."[19] So it's one thing for male leaders to proclaim that "real men don't hit women," even when they mean it. But how could they ever honestly campaign against the dangerous norm that men should be in control, when they are so often living examples of that ethos?

————

Once upon a time, domestic abuse was somebody else's business. Now it's everybody's business.

However, in a cruel twist, the increased attention on men's violence— amplified by the #MeToo movement—may actually be making perpetrators more dangerous. In homes across the globe, abusive men, furious that women are getting all the attention while *their* suffering is ignored, are taking out their humiliated fury on their girlfriends, wives, and children. The backlash is real, and it's violent. When I visited Safe Steps, then-CEO Annette Gillespie told me they had recorded an increase in the frequency and severity of assaults being reported, and had victims calling in to say that awareness campaigns were making their abusers more volatile. "Women will call and say, 'Can you get them to stop the ad on TV, can you ask them to stop talking about family violence? Because every time he sees that ad he goes nuts.'"

In this book, I focus mostly on men's violence against women, because in scale and severity, it is by far the most dangerous kind. But heterosexual men didn't invent abuse, and they're not the only ones to inflict it. Domestic abuse is also suffered, often in silence, by a high percentage (possibly as high as 28 percent)[20] of women in same-sex relationships, whose partners may convince them that if they report it they will be exiled from their community, bring shame on same-sex relationships, and be laughed at by police. It's suffered by gay men, whose subordination may be secured with threats to out them or to reveal their HIV status. In this way, same-sex partner abuse is produced by the same patriarchal conditions that produce men's violence against women. It is held in place by the heterosexism and homophobia that are central to patriarchy. Ultimately, domestic abuse is a pattern of power and control, and power imbalances aren't limited to heterosexual relationships. As one of America's leading sociologists on gender and violence, Dr. Claire Renzetti, argues, those who perpetrate violence in same-sex relationships still do so from a position of unequal power; the greater the power difference, the more severe the physical and psychological abuse.[21]

Meanwhile, in heterosexual relationships, domestic abuse is also suffered by a smaller proportion of men, who (like women) often stay in the vain hope that they can help their abusive partners, and who may be trapped by the fear that they won't be able to protect their children if they leave.

––––––––––

The recent awakening to domestic abuse threatens to initiate us into a dark reality: that tens of millions have inflicted pain, suffering, and even sadistic torture on people they professed to love.

We've faced a painful awakening like this before. In the mid-2000s, we went from believing that children were only sexually abused by a few bad priests to acknowledging that child rapists were not only endemic within the clergy, they were systematically protected by the Vatican. We're at a similar point now with domestic abuse. This is a historic shift in power and accountability, but it's a fragile one. Making it stick will require nerve and determination. In the words of world-leading trauma expert Judith Herman, "It is very tempting to take the side of the perpetrator. All the perpetrator asks is that we do nothing. The victim, on the contrary, asks the bystander to share the burden of pain. The victim demands action, engagement, and remembering."[22] If we flinch and decide that's too hard, domestic abuse may once again disappear from sight.

Domestic abuse is deeply disturbing and yet endlessly fascinating for what it tells us about ourselves: how we relate, how we love, and how we govern. That's why I've spent the past six years obsessing over it. I've never experienced domestic abuse myself, but in my quest to understand it, I have uncovered much about myself, my relationships, society, power, and justice.

In the chapters that follow, we will travel through an extraordinary landscape, from the confounding psychology of perpetrators and victims to the Kafkaesque absurdity of the family law system. Through the eyes of survivors and perpetrators, I've been taken into the horrific underworld of domestic abuse. Now is the time for all of us to see what is hiding in plain sight.

1.

The Perpetrator's Handbook

Humiliation is worse than physical pain.

THE TALMUD

It's a sparkling Saturday afternoon in a pretty suburban neighborhood. The people who live here have faith and money: the streets are immaculate, and the houses are huge. Outside one house, a pile of household items is all that blights the row of manicured lawns. As is typical in suburbs like this, there are signs of life but nobody on the street.

Nobody except for a slight man in an oversize white tank top, leaning into a car. As I approach, he waves. "My son's selling his car, so I'm taking off the most valuable part of it," laughs Rob Sanasi, triumphantly waving a toll pass above his head.

We walk into the house at the bottom of the driveway to find an elegant blond woman and two twenty-somethings milling around the kitchen, joking and making plans for the weekend. This is the house Rob shares with his wife, Deb, and their two adult children.

Deb puts on the teakettle, and Rob brings out some cookies, one of which has already been partially enjoyed. "Oh, nice," he says apologetically. "Someone graciously put that one back there."

Deb guffaws from behind the kitchen counter. "You don't want to feel the guilt of taking a whole one!"

Rob shrugs, smiling. "Yeah, it's the quirk in this family."

As the kids wave their goodbyes, new cookies are found, and tea is poured. Then we sit down together at the kitchen table to talk about Rob and Deb's history of domestic abuse.

Rob begins his story in 2006. It was a bad time: his business was failing; his family life was falling apart. "Deb and I were...well, when I say Deb and I were fighting, I was fighting more, but it looked like *we* were fighting. I remember driving along on the motorway... I was in a bad way. Actually, that day, I thought: this is probably going to be my last day."

Rob, a devout Christian, thought about driving his car into a tree. Then he put on a recording of a church minister addressing a large auditorium. "And he just said something... It was, 'Do you love your children?' And I answered in the car, 'Yeah, of course I do.' And then he said, 'Would you die for them?' and I said, 'Yeah, I would.' And he said, 'Well, you'll probably never have to die for your children, but if you're willing to die for them, why won't you change for them?' And when I heard that, I just thought, *Wow*." At that moment, Rob says, he realized he had to seek counseling.

Deb shakes her head. "Can I interject? The reason that Rob went into counseling was I went into the workforce. The control had been very strong in our relationship, but actually neither of us really realized to what degree Rob was controlling me, until I did something that he couldn't control. Within three weeks of me starting that job, Rob had a nervous breakdown. He lost thirty pounds, he was having anxiety and panic attacks, he became addicted to Xanax, he was suicidal. That's what drove him into counseling. He was a mess." Rob nods quietly.

During their first session, Rob says his counselor asked him a series of questions. "Do you raise your voice, do you yell, do you throw things, do you call your wife names, do you swear, do you bash things—not her, but *things*—and it was kind of tick, tick, tick," Rob remembers. "And then he went to a filing cabinet in his office and pulled out a piece of paper with a preprinted 'Cycle of Violence' on it, and he whacked that on the table, and he said, 'That's what you do. This is what we call domestic violence.'"

"So that was the first session. And he said, 'Take that with you and discuss it with your wife.' So I was like, *I don't think that's a very good idea, right?*"

Rob wasn't physically violent, but he behaved like a typical perpetrator: he constantly criticized and bullied his wife, tried to stop her from working, made it hard for her to see family and friends, and kept total control over their bank accounts. The bullying and criticism weren't always overt; sometimes Rob would use humor to demean Deb. But it was always sending the same message: he was more important than she was, and she was there to serve him. The only thing that wasn't typical about Rob was that he had sought counseling without being forced.

At first, Rob kept the piece of paper to himself. "And then eventually I thought, *Oh, I'll just bring it out casually, you know.* But when I brought it out, things got a lot worse. Because then Deb realized what was going on. It's kind of like the scales fell off our eyes—both of us."

I ask Deb what it was like for her to see that piece of paper. "I remember actually what Rob said to me. He said, 'What's going on in our relationship is domestic violence, and the type of violence that I'm using on you is called emotional abuse, which means I don't bash you with my fists, I bash you with my emotions, to keep you under control.'"

That shocked Deb. As she understood it, domestic violence was "the guy that goes down to the pub on a Friday night and comes home and beats up his wife. It doesn't happen in suburbs like where I'm from." (As Deb has since discovered, she wasn't the only anomaly in her suburb—or even her street. Later she told me that the items I'd seen on the lawn next door belonged to her neighbor, who had dumped them there before fleeing her violent husband.)

Now, after almost ten years and much intense counseling, Rob and Deb are happily married, and both counsel domestic abuse survivors and perpetrators: Deb in private practice, and Rob more informally, with abusive men who seek him out for advice.

Deb says one thing stands out about abusers: it's as if they've studied some kind of domestic abuse handbook. "They all have the same tactics. So, for example, they may not come out and say, 'I don't want you seeing your friends, or having hobbies, or being around your parents,' but they'll just make it hard. Like, 'What do you want to see them for? I don't think they're good for you.' And eventually women go *it's just all too hard*, because they don't want the fight. So that's how it starts over time... And then your world gets smaller. And then if the perpetrator becomes your main frame of reference, which is what happens, it's very much like a cult. Because you're essentially getting your main input from him."

"It's like you go to abuse school," says Rob. "They all do it."

———

Speak to anyone who's worked with survivors or perpetrators, and they'll tell you the same thing: domestic abuse almost always follows the same script. It's a truly confounding phenomenon: How is it that men from vastly different cultures know to use the same basic techniques of oppression?

That's something we've only recently begun to investigate. Domestic abuse may be as old as intimacy, but we only really started to understand it after the first women's refuges opened in the 1970s. When women in the thousands fled to these makeshift shelters, they weren't just complaining about black eyes and raging tempers. They told stories of unfathomable cruelty and violence, and what sounded like orchestrated campaigns of control. It became clear that, although each woman's story was individual, the overarching narratives were uncannily alike. As one shelter worker said at the time, "It got so I could finish a woman's story halfway through it. There was this absolutely eerie feeling that these guys were sitting together and deciding what to say and do."

In the early 1980s, researchers noticed something else extraordinary. Not only were the stories of victims uncannily alike, they also resembled the accounts of a seemingly unrelated group of survivors: returned prisoners of war. It may seem odd to start a book about domestic abuse with a story from the Cold War, but this is where our modern understanding of domestic abuse really begins.

On September 24, 1953, the Korean War was officially over, and Operation Big Switch was underway. In the back of open-built Russian trucks, twenty-three American prisoners of war (POWs) were being driven to a prisoner exchange complex in the village of Panmunjom, on the North-South Korean border. The atmosphere at the complex had been electric with anger for months, as American prisoners returned from North Korean camps with shocking stories of cruelty. But on this day, as the trucks drew closer, American observers noticed that something about these prisoners was different. They looked tanned and healthy, and were dressed in padded blue Chinese uniforms, each pinned with Pablo Picasso's dove of peace.

As the trucks screeched to a halt, the prisoners laughed and shook hands with their captors. "See you in Peiping, old man," said one, as they climbed down off the trucks. Turning to the shocked crowd who had gathered to greet them, the POWs clenched their fists and shouted, "Tomorrow, the international Soviet unites the human race!" Then, instead of walking over to their countrymen, they turned the other way and defected to Communist China.

These shocking defections were just the tip of the iceberg. In the North Korean camps, American POWs had cooperated with the enemy to an unprecedented extent. Not only did they inform on their fellow prisoners, but hundreds of POWs also gave false confessions to atrocities and made radio broadcasts extolling the virtues of communism and condemning Western capitalism. Never before had captured soldiers betrayed their country so flagrantly.

For America, this was the stuff of nightmares. What could have driven U.S. soldiers to align with this diabolical creed? Frantic newspaper reports described how the Communists had bewitched the American POWs with a sophisticated new weapon called *brainwashing*: a method of mind control that could render a man's brain a blank slate and implant new thoughts, memories, and beliefs. This wasn't a fringe conspiracy theory: it was the earnest belief of people in the highest positions of government, including the head of the Central Intelligence Agency (CIA). By the mid-1950s, hysteria over brainwashing was at fever pitch.

Albert Biderman, a social scientist with the U.S. Air Force, was not convinced. He thought "brainwashing" sounded like a lot of propaganda and not much science. As paranoia peaked in Washington, the Air Force—similarly unpersuaded—dispatched Biderman to uncover the real reason so many well-trained American airmen had cooperated with the Communists.

After extensive interviews with returned POWs, Biderman's suspicions were confirmed: their compliance was not won using an esoteric new technique. Instead, the Chinese Communists who ran the North Korean camps had used age-old methods of coercive control. These methods were based "primarily on simple, easily understandable ideas of how an individual's physical and moral strength can be undermined."[1] There was nothing new about them, but nobody had ever seen them used in war before. That's why the American soldiers were so unprepared to resist.

Biderman established that three primary elements were at the heart of coercive control: "DDD," or dependency, debility, and dread. To achieve this effect, the captors used eight techniques: isolation, monopolization of perception, induced debility or exhaustion, cultivation of anxiety and despair, alternation of punishment and reward, demonstrations of omnipotence, degradation, and the enforcement of trivial demands. Biderman's "Chart of Coercion"[2] showed that acts of cruelty that appeared at first to be isolated were actually intricately connected. It was only when these acts were seen together that the full picture of coercive control became clear.

In Biderman's chart, there was no category for physical abuse. Though it was frequently used, actual violence was neither "a necessary nor [a] particularly effective method" to gain compliance, and the more skilled and experienced interrogators avoided it. They only needed to instill the *fear* of violence, which they did with "vague threats, and the implication that they were prepared to do drastic things." The Chinese Communists were not like the Germans or the Japanese—they didn't want to just brutalize their prisoners or work them to death. They wanted to control their hearts and minds.

When Biderman released his findings, people were incredulous. Could people really be manipulated so easily? Was he sure there was not something he had failed to detect? But Biderman was adamant: "Probably no other aspect of Communism reveals more thoroughly its disrespect for truth and the individuals," he wrote, "than its resort to these techniques."[3] Before we go on, it's worth mentioning that their use of coercive control didn't prove Chinese Communism to be a uniquely debased form of state power. To cite a more recent example, in 2002, U.S. military trainers used Biderman's Chart of Coercion to train interrogators at Guantanamo Bay on the "coercive management techniques" for which the prison became notorious: sleep deprivation, prolonged constraint, and exposure. Remarkably, what was seemingly lost on the American military was that these techniques had come to fame for eliciting *false* confessions. Coercive techniques were used on a small group of prisoners at Guantanamo until 2005, when Congress banned them.[4]

But let's get back to our story. In the 1970s, when women began fleeing to newly opened shelters, they spoke about being isolated from friends and family, instructed on how to behave, degraded, manipulated, sexually violated, and threatened with death. Physical violence was common and could be sadistic in its extremes, but survivors insisted it was not the worst part of the abuse—and some were not physically abused at all. In her groundbreaking book *Rape in Marriage*,[5] Diana Russell presented two lists side by side: Biderman's Chart of Coercion and the common techniques of domestic perpetrators. The lists were virtually identical. The only difference was that whereas captors in North Korea deployed the techniques tactically, husbands appeared to be replicating the system of coercive control unconsciously.

In 1973, Amnesty International included Biderman's Chart of Coercion in its *Report on Torture,* declaring these techniques the universal tools of torture and coercion.[6] As Harvard psychiatrist and trauma specialist Judith Herman would later write, "The [coercive] methods that enable one human being to enslave another are remarkably consistent."[7] In situations of domestic abuse, the effect of coercive control is the same: the perpetrator becomes "the most powerful person" in the victim's life, and the victim's psychology is "shaped by the [perpetrator's] actions and beliefs.[8] Victims may even end up unconsciously adopting their perpetrator's worldview, in which certain beliefs, rules, and codes are inviolable. If this worldview overwhelms the victim's own value system, she may punish or shun others—friends, family, children—who break the "rules."

Domestic perpetrators don't need physical violence to maintain their power—they only have to make their victims believe they are capable of it. This threat is particularly effective, wrote Herman, when it is directed toward loved ones: "Battered women, for example, frequently report that their abuser has threatened to kill their children, their parents, or any friends who harbor them, should they attempt to escape." This atmosphere of threat is enough to "convince the victim that the perpetrator is omnipotent, that resistance is futile, and that her life depends upon winning his indulgence through absolute compliance."[9]

Today, thanks to the pioneering work of experts such as Herman, Lewis Okun, and Evan Stark, we know that the techniques common to domestic abuse match those used by practically anyone who trades in captivity: kidnappers, hostage-takers, pimps, cult leaders. This shows us that there is nothing uniquely weak, helpless, or masochistic about victims of domestic abuse. Faced with the universal methods of coercive control, their responses are no different from those of trained soldiers.

In fact, for victims of domestic abuse, resistance is even harder than for other captives. Hostages, for example, often know nothing of their captors, and generally regard them as an enemy. But, as Herman explains, a victim of domestic abuse doesn't have this advantage. She is "taken prisoner gradually, by courtship."[10] Before she feels trapped by fear and control, it is love that first binds her to her abuser, and it's love that makes her forgive him when he says he won't abuse her again. Abusers are rarely simple thugs or sadists—if they were, they'd be far easier to avoid or apprehend. Instead, like all men, they can be loving, kind, charming, and warm, and they struggle with personal pain and uncertainty. This is who the woman falls in love with.

Fairy tales and Hollywood movies have encouraged us to interpret the warning signs of domestic abuse—obsession, jealousy, possessiveness—as signs of passion, not danger. By the time this "passion" begins to morph into abusive and domineering behavior, the victim already cares deeply for the perpetrator and will minimize and excuse his behavior to protect him and their love. If she's to resist becoming captive to his abuse, she will have to do the very opposite of what we do when we're in love, as Herman describes:

Not only will she have to avoid developing empathy for her abuser, but she will also have to suppress the affection she already feels. She will have to do this in spite of the batterer's persuasive arguments that just one more sacrifice, one more proof of her love, will end the violence and save the relationship. Since most women derive pride and self-esteem from their capacity to sustain relationships, the batterer is often able to entrap his victim by appealing to her most cherished values. It is not surprising, therefore, that battered women are often persuaded to return after trying to flee from their abusers.[11]

What should surprise us about domestic abuse is not that a woman can take a long time to leave, but that she has the mental fortitude to *survive*.

————

Perpetrators exist on a spectrum: from family men who don't even realize they're being abusive, to master manipulators who terrorize their partners. Whether domination is the aim or simply the result of their abuse, many use similar methods, but to varying degrees.

Some perpetrators know exactly what they're doing; their abuse is premeditated and tactical. Rarely do you see this as blatantly as in the following exchange between two Facebook users. Says one: "Covertly reduce her self-belief and self-esteem to a point where she has to rely on you to survive, then threaten to dump her for being needy." Says another:

The place should be devoid of any cell phones or land lines, cars should be manual, neighbor should be fought on regular bases [sic] and cops should also be paid routinely! Behave for the first 6–8 months, she'll think he is the perfect one and when she's emotionally invested and reliant then start off as she's an easy picking now and has dropped her guard. An honest word of caution: Never introduce her to your friends as those Rambos might jeopardize the fucking plan. The power of suggestion over and over again will wear her down and no matter how empowered she is she will kneel! It's the way they're hardwired and oh they'll make the same mistake again and again. Luring them in is the best sport one can play.[12]

Most abusive men, however, would be hard-pressed to articulate such tactics: they reinvent the techniques of coercive control subconsciously, with an intent that is largely hidden even from themselves. This is perhaps one of the most confounding aspects of domestic abuse: whether an abuser is a cunning sociopath or a "normal" man afflicted by morbid jealousy, he will almost always end up using the same basic methods to dominate his partner.

This doesn't mean that all domestic abuse is the same. We will explore this in more detail in chapter 3, but for now, think of it this way: domestic abuse occurs on a spectrum of power and control. At the highest end, perpetrators micromanage the lives of their victims, prevent them from seeing friends and family, track their movements, and force them to obey a unique set of rules. This abuse is called "coercive control" (and sometimes "intimate terrorism")—the type of oppression Biderman first identified. Here, two patterns are commonly identified: the calculating abuser who knowingly manipulates and degrades his partner so he can dominate her; and the paranoid, emotionally dependent abuser who becomes more controlling over time because he's afraid his partner will leave. They both fit under the title of coercive controllers (though these distinctions are better understood as *patterns* rather than rigid *types*; these are people, after all, not neat specimens). At the lower end of the power and control spectrum, we have abusers who are not so intent on dominating their partners, to whom the term "insecure reactors" is better suited. But let's look at the coercive controllers first.

Coercive Controllers

According to Evan Stark, the American sociologist who popularized the term, perpetrators of coercive control make each household "a patriarchy in miniature, complete with its own web of rules or codes, rituals of deference, modes of enforcement, sanctions, and forbidden places."[13] Victims are commonly isolated from friends, family, and other supports, and "frequently deprived of money, food, access to communication or transportation, and other survival resources."[14] This kind of controlling abuse is rooted in a historical imbalance of power, which is why, in heterosexual couples, it is almost exclusively perpetrated by men (but is also replicated in same-sex relationships). "To make contemporary women their personal property, the modern man must effectively stand against the tide of history," writes Stark, "degrading women into a position of subservience that the progress of civilization has made obsolete. As batterers themselves have pointed out to me over the years, there would be no need for so many men to deploy elaborate means to control female partners if women still accepted subordination as a fate bestowed by nature."[15] Based on the available research, Stark estimates that 60 to 80 percent of female victims who seek help have been subjected to a type of coercive control.[16]

Coercive control is a very particular kind of abuse. Coercive controllers don't abuse their partners just to hurt, humiliate, or punish them. They don't use violence just to seize power in the moment or gain the advantage in a fight. Instead, they use particular techniques—isolation, gaslighting, surveillance—to strip the victim of their liberty and take away their sense of self. As Stark explains, the aim of coercive control is "total domination, rather than simply to win compliance on a particular issue."[17] In other situations of domestic abuse, the victim may feel degraded, angry, or helpless, but may not actually be afraid of the abuser. Coercive control is different. It is a strategic campaign of abuse held together by fear.

"Tom" is a typical coercive controller. He met "Melissa" when she was seventeen, and within six months, insisted that they get married and move to his farm, far away from Melissa's family. After promising a countryside idyll, Tom became controlling, jealous, and violent. When he wanted to punish Melissa—for disobedience, or whatever he'd just come up with—he'd drag her around the house by her hair. Any mention of Melissa going out was a provocation. "I was stuck there," she told me. "I had no friends, no family. I was in a prison, basically." Tom undermined Melissa's self-esteem so severely that she felt she had no options outside the relationship and was fearful of what he might do if she tried to leave. Then there were the apologies and promises from the Tom who really loved her, who needed her help to become a better man, who only hit her when she "provoked" him.

Over the next thirteen years, they had two children together. Each time Melissa became pregnant, Tom would stop the physical violence and assume the role of "protector." "If I wasn't eating right, he'd force me to eat," she says. "I'd be about to vomit, and he'd be forcing me to eat, saying, 'I don't want anything to be wrong with my child.'"

One day, Melissa told Tom she planned to go to the movies with a woman she'd managed to befriend on a rare trip into town. In thirteen years, Melissa said, she had never once been on a girls' night out. Tom turned on her, teeth clenched, and snarled, "You're not fucking going anywhere." For the first time, Melissa stood up to him. "I said, 'Well, I'm letting you know that I'm going on Friday, whether you clench your teeth or not. I'm not your daughter, I'm your wife.'" When Melissa returned home that night, Tom had locked her out of the house.

The next time Melissa decided to venture out, Tom came at her more ferociously than ever. He accused her of having an affair, and then punched her so hard she was thrown across the room. This time, Melissa fought back. "I just felt this power," she says, with a faint smile. "I jumped up and knocked him flying over the computer table. He was just so shocked that

I'd done it. I said, 'Don't you ever do that to me again. You ever touch me, or push me, or shove me again, I'm gonna divorce you and I will leave.'"

Tom didn't hit Melissa again for three years. The next time he did, she left.

Insecure Reactors

All domestic abuse is about power, in one way or another, but not all perpetrators enforce tight regimes of control. At the lower end of the power and control spectrum are men who don't completely subordinate their partners, but use emotional or physical violence to gain power in the relationship. They may do this to gain the advantage in an argument, to get the treatment and privileges to which they believe they're entitled, or to exorcise their shame and frustration. (This is a kind of domestic abuse women also perpetrate, as we'll read in chapter 7.) Evan Stark calls this "simple domestic violence"; Michael Johnson calls it "situational violence." Don't be fooled: although these terms can make this abuse sound benign, it can still be very dangerous—and insecure reactors can end up killing their partners, too.

Susan Geraghty, who has been running men's behavior change programs since the 1980s, says that no matter what culture they grew up in, the attitude of these men is the same. "It's the self-righteousness that kicks in, where if I don't get my way or you don't agree with me, or if this isn't happening the way I want it, I have every right to show my displeasure and punish you." However, these are also the men most likely to confront their own behavior. Those Geraghty works with are there by choice—not mandated by court order—and they are usually not coercive controllers. "To a large degree," she explains, "these are men who have lived with violence, have incredible issues around intimacy and have never learned to communicate. Their sense of frustration with that [is] profound."

"Nick," a burly man in his mid-thirties, is a typical insecure reactor. When I met him at the home he shares with his wife, "Ani," and their two sons, he was still serving the last weeks of a restraining order. A year earlier, during an argument late one night, Nick picked Ani up and threw her out of bed. Her screams woke up their eldest son, who came running into the room to find his mother sobbing on the floor.

That night, Ani called the police. As they were loading Nick into the police van, he turned to one of the police officers and said, "I'm not a criminal." It was the first time Nick had been physically violent toward Ani, and he certainly didn't consider himself an abusive husband. But Nick was about to discover that not only had he committed a crime that night, he'd been inflicting domestic abuse on his wife for years.

At a local men's behavior change program, Nick and the other men in the group were astonished to learn that verbal, emotional, psychological, and even financial abuse counted as domestic abuse. "I actually didn't know what family violence constituted, and a lot of people don't. Probably the biggest one was language—the derogatory language. That's the bit that probably really woke up most of the men in the program," he says. "I can assure you that the true meaning of family violence is misunderstood by 95 percent of men."

Nick may fit the profile of an insecure reactor, but he's not typical: he's one of the rare men who has committed to at least try to change. When I met him, he was trying to reconcile with Ani, who he said was willing to give him another chance. But regaining her trust was harder than he had anticipated. "Even recently she said, 'I'm scared of you.' I got really upset. I suppose it gave me a reminder to say, *hang on a minute, it could take you ten years to... It could be never. She could be always scared of you.* And that really eats me up."

———————

It would be much easier to police domestic abuse if perpetrators fit neatly into a particular category. Unfortunately, it doesn't work that way: the line between these two groups is very hazy and can be easily crossed. Insecure reactors, for example, may turn into coercive controllers, and coercive controllers may pretend—especially in court—to have merely overreacted, like an insecure reactor. Some perpetrators won't fit into either category, especially those whose violence is driven by psychosis. Despite this ambiguity, it's still vital to understand that not all domestic abuse is the same.

We Fight a Lot: Is It Abuse?

It can be hard to pinpoint where garden-variety fighting ends and domestic abuse begins. Most people have arguments with the person they love. Many of us have felt jealous at times and have said things we regret. We may have even screamed the house down. In a healthy relationship, both partners negotiate power: over money, housework, socializing, childcare, sex, and so on. Though one partner may have more power in a particular domain, overall power is reasonably evenly distributed between them. In relationships where one partner is abusive, these same power struggles occur. But if one were to animate these couples, the abuser would be depicted as twice the size of their partner. Outsiders, like police, may see that couple fighting and judge the violence to be mutual, but this is a dangerous mistake. Where there is a severe power imbalance, the "smaller" partner—the victim—is always at a severe disadvantage, no matter how fiercely they fight. Indeed, the perpetrator will often make it look like *they* are the one being abused.

So how can you tell? There is a simple test: relationship conflict becomes domestic abuse when one partner uses violent, threatening, or coercive behavior to gain power over the other person. Another test is that the victimized person will generally feel afraid of their partner, but even that is not a reliable way to measure it. Many victims start off feeling confused and anxious, even angry. Fear can build over time, sometimes imperceptibly—just as the heat builds slowly for the proverbial frog in the boiling pot. Little about domestic abuse is simple or straightforward.

The Blueprint for Establishing Power

Using Biderman's chart as a guide, here I outline the basic techniques used to varying extents by all abusers, regardless of culture or creed. People partnered with insecure reactors will recognize some but not all of these techniques. That's because such abusers are not seeking to dominate them entirely, and thus don't use all the techniques of a coercive controller. Others who recognize only a few techniques, however, may be living through the early stages of coercive control—even if they have been with their partners for years.

Under each technique, I have included some common tactics and behaviors, but it is by no means an exhaustive list. With each new technique that is deployed, the bonds of coercive control are fortified and become tighter over time. It's the cumulative effect of these techniques that is devastating for victims, not just the isolated incidents. The longer a person stays, the harder—and more dangerous—it becomes to leave.

Establish love and trust

The first stage of domestic abuse is the development of love, trust, and intimacy. With the exception of arranged marriages, it is love that first binds the victim to her abuser, and love that makes her forgive and make excuses for him. *This first stage cannot be emphasized enough when trying to understand the cycle of abuse.*

Trust is an essential component of coercive control. In the North Korean camps, the "most insidious" and effective technique the Communists used was false friendship. "When an American soldier was captured by the Chinese," wrote Biderman, "he was given a vigorous handshake and a pat on the back." The enemy "introduced himself as a friend of the 'workers' of America... This display of friendship caught most of the Americans totally off-guard."[18] The captors in North Korea were only being friendly for show, knowing full well the psychological horrors that awaited the soldiers in the prison camps. But domestic perpetrators—aside from those who set out to abuse and exploit—don't usually seduce a woman with the explicit aim of controlling her. When an abusive man says he loves his new partner, he probably means it. But it's not the kind of love nonabusive people feel—it is defined and distorted by his deeply held sense of entitlement. As longtime men's counselor Lundy Bancroft explains, "When an abusive man feels the powerful stirring inside that other people call love, he is probably largely feeling the desire to have you devote your life to keeping him happy with no outside interference, and to impress others by having you be his partner... The confusion of love with abuse is what allows abusers who kill their partners to make the absurd claim that they were driven by the depths of their loving feelings."[19]

Either way, whether the love is real or fabricated, the victim is lulled into a sense of security. Once the victim's guard is down and trust is established, the abusive process can truly begin.

Isolate

The first technique in Biderman's Chart of Coercion is to *isolate*. As long as the victim maintains meaningful social and emotional connections, the abuser's influence is diluted. To become the most powerful person in his victim's life, he must eliminate her external sources of support and silence voices that would question his behavior.

Take the story of "Jasmine" and "Nelson." Jasmine was fresh out of school when she met Nelson, who became her first boyfriend. She had been educated by Catholic nuns and spent most of her teenage years hanging out with her mother and sister. She was, by her own admission, incredibly naive, and at age seventeen, believed the only men she needed to be wary of were strangers. Early in their relationship, Nelson told her she shouldn't wear white pants because her underwear showed through and made her look like a tart. She was grateful for his advice— she certainly didn't want to look like a tart. When he said that wearing a dress would make her an easy target for bad people who wanted to touch her, she thought that was a bit over the top, but agreed not to wear dresses either. He was older and he'd traveled overseas. He knew how the world worked.

In a matter of months, Nelson's "helpful" advice had calcified into hard-and-fast rules about what Jasmine was allowed to do and who she could see. She shouldn't spend so much time with her sister, he said, and her male friends were a problem—he was worried she would be tempted to have sex with them. At first, Jasmine was flattered. *He really wants me all to himself,* she thought. She was right. Soon enough, he was threatening to harm her male acquaintances and forcing her to call male colleagues to tell them she hated them. This was just the beginning. Unbeknownst to Jasmine, Nelson was systematically isolating her.

Unlike prisoners of war, victims of domestic abuse are isolated gradually, in ways that can seem relatively harmless. A perpetrator may isolate his partner geographically, moving her far away from friends and family, to somewhere he can monitor and restrict her movements. Or he may isolate her in more subtle ways, by driving supportive friends and family away: he might make it difficult for her to see them, convince her they're no good for her, or behave so badly around them that they simply stop visiting. Weary and distressed by her reluctance to leave what they see as a toxic relationship, they may gradually stop trying to contact her. In this way, they do the perpetrator's job for him.

Alternatively, if the victim has a troubled relationship with her parents, the perpetrator may seek to collude with them—something that can isolate the victim to an even greater degree, as her family sides with and supports *him*. One survivor, Terri, says, "When he tried to reestablish regular contact with my family, I convinced myself that he was a nice guy who was trying to repair and strengthen my relationship with my family. I now believe that he recognized a kindred spirit in my mother. She essentially became his partner in crime."

Sometimes the victim remains in public, and to the rest of the world her relationship looks perfect. Here, she isolates *herself* by refusing—out of shame, fear, or the desire to protect her partner—to tell anyone about the abuse. She doesn't need to be isolated entirely for coercive control to be effective. All that's required is that her supportive connections—the ones most likely to question his behavior—are damaged or disconnected.

If an abuser decides to isolate his victim against her will, the campaign can become extreme: hiding car keys, intercepting messages and phone calls, threatening or assaulting friends and family. He may explain his possessive behavior as a sign of his passionate love or accuse her of cheating. Severing connections with others is the only way she can prove she loves him and allay his jealousy.

Monopolize perception

After the victim is isolated from friends and family, the perpetrator is able to *monopolize her perception*. In the North Korean POW camps, this was achieved by physical isolation and other sensory tricks: keeping the prisoner in complete darkness or bright light, restricting movement, and so on. The point of this was to fix the prisoner's attention on his immediate predicament, foster introspection, and frustrate all actions not consistent with compliance. Domestic perpetrators are rarely so explicit. Instead, like a magician working sleight of hand, the perpetrator redirects his partner's attention away from *his* abuse to *her* faults: if she wasn't so *this*, he wouldn't be so *that*. This can make a lot of sense to her, especially if, like many perpetrators, he seems to love and care for friends and family. If she's the only one he's attacking, it must be she who is provoking him.

While she's trying to figure out what *she's* doing wrong, he has the perfect cover. The walls creep up. He's better able to tell her who she should see and how she should behave; after all, he's only trying to help her overcome her faults and become a better person.

When she resists, the abuser changes tack. Maybe he tries to persuade her that she shouldn't see certain people and do certain things because he needs her devoted attention. Maybe he needs her to help *him* be a better man. He is wounded and lost, and she is the only woman who can help him. She's actually the strong one. But to help him, she will need to address her faults too—which seem to multiply by the day.

Over time, her guilt begins to morph into shame. When shame takes hold, she doesn't just feel bad about certain things she's done: she starts to feel that *she is* bad. This cuts her off from her instinct—which she can no longer trust—and makes the perpetrator's opinion even more important. From there, the shame becomes a spiral. Every time the perpetrator gets her to act against her instincts—by cutting off beloved family or friends, for example—the feelings of shame multiply. The more ashamed she feels, the more dependent she becomes on the perpetrator, and the less likely she is to seek help. After all, who would want to help a person like her?

Gradually the abuser draws his victim further away from the real world and into his version of reality. As she becomes more isolated, alternative viewpoints from friends and family that may alert her to the danger she's in slowly disappear. Indeed, she may drive them away herself: she is being conditioned into absolute loyalty, so she may resist any efforts to question her relationship, and draw away from those who express an ill view of her partner.

As the abuse escalates, she starts searching for clues to explain his behavior. It can't *all* be her fault, so why is he being like this? This leads her to the exact same questions we ask when we try to understand why men abuse their partners: Is he mentally ill? Is it his drinking? Is it drugs? Is he just stressed? There must be *some* reason for it.

The clues she finds turn into excuses. He's jealous because that bitch of an ex-girlfriend betrayed him. He doesn't like her going out because he's overprotective. He's got a temper, but everyone's got their demons—he just needs a good woman to help him overcome them. She makes these excuses because the idea that the man she loves would *choose* to inflict such cruelty on her is almost impossible for her to comprehend—just as it is for us. So she searches for ways to fix him, because that's what a woman is supposed to do for a man. Solve his problems. Care for him. Show him how to be soft. Show him how to love. The longer she takes responsibility for his abuse, and the longer she tries to fix him, the further she becomes trapped.

"Right from the get-go, you don't know it for what it is," explains Frances, who was a successful performer before her seventeen-year relationship with an abusive partner. "It seems like aberrant behavior, and then there is some more aberrant behavior. But it doesn't form a pattern until it has been there for a long time. You wonder if you're going mad a lot... [It's like] you are Alice in Wonderland [and] you don't know what's really real."[20]

The abuser's most skillful trick is to make his abuse invisible.

Induce debility and exhaustion

The captors in the North Korean POW camps specialized in *inducing debility and exhaustion*. "The Communists place great reliance on the poor understanding of the victim of what is happening to him," explained Biderman. "Deceiving, tricking, and confusing the victim are important."[21] The bewildered prisoner had to devote enormous mental energy to distinguishing fact from fiction. The further he fell down the rabbit hole, the more exhausted he became. Eventually, it was easier just to let the captor define his reality.

This process is replicated by domestic perpetrators, only we have a different term for it: *gaslighting*. Gaslighting is when an abuser *knowingly* denies, fabricates, and manipulates situations to make his partner doubt her own memory and perception. As she becomes more confused and anxious, she starts to believe that his interpretation of events may be more reliable than her own. The term comes from the 1944 film *Gaslight*, starring Ingrid Bergman as a woman driven by her abusive partner to believe she is insane. He does this by making small changes to her environment, like dimming the gas lights. When she notices, he denies it is happening and insists she is mistaken and, eventually, crazy. With her sanity in doubt, he convinces her that it's not safe to go out or have visitors, because she is imagining things that aren't real.

Survivor Terri describes an incident of gaslighting that occurred when she and her abuser first started dating:

We had been walking. He had his hand in the small of my back, and I ended up on the ground. I was sure he had pushed me over and I accused him of it, but he denied it, and was so nice. And even though I was really, really sure I had been pushed, I couldn't reconcile that knowledge with this charming, supportive man. Though confused, I chose to believe him. I remember asking myself why he would have pushed me over. Why would anyone do that? And because I couldn't work out why someone would do that, I convinced myself that what I knew to be true—that I was pushed—was wrong. The grooming started very early.

Gaslighting is remarkably common in situations of domestic abuse. Kay Schubach, then an art dealer working in affluent eastern suburbs, was with an extremely dangerous—and charming—serial abuser for two months, who gaslit her relentlessly. "My keys were there one second and then they weren't. Fifty dollars was in my wallet and then it wasn't. 'You must have lost it,' he said. 'Are you losing your mind? You just can't think straight. What's wrong with you?' He was always putting me on the back foot. In the end I thought I was going mad." Kay's abuser, Simon Lowe (who, in 2009, was sentenced to twelve years' imprisonment for the rape and assault of another woman), told her that, given how anxious and confused she was, she should go to his doctor and have something prescribed. Later, when it was clear she was planning to leave him, Simon said that he had kept the prescription for antidepressants and would use it to undermine Kay's credibility if she ever tried to take him to court.

Other techniques can range from prolonged interrogations over suspected betrayals to sleep deprivation, or they can be much more subtle. "Everything he did was geared toward making things as difficult as possible for me," says Terri. "My daughters have Asperger's, and when my second daughter was little, she had issues with routine and order; she needed dinner, bath, bed, in that order. So right after dinner he would shower until the hot water tank was empty. I would ask if he could wait until I ran a little water in the bath, but that would have ruined his game. I was too exhausted to see it for what it was." Mind games are common: an abuser may, for example, send his partner a loving text message, then chastise her for replying with the exact same sentiments. Alternatively, he may go completely silent for days at a time (even months or *years*), leaving her feeling intimidated and wondering what on earth she's done to deserve such treatment. His unpredictable responses lead her to "walk on eggshells," endlessly hypervigilant, alert to the need to adapt her behavior to prevent further abuse. Needless to say, the victim is left exhausted by constantly having to monitor her abuser's emotional state.

Each abusive strand is now being woven so tightly and imperceptibly that it can feel impossible to describe what's happening to outsiders, be they friends or police. Unless the abuser is brutish and clumsy and leaves evidence on her skin, she has no way to prove his violence. Without proof, it's her word against his, and her story is often so outlandish that it sounds implausible.

Enforce trivial demands

To develop the habit of compliance, the abuser starts to *enforce trivial demands*. Demands may adhere to a theme—like forbidding sexy clothing or speaking to other men—or be arbitrary and spontaneous, and enforced without warning. The victim's actions and behaviors are measured against these rules, which are ever-changing and often contradictory; to avoid punishment, she must know them by heart. This puts the victim in a hyper-alert state, her attention trained on how to anticipate and comply with the demands her abuser is likely to make. To do this, she must align her perception with his, so she can see through his eyes, and predict his next demand before he makes it. Only her compliance can prevent him from hurting her or her friends, family, or pets. The incredible mental effort this requires draws her further away from her own needs and wants, and deeper into his web of abuse.

Jasmine's life was governed by Nelson so completely that she could barely go a few minutes without reporting her whereabouts. Even when she was at home, she had to take photos to prove to Nelson which room she was in. If she bought the wrong shampoo, looked at him the wrong way, or used the wrong tone of voice, she would be criticized and denigrated. Repeatedly, Nelson would tell her, "You are a slut and will be treated accordingly."

Forensic social worker Evan Stark describes how such rule-setting can approach the level of fetish. "Rules given to women have extended to how the carpet was to be vacuumed ('til you can see the lines') and the height of the bedspread off the floor, to the heat of the water in the bath drawn each

night for a husband. Since the only purpose of the rules is to exact obedience, they are continually being revised."[22]

In an environment where the rules are constantly in flux, a victim
comes to feel as though she's living in a parallel universe. Her energy is
directed toward avoiding punishment and adapting her behavior to suit
his expectations. She may be so focused on compliance—and so exhausted
by it—that it may not even occur to her that she is being abused. As Terri
explains: "Between dealing with my two daughters and trying to avoid retal-
iation for all matter of perceived and manufactured things, I was too tired
to realize that I was walking on eggshells. Every moment was a moment to
get through."

Demonstrate omnipotence

In the North Korean camps, the captors would *demonstrate omnipotence*
by exhibiting complete control over the prisoner's fate. In domestic abuse,
omnipotence is demonstrated in a few ways, and it makes the victim feel
that no matter what she does, escape is impossible.

In many controlling relationships, the victim is subjected to relentless
surveillance. As her sense of self deteriorates, her abuser occupies and
defines more of her reality. If she has places she feels safe—work, church,
even the supermarket—he colonizes them, calling and texting her constantly,
for example, and punishing her if she doesn't answer. "If abusive relationships were filmed in slow motion," explains Stark, "they would resemble a
grotesque dance whereby victims create moments of autonomy and perpetrators 'search and destroy' them."[23] Over time, she may start to believe her
partner is somehow omnipotent, and that no external authority—not the
police, not the courts—can keep her safe. As in the POW camps in North
Korea, the abuser creates this impression for a distinct purpose: to convince
his victim that resistance is futile.

Some abusers do an impressive job of being all-knowing. They know which websites she's visiting, who she's calling, the exact route she takes to work each day. Assuming godlike powers these days is easy; they can be purchased online. One popular phone app costs less than $200 per year and, once installed, doesn't show up on the home screen, so the user can't see it. With this single app, an abuser gains remote access to that phone's text messages, call log, photos, emails, contacts, and browsing history. Such apps can even block numbers for inbound and outbound calls and delete everything on the phone remotely. The victim's phone becomes a tracking device thanks to its built-in GPS: a stalker can sit at the computer and watch her move from one place to another on a street map. Most terrifying of all, these apps can turn the targeted person's phone into a listening device. As one survivor told the BBC, "He would drop snippets into conversations, such as knowing about a friend's baby. Really private things that he shouldn't have known about. If I asked him how he knew these things, he'd say I told him and accuse me of losing it." Another said her husband would play mind games with her by repeating specific phrases she and her friends had used in private conversations. He was spying on her through her phone's microphone.[24]

Aside from physical surveillance, an abuser may choose to demonstrate his omnipotence by showing that he can control whether the victim lives or dies. Nothing proves this kind of total power like strangulation. From the moment he has his hands around her throat, the abuser controls his victim entirely. She can't talk back and she can't scream. He can prolong the assault by loosening his grip and allowing her to catch her breath before tightening it again, or he can choke her until she blacks out altogether. As he does this, he is free to chastise her for some perceived wrongdoing, or simply show her how easy it would be to kill her. Strangulation is an extreme form of violence that seldom leaves a mark. There's no black eye, no bloody nose. In fact, by the time police arrive, it's more likely the abuser will look like *he's* the one who's been violently assaulted, because victims will commonly bite and scratch their abusers as they fight for air.

Research shows that more than 65 percent of domestic abuse victims will experience near-fatal choking.[25] As one survivor recalls:

> The first time he was violent it came out of the blue. It was an intense, terrifying experience. He flew into a rage over something I've long since forgotten. What I do remember is his hands closing around my throat. I remember gasping, I remember the fear, and I remember the way he watched my eyes as I slipped toward unconsciousness. He would release the pressure just as I felt myself sinking into blackness, allowing me just enough oxygen so that he could begin the process again. I don't know how long he did this for, like a cat playing with a mouse, making sure just enough life remained to sustain the game for longer. I don't remember what happened afterwards. I just remember feeling petrified and trapped. I wanted him to leave then, I asked him to. He refused. What could I do?[26]

Traditionally, strangulation was classified as a minor assault—only recently have forty-five states made it a felony—but it is far more cruel and dangerous than a punch or a kick. Researchers at the University of Pennsylvania have likened it to waterboarding. The physical harm can be extremely serious: a victim can die from internal injuries days or even weeks later. Strangulation is also a big red flag for future homicide: abusers who strangle are almost eight times more likely to end up killing their partner.[27]

Alternate punishments with rewards

The key to coercive control is to *alternate punishments with rewards*. In the North Korean camps, the captors were master shape-shifters. "At various times and places, [the captor] may seek to achieve its purposes by representing itself as a kindly, solicitous, smiling creature—at others, it may wantonly display its brutality in all its nakedness... Many have been impressed by its abilities as a quick-change artist."[28]

Domestic abuse was certainly not in Biderman's mind when he wrote those words, but he could not have better described the mercurial temperament of the domestic abuser. Aside from extreme situations, in which the abuse is unrelenting, the perpetrator will at times profess his love, offer gifts, show kindness, and express remorse. This is what's known as the cycle of violence, where an explosion is followed by a period of remorse, then promises and pursuit, a false honeymoon stage, then a build-up in tension, a stand-over phase, and another explosion. The kindness expressed during the false honeymoon may feel genuine to the abuser, but this reward phase— like every other part of the cycle—is still all about maintaining control.

Periods of kindness, no matter how short, bond the victim to her abuser. Reminded even momentarily of the man she fell in love with, she is duped into letting her guard down and into sharing things—secrets, desires, perhaps even erotic photographs—that the abuser may later use against her. The victim is persuaded that if she changes her behavior and creates the perfect environment, his abuse will cease. She resumes her search for what it is that sets him off, and doubles down on trying to comply with his demands, to prolong the period of grace and win the approval of her harshest critic.

Even a small act of mercy delivered directly after an attack can elicit a deep sense of gratitude. Kay Schubach survived a particularly terrifying assault, during which her abuser drove wildly along a main road and punched her twice in the head. As she begged him to take her to the hospital, he screeched the car to a halt outside their apartment and ordered her to "stop making a spectacle." Upstairs, he continued to berate her until, all of a sudden, he changed. "He would just calm down," says Kay, "and you could see it was safe again. Then he's like, 'Oh, you gotta calm down, I'll make you a peppermint tea, everything is alright.' You're a nervous wreck by this stage, so that's when you break down and start crying, and then he comforts you, and puts you into bed and makes you a cup of tea, and says he's sorry, and he doesn't know what happened, and then changes the subject. You actually feel grateful that he is a warm, nice person again and he's going to deliver you from evil."

As Herman explains, this "kind" treatment does the job of undermining psychic resistance far better than simply feeding the victim an unchanging diet of degradation and fear. "The goal of the perpetrator is to instill in his victim not only the fear of death, but also gratitude for being allowed to live... After several cycles of reprieve from certain death, the victim may come to view the perpetrator, paradoxically, as her savior."[29]

In the light of his mercy, the victim shifts from fear to relief, or even admiration. "You get so attuned to what they're doing, for your own safety and survival," explains Schubach. "When they're good, you're incredibly grateful, you're incredibly in love with them, for bestowing their kindness upon you."

This, in the end, is what the controlling abuser is looking for: a willing and devoted submissive who loves him even more for setting the boundaries so clearly and expects to be punished if she disobeys. For centuries, this was just a basic expectation held by men in patriarchal societies. In 1869, the English philosopher and feminist John Stuart Mill described the despotic mindset. "Men do not want solely the obedience of women, they want their sentiments," he wrote in *The Subjection of Women*. "All men, except the most brutish, desire to have, in the woman most nearly connected with them, not a forced slave but a willing one, not a slave merely, but a favorite. They have therefore put everything in practice to enslave their minds."[30]

Orwell gave this same animating desire to Big Brother in *Nineteen Eighty-Four*: "We are not content with negative obedience, nor even with the most abject submission. When finally you surrender to us, it must be of your own free will. We do not destroy the heretic because he resists us... We convert him, we capture his inner mind, we reshape him. We burn all evil and all illusion out of him; we bring him over to our side, not in appearance, but genuinely, heart and soul."[31]

In the North Korean camps, Communist interrogators also looked for this form of total submission, telling prisoners: "You do not have the correct attitude. I am trying to help you adopt the correct attitude. You must change your attitude."[32]

As Herman observes, "the desire for total control over another person is the common denominator of all forms of tyranny. Totalitarian governments demand confession and political conversion of their victims. Slaveholders demand gratitude of their slaves... Perpetrators of domestic battery demand that their victims prove complete obedience and loyalty by sacrificing all other relationships." It's this fantasy of "total control" that forms the power dynamic at the core of most pornography. "The erotic appeal of this fantasy to millions of terrifyingly normal men fosters an immense industry in which women and children are abused, not in fantasy but in reality."[33]

Nevertheless, subjugation is not a condition that is natural to women, and it runs entirely counter to the phenomenal liberation we have fought so hard for. That's why abusers—especially coercive controllers—don't just beat their victims anymore. If they want to replicate the old conditions of submission and devotion, they need to create an environment of coercive control.

It's worth pausing here to remember that many perpetrators are not necessarily aware that they are orchestrating campaigns of control and degradation. Cold and calculating coercive controllers have an acute sense of dominance and a correspondingly acute propensity for violence, physical and psychological; with them, the system of control is conscious and ever-present. But coercive controllers who are consumed by morbid jealousy and paranoia are more likely to recreate these techniques spontaneously, and insecure reactors are even less intent on acting strategically: they move in and out of the control regime, as if switching channels. Once they have regained control, they can let the system go and feel genuinely restored to the relationship. Whether perpetrators abuse strategically or on impulse, however, they usually have one thing in common: a supercharged sense of entitlement.

Threats

As the abuse becomes more degrading and intrusive, the abuser uses *threats* to cultivate anxiety and despair and to prevent his victim from leaving or seeking help.

In the North Korean camps, captors would threaten their prisoners with death, endless isolation and interrogation, and harm to their families. In domestic abuse, the threats are just as terrifying. They are what render a woman captive and communicate to her that even if she wants to leave, she may never be safe.

In the case of Jasmine and Nelson, Nelson's coercive control reached toxic levels of intensity. Soon after Jasmine gave birth to their baby daughter, he forced her to spend most nights sleeping in the car with the baby, allowing her to come inside only for housework or sex. All through the night, Nelson would call her to make sure that she hadn't gone to her mother's house, which was forbidden. If Jasmine disobeyed, the consequences were clear: not only would she and her baby be killed, but several of her family members would die, and her cats would be killed too. By this point Jasmine had been coercively controlled for eight years, since she was seventeen.

Abusers may make grand threats, but many are also finely attuned to the limits of their power and averse to being caught. Harming friends or family would risk police involvement; it's less risky to hurt or kill the family pet. In an Australian study of 102 women with a history of family violence, more than half said their animals had also been abused.[34] These included a pet cockatiel beheaded for "singing too much," a cat hung by a leash, another cat put in a microwave, and other pets that were shot, stabbed, kicked, and thrown. Survivor Kim Gentle returned home one day to hear that her abuser (the same man who had abused Kay Schubach) had thrown the dog he gave her off a cliff. Why? Because she "loved the dog more than she loved him."

Abusers aren't always so coarse. Some are more covert: tampering with the brakes on the victim's car, for example, or cutting the telephone lines. Others will exploit their victims' loyalty and empathy by threatening to harm or kill *themselves*. No matter the abuser's method, the victim is left feeling that there is no safe place in or out of the relationship. As Schubach explains, "It's like being in a house with an assassin. You know there is someone there who's out to get you. You don't know how, when or where, but you're sure it's going to happen."

Degradation

In the North Korean camps, *degradation* of the prisoners was achieved through preventing personal hygiene; keeping them in filthy surroundings; administering demeaning punishments, insults, and taunts; and denying any privacy. The point of this was to reduce the prisoner to "animal level" and "make the cost of resistance more damaging to self-esteem than capitulation."[35]

In domestic abuse, degradation is obscenely targeted. Unlike other captors, a domestic abuser has intimate knowledge of his victim's fears, secrets, and insecurities, and uses this to hone his taunts and insults.

The psychological impact of degrading comments can be extreme. Abusers commonly tell their partners they're worthless, stupid, and unlovable, and after a while the woman may start to believe it. "[So many women have] said to me over the years, 'Give me a black eye any day. The bruise is gone in a fortnight. It's the words that hurt, the words that stay,'" says Karen Willis, who heads a national rape and domestic violence center. "In fact, all of our counseling and trauma work—99 percent of it—is about reversing the impacts of those words."

Returning to Nelson and Jasmine: after a separation of several months, Nelson lured Jasmine back, claiming he was miserable without her. Thinking they could "turn a corner," she accepted. When, soon thereafter, Jasmine revealed a brief sexual relationship she'd had during their time apart, Nelson seized this opportunity. He stopped addressing her by her name, referring to her instead as "Slut." After their daughter was born, Nelson was determined to make "slut" the child's first word.

Degradation is not always so overt. Willis describes a typical scenario: "[You're] at a party with some friends, laughing and joking and having a good time. There will be a whisper in the ear: 'They're not laughing with you. They're laughing at you because you're an idiot.'"

Sometimes degradation goes so far, it reaches a level of dehumanization. Evan Stark explains that women in his practice "have been forced to eat off the floor, wear a leash, bark when they wanted supper, or beg for favors on their knees."[36] In many of these sickening scenarios, both the perpetrator and the victim were known to friends and families as friendly, regular people. As the American philosopher David Livingstone Smith stresses, "You don't have to be a monster or a madman to dehumanize others. You just have to be an ordinary human being."[37]

One of the most powerful ways a perpetrator can degrade his victim is through sex. Commonly, survivors report being coerced into sexual acts they find humiliating, degrading, or painful. Others are simply raped. "Eleanor," a survivor with three children, was raped throughout her marriage. The first time, she remembers, her husband came into the bedroom and announced they were going to have sex. When Eleanor told him she didn't want to, he forced himself on top of her, ripped off her underwear, and shoved his hand over her mouth to stop her screaming. "I could hardly breathe," Eleanor says. "It was a matter of minutes before he ejaculated inside me and finished. I was sobbing, and I said to him, 'How could you do this to me?' He got off me, and I remember him looking at me like he was disgusted with me." Afterward, Eleanor confronted her husband and asked if he was going to apologize. "He said, 'Why? It was the best sex I've had in six years. The more you struggled the more it turned me on, and what you got was fucking great.' I remember vomiting in my mouth," says Eleanor.

Some abusers aren't satisfied until they have degraded their victim to the point of utter despair. In these extreme cases, the work of degradation is complete when, as Herman explains, the victim is "forced to violate her own moral principles and to betray her basic human attachments. Psychologically, this is the most destructive of all coercive techniques, for the victim who has succumbed loathes herself. It is at this point, when the victim under duress participates in the sacrifice of others, that she is truly 'broken.'"

Such a sacrifice may involve her children. She may feel forced to neglect them, as Terri did: "If I was caught spending time with my eldest, he would take it out on her. I felt forced to ignore her to protect her." Or she may start to dole out severe punishments, in the hope that this may protect her child from a worse fate at the hands of the father.

In this rare and candid account, an abuser relates an extreme example of how children can be used to degrade a mother:

I raped her daughters—my stepdaughters—right in front of her. I made her watch—every time I saw her look away, I threatened to shoot her and the girls. I had my .38 loaded and in my hand—that's how I made them all do what I said. I didn't do it for the sex. I didn't desire her daughters, really. I just wanted to make her feel terrible that she had watched me do that to the girls without her trying to protect them. I wanted her miserable. I wanted her to doubt herself as a mother, to think she was a bad mother. So I gave her the biggest failure a mother could have.[38]

Mothers who are being abused will frequently risk their lives to defend their children. However, others may be so thoroughly dominated that they allow or enable the abuse of their children, and even punish the children for trying to defend themselves. "At this point," says Herman, "the demoralization of the battered woman is complete."[39]

_____

In suburban houses, on remote farms, and in inner-city apartments, women of all backgrounds encounter the abusive man. It may be weeks or months— even years—before his abuse emerges. When it does, each woman will have her own reasons for staying. The strong, independent woman believes she is the only one who can help him defeat his demons. The woman who grew up with abuse may think she doesn't deserve any better. The woman recovering from an abusive partner seeks the protection of another man. A religious woman believes marriage is sacred. A woman from overseas is threatened with deportation if she leaves. A new mother is determined not to fail like her parents did. A young woman caught in the rush of her first love is eager to please and willing to change. By the time a woman realizes the threat she's facing, she may have no choice but to stay, because leaving either feels impossible, or has become too dangerous.

2.

The Underground

She wandered the streets, looking in shop windows. Nobody knew
her here. Nobody knew what he did when the door was closed.
Nobody knew.

BETH BRANT, *WILD TURKEYS*

In a city café, three women sit in close conversation. Two of them lean forward, their forearms on the table, looking intently at a woman who appears to be in her late forties. "He beat me, he beat me until I had bruises everywhere," she says, in a Russian accent. "And he put her in a cage!" The "her" is their daughter; after the marriage was over, she explains, her ex took their young daughter to the zoo and photographed her inside an animal enclosure. "She came home with three bruises, here, here, and here."

"This is terrible," says one friend.

The woman shakes her head. "That is nothing. You know *nothing*," she replies, direct but not unkind. "You've got pain after pain after pain, you know, but..." The woman pauses, and the table falls quiet. "Then his new wife—she took everything," she says.

"Good on her, good on her," the friends chorus.

Another café. As I write, a young woman nervously leans across and asks if I'm connecting to her computer by Bluetooth. When she sees my confusion, she apologizes. She's paranoid about being hacked because she's being stalked by her ex-boyfriend, who's a cop. She had to move across states to get away from him, but she's terrified he'll use his connections to find out where she is.

I go to court with a friend who needs protection from her partner; he held her and their young kids hostage for hours one night, taunting her and demanding that she become his slave. She is later devastated to discover that before she met him, the father of her beautiful children had been violent with other women.

Another old friend flees her family home with her mother after being attacked by her father and stays in hiding with us for a week. Turns out her father has a gun, and he blames her for making his wife leave him. We make sure the doors are locked at night.

I used to think I didn't know anyone who'd been through domestic abuse. Now I know that was never true. Now I see its traces all around me.

The women who are degraded and dominated by their partners occupy a deep underground. They walk on isolated paths—on the street, at the office, in the school playground, and at the shopping center—unseen and alone in their abuse. They are us—our sisters and mothers and friends and colleagues—and they are the women we'll never meet, whose lives we cannot imagine. Statistically, we all know at least one woman who's lived in this underground, because it has been home to a shocking number of women. According to the Centers for Disease Control and Prevention (CDC), almost 50 million American women alive today have, at some point, lived underground.[1] Some will never leave.

We think of domestic abuse as something that happens behind closed doors, but it's actually happening all around us; we just don't know what it looks like. Louisa, a forty-five-year-old with three children under ten, had her abuse paraded in front of strangers regularly at the supermarket. On the weekend, her partner would tell her where she could shop, and then tell her to wait there while he watched his nephews play football. Louisa would do the shopping, then wait in the supermarket with a full cart. When he arrived, he'd start going through the items one by one, pulling out everything she wasn't "allowed" to have, like baby wipes. "He'd say 'What do we need this for?' in front of people, and I'd be so embarrassed, humiliated—in fear all the time," she says. "I was so frightened, because his behavior was so erratic and controlling. You want to run but you don't know where to go, and you are thinking, *This is just completely ridiculous. Like, it's not normal, is it? Is it normal?*"[2]

Sometimes the most brutal acts of domestic abuse happen right in front of us. One senior police officer, Detective Superintendent Rod Jouning, told me about a particularly shocking assault at a local football game. A man who was there with his wife and child had spent the day watching the game with his friends. When it started getting late, his wife walked over to let him know it was time for them to go home, so they could get their kid ready for bed. "He turned around, said, 'Don't you dare disrespect me in front of my friends,' and then laid into her," said Jouning. "He broke her eye socket, fractured her jaw, then picked her up by the hair and one leg and dragged her to the car. *Not one person intervened.*"

People do intervene, of course, often at enormous risk to themselves. One night in 2017, around midnight, off-duty police officer Stephanie Bochorsky was watching television in her pajamas when she heard a "blood-curdling" cry coming from the property next door. When she ran outside, she found a woman in the driveway standing in a pink bathrobe, screaming. When Stephanie asked her if she was okay, the woman cried, "No, he's setting my kids on fire!" Stephanie told the woman to call the police and not let anyone else inside, and then rushed into the house. Inside, it was eerily quiet and reeked of gasoline. Seeing an unusual glow coming from one of the rooms, she entered to find three-year-old "Mikayla" standing in her cot, her head entirely engulfed in flames—not screaming, just moving her head with a "shocked look on her face." Stephanie grabbed a blanket and threw it over the toddler's head to extinguish the fire. Suddenly, behind her stood the girl's father, Edward John Herbert—a towering figure covered in tattoos, naked, eyes vacant, in a drug-induced psychosis—pouring gas on his seven-year-old daughter, "Tahlia." When he saw Stephanie, he said just one thing to her: "Why don't you take your fucking clothes off?" Stephanie reacted immediately. "Get the fuck away from her," she said, and with Mikayla in her arms, reached forward, grabbed Tahlia by the back of her pajama collar, and ran out of the room.[3]

Unbeknownst to Stephanie, Herbert was carrying a butcher's knife, and his six-year-old son was also in the house. Later, Herbert told a neighbor that he set his daughter on fire because she was "too fucking beautiful." "Don't worry," he added, "I wouldn't have lit my boy up." Thanks to Stephanie and neighbor Daniel McMillan, who managed to fight Herbert off, all three children survived. Mikayla suffered burns to 13 percent of her body. Herbert was sentenced to seventeen years in jail for two counts of attempted murder. His insanity defense was rejected by the court.

I don't share these stories to be gratuitous or shocking. I share them because they illustrate everyday horrors. The #MeToo movement jolted us out of our stupor by showing us what sexual harassment looks and feels like. If we're to get that same visceral sense for domestic abuse, we will need to doubly steel ourselves.

———

Most of what happens underground stays underground. However, in court-houses around the country, the public gets to glimpse the shocking reality of domestic abuse. Outside one of the courthouses I visit, people cluster on the footpath in twos and threes. Some pass the time with a cigarette, some on their phones, others locked in solemn conversation with the roaming advocates of the Women's Domestic Violence Court Advocacy Service (WDVCAS). Scanning the crowd, I feel something like anxiety rise in my stomach. Everybody looks so *normal*. Aside from a few neck tattoos, there's virtually nothing that distinguishes these men from others. *If you went on a date with one of these guys, how would you know?*

A policeman walks out of the court and calls for a "Mr. Pearson." A heavyset man in a long black coat looks up, nods, and follows him in. Inside, it's a full house: lawyers and police stand just below the bench, clutching folders and scanning the faces of the sixty or so seated men and women. Mr. Pearson sits alone in a chair at the front of the court, shoulders hunched and head bowed. The magistrate looks at the pile of notes in front of him and reads from the police incident report.

"Mr. Pearson came home from work," he starts, his tone matter-of-fact. "He went upstairs to his wife's bedroom, and went into the room without any clothes, placing his hand between her legs while she was laying face down, asleep. She then woke up and turned to face him. He then pulled her underwear away and attempted to open her legs by pushing her knees apart with his hands. She then kicked him and screamed for him to stop. He then continued to push her legs apart. She then covered her genitalia with her hands while continuing to scream at him to stop. As a result, one of his children entered the room, after hearing the alarm from the child's mother."

At this time, it's as if the entire courtroom is holding its breath. Did the man sitting in front of us hurt his own child? How bad is this going to get? I feel my jaw clench and am overtaken by a momentary illusion: if we sit absolutely still and quiet, maybe we can alter the course of these events and protect this child.

The magistrate goes on. "The son asked, 'What's wrong?' And he then said to his son that everything was okay." *Exhale.* "He then asked his wife,

'What's wrong? Why didn't you let me?' She was crying and upset and said, 'I don't want to do this, I don't want you, just leave me alone.'"

This feels too personal, too intimate, to be read out to a room full of strangers. Mr. Pearson is eerily still as the magistrate reads out what happened next.

Mr. Pearson accused his wife of "having someone," and said she was just using him. When she got up to pack a bag, he snatched it from her and left the room to get dressed. When his wife came out of the bedroom, he was waiting for her. Again, he accused her of using him for money, and when she told him to leave her alone, he slapped her twice across the face. She dropped to the floor, screaming for help and crying, "Call the kids!" Mr. Pearson stood over her and warned, "Don't do something silly, I will kill you." When she tried to run for the front door, he grabbed her from behind, pushing her to the ground. Mr. Pearson then paced back and forth above her, berating her for lying and accusing her and her family of damaging his property. She managed to scramble outside, where she lit a cigarette. She told him to leave. He warned her to keep her voice down, because "the neighbors can hear you."

The magistrate continues in terrifying detail:

He then pulled a knife from his side pocket and waved the knife toward her. The knife was a 30-centimeter black-handled kitchen knife. He told her to be quiet—"I don't want to hear you talking. This is what I'm going to do to you"—and he pointed the knife toward her stomach. She said, "Please don't do this. I don't want the kids to suffer. What you've already done is enough." He then told her, "Shut up, I don't want to hear from you." He called out to one of the children: "Where are you going? Why are you opening the door?" She said, "Don't do this, I want to hear my kids' voices, I want to see my kids." She walked upstairs with him behind her; he grabbed the back of her shirt, holding her as they walked up the stairs, holding the knife in his hand. They entered his room, he closed the door, and said, "If the cops come, I will chop you in half, I will slit you and let the cops do whatever they do. If they shoot me, I don't care." He kept looking out the window, holding the knife, saying, "I have a gun, I can kill us all. If you run away, I will find you, I will kill you." His wife was crying, thinking she was about to die. He kept pointing the knife at her. The police arrived and knocked on the door. He said, "What is it?" Police told him to open the door. He told her to keep quiet by putting his fingers to his lips. He then pulled the mattress of the bed up and hid the knife underneath. When the police spoke to him, he said, "I was just trying to have sex with my wife. She was asleep. I got home from night shift; I was trying to have sex. I'm a man, you know."

There's a pause as the magistrate puts the report down. He looks across the rows of solemn faces in the courtroom. These are serious offenses, he says, enough to warrant a period of imprisonment.

However, nothing brings home the awful practicalities of domestic abuse—and the vexed position of the court—like the letter the magistrate reads from Mr. Pearson's wife. They have seven children, she says, and have been married for twenty-two years. She is a stay-at-home mother, and he is the only financial provider for the children. He has "treated her like a queen" until this incident; not once has she been disrespected. He is a "loving, respectful, and hard-working man" who always helps anyone in need. He's been working two jobs, often has very little sleep, and yet she has never heard him complain. She came from a broken family, so she knows how much it hurts—and how hard it is—when families separate. Her children are now "confused and sad," and some of them are suffering from eating disorders. "There is a clear wish," says the magistrate, "for the family unit to stay together."

What is the "right" thing to do in this situation? Despite what the magistrate says, nobody can say from that letter alone that Mr. Pearson's wife has a "clear wish" to keep the family unit together. It's also impossible to know, from this one incident, just how dangerous this man is. Did he really switch, out of nowhere, from treating her "like a queen" to beating and threatening to kill her? That seems unlikely. Did she write that letter with him looking over her shoulder? Maybe. But in this moment, it's impossible to know. More to the point: What choices does she have? If she left, how would she provide for her children? Would he make good on his threats? How would they ever feel safe?

In this situation, what should the magistrate do? Lock up Mr. Pearson, and leave his wife and seven children with no income? If he *were* jailed, would that protect her? Or would he come out in a few months or years looking for revenge?

The magistrate takes a deep breath. "Taking into account that he has no prior criminal convictions, he is engaged with a psychologist, he is engaged in mental health diversion programs, he is in full-time work, and his wife expresses the need for financial assistance for her seven children, ultimately I am determining it is appropriate for him to serve his term of imprisonment by way of an intensive correction order." He asks Mr. Pearson to stand up. "You are to be on your best behavior," the magistrate tells him. "You will be regularly tested for drugs and alcohol, you will undertake thirty-two hours of community service for each month of your imprisonment, and you will engage in activities to address your offending behavior. Do you understand the terms of your imprisonment?"

In a quiet voice, Mr. Pearson says, "Yes, sir."

———

What is wrong with all these women? Why don't they just leave? If anyone ever did that to me, I'd be out of there in a heartbeat. When people hear stories of domestic abuse, this is a common knee-jerk response. We like to believe we would act immediately, that we would see what was coming. We think we're better than the women who end up in abusive relationships. We think we'd be smarter, stronger, quicker to act. We would never get trapped. Not like *them.*

But think back to the times you forgave a lover for wronging you, or trusted them against your better judgment. To do that, you had to believe that the better part of them—the part you were in love with—was dominant, and their wrongdoing an aberration. Maybe you did break up with them, but got drawn back by their pleading and promises, or simply because you missed them. Maybe you were right to trust them; maybe you weren't. It's the same for victims of domestic abuse. The only difference is that their perspective isn't just obscured by love and sexual attraction. It's been scrambled by the forces of degradation and coercion.

We're quick to judge women underground because we think their behavior is irrational. It doesn't make sense that a smart, independent woman would insist on staying with a man who brutalizes her. It doesn't make sense that after she leaves, there's a good chance she will go back to him. It doesn't make sense that a woman who is raped by her partner can continue to crave his affection. It doesn't make sense that a mother would stay with an abusive father and put her children in danger.

Maybe this does make sense to you. Maybe you scoff at those who ask why women don't just leave, and remind them: "Don't you know that leaving is the most dangerous time for a woman?" But if we're being honest, even the most empathetic among us (myself included) can sometimes find the behavior of victims bewildering (and deeply frustrating, if they are dear to us).

Even women who've lived underground can find themselves making snap judgments about other victims. Survivor Kay Schubach was at her abuser's trial when one of his victims was testifying. "I was sitting there and I was thinking, *This stupid girl, how did she let this happen?* You know, like, *Oh God, and then she got pregnant by him twice, and she went back to the house and kept going back, and this went on for months! How could she have been so stupid?* And then this penny drops. It was exactly my story, word for word." Kay had been impregnated by the same man, and she too had forgiven him after savage assaults. "[He told her] she was ugly, old, stupid, past her use-by date, that he was building a case against her, trying to discredit her mental health...[trying to line up] witnesses to testify to any scratches or marks on him. It was exactly the same."

Despite having made the same choices, Kay's impulse was to revert to the position we've all been culturally trained to take. For decades, victims of domestic abuse have been blamed by the public, maligned by the justice system, and pathologized by psychiatrists. Now many of us see just one logical binary: if your partner abuses you, you should leave. If you don't leave, there's obviously something wrong with you. That's just common sense, right?

But what *is* common sense? It's not some set of inviolable rules handed to us on stone tablets. Common sense is constructed for us, brick by brick, by academics, filmmakers, storytellers, experts—by *culture*. Every cliché we have about victims—from women's masochism to learned helplessness—was invented by somebody first before it was woven into the fabric of what is considered "normal" or "abnormal." If we trace these "common sense" positions back to their origins, we can see exactly how the dangerous logic of victim-blaming took hold—and how *illogical* it actually is.

Before we do that, though, let's start with a story that will test even the most compassionate among us.

———

Jasmine, whose story began in chapter 1, met her partner Nelson when she was seventeen, and stayed with him for more than a decade. Nelson's coercive control escalated to shocking levels of emotional sadism: aside from forcing Jasmine to sleep in the car with their newborn, he regularly traveled interstate to have affairs, and on his return would force Jasmine to watch videos of him having sex. One day, after Nelson left on another trip, Jasmine sent a message to his best friend, "David," asking David to come over. Predictably, David forwarded the message to Nelson. When Jasmine picked Nelson up from the airport a few days later, he launched into a terrifying assault.

Nelson later pleaded guilty to punching Jasmine repeatedly in the head on the drive home, then duct-taping her to an office chair in their bedroom, where he continued to beat her savagely in front of their eighteen-month-old daughter, Ruby, whom Nelson sat on the bed so she could watch. As Jasmine cried and begged for mercy, Nelson picked up Ruby, held a samurai sword to her chest, and told Jasmine that her punishment for being a slut would be to watch her daughter die. Unable to move and in a state of abject terror, Jasmine fainted. When she regained consciousness, Nelson forced her to eat her SIM card and then smashed her phone on the floor. Then, removing the tape from her wrists, he told Jasmine to get into his room and take off her pants. There, on the bed, he anally raped her. When he finished, he said: "You want to act like a dirty slut, you will be treated like one too." Then he took her to Ruby's room and told her to look after her daughter, threw in a loaf of bread, locked the door, and said they better be there when he got back. Using a pair of scissors to jimmy open the door, Jasmine was able to escape, and drove to where her parents were staying with friends. There, a family friend photographed her extensive injuries.

Jasmine did report the attack to police but refused to take it any further. Within two months, she had moved back in with Nelson. They even exchanged sexually explicit texts, and Jasmine sent erotic videos of herself telling him how much she loved him. They remained living together for five months, until January 2008, when Nelson sent Jasmine several threatening texts, trashed their daughter's room, and kicked them both out of the house. A few weeks later, after Jasmine had moved into a new place, Nelson was evicted, and Jasmine let him stay with her temporarily until he could find a new place. But when Jasmine asked him to leave, Nelson refused. Even when she stopped letting him sleep in the house, he would sleep right outside and plead to come inside. Eventually, Jasmine relented.

When Jasmine moved to another place, Nelson moved back in. They didn't sleep in the same room, but Jasmine continued to do all the housework and domestic chores. By this time, Jasmine really wanted to leave, but the more she said so, the more controlling he became, until he was locking her in the house during the day and taking her car keys to work with him.

In December 2008, almost eighteen months after the assault, Nelson finally agreed to move out. Then, just days later, when Jasmine was getting a security camera installed, Nelson arrived at the house unannounced, picked up Ruby, and walked off, telling Jasmine she would never see her daughter again. Jasmine, distraught and panicked, went straight to the police and begged them to get her daughter back, but they told her that with no family court order in place they couldn't intervene. When federal police did retrieve Ruby a week later, on the orders of a family court judge, she was still wearing the same clothes she'd been taken in, and her hair was matted to her head. When Jasmine set her down in the lounge room, three-year-old Ruby—usually a "chatty, happy girl"—refused to speak, and instead made "little wild animal sounds" and dragged herself across the floor with her legs behind her. "I'll never forget it," says Jasmine. That was the end of Jasmine's relationship with Nelson. She would spend another eight years in family court battling for sole custody of her daughter, even after Nelson was jailed for assaulting them both. Jasmine now has sole custody of Ruby.

———

What did Jasmine's story evoke in you? Sympathy, sadness, frustration, anger, disgust? Can you understand why she went back to Nelson, even after he viciously assaulted her and threatened to kill their baby girl? Why do *you* think she stayed?

For much of the twentieth century, until the late 1970s, responses to Jasmine's story would have been pretty uniform: most people would have dismissed her as a masochist. That was the expert consensus: victims of domestic abuse were frigid, controlling masochists who were secretly gratified by their abuse.

We didn't always think of survivors like this. In the late nineteenth century, victims of domestic abuse weren't "masochistic"; rather, they were seen as pitiful creatures living under the yoke of brutal, alcoholic husbands (but were nonetheless commonly reprimanded by the courts for "provoking" their husbands). But that relatively sympathetic view seemed to last only as long as women were willing to shut up and accept their fate. When, in the 1930s, wives started *complaining* about their violent husbands—and (shock-horror) even applied for divorce—they were no longer objects of pity: they were a threat to the sacred family unit.

Cue a new theory: women stayed with their abusers because they *liked* it. For the grand theory of women's masochism, we can telegram our appreciation to Sigmund Freud, who claimed—and was for a long time believed—to have discovered the essential forces driving human behavior. According to Freud, all women (who were lesser for lacking a penis, and envied men for theirs) were innately masochistic, and unconsciously sought to be punished. This wasn't just one theory jostling for primacy; for a time, Freud's was *the* dominant model. In her 1944 magnum opus, *The Psychology of Women*, psychoanalyst Helene Deutsch expanded on Freud, listing masochism as one of three essential traits for femininity, alongside passivity and narcissism.

In the 1940s and 1950s, when Freudian theories were at their peak, social workers came to believe that battered women actually *looked* for men who would abuse them. This idea gained particularly enthusiastic backing from abusive husbands. In the influential 1964 study *The Wifebeater's Wife*, three psychiatrists sought to understand the internal lives of *victims* by interviewing thirty-seven *abusers*. The responses of these violent men led the authors to conclude that, though their wives might protest their abuse, they secretly wanted it. In fact, their husbands' violence "probably" helped them deal with how guilty they felt about the "intense hostility expressed in [their own] controlling, castrating behavior."[4]

This shameless victim-blaming dominated popular thinking until the second wave of feminism crashed into the 1970s. In her bestseller *The Myth of Women's Masochism*, psychologist Paula Caplan delivered a broadside against Freud and his ilk. Women were not innately masochistic, she argued, they were simply acculturated to behavior that *appeared* masochistic, because the "ideal woman" was one who denied her own needs in the service of others. "Once females have been trained [to be nurturing, selfless, and endlessly patient], this behavior is then labeled masochistic," wrote Caplan.[5] As she told *The New York Times*, women stayed with abusive husbands not because they liked the abuse, but for myriad reasons, including fear that they would be punished for leaving. Among these reasons, they hoped that love would prevail. "Some of these women are so vulnerable that they are bonded not to the abuse," said Caplan, "but to the occasional affection these men express."[6] Her "revolutionary proposition" was that women were just as eager to be happy as men.

By the 1980s, when the opinions of abusive men were no longer counted as supporting data, the notion of the "masochistic" victim was thoroughly discredited. When researchers began to ask survivors about their own experiences, study after study returned the same result: "Women rarely provoked assaults and could do little to prevent them."[7]

Only fools and charlatans would solemnly invoke the *m*-word today, but its ghost still lurks. Two-thirds of Americans believe, for example, that most women could leave a violent partner if they really wanted to.[8] Some who contribute to this statistic believe that if a woman hasn't left, she must want to stay—because maybe she secretly likes the drama, she has a victim complex, she gets off on being abused, and so on. These assumptions are categorically wrong. The reality is far more complex, as we'll see.

Alongside the ghost of women's masochism thrives another wraith, the helpless victim rendered powerless by her partner's violence. She is the poster girl for domestic abuse: a typically white, middle-class woman cowering in a corner as her husband looms above, fist clenched. This figure emerged from the work of psychologist Lenore Walker, who with her landmark book, *The Battered Woman*, shifted the model victim from masochistic harpy to helpless child virtually overnight.

Walker's book declared that "battered women" had a unique syndrome characterized largely by "learned helplessness."[9] Walker drew this from the work of psychologist Martin Seligman, who found that dogs confined to a cage and subjected to electrical shocks at unpredictable intervals would, over time, stop trying to escape and instead become "compliant, passive, and submissive."[10] Victims of domestic abuse also became defeated by a "cycle of abuse": first a building of tension; then a phase of acute violence, followed by a "honeymoon period" of remorse, affection, and promises that it will never happen again; then another build-up phase, an explosion, and on and on it went. With each repetition of the cycle, the woman's motivation to resist diminished; she became passive, believed herself "too stupid to learn how to change things," and was prone to depression and anxiety. The reason she stayed with her abuser, said Walker, was because she was blind to the opportunities she had to leave.[11]

Walker's "helpless victim" rewound public sympathies back to the nineteenth century, when victims were pitied instead of scorned. But in doing so, she created yet another stereotype—and one that still laid blame on the victim for her abuse. It was the victim's passivity, Walker wrote, that drove the perpetrator to abuse her: "The batterer, spurred on by her apparent passive acceptance of his abusive behavior, does not try to control himself."[12] It is true that in controlling relationships, victims can become so degraded, and have their self-esteem so reduced, that they can lose the ability to do even simple tasks. They may even start to believe what their abuser tells them: that they won't be able to survive without the abuser. But they are not trapped simply because they can't see how to escape. As we will see, most victims are constantly strategizing and resisting the abuser, in their own way.

Despite clashing with the lived reality of victims, Walker's theory of learned helplessness dominated for more than twenty years and is still widely referenced. Explains one critic, the Canadian family therapist Allan Wade: "[Walker's] theory of violence became so popular because it failed to question the status quo in any meaningful way."[13]

———————

Nothing exposes the mythical thinking behind learned helplessness better than Stockholm syndrome: a diagnosis assigned to women who show affection for their captors and a distrust of authority. It's a classic throwaway line we use to describe the mental condition of domestic abuse victims, but it's also a term that's still taken seriously by some psychologists. "A classic example [of Stockholm syndrome] is domestic violence," says Oxford psychologist Jennifer Wild, "when someone—typically a woman—has a sense of dependency on her partner and stays with him."[14] But Stockholm syndrome—a dubious pathology with no diagnostic criteria—is riddled with misogyny and founded on a lie.[15] The psychiatrist who invented it, Nils Bejerot, never spoke to the woman he based it on; never bothered to ask her why she trusted her captors more than the authorities. More to the point, during the Swedish bank heist that inspired the syndrome, Bejerot was the psychiatrist leading the police response. He *was* the authority that Kristin Enmark—the first woman diagnosed with Stockholm syndrome—distrusted.

Enmark was twenty-three when, one morning in 1973, Jan Olsson walked into a bank in Norrmalmstorg and took her and three other clerks hostage. Over the next six days, the audacious heist became a blockbuster media event. Swedes had never seen anything like it, and neither had the police.

With no training in hostage negotiation, the police response was ham-fisted from the start. Early in the siege, they misidentified Olsson and, thinking they had found his younger brother, sent a teenage boy into the bank to negotiate, accompanied by Nils Bejerot, only to have Olsson shoot at him. As Olsson became more and more agitated, his accomplice, Clark Olofsson, whose release from jail was one of Olsson's first demands, reassured the hostages. "[Clark] comforted me, he held my hand," Enmark recalled in 2016. "He said, 'I want to see that Jan doesn't hurt you.' I can't say that I felt safe, because that's not the word, but I chose to believe him. He meant very much to me, because I thought that somebody cared about me. But there was no affection in that way. In some way, he gave me hope that *this is going to end okay*."[16]

There was no such reassurance from the police. Enmark asked to speak to Bejerot, but he refused. In a live radio interview from the bank, she blew up at the authorities. "[The police] are playing with...our lives. And then they don't even want to talk to me, who is the one who will die if anything happens." Sensing that their likelihood of survival was getting slimmer by the hour, Enmark took matters into her own hands. She called the Swedish prime minister, Olof Palme, and begged him to let her and another hostage leave the bank with their captors. "I fully trust Clark and the robber," she told Palme. "I am not desperate. They haven't done a thing to us. On the contrary, they have been very nice. But you know, Olof, what I'm scared of is that the police will attack and cause us to die." Palme refused to let her

leave, saying they could not give in to the demands of criminals. At the end
of the conversation, Enmark reported that Palme said, "Well, Kristin, you
can't get out of the bank. You will have to content yourself that you will
have died at your post." Enmark was appalled, telling Palme, "I don't want
to be a dead hero."[17]

Finally, police teargassed the bank vault and paraded the captors up
and down the street to cheers and jeers from the crowd. Enmark watched,
furious at this macho display. When she was told to lie on a stretcher, she
refused: "I walked in here six and a half days ago, I'm walking out."[18]

On the radio, Enmark criticized the police and singled out Bejerot. In
response, and without once speaking to her, Bejerot dismissed her comments as the product of a syndrome he made up: "Norrmalmstorg syndrome" (later renamed Stockholm syndrome). The fear Enmark felt toward
the police was irrational, Bejerot explained, caused by the emotional or
sexual attachment she had with her captors. Bejerot's snap diagnosis suited
the Swedish media; they were suspicious of Enmark, who "did not appear as
traumatized as she ought to be." "It is hard to admit," wrote one journalist,
"but the words that come to mind to describe her condition are: fresh and
alert." Her clarity was, apparently, proof that she was sick.

Enmark's savviness in establishing a personal connection with the bank
robbers was in fact confirmed after the siege by Olsson, who said that in the
early days of the siege he could have "easily" killed the hostages, and that
they survived not only because they'd been cooperative, but also because
they had gotten to know each other.

Four years later, when Enmark was asked to explain her actions, she
was indignant. "Yes, I was afraid of the police; what is so strange about that?
Is it strange that one is afraid of those who are all around, in parks, on roofs,
behind corners, in armored vests, helmets and weapons, ready to shoot?"

In 2008, a review of the literature on Stockholm syndrome found that
most diagnoses were made by the media, not psychologists or psychiatrists;

that it was poorly researched; and that the scant academic research on it could not even agree on what the syndrome was, let alone how to diagnose it.[19] Allan Wade, who has consulted closely with Enmark, says Stockholm syndrome is "a myth invented to discredit women victims of violence" by a psychiatrist with an obvious conflict of interest, whose first instinct was to silence the woman questioning his authority.[20]

In the 1980s and 1990s, Stockholm syndrome, battered woman syndrome, and learned helplessness became the dominant models for domestic abuse experts and lawyers. Victims were typecast as pure, timid, and submissive: the proverbial woman cowering in the corner. This "true victim" stereotype persists to this day in courts across the Western world. She is "a middle-aged, working-class white woman, a good mother and a devoted wife who has done everything in her power to appease her abuser and obtain protection from the criminal justice system."[21] When a victim fails to live up to this standard—if she is "difficult," addicted to drugs, uses violence to defend herself or her children, or exhibits the chaotic effects of trauma—she may be judged to be as or even *more* guilty than the man abusing her. Conversely, judicial officers may also discriminate against a woman who presents as strong and independent, because they can't reconcile competence and strength with their belief that true victims are vulnerable and helpless. Unless a victim's story matches "the standard melodrama of a virtuous female protagonist and a one-dimensional male villain,"[22] the legal system often doesn't know what to do with her.

In fact, the reality for women living underground is that they are, just like Kristin Enmark was in Stockholm, constantly strategizing and seeking ways to be safe. The research on this is conclusive. "Survivor theory" arises from a study of six thousand women who sought refuge at fifty women's shelters in Texas.[23] The study found that these women were precisely the opposite of "helpless": most had been extremely assertive in their efforts to stop the abuse. Other studies that followed[24] showed that not only were victims commonly assertive, they also had sophisticated coping strategies and frequently sought help. The obstacles these women had to overcome in order to leave weren't psychological: they were social. In case after case, it was the state authorities—in particular, police and welfare services—that had failed these women and made it harder for them to leave.

Throughout the nineteenth and twentieth centuries, while the patriarchal world of psychiatry was portraying victims as mad, bad, and pathetic, women living underground were doing what they'd always done: defending themselves, in whatever way they could. In Linda Gordon's study of social agency case records from 1880 to 1960, the same story appears again and again: a resourceful woman who, with little or no help from the state, is able to resist, and even at times overpower, her abuser.[25] Women underground have never been gratified by their abuse, and they've never been totally passive in the face of it.

We don't hear much about women's resistance, but every day women push and fight back, even in the face of terrifying consequences. "I argued back," says survivor Nicole Lee. "You get to a point where you're so exhausted, you've walked on eggshells so much—then he leaves a plate on the table, and you're just like, 'Can you just put that in the fucking sink?' And then you think *Why did I do that?* as the plate comes hurtling at you. You're fighting back tooth and nail, *Get away from me, stop.* But the physical power imbalance—there's no chance of me protecting myself against this man, none whatsoever. I tried." Even when women feel that they've surrendered their agency, they are still making the minute-to-minute calculations required to survive. As one survivor described it: "Before I met my husband, I was never a strategic person. He has taught me strategy. It was about survival."

Resistance is a human instinct. In the North Korean prisoner-of-war camps, even when the "physical and moral strength" of the prisoners was at its lowest, the will to resist remained, even if it had to be exercised subtly—like the American officer who made Communist propaganda films but indicated that he had "his tongue in his cheek."[26] Even acts that looked like capitulation were often carefully calculated. Some American soldiers who defected to Communist China after the war did so strategically, because they were afraid their coerced confessions and cooperation would get them jailed back in America. Defecting—an act Americans put down to brainwashing—was the only way they thought they could maintain their freedom.

Similarly, women may resist their abusers in imperceptible ways, and also often stay for strategic reasons. One I've heard time and again is that they are afraid of what might happen if their abusive partner fought for custody. Survivor Terri said, "I felt that the only way I could protect my children, as best I could, was to stay until they were old enough to be heard by the court. My oldest daughter had been pleading with me to 'get rid of him' from quite a young age. I explained to her that the best-case scenario would probably be that they would have to spend every second weekend with him, without anyone to witness or check his behavior. I don't think I will ever forget the look on her face when she realized what that meant."

As long as we portray women going through domestic abuse as passive and helpless, they will find it even harder to see themselves as victims. As Nicole Lee says, "We keep showing victims as this cowering person in the corner. I used to look at that and think, *Those poor women didn't do anything to deserve it. But me? I should have shut my fucking mouth. I shouldn't have provoked him.* We need to show it like it is. We keep painting the monster and the powerless victim, but they're not monsters—they're just a man that you work with, the dude next door, someone walking past you in the street. They're average people. I'm just a woman trying to protect myself, and he's just a man trying to exert his power and control."

———————

Once we've discarded all these discredited theories, it's actually not so hard to see why some women stay. Even Jasmine's reasons for returning to Nelson, though complex, are not impossible to understand. The reason she initially didn't want to press charges after the assault was because she was terrified that Nelson would either hurt her or punish her by hurting Ruby. After the assault, she was apart from him for two months and started to establish some semblance of independence—and she began to remember who she was before she met Nelson. However, just as she was reclaiming her life (and her mind), she started getting incessant calls and texts from Nelson's friends, who said he was becoming suicidal without her. Jasmine felt sorry for him and thought maybe he'd finally learned his lesson; that he might now become the man "he'd always promised he could be." Nelson also knew all the right buttons to push: he kept telling her it wouldn't be right for Ruby to grow up without a father, knowing that Jasmine was pained by the fact that her own father had left when she was little.

On top of all this, Jasmine was also suffering from complex trauma after a decade of living under extreme coercive control. She had no experience of adult life without Nelson, as they had gotten together as soon as she finished high school. "I had no self-esteem—I didn't know how to live separate from him," she says. "I have this image in my head—it's like a cobweb. You're just dangling on the outside of the cobweb, but your safety is *in* the cobweb. I was just swinging around on the outside of that cobweb, and I had nothing to hang on to."

The "cobweb" Jasmine describes is a metaphor used time and again by women underground. It's what Catherine Kirkwood calls the "web of abuse." In her book based on interviews of thirty abused women, Kirkwood writes, "The insidiousness and power of emotional abuse paralleled the invisibility, strength, and purpose of a spider's web… As in a web, the components were interwoven; no strand could be considered in isolation from the support and reinforcement of the other, and within this web...the struggle for change was complex."[27]

When a woman is subjected to extreme coercive control and sexual abuse, her mindset can become severely distorted.

When Jasmine left Nelson the first time, she did begin to reclaim her own perspective. "I started to go, hang on—I'm actually a person! I can make my own decisions, and I have a life! The longer I was apart from him, the more I started to resent him for what he had done to me," she says. "But I was still in love with him, and I was angry with him. I wanted him to be what he'd promised me all [those] years... I think I loved the idea of what he said he represented, if that makes sense. I just wanted him to be the husband, the provider—the man who looked after me. Well, forget that idea," she says, laughing. "I'm happy looking after myself now."

If the idea of loving someone who abuses you makes your head spin, think for a moment about what intimacy does to us. When we fall in love, we thrill at the potential for "oneness": the chance to have a true partner in life, someone who knows us better than we know ourselves, who can accept and love us for our flaws and vulnerabilities. To develop this kind of intimacy, we immerse ourselves in that person's life, and share our most secret thoughts and fears with them. Relationships with an abusive partner are no exception. In fact, unless the woman is there by force or arrangement, domestic abuse *needs* intimacy in order to thrive. Once intimacy is established, the perpetrator has everything he needs to hold his partner captive: trust, unique insights into her flaws and vulnerabilities, and her belief that the *true* him is the one she fell in love with, while the abusive him is just something to be fixed.

Abusers are notorious for rushing the first stage of intimacy, something that's often described by survivors as a kind of "love-bombing." This phase is electric and full of promise. Survivors commonly recall being swept off their feet by a man more passionately interested in them than anyone had ever been before. When survivor-advocate Leslie Morgan Steiner first met her partner, he idolized her. "Conor believed in me as a writer and a woman in a way that no one else ever had. And he also created a magical atmosphere of trust between us, by confessing his secret: starting at age four, he had been savagely and repeatedly physically abused by his stepfather," says Steiner. "If you had told me that this smart, funny, sensitive man who adored me would one day dictate whether or not I wore make-up, how short my skirts were, where I lived, what jobs I took, who my friends were and how I spent Christmas, I would have laughed at you. Because there was not a hint of violence or control or anger in Conor at the beginning. I didn't know that the first stage of any domestic violence relationship is to seduce and charm the victim... I had no idea I was falling into crazy love, that I was walking headfirst into a carefully laid physical, financial, and psychological trap."[28]

Sharing secrets and confiding intimate details is the kind of self-revealing behavior that bonds us to a partner. I don't want to override Steiner's interpretation of her ex-partner's behavior; I have never even met Conor. But it's important to note that men with histories of intense trauma don't necessarily start a relationship with the explicit goal of controlling their partner. Some do, but many others are terrified of being abandoned (or of being revealed as fundamentally flawed), and can be triggered into controlling and even sadistic behavior in part by the vulnerability that comes with close emotional attachment. Seducing and charming the victim *is* the first stage of domestic abuse, as Steiner says, but it is also the first stage of *any* intimate relationship. To suggest that all abusive men seduce their partner with the explicit aim to control and abuse is not reflected in the evidence, as I'll discuss in later chapters.

However, as Steiner alludes to, in any situation of coercive control or abuse, developing trust is the first component. Recall the Chinese captors lulling American soldiers into a sense of camaraderie with offers of cigarettes and kind words. When their captors later alternated between kindness and punishment, the prisoners were left disoriented and confused. Imagine, then, what it's like for victims of domestic abuse: They believe they know this person inside and out, they've made life plans with them, they may have had children with them. The sharing of confidences makes us allies and gets us invested in the journey our partners are on to over-come their "difficulties" and grow into the best parts of themselves. This alliance is exactly the protection an abuser needs; it persuades the victim that the abusiveness is just a "difficulty" he will overcome. Often, by the time the abuse starts, their captor is not just part of their family, but part of *them*. The process of realizing that the person they share a bed with—the person they have taken into their heart—is actually a mortal threat to them, and possibly to their children, is not only painful and frightening, it can be virtually inconceivable.

———

Before a woman starts to weigh up whether to leave or stay, she must first recognize that she is a victim of domestic abuse. This may sound strange to some readers. How could someone not know they are being abused? But it can take victims months or years to realize that their partner's "difficult" behavior is actually domestic abuse.

There are many reasons for this, but one of the most significant imped-iments to seeing the truth connects to the way women are socialized. There is a process that occurs around the time women reach adolescence that the feminist psychologist Carol Gilligan describes as "losing their voices."[29] In a five-year study of girls aged nine to sixteen, Gilligan observed how girls who had been "honest and confident and courageously outspoken" when they were young became, around the age of twelve, ambiguous and timid in their answers, "covering up what they knew."[30] When pressed, these timid older girls *did* know the answers to her questions, but were afraid to say what they really thought. As Gilligan explains, "We did some sentence completion tests where one sentence starts, 'What gets me in trouble is...' and a lot of girls [would] say, 'My big mouth.'"[31] This silence, Gilligan concluded, stemmed from a fear that if they expressed their opinion, they might lose their friends—but it was also for fear that boys wouldn't like them. Girls like Iris, a high school senior and the valedictorian of her class, felt they had to choose between having a voice and having relationships: "If I were to say what I was feeling and thinking, no one would want to be with me, my voice would be too loud." Iris then added, "But you have to have relationships." Gilligan calls this adolescent silencing "going underground"[32]—which is, coincidentally, the same metaphor I use for living with domestic abuse. The metaphors line up because they describe a similar phenomenon: women occupying a parallel reality, in which the truth of what they are experiencing is hidden from the outside world—and even from themselves.

Women aren't just socialized to shrink their voices; they're also taught to conceal their pain and discomfort, especially when it comes to sex. One learns as a teenager that there is nothing more important than a man's pleasure and satisfaction. When I was growing up as a teenager in Sydney, resisting sex with a guy was tantamount to a human rights abuse. Being "frigid" wasn't just disappointing, it was a medical problem that caused boys great pain. Orgasms for girls, on the other hand, were inconsequential—girls didn't *need* to orgasm like guys did. If sex caused you pain, that was not important either. Unless you had an unusually thoughtful boyfriend (as I did), the pain of losing your virginity was something you were not only expected to endure, but also to pretend you were enjoying.

This early training—to focus on a man's pleasure and satisfaction and ignore our own pain or discomfort—can follow young women into adulthood. A national research study in the U.S. showed that although 30 percent of women report pain during vaginal sex and 72 percent during anal sex, vast numbers of women do not tell their partner when sex hurts. "Everyone who regularly encounters the complaint of dyspareunia (pain during sex) knows that women are inclined to continue with coitus," reported another scientific study, "if necessary, with their teeth tightly clenched."[33]

There's even a sense that women *deserve* to feel pain—and that their desire to avoid pain is proof of their weakness. In 2009, one of Britain's most influential midwives, Dr. Denis Walsh, said that women should endure the pain of labor, and criticized hospital staff for being too quick to offer pain relief. "More women should be prepared to withstand pain," he told the *Observer*. "Pain in labor is a purposeful, useful thing, which has quite a number of benefits, such as preparing a mother for the responsibility of nurturing a newborn baby."[34]

The message girls and women receive time and again is that pain is *normal*. Want to be sexually attractive? Best you ignore how much those high heels hurt your feet and those skinny jeans dig into your hips. Best you get rid of that unsightly pubic hair, too—preferably not by shaving it, but by pouring hot wax over the most sensitive part of your body and ripping out the hair by the root. And if you have a vulva that doesn't look "normal" (i.e., it doesn't fit the standard set by porn), you should feel ashamed—or look at ways to fix it.

Is it any great mystery, then, that some women can take months or years to even realize they're being abused? How do you privilege your own pain over the apparent needs of your partner when you've been trained to do the opposite since adolescence? As the journalist Lily Loofbourow writes: "Next time we're inclined to wonder why a woman didn't immediately register and fix her own discomfort, we might wonder why we spent the preceding decades instructing her to override the signals we now blame her for not recognizing."[35]

Deb Sanasi had to google "emotional abuse" when her husband, Rob—on the stern advice of his counselor—told her that his controlling and degrading behavior was defined as domestic abuse. "Then up came this list of behaviors," says Deb, "and I actually saw my whole life in a list on a computer." She was astonished. "I thought, you know, I'm a high-functioning, intelligent person. How could I have been in an abusive relationship and not even known?"

It's not that they don't know they're being badly treated, they just don't see it as "abuse." In her TED talk, Leslie Morgan Steiner explains why she stayed for years in an abusive relationship with Conor. "Even though he held those loaded guns to my head, pushed me down stairs, threatened to kill our dog, pulled the key out of the car ignition as I drove down the highway, poured coffee grinds on my head as I dressed for a job interview, I never once thought of myself as a battered wife. Instead, I was a very strong woman in love with a deeply troubled man, and I was the only person on earth who could help Conor face his demons."[36]

This disconnect is *vital* to understand. Before women realize they're a victim of domestic abuse, they see themselves as just another woman in a difficult relationship, albeit one that may be more difficult than most. Often, it's a relationship they've invested a lot of time in, with someone they think they know better than anyone else. Most don't want to give that up until they are sure there is no way to save it—even when they know their lives are at risk.

This is what makes domestic abuse the most insidious and dangerous version of coercive control. People taken hostage against their will generally can't wait to be released, so they can go back to their old life. In domestic abuse, the relationship in which they are captive *is* their life, and they will go to great lengths—and suppress severe pain and distress—to preserve it.

In a study of more than one hundred female survivors in the United States, Kathleen Ferraro and John Johnson found that women rationalized the abuse in six ways:[37]

"I can fix him": The abuser is deeply troubled and needs a strong woman to get better. As the author Ali Owens writes:

"Occasionally—generally after a particularly cruel incident...he would promise me that he'd get counseling, that he'd do whatever it took to get better... [I]n those moments, he seemed to me like a lost, broken boy—and I would ache for him. I loved him so much that seeing his pain felt far worse than the pain he inflicted on me."[38]

"It's not really him": If he weren't [insert problem here], he wouldn't abuse me. The "problem" might be drugs, drink, mental illness, unemployment—the list goes on. Once the problem is fixed, the abuse will stop, or so the thinking goes. Sometimes they may be right, but more often than not the "problem" goes but the abuse persists.

"It's easier to try to forget": The knowledge that their partner has intentionally hurt them can be so inconceivable, some women refuse to acknowledge it. Their attention goes toward "getting back to normal"; even while the evidence (cuts, bruises) is still visible, the routines of daily life soon "override the strange, confusing memory of the attack."[39]

"It's partly my fault": Some women believe the abuse will stop if they work out how to change their own behavior—how to be more passive, more agreeable, more sensitive to their partner's needs.

"There's nowhere to go": For many women, it's just not possible to leave—there's nowhere to stay, no money, and so on. Some may believe that nobody else will ever love them and find the prospect of being alone too awful. Others, especially those from poor or violent backgrounds, view the world in general as an unsafe place, and they feel relatively protected by the abusive partner.

"Until death do us part": Some women are determined to endure the relationship, no matter what, because they see it as their duty to God, or to the notions of family and tradition. As one investigation in 2018 found (perhaps unsurprisingly), religious leaders from many faith groups still encourage women to stay with abusive partners, deny them access to religious divorce, and prevent them from leaving the marriage. Women who want to leave their abuser are threatened with exile from the community and punishment in the afterlife.[40]

Women can spend months, years, or even their entire lives rationalizing the abuse they're suffering. To distract themselves from their unbearable reality, they may turn to drugs or alcohol, develop eating disorders, harm themselves, become addicted to gambling—anything that provides a psychological escape from the abuse. Cruelly, this will likely render them untrustworthy in the eyes of friends, family, and the courts if they do try to leave.

As long as victims are rationalizing their abuse, they will commonly refuse help, withdraw testimony when their partner is charged, and otherwise resist efforts from friends or family to get them to see what's really happening to them. This can be incredibly difficult and painful for the people who love them. But there's something important to know about this process: what may look like stubbornness or naivete is, according to the Harvard psychiatrist Judith Herman, actually a sophisticated coping mechanism. "People in captivity become adept practitioners of the art of altered consciousness," she writes. "Through the practice of dissociation, voluntary thought suppression, minimization, and sometimes outright denial, they learn to alter an unbearable reality."[41] Herman calls these complex mental maneuvers "doublethink," borrowing George Orwell's term to describe "the power of holding two contradictory beliefs in one's mind simultaneously, and accepting both of them."[42] Doublethink is not just something victims use to cope: it also helps them to survive. To evade punishment, a victim needs to get inside her abuser's head, so she can be meticulously attuned to what makes him angry and what will calm him down. Over time, as the abuse worsens, his perspective becomes more important, to the point where she may start to see the world through his eyes more than her own. She does this not because she is helpless, but because she needs to be constantly one step ahead of him if she's to protect herself (and possibly her children).

But doublethink is *fragile*, as are the rationalizations that underpin it. If something about the abuse changes—if it becomes physical or is witnessed by an outsider—a victim may be startled into seeing her situation with fresh eyes. The best thing friends and family can do is give judgment-free, unqualified support, even when the victim is trying to push them away. Connections with family and friends are the best protection a victim has.

Of course, sometimes the catalyst for change is straightforward: she may just get the money, accommodation, or protection she needs to leave. Others simply reach a point of despair, where the promises to change finally ring hollow, and they have no faith left that things will get better. At this point, they may—finally—allow themselves to admit that they are victims of domestic abuse.

———

Some women recognize their abuse, leave their abuser, and go on to lead happy lives. Some may even go on to live happy or at least peaceful lives *with* their abusive partner, if he does the extraordinary emotional work required to change his behavior. But if an abusive man is determined to keep abusing her, nothing a woman does will guarantee her safety. Whether a woman stays or leaves is irrelevant to a man who is determined to punish and control her.

"Sarah" knew exactly what domestic abuse looked like. As a doctor in a trauma hospital, she dealt with injured victims of abuse every other day. One memory in particular stands out. "A woman came in who had just had a baby. She was in her twenties, and it was thought that her partner had attacked her with the back of a hammer. She had multiple entry wounds all over her head, and I remember just struggling to compute the reality of so many deep and intentional puncture wounds to her face and skull. It was heartbreaking—her prognosis was grim. I don't think she was expected to regain consciousness."

Sarah's own fiancé, "Carl," turned violent the day after he found out she was pregnant. "Suddenly my charming, charismatic partner—a man who often made fun of himself—turned into someone I didn't recognize," she says. "The anger, the entitlement, and the vitriol—it seemed to come out of nowhere." What made it even more bewildering was that up until then, Carl had been an avid supporter of female empowerment. "He really respected the fact that I was well-educated and independent," she says. "But after I got pregnant, that all changed—he expected all of my focus to be on him. He tried to control what I wore, what I did, where I went, how tidy the house was, and when I saw my family and friends. He became obsessed with the minutiae—from what I ate to what time the blinds were drawn."

After Sarah gave birth to their daughter, "Alice," the situation became even more dangerous. Alice had a medical condition that sent her to the hospital multiple times in her first year and meant that her breathing required constant monitoring. "It was an incredibly stressful time. I was walking on eggshells, trying to keep him calm, while also managing a baby who found it hard to breathe." As Sarah made repeat visits to intensive care, Carl grew increasingly erratic and malevolent. "At times, he stopped me calling an ambulance for Alice; another time he insisted that she wasn't really unwell and disconnected her breathing monitor. He photographed me if he thought I wasn't supporting her head properly, as evidence of my inadequate parenting, and would purposely squeeze my breasts so that I wouldn't have enough breast milk for her. Life was very difficult, and I tried to make sure

Alice would cry as little as possible when he was home, because when she cried, he reacted like there was an air raid siren going off."

Sarah knew she was being abused and sought help straightaway. "I was very vocal about what was going on for us. He assaulted me a number of times during the pregnancy, which I told my GP and the obstetrician," she says. "The maternal child health nurse knew, the social worker at Alice's hospital knew, even our friends and families knew. Everyone knew. I told *everyone*. He was seeing a domestic violence specialist psychologist and we went to a relationship counselor. I was trying to get him help. But while these professionals pointed to small improvements he was making, his behavior actually just kept escalating."

When I ask Sarah to describe some of the things Carl did to her, her tone is matter-of-fact. "You know, he did awful stuff to me. He raped me twice while I was in labor and ripped my episiotomy stitches because he wouldn't wait for me to heal after the birth. After Alice was born, he would ejaculate in my face in the middle of the night while I was asleep, and I would wake up choking on his cum. I was still breastfeeding Alice, so I would just quietly go and wash the semen off myself, out of my hair and nose, before the next feed. It was too dangerous to protest because there was always a baseball bat beside the bed."

As is common in coercive control, Carl's violence was just part of his broader campaign to dominate Sarah. "He'd tip expressed breast milk down the drain and control how much I was 'allowed' to give her. He threatened to 'crush the dog's skull.' He cut off Alice's private health insurance, and while I was at Alice's bedside in the hospital, he engaged a sex worker to come to our house, then demanded that I change the bedsheets as my first priority when I got home."

Despite all this, Sarah was still determined: she was going to do everything she could to return Carl to the man she had known before she was pregnant. Like a psych nurse with a patient, she managed his routine to ensure that he encountered minimal stress and had all the help he needed. "He went to the gym every day, he had all his meals cooked for him," she says. "I thought if I did all of the parenting, if I encouraged him to see a psychologist, that things would get better." But no matter what Sarah did, Carl's abuse just got worse.

One night, when Sarah was watching a special TV program on domestic violence, Carl exploded. "He watched that episode and got very angry, storming around the house, swearing and insisting that the women that had died that year all deserved to be killed, and that the men in their lives were the real victims." The next day, Sarah went to the police for advice, and called Carl's psychologist—a specialist in domestic violence—to tell him how Carl had reacted. "He basically said that he thought lots of men would have struggled with that episode, and that Carl's behavior wasn't that abnormal."

Over the next week, Carl continued to escalate, until one night, when seven-month-old Alice was unusually difficult to settle, Carl lost it with Sarah. When Alice suddenly started crying again, Carl jumped out of bed and ran into the nursery. "I heard the baby gate open, and then I heard a thud," says Sarah. "I looked at the baby monitor next to my bed, and I could see that he had jumped completely into the cot—he was crouched and had his hands around Alice's torso, and he was shaking her from above his head to the base of her cot very, very rapidly while yelling, 'Shut up, shut up, shut up!' I ran into the room and grabbed Alice away from him." Carl sheepishly got out of Alice's crib and admitted that he had "made a mistake" before returning to bed. Sarah, petrified that Alice had suffered an intracranial hemorrhage, secretly called an ambulance. As she would later write in her victim impact statement, the minutes before help arrived were "long, arduous, and terrifyingly slow... One of my greatest fears was that these would be the last moments that I would spend with Alice before she succumbed to potentially fatal intracranial bleeds. I said a private goodbye to my baby, telling her that everything would be okay and that whatever happened I loved her with all my heart." As Sarah held Alice, she steeled herself for another attack from Carl, knowing he would be furious if he discovered that she had called an ambulance and might try to injure or kill them both. This was no idle fear: Sarah knows in her bones that if she hadn't stopped him from shaking Alice, Carl would not have let go until the baby lost consciousness.

By the time Carl attacked Alice, Sarah had endured his abuse for sixteen months. While Sarah was giving a statement to the police, Alice was being examined in the hospital, undergoing procedures that left her with temporarily impaired sight. "Alice was left alone in a hospital cot, in a loud room, unable to see. When I realized and found her, she was crying hysterically and very difficult to console. She was desperately rubbing her eyes and trying to feel my face with her hands. It took some time for her to recover from this, and she stopped crawling for a period." After twenty-four hours of heart-stopping uncertainty, Alice was found to have no intracranial injuries. "In that moment, the sky was brighter, and I felt a rare surety of an omniscient, omnipotent, benevolent god."

For his assault on Alice, Carl was charged with several offenses, including conduct endangering life, serious injury, and unlawful assault. The sentence he received was typically mild: "He was offered a diversion program [an alternative to prison] and all he had to do was be on good behavior for nine months and complete a men's behavior change program. He broke the good behavior part within months, and he got expelled from his first behavior change program." After violating the conditions of the diversion program, Carl pleaded guilty to the charges and was found guilty. He received a $350 fine but served no jail time.

Although she is out of the relationship, Sarah continues to suffer ongoing abuse from Carl, only now it is utterly unpredictable. "When I lived with him, I knew what level of risk he posed to me. Or I had at least more ability to predict it, because I could see him and make a risk assessment.

Now I don't know." Sarah lives in constant fear of what Carl might do. He's considered such a threat to her and Alice that they have had to be moved into crisis accommodation five times in just twelve months. Today, they live in a location Sarah keeps secret. Nevertheless, police have told Sarah she should presume that Carl knows where they live.

When she isn't working, Sarah spends almost all her time and money managing Carl's ongoing abuse. "These days my entire life is keeping my daughter safe. When I leave Alice at daycare, there is a safety plan in place that the center has discussed with police. I've also got five concurrent court cases running, and every day there is a new legal letter or something that has to be sent, or a new affidavit." The ongoing abuse from Carl has left Sarah—formerly a successful doctor—living in virtual poverty. "I have a list of all the places in my suburb that give out grocery vouchers or free food, and over the month I go around to each one of them in turn. That's how I save for legal fees. I don't qualify for Legal Aid, because I still work. I would actually be much better off exclusively on welfare."

Despite this extraordinary situation, Sarah still gives Carl access to Alice once a week, supervised by her parents in a public place. As she did during their relationship, she manages every detail of their interaction to make sure her daughter is as safe as possible. "I stay outside, and I monitor the one exit. It's only an hour, she's got a clean diaper, she's fed, slept—everything is positioned so that there will not be a problem." From the supervised access visits, Carl is able to present himself as the perfect parent. "For Alice's birthday, Carl brought a cake, a tablecloth, lots of presents, and all the trappings of a party to the access visit. Carl changed Alice's clothes a couple of times, so it looked like he had seen her on more than one occasion, and he took lots and lots of photos. It's all about maintaining the facade of being an excellent parent to Alice for the outside world."

Sarah is trapped in this dangerous situation because if Carl were to apply for legal custody, things could get even worse. "I have been advised that if he does a short parenting course and a period of professionally supervised access visits, he'll likely be granted unsupervised access to Alice by the family court." Carl presents well; he is charming and looks like a doting father to Alice in public, but in private, she knows he is capable of sadistic cruelty.

Faced with the threat of having to leave Alice alone with Carl, Sarah has seriously considered going back to the relationship, because she feels it's the only way she can reliably protect her daughter. "He would need to get through me to get to her. If he gets unsupervised access, and there's just nothing..." She trails off, as though the end of that sentence is too horrible to utter. "I am seriously concerned that Alice will be killed if she is left alone with Carl. I know that he is capable of life-threatening violence toward Alice—I've seen and felt his impulsive aggression firsthand. It may not happen the first time, but there would be a trigger—she'd cry, she'd impose her will against his, something would happen, and he'd lose it," she says. "No parent should be asked to hand their child over to someone who almost killed them." Sarah is even more vigilant now because she feels the true danger Carl posed to Alice was a blind spot for her. "I did not ever predict during the relationship that he would attack her... I knew that I was going to be the victim of his horrendousness, but I never thought it would be her."

Despite all of this, Sarah is remarkably upbeat. "Look, I'm really grateful to him for some extent that I have Alice. I don't spend a lot of time being angry toward him or hating him, because there's just not a lot of point. I'm a really good [mom], and I love being a [mom]. That's basically the only thing that matters to me anymore. So in lots of ways I'm incredibly lucky, but my life is now all about surviving. There's no end in sight to this. And there's a significant concern that it can only get worse."

Sarah wants people to understand how difficult it was for her to leave. "I would never have left unless Carl had assaulted Alice," she insists. "And he was assaulting me sexually almost every day. I used to leave work and I would be scared to go home. I couldn't even put a finger on what I was scared of some days. In the months before leaving Carl, Alice and I were assessed as 'in need of immediate protection,' but still, [leaving] would have felt like giving up, and I don't give up. No matter what he did to me, I was fighting for my family. I'm very stubborn. I thought, *I can do this, I can put up with this*. Because I was expendable."

For now, Sarah remains on edge, and the car is always packed with an emergency bag. "We live in the moment, without an obvious future, but with a plan to stay as safe as we can. It is empowering for me to know that I have managed for as long as I have. The person who gets me by is ever-present; she is at my side, hugging my legs or sitting on my shoulders. She is the most beautiful soul I have ever known. She loves pink, painting with her fingers, Play-Doh pretend cookies, dinosaurs, Thomas the Tank Engine, and Peter Rabbit. I live in fear every day that her future will be taken away from her by her own father. I cannot imagine my life without her."

The underground does not discriminate, but for some women it is deeper and harder to escape. In this deep underground, women are oppressed not only by their abusers, but also by the compounding oppressions of racism, poverty, stigma, transphobia, insecure residency, and disability.

Advocates in the domestic violence sector have fought long and hard to make people understand that domestic abuse can happen to anyone, not just to poor women. Their efforts to shift this view—which they started back in the 1970s—have met with stunning success. The image of a "typical" victim is now a middle-class white woman. She is someone policymakers are urged to imagine as their friend, sister, or daughter; someone they might be willing to spend money to protect. (This tactic—foregrounding the "virtuous oppressed"—is common in human rights activism, notably the "respectability politics" of the civil rights movement.) However, since this "respectable" victim was created, it's become almost taboo to suggest that domestic abuse does not affect all women equally. As Professor Leigh Goodmark writes, "the movement's 'every woman could be a victim' rhetoric [has] pushed the concerns of marginalized women further to the sidelines of debates about how to address domestic violence."[43]

Yasmin Khan knows the deepest sections of the underground like the back of her hand. As the director of a community services center, Khan is a lifeline for women from culturally and linguistically diverse backgrounds. When we speak, she's in the middle of a frantic mission to get a residential visa for "Vivian," a Fijian woman who is being coercively controlled by "Neil," her older husband who has citizenship.

Everything was going well, says Khan, until one of the residency tribunal members questioned the validity of the relationship. Khan was incensed. "I said, 'Do you mean to say that after arriving here in 2015 and living in the same bloody house, there's not a relationship? There's a child that's come out of it—how can you deny that there's a relationship?'" But the tribunal wasn't satisfied. "And what was really disappointing," says Khan, "was that this woman—privileged, well-paid, blond-haired, blue-eyed—turned to this applicant, a covered Muslim woman, and said, 'Why did you think this relationship would last if he's of a different religion and culture to you?'" Khan was having none of it. "Did she ever say that to the white fella? Like: Why are you going overseas as an old man to get a forty-year-old Fijian woman? Just to look after you in your old age?" Apparently, no such questions were posed to Neil, because when Vivian got home, Neil said, "That woman was really nice to me on the phone. I'm going to tell her to cancel your visa and your passport."

Neil—a sixty-something white man who's lived on worker's compensation since injuring his back—kept Vivian a virtual prisoner for four years. He didn't let her leave the house and gave her no access to money; when she needed sanitary pads or underwear, she had to ask him to buy them. After Neil assaulted her, Vivian made the incredibly brave move of calling the police; then Yasmin was called, because she's the woman people call to handle cases like this.

Getting residency for Vivian will be an uphill battle: Neil burned and deleted any photographs of them together and destroyed every bit of paperwork she will need to verify her claim. "He's a citizen—he knows the system, and how to exploit it," says Khan. Doctors have assessed their young child as likely having a serious medical condition, but Vivian has no record of that assessment, because Neil tore it up. Now Khan has to persuade the hospital to provide her with the records, and she'll have to lean on her connections with the police to get proof of the three trips Vivian and Neil made overseas. Going home is unthinkable now for Vivian: "The child is a citizen. He's never going to get the medical attention he needs back in Fiji. They have to stay."

Khan talks a mile a minute and has a finely tuned radar for nonsense, obfuscation, and outright lies. She knows the system back to front, but also has a deep understanding of the cultural issues confronting the women she helps. "Many of [the perpetrators] don't use much physical violence," she says. "The women might get a cup of hot tea thrown on them, but they're not getting a smack in the mouth. A lot of it is threatening behavior and restricting them from socializing." These women may earn their own money—"they've all done beautician courses, so they're doing a bit of eyebrow threading at home"—but it all goes to him. The standard script for husbands is a porn addiction and a girlfriend on the side.

Religious abuse is common too: "It could be 'you can't wear the hijab' or 'you have to wear the hijab.'" And then there's the issue of getting a "religious divorce"—a process separate from a civil divorce that has to be approved by an imam or a religious body. "She has to go and ask an imam who she has no connection with, and who probably has a connection with her husband,

and she has to explain everything. Imams have no idea. They're more voyeurs than anything: 'Oh, tell us all the details. Did he do this to you, and how many times did he do that to you?' And then they'll say, 'Well, we have to ring him now and hear his side of the story.'

"Actually," says Khan, "you don't need to listen to his side of the story, especially if there has been ongoing abuse and neglect. Islam is quite simple. God says in the Qur'an, if two people don't get on, then part amicably and equitably."

However, it's not just husbands abusing these women. It might also be someone in his family, whom she and her husband are usually living with. In Indian communities worldwide, dowry abuse is a particularly chilling type of family-perpetrated violence, in which the groom's family demands additional payments after the initial dowry. Often, the new wife is essentially held for ransom: payments have to be made to stop the husband from beating her.[44]

These are the delicate and complex issues Khan deals with every day, using her clout and connections to help women navigate a Byzantine system. "I'm in a position of privilege. I use it sparingly, but for the ones who are genuine, I make sure that I pull out all stops. Yesterday, I had a long talk with the state manager of immigration and I said, 'These are a couple of cases that have fallen through the cracks.' Now we're working through some of them. I'm not a psychologist, and I'm not there to counsel. But I've got networks and support mechanisms available to help women work their way through the system."

———————

Living deep underground are another group of women we don't like to talk about: those in serious disadvantage, many of whom have lived their entire lives surrounded by violence, neglect, and abuse. Although the domestic violence sector rejects the idea that violence is born of poverty, studies do indicate that, particularly when it comes to physical violence, women living in poverty are disproportionately affected. The British Crime Survey—a nationwide computerized survey that has provided "the most reliable findings to date" on interpersonal violence in England and Wales—found that women in poor households were more than three times as likely to be living with domestic violence.[45] The British researchers who analyzed these results resurrected explanations that have long been rejected by feminists: "namely, the possibility that...where perpetrators are frustrated by an inability to establish power in an employment context, or where tensions and frustrations around a lack of money are already present, [that] may increase the propensity for some men to use violence."[46]

For the women these men target, it can be very hard to find a place of safety, or even to imagine that such a place exists. Australian Indigenous author Melissa Lucashenko demonstrated this in her searing essay on women living in Brisbane's "Black Belt" of Logan City, which is home to more than 150 ethnic groups. Poverty for the three women she interviewed had been entrenched in large part by "the violence and mental illness of parents and partners... All three—either openly stated or by strong implication—[had] been molested in childhood and/or raped at least once."[47]

Selma—"twenty-seven years old, dark-haired, doe-eyed and slender"—had four children under the age of ten. The man she still called her partner (the children's Indigenous father) had done several stints in jail and was now in rehab for his addiction to amphetamines. Selma's family were refugees from the war in Yugoslavia, and she grew up around severe domestic violence. She was "deeply humiliated at finding herself a victim" as an adult, and isolated herself to prevent her family finding out, and to protect her mentally ill brother from intervening and getting himself hurt. One day, heavily pregnant, she went to see her mom, forgetting "he'd flogged me with a stick of bunya pine the day before. I had big black welts across the back of my legs and two black eyes. I was at least eight months pregnant—I protected the belly—and I'd forgotten the bruises were there. It was like, *that was yesterday and this is today*. And I remember the look on my mom's face. I felt huge shame, like I was piss-weak. Because I always felt like I had nobody and was nobody since I came here." Like many women who have fought to survive poverty, alienation, addiction, and abuse, Selma drew power and strength from her experience of being a mother. "In the end I just had no more fear, because what else could he do to me that he hadn't already done?" she told Lucashenko. "He was chasing me with an ax this day, and then I just had enough. I said to him, 'Just do it cunt, ya dead dog. If ya gonna be a big man, just do it and put me outta my misery.'" It shocked Selma's partner enough to stop him in his tracks that day, but not enough to stop him beating her.

Despite the crushing pressures of poverty, violence, and raising young children, Selma overcame an addiction to marijuana and enrolled in technical college. She kept resisting her husband's violence and protecting her boys as best she could until, one day, the school reported that her eldest (seven years old) had said he wished he was dead. For the next three days, Selma rushed frantically to finish her assignments, then "jumped in the car and fucked off with nothing. No money, car on its last legs, no house, nothing." When Lucashenko spoke to her, Selma was living in poverty with her kids. "I don't think people realize how hard it is, not being able to provide," she said. "If I have to put my phone into hock so the kids can go on excursions, then I will. Nobody rings you anyway, there's no gas to go anywhere and no money to do anything, so you just sit home." Still, Selma had hope. When Lucashenko asked her if she had any dreams for the future, Selma surprised her by quoting Martin Luther King Jr.: "*If you can't fly, run. If you can't run, walk. If you can't walk, crawl.*" She wanted her boys to complete high school, and she wanted to go to university and then work in the domestic violence sector so she could help other women.

For those like Selma, the lived experience is clear: violence is directly compounded by poverty. "Poverty breeds hate to the other side; it breeds hate in your own little life. You are 'free' but you're not really free. You have no options."

———

Even the wealthiest victim of domestic abuse, however, may not have access to money. Abusers commonly control bank accounts, and often women flee their homes with little but the change in their pocket. Many middle-class women spend so much on the process of leaving that they are left practically destitute. On average, leaving an abusive partner is estimated to take around 141 hours and cost around $18,000.[48] If the abuser wants to keep controlling her through the legal system, that amount can quickly rise into the tens of thousands. If children are involved, the costs can be astronomical: family law cases easily run into the high tens and hundreds of thousands of dollars, and even if you "win," you still have to pay your own legal and court costs.

In a 2017 survey of domestic abuse victims, fear of destitution was the leading reason women were afraid to leave their abuser,[49] polling well ahead of fear of physical violence. This comment from Sophie, a mother of two girls, was typical: "I ended up leaving the relationship scared witless in terms of the financial abuse with a one- and a two-year-old [and] with $1.57 in my bank account. A friend had to put $150 in my bank account... I think the week before I left, I had $15 and he canceled the credit card."[50]

The vast majority of domestic abuse victims—between 80 and 90 percent[51]—have experienced financial abuse, an often vicious type of control and exploitation that leaves many impoverished. "Erin," who had two children by her abusive husband, "John," worked so hard juggling child-care and full-time work that she almost had a nervous breakdown, and ended up in the hospital. Determined to give John the freedom to build his business, Erin paid for everything: the mortgage, the groceries, and every other expense came out of her wages. But after witnessing one suicide and then another attempt at work, Erin needed to take leave, which meant the family had to struggle to survive on John's apparently meager income. Erin had to beg John for money, even for essentials. She had to write shopping lists for him to approve, and when she developed an abscess in her tooth he refused to pay for the dentist, forcing her to go to her parents for money. When Erin finally worked out how to leave John safely, he refused to pay child support. When Erin went to formally challenge this, she was astonished by what she found. The entire time she had been working herself into the ground, John had been earning $250,000 a year from his business. He was still receiving that income when he was making her submit shopping lists, denying her money for the dentist, and forcing her to beg for gas money.

Women encountering financial abuse typically describe three types of abuser: controllers, exploiters, and schemers. Controllers and exploiters— the two most common types—"use financial abuse as one of a range of behaviors to control their partner and get their needs met within the relationship." Schemers, in contrast, don't enter a relationship for love: they focus purely on stripping the woman of her money and assets. When they're done, they leave. Emma, a thirty-eight-year-old hairdresser, spent seven years with a schemer and lost all her savings and her hairdressing business as a result. "I was completely financially secure and living the life I had always wanted to...until about seven years ago I met a guy and began a relationship. It got to the point where if I asked about his situation he would just blow up. In that time, he was siphoning money; he gambled...he just dismantled me in every way... I ended up with nothing but financial debt. I lost my home, my business, most of my friends."

The instinct most of us have to avoid conflict is the cover financial abusers need to hide what they're doing. In many cases, women just stop talking about money, for fear it will end up in a fight, or worse. "Jennifer," a forty-year-old police investigator, explained: "A lot of the time I wouldn't end up having the conversation about finances because to me, he was a volcano ready to erupt and God knows what he'd get up to."

The damage wrought by financial abuse can profoundly alter the course of a life. "Susan," a fifty-three-year-old with four children, was told by her partner in no uncertain terms that in return for her leaving him he intended to "destroy" her through the legal system. "He has all the assets and he is saying to friends that he is not going to stop," she says. "He has said that he is going to use everything in the court system to destroy me financially because I cannot afford the legal fees. I have paid $65,000 so far."

Despite hoary old gender stereotypes about men being "naturally" better with money, women in these relationships are not only able to manage a household on an abusively rationed budget, they are often incredibly resourceful money managers once they leave—even in the face of torturous and costly legal abuse from their partners.

———————

No matter how clearly we depict what domestic abuse is like for women living underground, most people will resist understanding it. This resistance is deep and instinctive: we don't want to know that the same forces that so blissfully draw us together can also become our single greatest threat. We need to believe in love, and we need to believe that any threat to our well-being would come from someone unknown to us, from outside forces. We persist with the question "Why doesn't she just leave?" because it's easier to separate "us" from "them" if we can frame "them" as illogical. It is too frightening to believe that this could happen to any of us.

As we've seen, however, it's not so hard to understand the behavior of victims. In the years I've spent writing this book, I've found that it's the questions we *don't* ask that are the most confounding: Why does *he* stay? Why do these men, who seem to have so much hatred for their partners, not only stay, but in fact do everything they can to stop their partner from leaving? Why do they even do it in the first place? It's not enough to say that perpetrators abuse because they want power and control. *Why* do they want that?

These are questions that take us down a much deeper rabbit hole.

3.

The Abusive Mind

I lived through hell at the hands of this man. I want people to understand how easy it is to feel trapped. I was immobilized through terror, through hopelessness, through absolute powerlessness. I want people to stop asking "Why does she stay?" and start asking "Why does he do that?"

SURVIVOR

There are some things that, once read, we wish we could unread. Each time I've gone to write a graphic account of violence, I have hesitated. I don't want to disturb readers unnecessarily, and I am painfully aware that many will have experienced horrors of their own. So I don't write these accounts lightly. But I *do* write them, because as long as we conceal domestic abuse under umbrella terms like "rape" and "assault," we will never fathom its true, visceral horror. We need to look this phenomenon square in the face. The bare facts of a violent incident—a hit, a slap, a threat, a rape—tell us very little. The real devil of domestic abuse is in the details. Of the hundreds of accounts from survivors I've heard or read, this one has seared itself into my memory.

"My head was pounding," she begins. "He was ripping out my hair. I had big chunks of hair missing... I was screaming the whole time. The neighbors didn't call anyone. When I tried to scream, he would smother me. Then I blacked out. When I woke up, he was on top of me and he started having sex with me. I was like, *stop it, everything is hurting, I can't move, stop it, you're hurting me.* I was crying. He was like, *shut up, shut up, I'm just using you, shut up, you slut.* I was like, *please stop, please stop.* He was like, *I'm doing this because I love you.* Then he obviously didn't stop. I just blacked out... Then when I woke up again, he was yelling at me to get up because he had to go to work."[1]

I'm doing this because I love you. That's the line I couldn't stop thinking about. How had this man's "love" become so dangerously perverted?

For most readers, the violence and insanity of this assault will be as foreign as it is shocking. And yet the evidence tells us that such scenes play out every day and night around the world: in suburban homes and small towns, apartment blocks and mansions. The abusers are men who are prominent and successful, men who work regular jobs, men who are mentally ill, men with drinking problems, men who work their guts out for minimum wage, and men who expect their partners to earn all the money *and* do all the housework. Men who say they love their partners. Men who say they want equal rights for women. Men who think most "chicks" are dumb sluts begging to be raped. Men who often show no signs they are capable of such sadism. Just as an infinite variety of women end up as victims, there is no such thing as a typical male perpetrator.

So how does it happen? Why do so many different kinds of men abuse the women they claim to love?

The answer to that question depends on who you ask. Let me be clear at the outset: Explaining abusive behavior is not an exact science. It's a battle of ideas being fought on territory we've only just begun to map. It's been about fifty years since scholars started taking domestic abuse seriously, and ever since, competing factions have clashed over how to explain it.

First, as we've seen, we make a terrible mistake when we treat "domestic abuse" as one homogeneous phenomenon. Those two words cover behavior that ranges from cold and systematic to reactive and haphazard.

Perpetrators may use predictable behaviors and tactics—as though they've studied some "perpetrator's handbook"—but the intensity of their abuse, and their *reasons* for abusing, vary wildly. A sociopathic coercive controller who exploits his wife for money and domestic labor is very different from the morbidly jealous man who controls his wife because he's terrified she will leave. Add other variables, such as mental illness and substance abuse, and you have yet another set of circumstances.

That's why researchers have attempted to arrange the behavior of abusive men into a few distinct categories. These categories, which in academic terms are known as *typologies*, are an attempt to distill the chaos of abusive behavior into clear, observable patterns. They've had some success: in study after study, researchers have repeatedly landed on similar ways to describe different "types" of abusive men. It's tempting to treat these types as diagnoses (*Oh, he's definitely this type, not that*). But a caution before we begin: even the researchers who've defined these types say it's often impossible to slot individual abusers definitively into one single type. As we saw in chapter 1, some men may start out acting like one type and shape-shift into another; others may seem like a combination. Human complexity defies neat categorization. We'll have more to say on this later, but for now, here's how the world's leading researchers have tried to illustrate that perpetrators are not all the same.

In 1995, two psychology professors at the University of Washington made a surprising discovery. Doctors John Gottman and Neil Jacobson were trying to solve a riddle that had long bewildered researchers: Why are some men violent toward women? To do this, they invited two hundred couples into a laboratory—nicknamed "The Love Lab"—to examine their arguing styles. They connected them to polygraph machines to record physiological responses such as heart rate, respiration, and blood pressure. Then they asked them to fight.

Late one Saturday night, they were crunching the data on sixty-three couples where the men had a history of controlling behavior and physical and emotional violence. These sixty-three men were *coercive controllers*: they sought to dominate their victims by isolating them, micromanaging their behavior, humiliating and degrading them, monitoring their movements, and creating an environment of confusion, contradiction, and extreme threat.

The data showed something Gottman and Jacobson weren't expecting. Usually, when people argue, they experience a range of internal responses: their heart rate goes up, their blood pressure skyrockets, and so on. And that's exactly what the data showed for the large majority of those men, around 80 percent. But, for the other 20 percent, the physiological results showed precisely the opposite. As these men became increasingly aggressive toward their partners, their heart rates *dropped*. On the outside, they looked just as angry and worked up as the other men, but internally they were perfectly calm. In fact, as they verbally abused their partners, the measurements indicated that they felt *calmer* than earlier in the study, when the doctors had asked them to close their eyes and relax.

Gottman and Jacobson replayed the tapes again and again, casting a forensic eye over the differences between how these two distinct groups of men fought. Each behavior and physiological response, from flickers of disgust to clammy hands to audible sighs, was meticulously coded and recorded. From this elaborate dataset, the doctors devised two profiles: "Cobras" and "Pit Bulls."[2]

Cobras

The smaller group of men—those who were internally calm when arguing—were observed to be more aggressive and even sadistic toward their partners. Their behavior was akin to that of the cobra, which sizes up its victim, then becomes perfectly focused, before striking hard and fast. By calming themselves internally, the Cobras remained in complete control even when they looked like they were losing it, enabling them to be swift and ruthless with their partners. They also displayed fewer signs of emotional dependence; some would even goad their wives into cheating on them. They were very frightening to their wives, the researchers noted, "and yet at the same time captivating."[3]

"George" was a Cobra. He liked unsettling people with his dry, dark humor and was a cold and systematic abuser who dominated his wife, "Vicky," in terrifying ways. Gottman and Jacobson describe a typical scene from their life:

> George came home late after drinking with his buddies and found Vicky and Christi (their young daughter) sharing a pizza. Vicky was angry at him for missing dinner and ignored him when he arrived. Her silence angered him, and he shouted, "You got a problem?" When she remained silent, he slammed his fist into the pizza, knocked her off the chair, dragged her across the room by her hair, held her down, and spit pizza in her face. He then beat her up, yelling, "You're a bitch! You've ruined my life!" Vicky described the argument as typical: "powerful, mean, and fast."[4]

George thought nothing of the assault: he minimized it and said he didn't remember the details "because it's not important." Besides, "[s]he was a bitch and she deserved it." Gottman and Jacobson wrote that "George was not emotionally dependent on Vicky...[but] in a peculiar way, he did need her. It seemed to us that his need for her was so infantile, a need to know that he had the power to control her. Having this power was important to him, perhaps because as a child he was so powerless." George was attached to the experience of having power over someone but was not emotionally

attached to Vicky herself. She could be anyone—so long as she was someone he could dominate.[5]

Pit Bulls

The majority of coercive controllers in the study behaved quite differently.
Their heart rates increased when they fought. Their anger built gradually,
and they became more domineering and threatening over time, until they
were in such a state of rage that they couldn't calm themselves. Searching
for another animal analogy, Gottman and Jacobson decided they were
akin to a breed of dog, the pit bull, because their hostility slowly increased
until, finally, they attacked. Unlike the cold and avoidant Cobras, Pit Bulls
were codependent and profoundly insecure, twisted by morbid jealousy
and paranoia.

A soft-spoken, artistic man called "Don" was a typical Pit Bull. He
was obsessively jealous with his wife, "Martha," and terrified she would
abandon him. This made him resent how dependent he'd become on her
and how vulnerable she made him feel. Things weren't all bad with Don:
he loved to buy Martha presents and take her to expensive restaurants.
But once they were married, Don's violence became an almost daily event,
and the honeymoon periods of remorse shrank until he stopped bothering
to apologize at all. Don was a textbook coercive controller: he monitored
Martha's movements obsessively and called regularly to check on her.

Don wasn't charismatic and charming like George; in fact, when he
met Martha, she was struck by how candid and raw he was about his terrible childhood, during which he'd been routinely humiliated and beaten
by his preacher father. He was tender and attentive with Martha at the
beginning. When Don's violence began to emerge, it was short-lived: he
would be mortified by his behavior, apologize sincerely, and return to
doting on her—until it happened again. At first, Martha fought back and

tried to hold Don accountable for his violence. But as the abuse became more frequent and severe, she grew increasingly afraid of him and withdrew into a state of hypervigilance, exhausted by her constant efforts to try to keep the peace. There was no respite for Martha; managing Don's volatility became a full-time job. His emotional needs, as the researchers noted, "were constant... [He] needed Martha to fill a void that could never be filled." Don had a "compelling need to feel connected to others." But after growing up in a family where emotional intimacy was cauterized by abuse, the relationship soon reached the point where "the only way that Don could connect with Martha was through violence."[6] By the time they showed up at the laboratory, Don was beating, humiliating, and abusing Martha every day. There was no latitude for her to resist: even when she tried to calm him down by asking, "Can we just drop it for now?," Don would blow up and accuse *her* of being abusive. His public face was very different: to the doctors, he appeared "meek and mild-mannered." In their interviews with him, he insisted it was he who was the victim, not Martha, and claimed that she loved to make him angry and "got off on it" when he reacted.[7]

This was, the doctors found, one of the key distinctions between the two groups of coercive controllers. Like many Pit Bulls, Don "didn't know he was dangerous." Cobras like George, on the other hand, knew they were dangerous—they just didn't care.[8]

Telling the Difference

From the fights they observed and their interviews with each couple, Gottman and Jacobson listed the differences between the two basic types of coercive controller. Cobras were generally hedonistic, impulsive, and blighted by an overblown sense of entitlement. They abused and dominated their wives to get what they wanted, whenever they wanted it. They had little interest in intimacy and did not fear abandonment. Instead, they appeared interested only in the benefits their wives could provide: sex, money, social profile, and so on. They were in the relationship for instant gratification and the thrill of being dominant. Cobras were the abusers most likely to answer the door calmly to police and fool them into believing it was really the agitated and hysterical wife who was the problem, not them.

Statistically, Cobras were also the ones most likely to have antisocial personality disorders, being sociopathic/psychopathic types relatively untroubled by messy feelings of guilt, remorse, or empathy. They were also most likely to have had severely problematic childhoods, in which at least one parent had abused or neglected them. These experiences in childhood, the researchers surmised, had perhaps "led the Cobras to vow that no one would ever control them again." Seventy-eight percent of Cobras in the study had grown up with violence, compared to 51 percent of the Pit Bulls.[9]

George came from a divorced family and grew up being beaten and neglected by both parents. His mother was a sex worker, and George was sexually abused by her male clients. As a vulnerable, dependent child living in this frightening environment, George worked out how to go cold when he was in a state of stress: when his mother hit him, for example, he would "leave the scene" in his mind (a process called *dissociation*).[10] Vicky could see how wounded George was, and—like so many other women devoted to their abusers—was determined she would be the woman to help him heal. But her devotion was simply another source of amusement for George. As he yelled at her while they argued in the lab, "Don't you see? It's all a game! Life is a game."[11]

The violence of George and other Cobras was typically more severe than that of the Pit Bulls. Thirty-eight percent of the Cobras had threatened their wives with a weapon, compared to only 4 percent of Pit Bulls. In the twelve months before their time in the lab, George had threatened to kill Vicky repeatedly, and had kicked, pushed, shoved, and choked her more than a dozen times. Nine percent of the Cobras *had* actually stabbed or shot their wives; not one Pit Bull had done this. The majority of both groups had, however, used severe physical violence against their wives, including beating and choking them.[12]

Whereas Cobras were generally difficult or intimidating, Pit Bulls were the kind of men who neighbors and friends would describe as "nice guys." Few would ever see their dark side, because their abuse only surfaced in intimate relationships. But they were no less controlling than the Cobras; they were often jealous to the point of obsession, and prone to converting the most unlikely clues into evidence of betrayal. These were the men who, once wounded, were more likely to stalk and potentially kill their partners after they'd left. "Although one is safer trying to leave a Pit Bull in the short run," the researchers wrote, "Pit Bulls may actually be more dangerous to leave in the long run."[13] Cobras were less interested in chasing; they were at their most dangerous when they were about to be exposed and left: for instance, if their partner threatened to call the police or take them to court. Cobras are emotionally attached to the need for control, but not necessarily the individual they are controlling. If she leaves and doesn't seek to reveal his abuse, a Cobra can simply move on to the next woman.

Two years after the initial study, Gottman and Jacobson interviewed their subjects again. The marriages of the Pit Bulls were highly volatile—almost half of them had ended—but not a single Cobra had separated or divorced. That's because the women married to Cobras were, the researchers deduced, too terrified to leave.[14]

When I spoke to John Gottman about this experiment, he was on the other end of a phone line in Seattle. There, he and his wife, Dr. Julie Gottman, head up the world-renowned Gottman Institute, which specializes in couples therapy and takes a "research-based approach to relationships." Gottman has been in the love business for more than forty years. He started out as a mathematician, studying at MIT, and became famous for (among other things) being able to predict whether a couple would be together in fifteen years, simply by watching them talk for one hour (his success rate is up to 94 percent).[15] Today, his research findings form a key part of what many psychotherapists understand about marriage and divorce.

Gottman talked about this particular study—one of hundreds he's carried out over the past twenty-five years—with such enthusiasm and detailed recall, it was as if the results came in yesterday. "Here's another thing that surprised us," he said. "The violence decreased over time, so we thought, *Oh, maybe this problem just takes care of itself.* But it turned out we were wrong. Once a perpetrator has frightened the victim, they don't have to use as much violence to get control. So, for example, a guy can just swiftly move his head—this is what the Cobras do, swiftly move their head and have an intake of breath, and just glare—and it reminds the partner that they're capable of sudden changes that's enough to keep them in line." I asked, "Is that partly why some victims talk about being so traumatized in court? Because the perpetrator is sending those subtle signals to intimidate them, but nobody else can see what they're doing?"

"That's right," Gottman replied.

Gottman and Jacobson noticed something else about coercive controllers in their lab. "They all think they're undiscovered geniuses," said Gottman. "Like, one guy that we studied, who is a Pit Bull; he was sure that he was going to become really famous internationally for his coin collection. That was his claim to fame. All of them had this ethos: 'I'm an undiscovered talent, and the world has abused me by not recognizing my great talent.' They get the woman to go along with this. They're on their side, that this person should be a celebrity. In reality, a lot of these guys don't do very well."

However, the guys who *did* do well, Gottman added, were "really terrifying." "They're not criminals, and they're not losers," he said. "They're CEOs, detectives, judges, entrepreneurs. Like this guy [Rob] Porter [former Trump White House staff secretary] who just resigned from the White House. He was violent toward three women. Those guys are really terrifying, because when the women leave, [these men] try to get even, and they make sure they ruin these women's lives. So you can't think of Pit Bulls and Cobras as criminal losers; many of them are very successful. I think our president [Donald Trump] is one of them."

––––––––––

The two basic types Gottman and Jacobson identified are seen time and again by other researchers and by people who work with perpetrators. Andre Van Altena has spent more than two decades working with violent men in prisons. He's a hulk of a man who has spent most of his adult life trying to get some of the state's most dangerous men to own up to their violence and change their behavior. Over the years, he says, he too has observed these two types. The codependent men—the Pit Bulls—"are often the ones who are very erratic, hostile, needing lots of support, and demanding support." These men are very different from the "more calculating, controlled offender." These offenders—Gottman and Jacobson's Cobras—are what Van Altena refers to as "the extreme end": the guys with antisocial disorders like psychopathy or sociopathy, who would typically avoid a program like his. "Some will tell you that they're selective on who they get involved with in their relationships—they're looking for someone that they can violate, that they can groom, and [they're looking] for the opportunity to control them."

"For these guys, the lack of empathy, the lack of regard for the victim… You're banging your head on a wall to have them in a therapeutic group. In fact, they will often try to collude with the facilitators, and speak on behalf of the other guys." Appealing to their sense of empathy or remorse is a waste of time, though they may show glimmers of both (generally as a tactic, says Van Altena). Instead, these offenders need to be treated one-on-one, and any appeals for them to change have to speak to their self-interest.

How do they feel about what's happened to them as a result of their crime? Do they really want to keep landing back in jail? Aren't they smarter than this? "The motivation [for change] will be freedom," says Van Altena, "what quality of life he's looking for, and what the community expects from him."

————

In summation, Gottman and Jacobson's research suggests that there are two types of coercive controllers: a big group, called Pit Bulls, whose anger and hostility build slowly and then explode; and a small group, called Cobras, who are always in control, even when their violence looks frenzied. When Pit Bulls fight, their heart rates go up; when Cobras fight, their heart rates go down.

There's general agreement from other researchers on the description of these two categories, but subsequent studies have failed to replicate the results exactly.[16] One study did succeed in replicating the division in heart rate (20 percent of their abusive participants also showed decelerated heart rates), but drew different conclusions about what that indicated about the men's style of violence. When I asked Gottman why his study had never been duplicated, he pointed to the different research methods used. "It's very hard to replicate things when you don't have the kind of high-tech laboratory that we had," he said. "That includes very good observational measurement—looking at facial expressions, how the body works, and how they work interactively."

One of the leading researchers who tried and failed to replicate the study is Amy Holtzworth-Munroe, a professor of psychology at Indiana University who has developed what are perhaps the best-known typologies for abusive men. She says that although she thinks there may be problems with the study's heart-rate conclusions, there hasn't been enough funding to investigate it properly. What *was* supported by her research were the basic categories: Cobras, who are cold and calculating, and Pit Bulls, who are paranoid and reactive. These two types were very similar to the typologies she identified.

Holtzworth-Munroe wrote her now-famous paper in 1994,[17] a year before Gottman and Jacobson, when domestic abuse researchers were starting to realize that not all offenders were the same. Munroe looked at three different factors:

1.   The severity and frequency of the abuse.
2.   Whether the abuser was violent outside the family or had a criminal history.
3.   Behavioral traits that matched certain personality disorders, like psychopathy or borderline personality disorder.

"When we put that together, we proposed the three types," Holtzworth-Munroe told me from her home in the Midwest. "I don't like the names for them, but these are the names that have stuck."

The first type—the "generally violent/antisocial"—are essentially the men Gottman and Jacobson defined as Cobras. These men aren't just a threat to their partners: they have a criminal nature and may also be a threat to the public. They are the abusers most likely to have had violent childhoods, they act on impulse, and though they have hostile attitudes toward women, they're also just hostile in general and are used to behaving violently. These are classic sociopaths, psychopaths, and malignant narcissists. What we know, however, is that many seemingly disordered perpetrators don't actually have a personality disorder. They just behave as though they do.

Lindt Café gunman Man Haron Monis is a classic example of a "generally violent/antisocial" perpetrator. Grandiose and deluded, Monis was a self-styled sheikh who first abused his wife and then, after they'd separated, arranged for his new girlfriend to kill the wife. In December 2014, when he took eighteen people hostage at the Lindt Café in Sydney's Martin Place, he was awaiting trial for the murder of his ex-wife and had also been charged with sexually assaulting several women who had come to him as a "spiritual healer."

The connection between domestic abuse and mass shootings is now explicit, especially in the United States, where mass shootings (defined as killing four or more people in a single incident) have become so commonplace, they occur on nine out of every ten days on average. Between 2009 and 2016, more than half of American mass shootings started with the murder of an intimate partner or family member.[18] Many other mass shooters have had histories of domestic abuse, including Omar Mateen, who killed forty-nine and wounded fifty-three at a gay club in Orlando, Florida; Mohamed Lahouaiej-Bouhlel, who killed more than eighty people when he drove a truck into a crowd in France on Bastille Day; and Robert Lewis Dear Jr., who shot three people dead at a Planned Parenthood clinic in Colorado. As Rebecca Traister wrote in New York Magazine: "What perpetrators of terrorist attacks turn out to often have in common, more than any particular religion or ideology, are histories of domestic violence."[19]

The second type, which correlates closely with the Pit Bulls, Holtzworth-Munroe called "dysphoric/borderline" (she did warn you that the names aren't catchy). Their abuse is normally confined to the relationship, which is why neighbors and friends find it hard to believe they could ever be abusive. Typically, a traumatic upbringing has left them terrified of abandonment, codependent, and morbidly jealous. Many fantasize that their intimate relationships will dispel the feelings of insecurity and worthlessness that have plagued them since childhood. "They're very worried about losing the relationship, so they become hypervigilant to cues that maybe their wife is screwing around and is going to leave them—even when there's no logical reason for them to perceive that," says Holtzworth-Munroe. "We don't know if they're using the violence because they're trying to get control over her, or because they're so emotionally dysregulated that they just can't control their upset and anger." These emotionally dependent men are the most likely to kill themselves after they've killed their partners.

The third type Holtzworth-Munroe identified is the "family-only batterer" (a type I loosely described as an "insecure reactor" in chapter 1). The family-only batterer is not a coercive controller. Essentially, their violence is an expression of frustration, anger, and sometimes rage that arises from stressors in their lives; once expressed, their abuse and the emotion that led to it seem to disappear, leaving them feeling back to normal until the next eruption. When they express remorse, they often mean it, and they are more likely to volunteer for and complete treatment. But even these men—the most receptive to treatment—are often reluctant to change.

Holtzworth-Munroe says that of the three types, family-only batterers are the most mysterious. Why do they abuse, when other men—who also deal with stress in their lives—do not? "Maybe it's cultural factors, maybe it's substance abuse—we don't know." What she can say is that their stress-related abuse usually corresponds with other risk factors, such as growing up with domestic abuse or having poor communication skills. But here's another thing. Unlike the other two types, these men are *not* overtly misogynistic—certainly no more or less than other nonviolent men. This should be a major consideration when we talk about *why* men are violent toward women, as we'll see a little later in this chapter.

————

There is no hard and fast border between these typologies. Just because a man fits a family-only batterer description now doesn't mean he won't develop over time into a coercive controller.

Typologies can be a great force for good. As Professor Jane Wangmann writes, they offer a vital insight, and can highlight "whether the use of violence is motivated by coercive control; whether it is one-off or conflict based...whether the person uses violence beyond the family setting; and whether there are other factors (for example, psychological) which are also important to understanding that person's use of violence."[20] This, she writes, has huge ramifications for how we respond to perpetrators: it tells us that a one-size-fits-all approach to reforming them is almost certainly doomed to fail; it helps us to devise better interventions and treatments for victims; and it has the potential to help us make better decisions in family law disputes.

Unfortunately, typologies can also do a lot of harm. As Wangmann notes, there are serious concerns about how they are applied, and most revolve around a single question: Do they make victims more or less safe? What if, for example, a judge in a family law case decides to grant access to children after being persuaded that the father was a family-only batterer, when he was in fact a coercive controller and was therefore a far greater danger to the children and their mother?

Holtzworth-Munroe is also disturbed by how her typology has been misused in the justice system. "I was told that, for example, a judge was trying to make those decisions from the bench—'Oh, you're a family-only man,' and 'Oh, you're a borderline-dysphoric man'—and then making decisions based on that. That was very concerning. Because even I couldn't do that!" she says with a laugh. "Except for extreme cases, you're not going to find people who are like, 'Oh, that's definitely this kind of man.' They're more *dimensions* than clear types."

For some who work with men in behavior change programs, the very notion of typologies is regressive and offensive. "Reducing people to negative categories or stereotypes in that way is offensive, humiliating, and against the entire spirit of why we do this work," says Allan Wade, a Canadian therapist whose work with survivors and perpetrators centers around dignity. "I can understand why people want to categorize. On the other hand, it doesn't seem to be very successful. And one of the reasons for that is that all typologies ignore the context around the person." Wade tells me that although typologies are seductive, they give the illusion of clarity—that we have some kind of perfect theory to explain domestic abuse. They also imply that men who abuse do so in a vacuum. "What we seem to want is a narrow description that absolves all the rest of us from examining the practice of our public institutions—the criminal justice system, family law system. That's where patriarchy, power, social class, gender bias...that's where that all exists. So we need explanations [for men's use of violence and control] that take the institutional responses to it into account."

Lizette Twistleton, who has been working with abusive men for more than fifteen years, says that when she's sitting with a man who's used violence and control, typologies are a wall up against his humanity. "When I read them, I think, *Yep, I've definitely worked with men who I could say, 'You're a bit of a Cobra, you're a bit of a Pit Bull.'*" But these "types" can easily pigeonhole people; they don't take into account the depth and breadth and complexity of them as human beings, and how that complexity influences how they behave and how they interact in a relationship. Twistleton herself has "pretty serious lived experience" and has for decades worked with women and young people, mostly victims of violence, who were "really struggling in their lives." Since working with young men, she's known that nothing will change as long as the sector—and society—insist on "otherizing" men who use violence and control.

"A good majority of the men who end up in the groups, you watch them have those moments where they go, *Holy shit, that's me—that's what I'm doing to my kids, to my partner...* You sit in that really heavy, deep space where someone's letting in that shame. If we put a label on them and say, 'Oh, you're a Cobra' or 'you're a Pit Bull,' we're casting them out as some scary thing people don't want to go anywhere near. All we're doing is pushing them to a more extreme place."

Shaming is precisely the opposite of what Lizette is trying to do in men's behavior change groups. "We want him to recognize his human connection to the people he's harming. We want him to develop empathy and to understand that the people he is harming are actually people he loves and who love him."

For Lizette, typologies shrink impossible complexity to a bit of "pop psychology." So, I ask, how does she explain the various patterns commonly observed in men who use violence and/or control? "I just say there's no quick answer. It's way too complex. We can identify patterns of behavior (like coercive control) and how different individuals will apply those patterns of behavior. But for them, part of the *how* might be about their personality and what kind of family they grew up in. Were they wealthy or not wealthy? Were they religious? Was it a family with a lot of traditions? You start to create a much richer picture of that person rather than a one-dimensional 'type.'"

———

To give you a sense of just how slippery and misleading types can be, let's look at the story of a twenty-one-year-old white British man called "Glen."[21] He'd been in and out of jail since he was a teenager for multiple offenses: arson, burglary, assaulting a police officer, attempted robberies, assaults, possession of weapons, and theft. Glen sought help soon after he grabbed his girlfriend, "Michelle," by the throat. He had been with Michelle for three years, a relationship he described as the best he'd ever had, despite it being wracked by violence from both sides. Glen had never hit Michelle, he said, even when she hit him. But he had thrown their puppy across the room when they were arguing and held her by the throat to restrain her when she hit him.

Speaking to Glen about Michelle, researcher Mary-Louise Corr may have concluded that this was just a volatile relationship, in which both

partners were unable to control their anger. But although Glen had not
been overtly violent toward Michelle, he *was* controlling—just as he'd been
with his two previous girlfriends. Exploring Glen's other relationships, the
researchers discovered a pattern: with all three girlfriends, he would get
"wound up" when they wore revealing clothing or got attention from other
guys. His way of dealing with his paranoia was to "always be with them, like
I wouldn't let them out of my sight 'cause I used to get paranoid and seeing,
thinking, what they're fuckin' up to. I think I used to force them to change
[their clothes] as well. Like say, 'You better flippin' change or I'll change
you myself.'" When he was asked to talk more about his other girlfriends,
Glen's answers revealed a remarkably violent history. When his ex, "Karen,"
made him wait outside a nightclub one night, he headbutted her, threw food
in her face, and then poured a drink over her because she "tried to make
[him] look like a dickhead in front of [his] mates." When Karen threatened
to leave him after she heard him tell an ex-girlfriend he still loved her, Glen
retaliated by strangling her, holding her hostage, and almost killing her:

> I grabbed her by the throat, threw her onto the bed, like shut the
> door. And my cousin and his girlfriend [were] in the room as well.
> Shut the door, told them none of them were leaving. Then told my
> other cousin to come round and get me. When he come round to the
> back of the house [I] went to the window and said, "Get me some
> petrol from the petrol station, I'm going to kill them all." But he didn't
> end up doing it. Then I just remember hitting her and stuff. And
> then—because I have anxiety attacks as well when I get stressed—
> then I had an anxiety attack and the ambulance, the ambulance
> come. And then I lashed out at the ambulance people as well.

Glen reacted violently when Michelle threatened to leave too, but in a
markedly different way: "She tried to leave so I grabbed her by the throat.

But obviously I was upset, crying, when I grabbed her by the throat, so I sat back down and tried speaking to her."

Glen explained that his violence came not from righteous anger, but from a deeper fear of abandonment, and a reaction to feeling disrespected and humiliated. "I've got paranoia and I end up thinking things and then if I think they're true I end up hurting them, lashing out and stuff like that. Or when they try and take the mick out of me, I end up hurting them." Glen spent much of his childhood feeling shamed, humiliated, and abandoned. His parents separated when he was two, and his father was in and out of jail so often that Glen barely knew him. His dad was never violent toward his mom, as far as Glen knew, but a later boyfriend hit her and dragged her by the hair. Violence was commonplace in Glen's family: he and his older brother fought severely. When Glen was about seven, his brother kicked and punched him so hard he had to be taken to the hospital with an appendix close to bursting. When Glen became a teenager, his older brother would do things to make him "tougher," such as directing him to bash random strangers in the street. When Glen disclosed that his older brother had masturbated in front of him when Glen was in primary school, Glen was put into foster care and his brother was sent to jail. When Glen told his mother that he had also been sexually abused by a relative when he was six, she went "mad" and refused to believe him.

Looking at Glen's history of domestic abuse, how would you categorize him? If you were to look only at Glen's relationship with Michelle, you would, as researchers Mary-Louise Corr and David Gadd point out, see someone who resorts to violence during times of stress—a typical "family-only" type. This is further borne out by Glen's attitudes to violence: when Michelle attacks him over his infidelities, he restrains but never hits her, he says, because men who are violent toward other women are "sick." The violence goes both ways, and there doesn't appear to be a serious power imbalance. Indeed, write Gadd and Corr, based on this relationship, police *had* assessed Glen to be a "family-only" type. But when you look at Glen's history with other girlfriends, a much more threatening pattern of coercive control emerges, and Glen starts to look a lot more dangerous. "Glen's tendency to perpetrate strangling, headbutting, hostage taking, and death threats place him at the most dangerous end of the spectrum," write Gadd and Corr, "and capable of behaviors that are hardly normal."[22] Glen—and the many other men like him—should be a cautionary tale to anyone who thinks they can categorize abusers based on their behavior in one relationship.

So what to make of the typologies? We may not be able to slot abusive men confidently into one type or another, and referring to types does inhibit our ability to see these men as individual people with their own complex behaviors and histories. Nevertheless, understanding these common dimensions does at least help us understand that there's more than one kind of perpetrator.

We find ourselves on even shakier ground, however, when we ask *why* these men feel and behave the way they do.

———

At this point, it's worth stepping back to remind ourselves just how complex and random the organism is that we're trying to understand. In the words of Nobel Prize–winning neurophysiologist Sir John Eccles, "the brain is so complicated it staggers its own imagination."[23] We're talking about a system of 86 billion neurons, each of which can form around five thousand synapses (connections) to other neurons. That means the helmet-shaped lump of watery fat and protein between our ears can produce hundreds of trillions of synaptic connections. They shape our identity: from our sense of smell to our personality, what we like and dislike, how we respond to our environment, and whether we're likely to be violent. These synapse formations are shaped by genes, hormones, experience, and culture. Neuroscientists can watch these neural pathways in action, but they can't put them in a petri dish and whip up a sample of consciousness. Consciousness is formed in a place neuroscientists can't even find. How does the activity of neurons give rise to the sense that we are conscious human beings? Why does human behavior seesaw between acts of altruism and sadism? Might our mood and behavior change according to the bacteria in our guts, as scientists at the University of California have started to explore?[24] What about other random factors, like research that suggests exposure to lead in childhood is associated with an increase in violent criminal behavior?[25]

We have theories to help us put this complicated picture together, but, scientifically speaking, we can't *prove* them. We can't even say for sure what a "self" is. It's in this unforgiving and deceptive terrain that we go looking for answers to this vital question: Why do so many men abuse the women they claim to love?

————

Since the 1970s, this controversial question has fueled an intellectual turf war. I could devote an entire chapter to the various models that attempt to explain men's violence, but let's just stick to the dominant two: the "feminist" model and the "psychopathology" model. The more strident devotees of each of these models insist they know the *real* reason men abuse women—and they alone know how to stop them.

So how do their theories stack up?

It's All in the Mind

Strict adherents to the psychopathology model insist that domestic abuse is rooted in mental illness, substance abuse, and childhood trauma, and has little (if anything) to do with gender or patriarchy. In fact, many dismiss gender as an irrelevant distraction. "There is no scientific truth to a

gendered approach whatsoever," Peter Miller, professor of violence prevention and addiction studies at Deakin University, told *The Spectator*. "The
real key is psychological predisposition around people with aggression: the
'Dark Triad'...narcissism, psychopathy, and Machiavellianism. These are
found in people of both sexes."[26]

Unlike the feminist model—which asks "Why do *men* beat their
wives?"—the psychopathology school asks: "Why did *this* man beat his
wife?" There *must* be something identifiably wrong with an abusive man,
because he displays aberrant behavior that is fundamentally incompatible
with a "normal" mind. The psychopathology model looks first for clear
signs of disorder, illness, or addiction. If these are absent, it will look for
other factors: abuse or neglect in childhood, or other traits that distinguish
the abuser, such as narcissism, immaturity, or sadism. In other words, from
a strict psychopathology perspective, only "sick" individuals would harm
people they claim to love. (Some psychiatrists may even believe that if a
"sickness" can't be found, then that person is probably not abusive—and is
therefore being falsely accused.)

How to fix this "sick" abuser? The psychopathology school says the
answer is cognitive behavioral therapy (CBT): treatment that identifies, challenges, and is ultimately supposed to change the distorted thought processes
that lead perpetrators to abuse. This treatment is done either one-on-one or
in groups, in which therapists or facilitators also teach abusive men new skills
for communication and anger management and give them coping strategies,
such as taking "time-outs." The idea behind this model of change is that since
perpetrators have "learned" to be abusive, they can also "unlearn" it.

As you would expect, studies of domestic abuse perpetrators *do* show a
higher-than-average incidence of personality disorder, especially so-called
"antisocial" disorders such as sociopathy, psychopathy, and borderline personality disorder. Thus far, though, the psychopathology view that abusive
behavior can be detected like a pathogen has been shown to be false.

Edward Gondolf, an American expert on abusive behavior, put the psychopathology model to the test. In his study of 840 abusive men across four cities,[27] he found only a small subgroup of abusers who were technically "disordered" (most with narcissistic or antisocial disorders). The vast majority of the abusers in Gondolf's study were no more disordered than regular people. As for the notion that violence is a behavior boys learn in childhood, other research has shown that theory to be incomplete, too. Boys who grow up in violent homes *are* more likely to become perpetrators than boys who don't, but, according to a review of multiple studies, there is only a "weak-to-moderate relationship" between experiencing violence as a boy and becoming an abuser as a man.[28] One area that requires much closer study is how attachment disorders—or even merely attachment disruption—can underpin abusive behavior.

In his bestselling text *Why Does He Do That?*, long-time men's behavior change facilitator Lundy Bancroft says it's no surprise that people believe abusers' thinking *must* be disordered. "When a man's face contorts in bitterness and hatred, he looks a little insane," writes Bancroft. "When his mood changes from elated to assaultive in the time it takes to turn around…[it] is no wonder that the partner of an abusive man would come to suspect that he was mentally ill."[29] However, the vast majority of the abusers Bancroft has worked with have been what he regards as "normal": "Their minds work logically; they understand cause and effect; they don't hallucinate. Their perceptions of most life circumstances are reasonably accurate. They get good reports at work; they do well in school or training programs; and no one other than their partners—and children—thinks that there is anything wrong with them." According to Bancroft, it is the abuser's value system that is unhealthy, *not* his mind.[30]

Applying a pure psychopathology lens to domestic abuse has been widely discredited, but its influence is still remarkably strong. Over the past fifteen years, this model has risen to dominate American public policy on domestic abuse research. That is a problem for the rest of the world, because before this policy shift, the United States was where much of the best research was coming from. Now, much of that funding has dried up, redirected away from experts on domestic abuse and put toward research on personality disorders instead. "We haven't done any more research," John Gottman told me, "because it's almost impossible to get a research grant from the federal government to study domestic violence. [It has] decided that all of these problems are in the brain, so they won't study relationships between two people anymore." Holtzworth-Munroe said she had noticed the same trend. "Somewhere along the way, a lot of the funding agencies changed and said they primarily wanted to do research on diagnoses in the *DSM* [*Diagnostic and Statistical Manual*]. I'm seeing that there's less research on violence, period." It would be easier for us to believe that domestic abusers are sick and recognizably different from normal men. Nevertheless, we cannot avoid the uncomfortable truth that violent and sadistic behavior can come from otherwise "normal" minds. More than fifty years after Hannah Arendt revealed the banality of evil in Adolf Eichmann—the Nazi organizer of the Holocaust who was certified as "normal" by half a dozen psychiatrists—we still struggle to believe that psychologically ordinary men can commit sadistic acts of cruelty.

It's the Patriarchy

To strict adherents of the feminist model, the psychopathology theory is simply a Trojan horse for protecting the patriarchy. Their suspicion is understandable: for much of the twentieth century, the field of psychiatry was dominated by misogynistic figures who blamed victims for their perpetrators' abuse and commonly misdiagnosed them as masochists and hysterics. According to the feminist model, domestic abuse is a natural byproduct of *patriarchy*, a system in which men feel entitled to dominate, discredit, and disregard women. This model says that an abuser's personal history is not the decisive factor in his abuse: pathology, upbringing, substance abuse, and even class may influence an abusive man's behavior, but they don't *cause* it.

Think of the feminist model this way: if an abusive man is a room, then toxic gender attitudes and beliefs—such as "women belong in the home," "real men don't cry," "women often make up false rape reports to punish men"—are the floor. The abusive man's "floor" may have a lot of heavy furniture on it: alcoholism, drug addiction, mental illness, child abuse, unemployment, and so on. The furniture in each abusive man's "room" makes it look unique, and sometimes the room is so crowded you can barely see the floor. But that floor—the gender stereotypes that form the foundation of this man's expectations and behavior—is still there. It's what all that furniture is sitting on.

This perspective has been developed over decades of research and work with victims, in shelters, hospitals, and courthouses, and the central assertion—that men who subscribe to rigid gender stereotypes are more likely to abuse their partners—is backed up by decades of research. Study after study[31] finds that men are more prone to abusing if they've (a) been socialized into rigid gender roles, (b) believe that men are naturally superior, or (c) feel their masculinity or authority has been threatened, particularly if women have not complied with their gender-role expectations. The feminist model is clear on how to reform these men: they must first take responsibility for their abuse, and then they must be shown how their male privilege and entitlement are part of a broader—and damaging—system of patriarchy.

Karen Willis, a legend of the domestic abuse sector who's worked with both victims and perpetrators for more than thirty years, explained the feminist model to me when I first started researching domestic abuse. As we sat down to chat, I was fixated on one question: Why do men *still* do this? "We know that those who use violence in their relationships use it not because they're mad or because they have anger management issues or any of those sorts of things, but because they're into power and control," Willis explained. "They want to hurt, humiliate, and dominate. They see that they're entitled to be completely and utterly in control and that everything revolves around them. Others in the family have an absolute responsibility and obligation to keep them happy at all times and do whatever it is that they want."

"But where does this sense of entitlement come from?" I asked. "Why this need for control?"

Willis didn't miss a beat. "Oh, good old-fashioned patriarchy," she replied. "It's all part of a social system where men have positions of power and women are seen as second-class citizens. Most men behave in absolutely ethical ways toward the women and children in their life. But what the system of patriarchy gives *some* men is what they perceive as permission to use power and control and be dominant...[T]hey are top of the pecking order, and...women and children within their families should be subjugated to them."

This is the explanation that—after decades of grinding, tireless advocacy—has been adopted by the United Nations, the World Health Organization, and many political leaders from across the world, including the UK, Canada, Spain, and Australia. Unlike the United States, where public policy is closely aligned with the psychopathology model, they are clear on one point: domestic violence is a cultural phenomenon that arises out of rigid gender norms and gender inequality. That's the thinking behind comments like this one, from former Australian prime minister Malcolm Turnbull: "Disrespecting women does not always result in violence against women. But all violence against women begins with disrespecting women."[32]

When feminist scholars developed this theory back in the 1970s, they did more than just revolutionize our understanding of men's violence against women. They also raised a figurative middle finger to all those psychiatrists who had insisted for decades—without proof—that domestic violence was a response to provocations from masochistic women who *wanted* their husbands to abuse them. When these psychiatrists bothered to examine the actual abusers, they reverted to the simplistic conclusion that their violence was the product of a sick and disordered mind. As the newly formed women's refuge movement proclaimed loud and clear: It's not pathology, it's society! What could be "disordered" about behavior that had been permitted—and encouraged—for centuries?

So how does the feminist model stack up? As we might expect, coercive controllers commonly score high on scales measuring misogyny and rigid gender stereotypes. They are the most dangerous abusers, and it's their victims that advocates who work in shelters and other emergency programs deal with the most. But when we look toward the lower end of the power and control spectrum, to the "family-only" abusers (whom I've also called "insecure reactors"), surveys show very different results. These abusers are no more or less misogynistic than nonviolent men. They're also unlikely to have any kind of mental disorder. They are not generally the most dangerous offenders, but they *are* violent and can still pose a serious threat to their partners. How do we explain their behavior?

Let's return briefly to the story of Glen, the young British man who by the age of twenty-one had abused three girlfriends. How can one explain why he did this? The researchers suggest a few possibilities. Did he obsess over what his girlfriends wore because he's a misogynist who felt entitled to control them, or was his behavior driven by the insecurity around intimacy that stemmed from his troubled and brutal childhood? Is it misogyny when Glen expects his girlfriends to adjust their behavior to soothe his paranoia, or is he grasping for the kind of care he never received as a boy? Is he paranoid about his girlfriends cheating on him because he feels entitled to own them, or is it the result of having his trust routinely betrayed in childhood?

The most likely answer is that it's all of these things. We cannot truly understand why Glen is abusive—or figure out how best to help him change—without looking at his behavior through the lenses of *both* gender *and* psychology.

I've spent years wrestling with misgivings over how to understand—and attempt to explain—the abusive mind. For four years, I've listened to survivors bravely recount stories of unfathomable cruelty. I've spent countless hours studying men's historical dominance over women, and how our patriarchal system has for centuries ignored—and *continues* to excuse—domestic abuse. My rage over the injustice of this has many times threatened to overwhelm me. To then turn around and look at domestic abuse through the eyes of the *perpetrators*—and to see them as complex humans with their own needs and sensitivities—has been so difficult that it has sometimes literally made me feel ill. It may be painful—even infuriating—for some readers to confront this as well, but it's essential that we do so, because getting clear on what causes men to abuse—and how to prevent and stop them from doing it—is urgent. As the renowned violence expert James Gilligan says, to simply condemn violence "is as irrelevant as it would be to 'condemn' cancer or heart disease."[33]

This is something that criminologist Michael Salter also anguishes over. His research focuses on men's violence toward women and children, and he's consulted with government organizations on strategies to reduce domestic abuse. Over the past few years, he has seen the public discussion about men's violence against women become increasingly narrow. "We've moved into a neoliberal feminist analysis of violence, which assumes that perpetrators have no depth; that they are all just surfaces that are written upon by TV and pornography and culture," he tells me. "I think the populist discourse on domestic violence has turned into a total shitshow. Those of us who appreciate a bit of complexity in our analysis have just stepped back to shut our mouths."

The problem with this narrow approach—which prescribes changing sexist and violence-supporting attitudes as the cure—is that it is dangerously missing the mark. Salter emphasizes: "Treatment based on these liberal feminist principles is not working. It's not working! At this point, why on earth wouldn't we swivel to recognize that these guys have an inner world?"

What's particularly odd about this increasingly narrow approach is that the "swivel" Salter is talking about was actually made, almost twenty years ago, by the cofounder of the feminist model for men's behavior change. The late and legendary Ellen Pence, codesigner of the Duluth model—the world's leading model of behavior change—was one of the most influential exponents of the feminist model (which holds that men abuse women because they want power and control). At the turn of the twentieth century, however, she decided the strict feminist model was incomplete—and, for some abusive men, not accurate at all. The idea that all abusers were *driven* by a need or desire for power "did not fit the lived experience of many of the men and women we were working with," wrote Pence in 1999. "I found that many of the men I interviewed did not seem to articulate a desire for power over their partner. Although I relentlessly took every opportunity to point out to men in the groups that they were...merely in denial, the fact that few men ever articulated such a desire went unnoticed by me and many of my coworkers."[34] Notice that here Pence is talking about what abusers feel *driven* by. She's not saying abusive men weren't seeking power over their partners, just that getting power was not what they felt was *driving* their abuse.

Pence wrote that for a long time, when she and her colleagues were running men's groups, they regarded the views of the men as inconsequential. These were abusers who denied, minimized, and justified their abuse, so anything they had to say about the reasons behind their abuse was probably just another excuse. "Like those we were criticizing, we reduced our analysis to a psychological universal truism [that battering was motivated by a need or desire for power]. Like the therapist insisting it was an anger control problem, or the judge wanting to see it as an alcohol problem... [we] remained undaunted by the difference in our theory and the actual experience of those we were working with."[35]

By framing abusive men as two-dimensional control freaks, Pence and her staff had reduced them to mere foot soldiers of the patriarchy, faceless enforcers of the system of male domination. This approach, Pence wrote, reduced "complex social relationships to slogans... 'He does it for power, he does it for control, he does it because he can'—these were advocacy jingles that, in our opinion, said just about all there was to say."[36] In going back to the individual cases, Pence and her colleagues realized that they needed to make a fundamental change to their approach. They began to formulate a theory that would apply to all abusive people, no matter their gender: namely, that domestic abuse is rooted in the entitlement some people feel over their intimate partners, a sense of entitlement that is formed by society and connected to patriarchy.

Once they had made this shift, it also became clear to Pence that different abusers needed different kinds of treatment. In relationships where the violence happened randomly—and not as part of a broader system of control—it could be the case that treating the perpetrator's addiction or mental illness *would* actually stop his violence. Such treatment would not be sufficient, however, for a coercive controller who was *also* an alcoholic: abusive men intent on domination would not stop simply by getting sober. Additionally, there was no point trying to get Cobra-style abusers to reform through group therapy: they are "singularly resistant to change" and often have little capacity to feel shame or remorse for their victims. These men needed a different approach altogether.[37]

In acknowledging the diversity of men's violence, Pence wasn't abandoning the Duluth theory of power and control. There was no doubt that many abusers wanted power and dominance, and that they felt entitled to it. In itself, though, the stock feminist answer for why men abuse—because they want power and control—doesn't go far enough.

The more interesting question is: Why do men *want* this power and control? And why do they go to such extreme and destructive lengths to get it?

———

The feminist movement had a clear goal in the 1970s: to ensure that domestic violence became a political issue that connected modern violence against women with a history of systematic male power and privilege. That approach has taken the movement—and society—a long way. Now, in the shift toward a more complex understanding of why men abuse, the feminist movement can also give us insight into what is happening inside the minds of men. It was feminist academics, after all, who first showed men that patriarchy hurts them, too, because it makes them sacrifice rich emotional lives in exchange for a phony promise of power and success.

Indeed, feminist academics were the first to even study masculinity, and they developed much of what we know about men's inner emotional lives. "Back in the 1970s," says Salter, "feminist psychoanalysis was looking at issues around men, vulnerability and dependency, and the high level of sensitivity among men that their basic needs can't be fulfilled, and that they will be overwhelmed and betrayed in their interpersonal relationships. Those sorts of approaches are now excoriated as 'anti-feminist.' Well, they're not anti-feminist: this was foundational feminist work, and it was very prominent in the 1980s in understandings of male violence."

It's to this work that we must now return.

It's indisputable that traditional notions of masculinity—particularly male entitlement—are at the core of men's violence against women. Abusive men obviously take power and control in their relationships. But there are many other questions that we still need to answer. What are the different reasons men have for needing to dominate their partners? What is happening in the minds of these men to make them sabotage the lives of their partners and children—to the point where they destroy even their *own* lives? These are critical parts of the puzzle that are missing from our public conversations about domestic abuse.

We'll talk more about patriarchy later and how it governs the forces that create an abusive mind. However, because it's the *mind* we're trying to understand, we'll also take a close look at some dark corners of the human psyche. It's only by integrating *both* viewpoints—feminism and psychology—that we can start to truly comprehend the phenomenon of men's violence against women and find effective ways to stop it.

––––––––––

There's an oft-quoted phrase from the novelist Margaret Atwood that made me look at the abusive mind with fresh eyes: "Men are afraid women will laugh at them, and women are afraid men will kill them." Atwood says this line was based on a straw poll she conducted among her friends and students. "I asked some women students in a poetry seminar I was giving, 'Why do women feel threatened by men?' 'They're afraid of being killed,' they said. 'Why do men feel threatened by women?' I asked a male friend of mine. 'They're afraid women will laugh at them,' he said. 'Undercut their world view.'"[38]

We could look at this contrast with derision, scoff at the fragility of men's egos, and rage at how pathetic they are for being preoccupied by petty concerns while women have *real* things to fear. Or, given how destructive those fragile male egos can be, we could take it seriously. Why is it that men are so afraid of being laughed at? This is what led me to the study of shame—and humiliated fury.

4.

Shame

With David Hollier

Between shame and shamelessness lies the axis upon which we turn; meteorological conditions at both these poles are of the most extreme, ferocious type. Shamelessness, shame: the roots of violence.
SALMAN RUSHDIE, *SHAME*

Professor Neil Websdale is like a domestic violence detective. As head of the National Domestic Violence Fatality Review Initiative in Flagstaff, Arizona, he spends his time reconstructing what happened in the days and months leading up to a domestic homicide. To find out how and why the homicide occurred, Websdale examines the case through both the eyes of the victim—via the evidence she leaves behind, testimony from friends and relatives—and the eyes of her killer. He applies a historian's lens to the killer's life, and sometimes he interviews them in jail. This is not a police investigation; instead, a fatality review looks to better understand homicides in order to design interventions that may stop them from happening. Websdale is the first to admit his work is inexact. "Women and family members take their secrets to the grave, as do perpetrators. We're working with the haunting presence of the inexplicable."

After decades studying perpetrators, Websdale says none of the standard models get to the heart of what he's seeing. In the hundreds of killers he's profiled, he doesn't see men driven solely by a desire for power and control, nor has he found a unifying thread of disorder or mental illness. However, his investigations *have* time and again brought him back to one recurring element: shame. "A lot of these guys struck me as deeply ashamed men," he says, and the majority had life histories that were "steeped in shame—particularly compromised masculinity."

For his book *Familicidal Hearts*, Websdale conducted a detailed study of seventy-six coercive controllers who killed their families.[1] His analysis of their lives and motives is critical to our understanding of abusive men. This is because, despite exerting enormous power over their families, these men didn't actually appear to *be* powerful. They certainly got a "fleeting sense of ascendancy created through force, intimidation, and instilling a deep fear in loved ones," as Lundy Bancroft describes, and they clearly benefited from that by "receiving various services, labor, and privileges": the luxury of never compromising, control over finances, having their goals prioritized, domestic service, and so on.[2] Still, their abuse wasn't driven by a simple desire for power and privilege. The driver of their abuse was buried deep inside, where an insatiable hunger for intimacy and belonging had mutated into violence through contact with another powerful emotion: shame.

This deep, long-buried shame was much too painful for the men to acknowledge, let alone address. When their shame was triggered (in ways we will soon explore), the only way they could override its intolerable pain was to overwhelm it, even momentarily, with a feeling of power. This they achieved through lashing out, abusing, controlling, or terrorizing their loved ones. This is the destructive force of *humiliated fury*.

The concept of humiliated fury dates back to 1971[3] and was coined by the American psychoanalyst Helen Block Lewis. Lewis was a pioneer in the field of psychology when female psychoanalysts were still very much a minority. She was the first to clinically study guilt and shame. She introduced the idea that some men used "humiliated fury" to protect themselves against feeling powerless and defective; by blaming others, they were able to regain a sense of power and avoid unbearable feelings of shame. Picture, for example, the schoolyard bully who gets up in a smaller boy's face, daring him to repeat what he just muttered under his breath; this is the schoolyard version of the man who beats his wife for daring to challenge his opinion. Lewis, a staunch feminist born and raised in New York, branded shame the "sleeper emotion" that lurked behind depression, obsession, narcissism, and paranoia. Shame was a "sleeper" because it was virtually taboo, even in the therapy room; in her study of hundreds of hours of therapy sessions,[4] Lewis found that psychoanalysts rarely, if ever, discussed shame with their clients. Instead, when faced with shame-ridden clients, these psychoanalysts were simply (and wrongly, according to Lewis) diagnosing them with borderline or narcissistic personality disorders. This problem persists.[5] As shame and violence expert James Gilligan suggests, it's as though we're so ashamed of shame that we can barely bring ourselves to talk about it.[6]

Let's clarify a few basics about shame. First, perpetrators who have antisocial personality disorders such as psychopathy or sociopathy—the group identified as "Cobras"—are *not* driven by humiliated fury. From his case reviews and interviews, Websdale has noticed that perpetrators with antisocial personality disorders "appear less vulnerable and dependent, suffer less abandonment anxiety and sensitivity to rejection, and seem to have more narcissism, grandiosity, and emotional isolation." In fact, Websdale says he has interviewed killers who have coldly described their murderous acts as "transcendent" or "spiritual" experiences. Whether or not shame plays a part in these men's perpetration, says Websdale, is something that requires more research. Psychopaths *can* feel empathy and shame, but they don't feel it spontaneously, and it doesn't overwhelm them.[7] As one diagnosed psychopath explained, "If most people feel an emotion between seven and eight on a dial of ten, I feel it between zero and two."[8]

Now to the next point: shame is not guilt. *Guilt* is the feeling we've done something bad or have wronged someone. When we have guilt, we can apologize and, if we are forgiven, we may be absolved of our guilty feeling. In contrast, no one can absolve you of shame. You have to do that work yourself. That's because shame is not just a feeling that we've done something bad; it's the unspeakable (and often deeply buried) feeling that "I *am* bad"—the feeling that we are "unloved and unlovable."[9]

"What does shame require?" Lewis asked. "That you be a better person, and not be ugly, and not be stupid, and not have failed? The only thing that suits it at this moment is for you to be nonexistent. That's what people frequently say. I could crawl through a hole, I could sink through the floor, I could die. It's so acutely painful."[10] There is no easy way to be rid of shame. It persists like a chemical burn.

Guilt and shame produce diametrically opposite effects in violent people. Studies of convicted criminals in Germany and the United States show that "guilt is more likely to convince prisoners to avoid crime in the future, whereas shame...produces a desire to lash out against unfair emotional pain and social blame. And this can lead to more bad behavior, not less."[11]

Before we interrogate the destructive force of men's shame and humiliated fury, let's take a minute to talk about shame itself. Shame is an emotion that everybody has to deal with (even if, in psychopaths, the effect of it is deeply muted). The way we respond to it has a lot to do with how we were raised, the culture we live in, and—first and foremost—whether we are male or female.

Though our culture excels at finding ever more sophisticated ways for us to feel shame, it's important to understand that shame itself is not a learned emotion. It is one of the nine primary "affects"[12] we are born with, on the same level physiologically as anger, sadness, fear, joy, anticipation, surprise, dissmell (the avoidance of bad smells), and disgust. These are the basic affects defined by the psychologist Silvan Tomkins, one of the most influential figures to have studied shame. Affect is, according to the Tomkins Institute, "an innate, biological response" that underlies emotion. The nine affects are with us from birth; they help us to survive. For example, a baby seeking contact with her mother may, if the mother doesn't acknowledge her, display classic shame responses: her body slumps, she turns her face away, and looks downward, away from her mother's face. Having her strong interest in connection rebuffed, she feels a type of shame.[13]

Why is this important to understand? Because it tells us there is an evolutionary purpose to shame. It's not just there to make us miserable; rather, it is fundamental to our survival in social groups. Researchers from the University of California say that just as pain exists to prevent us from damaging our tissue, "the function of shame is to prevent us from damaging our social relationships, or to motivate us to repair them." When we were hunter-gatherers, our survival depended on being included in social life: on having the other members of our small group value us enough to share food, protection, and care with us. Shame was one emotion that regulated our behavior and made us weigh up the possible consequences of our actions— which, if weighed incorrectly, could lead to being exiled, hurt, or killed.[14]

Today, it's far less likely that you'll die if you're exiled from your community, but the fear of becoming a pariah in the eyes of people we love and trust is still acute. To protect us against shame and exile, we keep our own internal records of acts that will make us liked or disliked. This is why, for example, victims of domestic abuse often keep their abuse a secret, and victims of child sexual abuse can take decades to tell anybody. The fear that they will be devalued in the eyes of their community is so great that they feel a need to bury what was done to them.

In the modern world, the list of shame-triggering behaviors has grown exponentially. For women, the potential sources of shame are kaleidoscopic and ever-changing. Modern culture has women walking a tightrope: be sexy but not *too* sexy, be smart but not intimidating, assertive but not pushy, and on it goes. Fall just an inch over the side of what has been decreed acceptable and you haven't just done something wrong, you *are* wrong. Even emotionality—a supposedly approved trait in women—can be evidence of women's inherent defectiveness: proof that females are innately irrational and not to be trusted in positions of power. So plentiful are the triggers for women's shame that they're almost impossible to avoid. "For women," says Brené Brown, a high-profile researcher on shame and vulnerability, "shame is, do it all, do it perfectly, and never let them see you sweat."[15]

Male shame, in contrast, is built around one unbreakable rule: do not be weak. To *be a man* is to be strong, powerful, and in control. Weakness, vulnerability, dependency: these all break manhood's number-one rule. For some men, the merest emotional disturbance—the slightest hint of vulnerability—can be so intolerable they must immediately expel it, usually by finding someone or something else to blame. In this moment of pain, they may also feel an urgent need to be cared for, even by the very person they are attacking.

The more closely one identifies with strict gender norms, the more likely one is to feel shame for disobeying them. In both sexes, the reactions to these feelings of shame can be extreme, but the way men and women respond to shame is itself gendered, as we will see.

———————

Shame is no excuse for men's violence. Many men who feel shame or jealousy, even acutely, don't respond in violent or abusive ways. Consider the men who, after suffering childhoods of abuse, shame, or neglect, grow up vowing never to repeat their mother's or father's violence; these are men whose pride stems from modeling love and tenderness with their lovers and their children. Others are those who have spent years working through their deep shame and anger so they *don't* end up taking their pain out on others.

However, when abusive people are confronted with feelings of shame, they take the path of least resistance. Instead of acknowledging their own sense of powerlessness and dealing with the discomfort, they blame others and, like the schoolyard bully, use violence to achieve a phony—and often short-lived—feeling of power and pride. Women and children suffer horrific abuse—and sometimes death—at the hands of men who refuse to confront the true source of their own pain and frustration.

It's a basic human instinct to defend ourselves against shame, because by its very nature shame is an unbearable feeling. Nevertheless, as therapists never tire of repeating, it's not the feeling that causes all the trouble, it's the way we respond to it—and the way individuals respond to shame differs enormously. In his 1992 book *Shame and Pride*, prominent American psychiatrist Donald Nathanson identified four basic human reactions to shame: withdrawal, attack self, avoidance, and attack others. Within each of these responses is a "library of methods people use when shame strikes."[16] Someone reacting to shame by going into withdrawal may do something as mild as look at the ground or as extreme as avoid human contact altogether. The withdrawal response is driven by the fear that if we are seen in our experience of shame, people will hold us in contempt. It is actually the most courageous way to deal with shame: people who tend toward withdrawal are the ones most likely to do the emotional work necessary to process their shame and move through it without harming themselves or others.

Another reaction is to "attack self"—to negate or annihilate oneself in an effort to control the punishment that one feels is not only inevitable but also deserved. A mild version of this is self-deprecating humor (to make fun of yourself before others get the chance). When the shame becomes overwhelming, though, the responses become more intense: self-loathing, self-harm, and (at the furthest extreme) suicide.

Perhaps the most invisible response to shame is avoidance. In extreme cases, this is the province of narcissists, people who have constructed their entire identity and lifestyle to avoid ever feeling shame. If you think shame and narcissism are polar opposites, think of the contradiction at the core of the narcissist: despite their grandiosity, attention-seeking, and seemingly unassailable high self-esteem, narcissists continually seek approval and flattery from others and will respond aggressively to the merest hint of challenge or humiliation. This is not a confident and powerful personality type; instead, as Lewis writes, narcissism is "a defense against the hatred of the self in shame."[17] This is what makes narcissistic men particularly dangerous. If the narcissist is prepared to build his entire personality—his hubris, excessive self-love, and grandiosity—as a firewall against feelings of shame or guilt, what might he do to someone who threatens to demolish this wall and expose his true self?

The fourth and final shame response—attack others—is the most destructive of all. Attacking others can replace feelings of shame with pride. However, that pride may be short-lived, and the act of attacking can lead one to feel even *more* shame. This is where we see shame at its most destructive: as humiliated fury. As Nathanson explains, "These are the people in our society most of us find truly dangerous, for no one can really avoid shame successfully, and we live at risk of their wrath. Those who must attack rather than withdraw make our common turf into a terrain of danger."[18]

————

Most often, those who react to shame by attacking others are men. Which begs the question: Why? The answer is usually summed up in four syllables: testosterone. Common belief has it that testosterone, which is vastly more abundant in men than in women, is the "aggression hormone." It's the reason men are more violent than women—case closed.

Well, if that's what you've always thought, it's time to reopen the case file on men's violence, because it's *not* testosterone that *causes* it. Hang on, I hear you say, "Surely there's something to the idea that testosterone is connected to violence?" Well, yes and no.

Weighing up the role of testosterone in male violence, one of the world's leading experts on biology and neurology, Professor Robert Sapolsky, lays out the essential point: when testosterone rises after a challenge, it doesn't *prompt* aggression. "Instead," writes Sapolsky, "it prompts whatever behaviors are needed to maintain status."[19] In other words, testosterone is not an *aggression* hormone, it is a *status-seeking* hormone. Male primates maintain status through aggression. But what happens, Sapolsky asks, "if defending your status requires you to be nice?"[20] Here we see how our biological reactions are shaped by the culture in which we live. If men truly believed their status would rise upon becoming the World Toilet Cleaning Champion, their testosterone levels would surge as they knelt before the bowl. "The problem," says Sapolsky, "isn't that testosterone can increase levels of aggression. The problem is the frequency with which we reward aggression"[21] rather than clean toilets.

Today, there may be no greater status for men than the appearance of being in control.

———

James Gilligan has spent much of his adult life working in prisons across North America and Britain, treating thousands of criminally violent men. Among the men he has worked with, Gilligan has found one common element. "Universal among the violent criminals was the fact that they were keeping a secret. A central secret. And that secret was that they felt ashamed—deeply ashamed, chronically ashamed, acutely ashamed."[22] Gilligan, who grew up with a violent father (and is married to "rock star"[23] feminist, ethicist, and psychologist Carol Gilligan), was struck by how often his prisoners and mental patients gave exactly the same reason for having assaulted or killed somebody. "Time after time, they would reply 'because he disrespected me.'" In fact, prisoners used that phrase so often, they abbreviated it into the slang phrase, "He dissed me."

Of the small group of scholars who look at the connection between shame and violence from the perpetrator's perspective, Gilligan is the most widely respected. After more than thirty-five years working with violent perpetrators, he has arrived at a compelling idea: all violence begins with shame. In fact, he argues, the very purpose of violence is to banish shame and replace it with pride.

Shame is a concept few people understand, so Gilligan lists its synonyms (and there are dozens): being insulted, dishonored, disrespected, disgraced, demeaned, slandered, ridiculed, teased, taunted, mocked, rejected, defeated, subjected to indignity or ignominy; "losing face" and being treated as insignificant; feeling inferior, impotent, incompetent, weak, ignorant, poor, a failure, ugly, unimportant, useless, worthless.[24] Envy and jealousy are siblings of shame, says Gilligan, because they also trigger—and are underpinned by—feelings of inferiority.

Like Gilligan's violent criminals, domestic abuse perpetrators are often exquisitely sensitive to the merest hint that they are being dissed, and commonly interpret harmless behavior from their partners as a deliberate personal attack. Phone counselors on the National Men's Referral Service helpline hear this kind of talk from offenders all the time. I met with a group of phone counselors at their head office. Its address is not listed, to protect staff from aggrieved perpetrators looking for someone to blame. When men call this helpline, it's usually because their partner has either urged them or given them an ultimatum. A typical call goes like this: "I just had an argument, I behaved violently; I'm not sure why I did that or what's going on. My partner has been telling me for a while that this has been an issue, and she gave me this number. But now it's just escalated and blown up, and I'm a mess and I don't know what to do."

More often, though, the calls are outgoing. Phone counselors here call men who have recently been charged with a domestic abuse–related offense. Their numbers are provided to the helpline by police. Guy Penna is the helpline's team leader, and he's heard every excuse under the sun. "I've had guys have [violent] incidents—where the police have been called—about how their partner's put the trashcan out. 'It wasn't straight to the curb, it wasn't square.'" The real cause almost never gets written on the police report. "Sometimes it takes you a little while to get to the why, and the 'why' might be that, 'Oh, she disrespected my mother three weeks ago,'" adds counselor Brett Tomlinson. "Or, 'She went out with her girlfriends four months ago and didn't say sorry, and I just haven't let it go since.'"

These are the real stories behind ludicrous headlines like "Man Murders Wife for Burning Toast." Consider the very public throttling of celebrity chef Nigella Lawson by her art collector husband Charles Saatchi, at an upmarket London restaurant in 2013. Lawson later testified in court that she had noticed "a sweet baby" in a stroller nearby and had casually mentioned to Saatchi that she was looking forward to becoming a grandmother. At that, Saatchi grabbed her by the throat, growling, "I am the only person you should be concerned with—I am the only person who should be giving you pleasure." He described the incident to the press as a "playful tiff."[25]

That violent men feel shamed for such trivial reasons further compounds their shame, writes Gilligan, and drives it deeper underground, to a place where, deeply concealed, it is even less likely to be acknowledged and more likely to manifest as violence. They feel "acutely ashamed, over matters that are so trivial that their very triviality makes it even more shameful to feel ashamed about them, so they are ashamed even to reveal what shames them."[26] Penna says one of the most common phrases the phone counselors hear is "pushing my buttons." "If you're not agreeing with me, if we're not in 100 percent solidarity in everything I say and do, then you're challenging me," he says, describing the mindset of many male callers. "If you're challenging me, you're undermining and attacking me. There's this sense that *my worldview is the only view*, and any challenge to that is automatically unsettling and requires [them] to react, as opposed to respond."

Shame can create terrible distortions in the way we perceive what is said or done to us. As Judith Graham, from the University of Maine, describes: "A shame-obsessed person hears ridicule even when none was intended. A shame-obsessed person loses the ability to distinguish between their inner feelings of worthlessness and everyday happenings." They see themselves as "objects of derision."[27] In their minds, abusive men sense that they've been somehow shamed by their partners, however ridiculous that may be. That is why perpetrators commonly see *themselves* as victims of their partner's "abuse."

Since they've already been attacked, the thinking goes, they are well within their rights to strike back—either in the moment, or by devising an ever-tighter regime of control to stop their partner hurting or disrespecting them again. As the feminist writer Germaine Greer notes in her essay *On Rage*, "A red-blooded man is not supposed to take insult and humiliation lying down. He should not let people get away with doing things he thinks wicked or unjust. He demands the right both to judge and to act upon his judgment."[28]

The victimhood of abusive men can be astonishing. For her doctoral thesis, Michelle Jones interviewed sixty-six men who'd agreed to attend a twelve-week behavior change program for domestic abuse.[29] One man, Peter, took what he'd learned about the various kinds of abuse and twisted it into proof that it was *he* who was being victimized. As Jones writes, "Peter claimed that he was the victim of his partner's sexual violence, as she had refused to have sex with him."[30]

Abusive men—many of whom have actually been charged—commonly play the victim card while on the phone to the Men's Referral Service. Brett Tomlinson says these calls usually have a distinctive tone: "A woman rings up and she wants the violence to stop. A man who rings up and says he's a victim; he wants her punished. There's a big difference. You can tell by the tone of her voice—the way she apologizes for what she's about to say, doesn't want to make him look bad, but just wants it to stop. Whereas he rings up and says, 'I'm the victim, punish her. Where can I send her?'"

For Matt Boulton, being dissed was a major ignition point for his own violence. "I didn't see [respect] as something I had to earn—I just saw it as one of my rights." Boulton looks back on his time as an abusive man as a period of deep insecurity. "We were married when we were twenty. I came straight from my parents into married life. I didn't know how to be a husband or even really what it meant to be a man. Looking back, I was a boy trapped inside a man's body, just playing the game, as a lot of guys are, at that age especially." When he started to feel like he wasn't getting the unconditional respect he "deserved," he began "crossing lines." It started gradually, he says—"raising my voice, swearing, and name-calling"—but with each conflict, it got a little bit worse, until the abuse became physical. "Again, that began with lower-level [acts]... It might have been locking the door, saying, 'No, we are going to talk about this now,' hitting the wall, physically lashing out at things, and then restraining and that sort of thing."

Today, Boulton runs his own behavior change program for abusive men who come voluntarily to deal with their abusive behavior. "What we're dealing with is a national epidemic," says Boulton, "and there's not enough experts in the field to deal with it." Early in the program, the men are asked to describe why they feel the need to control their partners. Over and over, Boulton gets the same response. "If a guy has been powerfully controlled—could be bullying, growing up with DV [domestic violence], sexual abuse—all of that can flick a switch where he says, 'I'm never going

to be controlled again. From now on, I'm going to be the one in control.'"
This kind of "trauma-based entitlement" is common in people who become
abusive—the notion that *I had to go through so much, so fuck you, you just have
to deal with whatever I do to you.* When that entitlement is thwarted, there
is the feeling of being defied, of being humiliated, of being shamed. This is
humiliated fury, when insecurity, toxic shame, and entitlement combine.

At the same time, many of these men also have an almost infantile need
for their partner to love them: a sense of vulnerability and dependency that
drives their controlling abuse. Andre Van Altena has, through leading men's
behavior change programs in jails and detention centers, often worked with
abusive men who have struggled through life. When these men finally find
someone who accepts and loves them, he says, they're not giving that up in
a hurry. "The fear is, 'If I let go of the control I have over this person, then
she will leave me. I will be abandoned, and I know what that feels like. I'll be
disrespected, because she'll hook up with someone else.' So to prevent that
from happening, you hold on tight. You keep every other bastard away, and
tuck her under your arm and protect her from the wider world. Of course,
if you hold on that tight, smother people, and violate them when they step
out of line...they're going to lose any love they had for you."

This sense of dependency and powerlessness—one of the strongest
triggers for male shame—can often (though certainly not always) be traced
back to the perpetrator's childhood. However, their childhood needn't have
been overtly abusive. In their book *The Batterer: A Psychological Profile*,
Donald Dutton and Susan Golant identified two parental types that most
commonly lead boys to become abusive as men: a cold, rejecting mother
or a shaming father. For boys in particular, this type of upbringing can set
a future trajectory:

There is a pool of shame in such an individual that can find no
expression—that is, until an intimate relationship occurs, and with

it the emotional vulnerability that menaces his equilibrium, the mask he has so carefully crafted over the years. Perhaps it is the mask of a "tough guy," or a "cool guy," or a "gentleman." Whatever identity he had created is irrelevant. Now a woman threatens to go backstage and see him and his shame without the makeup. Then, to his own surprise, the rage starts. He feels it like an irritation, and sometimes like a tidal wave. He is shocked and surprised. He may apologize and feel shame immediately after, but he can't sustain that emotion; it's too painful, too reminiscent of hurts long buried. So he blames it on her. If it happens repeatedly with more than one woman, he goes from blaming her to blaming "them." His personal shortcomings become rationalized by an evolving misogyny...[At this point] the man is programmed for intimate violence. No woman on earth can save him, although some will try.[31]

When abusive men emerge out of violent childhoods, in which they watched their fathers beat and humiliate their mothers (or vice versa), they are doing more than just repeating learned behavior. Rather, as Dutton and Golant write, abusiveness is "a learned means of self-maintenance. The abusive man is addicted to brutality to keep his shaky self-concept intact. The only times he feels powerful and whole is when he is engaged in violence."[32] Psychoanalyst Erich Fromm is more direct: "The passion to have absolute and unrestricted control over a living being is [the] transformation of impotence into omnipotence."[33]

"Kevin" learned about shame from his father at a young age. On the isolated family farm where he was homeschooled by his father—a Baptist preacher with a background in sales, police, and the military—Kevin was whipped for being dishonest and lashed with harsh put-downs if he screwed up his chores. In the motel room where nineteen-year-old Kevin choked his fiancée to death, investigators found a note addressed to his father: "I'm sorry I was a disappointment to you, but I love you."

Professor Neil Websdale was part of the team that reviewed the killing, and the details here come from Websdale's report.[34] It is a rare forensic analysis because it includes the perpetrator's point of view. The report describes a young man, raised on a rigid code of southern paternalism, who "failed" to live up to its expectations of masculinity. In adolescence, the young farmhand was chronically ashamed of a limp he got from falling off a horse and embarrassed by his short stature, which drew "harassment" from his peers and turned him off sports. At fourteen, he began a "destructive relationship" with beer and whiskey, against the stern admonishment of his father, who told his children that alcohol was "from the devil." Soon he was getting into trouble: fighting, accruing speeding tickets, and getting arrested for drunk driving. Kevin was "enraged" by his failures, and despite looking like "one of the boys" and crowing about his sexual prowess, he was actually extremely isolated and prone to fits of anger. For relief, he would take his twelve-gauge shotgun to the back paddock and "just shoot something like the end of the stock tank or whatever," or "beat the shit out of something—not somebody."

Kevin's attitude toward women was not obviously misogynistic; indeed, it appeared to be quite the opposite. Raised "not to hit a woman," he went out of his way to look after female friends. As his childhood friend wrote in a letter to the judge: "Kevin would take me home so I would not have to walk alone... He was always a gentleman. Every time we went somewhere, Kevin would always pay, no matter what."

This chivalry, however, hid something darker. Taken to the extreme, this kind of rigid, protective masculinity—a trait coveted by some women—can mask something just as destructive as brutish misogyny. As men's behavior change facilitator Rodney Vlais explains, abusive men commonly cite their duty to protect as the reason for their abuse. "We don't just go into the work assuming that men don't care about the safety of their partners and families," he says. "Yes, some men certainly don't. But for other men, it's like, *I'm here to protect.* But it is that hypermasculine form of protection: *I guard the family from the perils outside, I guard the family's finances.* If the woman gets in the way of that by disobeying him, then another attitude takes hold: one where he believes she needs to be brought back into line—supposedly for her own safety." If she refuses his protection—that is, if she shames him by disobeying—then she risks becoming that other type of woman: a slut who warrants no protection and deserves whatever she gets.

The chivalrous Kevin joined the U.S. Air Force against the wishes of his father, and that's where he met Joanna—an independent, ambitious woman who had joined the force "to see the world." Kevin idealized Joanna—she was more competent, sexually experienced, and mature than he was—but was afraid that she would "see my weakness, my lack of worth, and leave me." After a monthlong whirlwind romance, Kevin asked Joanna to marry him. When she agreed, he began pressuring her to agree to a wedding date, worried she would soon discover that he was immature and "not very capable." These were not traits immediately obvious to other people; Kevin was described as an easygoing "nice guy." One friend of Joanna's, however, did glimpse his dark side: she described Kevin as "tightly wound" and said that in explaining his goal to become a technical instructor in the Air Force, he had told her that "getting in people's faces and screaming at them was exactly what he wanted to do."

There were red flags early on: excessive jealousy toward Joanna's ex-boyfriend, an incident in which he shoved Joanna up against a wall, and another where he raged and swore at her. Around three weeks before the murder, Joanna's roommate heard her yell at Kevin, "Don't you ever grab my face like that again!" When she asked if Joanna was all right, Joanna complained that Kevin was being "childish."

Then there was Kevin's excessive drinking. Joanna advised him to get help, but later bought alcohol for the underage military police officer so they could get drunk together on raunchy weekends off base. That's not to say that Joanna was somehow under Kevin's spell. As Websdale notes, Joanna "was clear about what she wanted from the relationship and equally emphatic about what she would not tolerate."[35]

This assertiveness and emotional strength, witnesses later testified, may have contributed to Kevin's decision to strangle her to death. The day before he killed her, Joanna and Kevin checked into a motel to drink and have sex. Joanna was alert to the serious increase in Kevin's drinking, his claustrophobic attentiveness, and his volatility. That night, Kevin ruined their evening by getting so drunk on Southern Comfort that he passed out. The following morning they fought. Joanna told Kevin she didn't want to marry an alcoholic and threw her engagement ring at him. Kevin later reported to the prison psychiatrist that as they argued, "rage shot through my entire body. My fists balled up. My legs went numb." Still drunk from the night before, Kevin threw up on the carpet. Joanna, who didn't want to pay a cleaning charge, asked her friend Mary to bring carpet cleaner to the motel. After the women cleaned up, Joanna asked Kevin—who was half-asleep in bed—if it would be okay if she and Mary went to lunch. Kevin sarcastically agreed, and the two left.

While they were gone, Joanna told Mary she was planning to break up with Kevin. When Mary dropped her back at the motel, Kevin asked Joanna if she was planning to stay. Her answer sounded "evasive," and Kevin was overwhelmed with the sickening thought of her being with somebody else. At this point, Kevin says, "Joanna, lay down on the bed." As he put his hands around her neck, she replied, "Oh, Kevin, don't," and bit his finger. As he applied more force, she screamed, struggled, and fought against him, until they fell off the bed, where Kevin killed her. Speaking to investigators, Kevin said, "She indicated she wanted nothing to do with me anymore. I was scared, angry, and nervous. As a snap action I choked her until she died."

However, Kevin was *not* out of control when he killed Joanna. His own testimony reveals that in the minutes he spent choking her, he went from reactive rage to a moment of conscious choice. To the detective who drew out his confession, Kevin admitted he did "at first" get a rush from strangling Joanna. "But at the end, I really wanted to let go, but I knew I couldn't 'cause she'd have jumped up and went straight to you." In the six to eight minutes it took Kevin to kill Joanna, Neil Websdale says that the shame and "humiliated fury" Kevin felt at the sense that he was about to be abandoned was replaced "with a rage that quickly and temporarily restored a sense of pride and a sense of control. His act of killing temporarily dissipated his anxiety and fear."[36]

Any pride or feeling of control Kevin might have had was short-lived. With Joanna dead on the floor, Kevin became "scared" and tried "to make it look like an accident." After lifting Joanna's body back onto the bed, Kevin violated her corpse to make it look like she'd died after a session of rough sex: removing her clothes, biting her nipple and breast, and digitally penetrating her. This desecration, Kevin later said, was something he felt more shame about than anything he had ever done. Over the next day, Kevin says he tried several times to kill himself, finally by attempting to drive Joanna's car into an oncoming tractor-trailer on a rural highway. When he was caught fleeing the scene by police, he confessed to killing Joanna and told them where to find her body.

If we were to look at this homicide through the lens of the feminist model, we might dismiss Kevin's testimony about his difficult childhood and subsequent fear of abandonment as just lousy excuses from a man seeking to minimize his crime and get a more sympathetic hearing. From this viewpoint, Kevin is just another man whose murderous rage was driven by a desire for ultimate power and control.

That's certainly what it looks like from the perspective of the victim. But as we've read, there is often a big difference between how powerful abusers *look* and how powerful they *feel*. This, I believe, is one of the major elements missing from the mainstream understanding of domestic abuse: the fact that in the moments before a man takes control, he may feel at his most vulnerable and powerless, just milliseconds before feeling the flush of power and pride that comes from reinstating dominance.

Consider the results of a 2004 study of twenty-four abusive men conducted by the psychologist Jac Brown in New South Wales.[37] The men in Brown's study said their violence generally followed an emotional sequence: first they felt vulnerable, then scared, and then angry. This cascade of emotions—from the initial feelings of shame, humiliation, and vulnerability through to the abusive reaction—can happen in a split second. Think of what occurs when you turn on a light. You flick the switch, which triggers a surge of electricity that gets conducted through the wires and down into the bulb itself, where the electric charge ignites the filament that creates the light. We don't see electricity's journey from the switch to the filament; we just see the light coming on. Similarly, the cascading emotion in an abusive man can happen so quickly that the only thing visible is the rage that erupts: the cold fury, the degrading remark.

As Websdale, Gilligan, and others have argued, the actual exertion of power and control over an intimate partner is often motivated by a feeling of underlying powerlessness and a fear of vulnerability—essentially, of shame. The notion that deeply shamed people "feel" shame, however, is not quite right, writes Gilligan. "While shame is initially painful, constant shaming leads to a deadening of feeling... When it reaches overwhelming intensity, shame is experienced, like cold, as a feeling of numbness and deadness. [In Dante's *Inferno*] the lowest circle of hell was a region not of flames, but of ice—absolute coldness."[38] (This raises interesting questions about the role shame plays in an antisocial personality disorder like sociopathy, and how shame may underpin the sadistic coldness of men whose behavior aligns with the "Cobra" type.)

If we carefully consider Kevin's testimony, a picture emerges that we don't often recognize in domestic abuse. Kevin didn't feel powerful or privileged. This was a young man who fantasized about guarding nuclear weapons, and who was raised to protect women as a point of honor. But his machismo covered a "tenuous sense of self, a precarious masculine identity...soaked in a level of alcohol consumption subconsciously or consciously directed at soothing his fear, rage, and anxiety."[39] Alongside Kevin's desperate attempts to control Joanna, and his intimidating behavior, "we also witness searing levels of personal vulnerability, powerlessness, dependency, and fear of abandonment."[40] This fear of abandonment—common to obsessive, paranoid abusers—is not simply a fear of being alone; it is a shame-based fear of being exposed as defective and unworthy of love. In Kevin's case, the violent disdain of his father left a legacy of shame and insecurity. It was, as Websdale concludes, Kevin's humiliated fury at the likelihood that his fiancée was about to abandon him that triggered his murderous act.

Men who attack others when they feel shamed are not doomed to do so forever. However, in order to change this pattern, they need to be able to see it. Nowhere have I heard of this happening more powerfully than in the men's behavior change groups led by Kylie Dowse. A qualified narrative therapist and domestic abuse advocate, Dowse describes herself as an Aboriginal feminist. A decade ago, after working for twenty years with women and child survivors, Dowse made the atypical move to work with abusive men, too. She did this because survivors were telling her, time and again, that they wanted the abuse to end, not the relationship. What these women needed, more than anything, was for their men to stop abusing them. So Dowse set about trying to find a way for that to happen. This marked the beginning of

"Insight"—group programs for abusive men that consisted of twice-weekly meetings for twelve weeks.

When Dowse started running the groups, she noticed one particularly strong theme: the men's sense of shame was stopping them from being honest about their abusive behavior. They insisted on blaming their partners: "If she hadn't said this," "If she hadn't done that," "She knows what I'm like." That's what got her thinking about the role of shame in men's abuse.

To investigate this, she changed tack. In one group, Dowse asked the men to try an experiment: If shame were in the room, what would it look like? To her surprise, the men all said that shame was male. "I thought it might have been a belligerent mother or something, but the men identified that shame was very male, hypercritical, and that this male shame got into their thinking—they're no good, they can't change, so they're better off just pretending it didn't happen or blaming someone else." Shame told these men that if they spoke about what they had done, they would be ostracized, says Dowse, because what they had done was so despicable that nobody would ever look at them the same way again.

Once shame had a face and a voice, the group started playing around with how to make shame visible. "These ideas came from the men in the group. We said, 'How about we put shame on this seat?' So we had a chair, and we stuck a piece of paper on it that said 'shame sits here.'" One night, they had shame seated in the circle, and one of the men said, "I just can't even stand shame sitting there looking at me like this." So the men agreed: Shame was to be put outside the room. "What I noticed," says Dowse, "was that once the shame seat was outside the room, men were saying things like 'thank god that idiot's gone,' and 'get out of here, we don't want you here.'"

Something about this didn't feel right. Dowse went home that night and thought about what had happened. Suddenly it dawned on her. "What had we recreated here? We don't like something, so we physically remove it from the room and abuse it." The following week, she went back to the group with a suggestion. "I was thinking about how we treated shame once he was asked to leave the group," she said. "What if we were to send shame to a support group? Because it sounds like he's got a whole bunch of things going on." With the backing of the group, she went over to the broom cupboard and tacked up a sign that said, "Shame Support Group." That started a whole new dynamic: when men would arrive at group, they would drop shame off at his support group, so they could meet as a group "without shame."

This might sound silly, but what Dowse and the group were doing was groundbreaking. Not only were they making shame—an unbearable and usually hidden emotion—*visible*, they were making it something to be *playful* with. When someone in the group would make a comment driven by shame—minimizing his abuse, blaming his partner, and so on—other men in the group would intervene, saying things like, "Uh-oh, I think we've got a problem—I think your shame got out of the room." Suddenly, instead of these men hiding behind their shame, they were talking openly about it and holding each other accountable.

What Dowse started to notice was a direct relationship between shame and responsibility: in releasing men from their shame, they were able to finally take responsibility for their abuse. But that wasn't the only major change in the group. "We'd start out with blokes telling war stories of how cool they are, how tough they are, how nobody could get anything over on them, particularly if they'd been to prison. Without shame in the group, tears became possible. We lost the bravado." When men spoke without shame or bravado, something else happened: they began to talk about the abuse in ways that more closely matched the women's accounts, positioning themselves as the ones at fault. When they gave up the need to blame their partners, it became easier for them to think about how their abuse had harmed their partners, their children, and themselves.

One of the most remarkable turnarounds was seen in a man called "Paul." He and his partner, "Crystal," had a long history of violence, which had landed him in jail several times. One night in the group, Paul started talking about something that had happened with his partner. He started saying, almost mechanically, "Yeah, well she..." and then interrupted himself. "I almost did that—my shame must be back. Let me just get rid of shame and start again." Paul took a moment, and said, "I was going to say that she pushes and pushes and pushes until I snap. But what I really want to say is that I snapped, and I feel terrible. I shouldn't have done it; it's not her fault, it's never been her fault."

In a video where Paul talks about this moment, he's able to talk about his abuse in a way "that didn't relieve him of responsibility, but relieved him of shame," says Dowse. "He was able to talk about being responsible without having his shoulders slump, or talk of being hopeless, helpless, a terrible man."

The next day, Dowse got a phone call from Crystal. "Whatever happened in group," she said, "keep it coming." The night before, she said, Paul had come home from group and asked if she wanted a cup of tea. Then, as he brought her tea, he told her he was thinking of moving out for a while. But he wasn't just telling her—he was asking her, checking to see if this was okay, and asking her if she wanted space. As Crystal recalled, Paul said, "I never really gave you a chance to say what you want. Maybe you don't want me to be here for a while." Paul was still up on charges from his last assault on Crystal, and they were both soon to return to court. But instead of planning to contest the charges, as he usually did, Paul called the police that night to ask what he would need to do to protect Crystal from going to court. On their advice, he turned himself in and was sentenced. "He wrote to the group from prison," says Dowse, "and explained what had happened. He said he just couldn't make her turn up to court anymore and have everyone look at her like she's no good, and have her worried about having the kids removed. He just turned up to court and said, 'Yeah, I did it,' so she didn't have to go."

The response from the group was equally surprising. The men weren't angry that Paul had been sent back to jail, and they didn't blame his partner for it. Instead, they were deeply moved. "We had a few men getting a bit teary and talking with real emotion in their voices about what had happened. What they wanted to know most of all was 'is his partner okay?'" Paul's act of taking responsibility had a ripple effect for the other men in the group, who started workshopping how they could do the same. "For one of the men in that group, that meant paying his child support debt and not whining about how she spent it. Other men agreed to just put their weapons down, in a way, and agree to stop doing something: badgering their former partners about access to their kids, humiliating her on Facebook, and so on."

There's been no formal study of Kylie Dowse's program, though she's had feedback from others in the field that its retention rate (the percentage of men who stay with the program) is unusually high. Whereas many men's behavior change groups focus on highlighting men's privilege and teaching skills for anger management, the Insight program did something highly unusual: it took its participants' top-secret fears—of their shame, dependency, and vulnerability—and brought them into the light.

———

The explosive cocktail of shame and entitlement in violent men like Kevin is a vital clue to solving one of the most confounding riddles of domestic abuse: Why do so many men sabotage not only the people they claim to love, but also themselves? Over and again, we hear of "nice guys" committing unthinkable violence against women and children. When another "nice guy" drowns his children or kills his wife, neighbors and newspaper headlines insist that this man was a good father, a successful worker, a pillar of the community, a tower of strength, a quiet neighbor.

We're not the only ones left in horrified bewilderment. Remember, Kevin tried several times to kill himself before ultimately confessing to

Joanna's murder. In 2015, a man named Robin Michael viciously beat his wife, Kerry, to death while they were hiking. Michael wrongly believed his wife was having an affair with his close friend. In a Facebook post written a few hours later, Michael wrote: "I have committed an act which should attract no pity, no sympathy, not even any understanding. I can't understand it." He said he had killed her in a jealous rage and was "so far gone it was surely insanity at its greatest." Michael killed himself in prison four months later.

Both Kevin and Michael were twisted by morbid paranoia, jealousy, and desperate need. Michael had a history of controlling and abusing his female partners; notes written by Kerry described how "trapped" she felt by his jealousy and possessiveness. Both men seemed "normal" to the outside world: Kevin was apparently an "easygoing, nice guy" working his way up the ranks of the military; Michael was a national figure in health care and general manager of an Australian hospital. We like to think only a certain type of man is capable of committing murder, but Kevin and Michael and the countless other men who've committed unthinkable violence toward women and children are the same kind of men we work with, are friends with, trust—men who *seem normal*. We almost never see their violence coming. As the renowned sociologist Allan Johnson writes, this is a profoundly disturbing realization calling into question a worldview we depend on for predictability and order in our lives.[41] If this man—this colleague, son, husband, or father—can commit such acts, then why believe another man will not?

Shame is felt by both genders. In fact, women have it drummed into them that their very femaleness is a shameful thing. Shame is something many women spend their lives trying to overcome. But women do not commit most of the world's violent crime. Men do.

The feeling of shame is biological and psychological, and the way we react to it is gendered. We may be born with the same physiological apparatus for feeling shame, but the way we experience shame is distinctly gendered. As Brené Brown explains, "Shame, for women, is this web of unobtainable, conflicting, competing expectations about who we're supposed to be. And it's a straitjacket. For men, shame is not a bunch of competing, conflicting expectations. Shame is one: do not be perceived as weak."[42] Numerous studies have shown that as soon as we identify a baby's sex, we bring our culturally biased expectations concerning gender to bear. The demand that boys be strong feeds into the expectation that one day, the baby boy will need to become a man who can be in control, so he can not only "succeed," but also defend himself against the violence of other men. From the very moment a young boy experiences shame, his response to it—and our response to him—is already being influenced by gender.

Now, having explored men's violence through the lens of biology and psychology, we need to take a closer look at it through the lens of gender. It's time to talk about the patriarchy.

5.

Patriarchy

there have been so many times
i have seen a man wanting to weep
but
instead
beat his heart until it was unconscious.

NAYYIRAH WAHEED

Patriarchy is an invisible mainframe that regulates how we live. It sets parameters around "acceptable" behavior for both genders: men should be "strong, independent, unemotional, logical, and confident," and women should be "expressive, nurturing, weak, and dependent."[1] This artificial construct, which we mistake as natural, also renders various injustices unavoidable: the violence of men, the domestic servitude of women, the dominance of men in power, and so on. Under patriarchy, this is all unfortunate, but "normal." Natural. Invisible.

Since the 1970s, the status of women in society has changed radically, and mostly for the better. But the patriarchy didn't vanish...we just stopped talking about it. When I began writing this book in 2016, *patriarchy* was still a dirty word; *gender equality* was the polite euphemism used by politicians and the feminist advocates trying to work with them. But even as gender inequality became the popular rallying cry against domestic abuse, I knew in my bones that it alone could not explain men's abuse of women. As the violence prevention expert Professor Bob Pease told me at the time, "gender inequality cannot capture the nuance, complexity, and multidimensional nature of patriarchy." Besides, if solving gender inequality is a panacea to domestic abuse, you'd expect domestic abuse statistics across the Nordic countries of Denmark, Finland, Iceland, Sweden, and Norway—the closest we have to gender-equal utopias—to be much lower than average. Shockingly, however, the number of women in these countries who have been subjected to physical or sexual violence from an intimate partner hovers around 30 percent[2]—*higher* than the European Union average of 22 percent and just above America's rate of 29 percent.[3]

Even with all this in mind, I was still reluctant to write about patriarchy, for fear I'd be pegged as having some anti-male agenda. Then, in late 2017, the #MeToo movement went viral. Millions of women worldwide shared raw and unflinching accounts of being harassed, assaulted, and raped. Sexual harassment, long considered "normal" and "unavoidable," was suddenly intolerable. Since then, the paradigm has shifted: "normal" gendered behaviors are being exposed and scrutinized as a matter of urgency, and "patriarchy" is the subject of countless op-eds and dinner party conversations. *The invisible mainframe has been made visible.*

Critically, aside from proving to women that the patriarchy still exists, #MeToo also proved it to some *men.* As the brutal stories of female friends filled their newsfeeds, men were genuinely shocked to learn that such behavior was not only commonplace, but had been suffered by virtually every woman they knew. "Until now, I thought I was awake," wrote journalist David Leser, "but the truth is I had absolutely no idea what women faced. No idea what it was like to feel afraid walking to my car or jogging at night; to be pressed against on a crowded train; to be ignored or talked over repeatedly; to know that my value at work was often predicated on my sexual attractiveness to my boss. No idea what it was like to have someone indecently expose themselves to me; to have to devise strategies each day, often unconsciously, to just feel safe."[4]

The nineteenth-century German dramatist Karl Georg Buchner observed that "revolutions often eat their children"; in other words, the people who bring down the status quo often fall victim to the forces they unleash. We've certainly seen that in recent revolutions—particularly the Arab uprisings—and it's impossible to predict how the #MeToo movement will evolve. But the ground has already shifted in ways unseen since the 1970s. After centuries of pathologizing women's fury as "hysteria," some men are finally starting to see that much of this fury is *legitimate*. Among this small but growing group of men, a new conversation is starting: *Why do we do this, and how can we change?*

For men, this conversation is fifty years late. While women have spent decades redefining what it is to be female in the modern world, men have clung stubbornly to old—and failing—definitions of patriarchal manhood. This, writes actor Michael Ian Black, has led "too many boys [to be] trapped in the same suffocating, outdated model of masculinity, where manhood is measured in strength, where there is no way to be vulnerable without being emasculated, where manliness is about having power over others. They are trapped, and they don't even have the language to talk about how they feel about being trapped, because the language that exists to discuss the full range of human emotion is still viewed as sensitive and feminine."[5] In other words, as feminists have been trying to tell men for decades, patriarchy is a dud deal for men, too.

Black is talking about decent men who aren't sure how to change but are willing to try. Yet plenty of other men aren't soul-searching, they're seething. Everywhere they look, people are carping on about "toxic masculinity" and male privilege, and some woman is whining about sexual harassment or unequal pay. These men nod along vigorously with statements like this one, from ACT Liberal politician Mark Parton in 2017: "If you are a heterosexual, employed, white male over the age of thirty, you're not really included in anything."[6] In homes everywhere, men like this are taking out their humiliated fury on their girlfriends, wives, and children, furious that women are getting all the attention while *their* suffering is ignored.

So we're talking about patriarchy again, and not a moment too soon. Men's violence against women is a global epidemic, and though gender inequality is a big component, this alone does not explain it. To get to the heart of why men abuse women they claim to love, we need to define and discuss the system that entraps *both* sexes. Domestic abuse doesn't really start with men disrespecting women. Its roots go much deeper: into men's fear of other men, and the way patriarchy shames them into rejecting their own so-called "feminine" traits, such as empathy, compassion, intuition, and emotional intelligence. We need to talk about how, for too many men, patriarchy makes power a zero-sum game and shrinks the rich landscape of intimacy to a staging ground for competition and threat. This is the realm of men's violence, with its underworld of male shame and humiliated fury.

Men have been sold a lie. They were brought up to believe that as long as they obeyed the rules of masculinity, they would be rewarded with power and privilege, limited only by how hard they were willing to work for it. But that system no longer exists (and for some, especially Indigenous men living under colonization, it never did). Men can no longer rely on a job for life, and they're no longer guaranteed that hard work will get them a house with a white-picket fence. Generations of men are frustrated, angry, and ashamed that despite following the rules—and despite sacrificing the tender, emotionally connected boys inside them—they're not getting what was promised to them. Thus, some of them are looking to their own home as a place to restore their lost power.

This is why we need to talk about patriarchy. First, though, we need to ask: What *is* patriarchy? I tracked down one of the world's most famous thinkers on the question and asked him to explain this notoriously slippery concept. Michael Kimmel is the SUNY Distinguished Professor of Sociology and Gender Studies at Stony Brook University in New York, and the best-selling author of several books about modern masculinity. Talking to him on the phone late one night, I asked him to start at the beginning. To people who've never even heard of patriarchy, how do you explain it?

"I explain patriarchy as a dual system of power: men's power over women, and some men's power over other men," he began. *Some men's power over other men*—that wasn't something I was expecting to hear. It immediately struck a chord.

Before we investigate the competition between men, though, let's unpack the most obvious aspect of patriarchy: men's power over women. To see how patriarchy entrenches male dominance, let's turn to renowned sociologist Allan Johnson. In his book *The Gender Knot*, Johnson breaks down patriarchy into four elements.[7] First, society is "male-dominated": positions of power are held predominantly by men. Second, and more subtly, society is "male-identified": patriarchy sets masculinity as the benchmark for what is good, desirable, or normal. That means our society privileges a certain set of "masculine" values: "control, strength, competitiveness, logic, decisiveness, rationality, autonomy, self-sufficiency." In opposition to these are the values considered to be "feminine": "cooperation, equality, sharing, empathy, vulnerability, and intuition." These so-called feminine values are not the values of power; they are the values attributed to people such as stay-at-home moms and people who do volunteer work and get paid minimum wage to care for children or the elderly. In other words, they are values that are at best underappreciated and at worst treated with contempt. Third, society is "male-centered," which means that we focus primarily on the exploits of men and boys—in the news, in movies, in art and culture, and in sport. Finally, the entire system of patriarchy is organized around an obsession with control. This is critical to our understanding of perpetrators of domestic abuse. The capacity to show power and control is the standard by which men are measured: whether it's their ability to master technology, run vast business empires, dominate conversation, rob a bank, or exhibit physical and emotional mastery. How and what they control doesn't matter, so long as they create the *impression* of being in control.

The way men exert power and control occurs on a spectrum. At the extreme end, it shows up as violence and abuse, but a little further down the spectrum this exact same behavior fits the definition of a successful man. "In a big corporate entity, you've got men who are exerting power, exerting control, are narcissistic, are audacious, they're not willing to compromise on their ideals, they're used to having their way, they bark orders, they expect to be listened to, they show no remorse. You know, that's what makes a successful man in a corporate world," says domestic abuse survivor-turned-advocate Kay Schubach. "Those behaviors are completely inappropriate in the family, and yet you see it time and time again; you've got these kids who are walking on eggshells when Dad gets home, Mom is completely terrified that everything needs to be perfect, and if it's not you're upsetting this incredibly powerful man with powerful friends, and everyone's on his side because he is bringing home the bacon, and he's provided this incredible lifestyle."

As a group, men are dominant and privileged in relation to women. As individuals, though, men pay a price for this privilege: to be considered "real men," they have to live up to patriarchy's standards and abide by its rules. These standards and rules are regulated—through fear, control, and violence—by other men.

This leads us to the second part of patriarchy: *some men's power over other men.* This is the side of patriarchy we rarely talk about, and it is the key to understanding the abusive mind. Here's why: Traditionally, feminism has equated manhood with power, and has thus positioned *all men* as powerful and privileged. From this viewpoint, violence against women is just a tool whereby men express, maintain, and restore male power and privilege.

However, Kimmel says that although it's understandable that women would see male power in this way, it doesn't describe how men actually *feel*, which is why men commonly reject it. "A lot of men will often try to opt out of the idea that men have power over women by saying, 'I don't have any power; my wife has all the power, my kids, my boss,'" says Kimmel. Although men are powerful as a *group*, they do not necessarily feel powerful as *individuals*. In fact, many individual men feel powerless (whether they actually are or not). The essence of patriarchal masculinity, says Kimmel, is not that individual men feel powerful. It's that they feel *entitled* to power.

This one statement, to me, makes sense of men's violence. When men feel powerless and ashamed, it's their *entitlement* to power that fuels their humiliated fury and drives them to commit twisted, violent acts. That entitlement to power is the key to understanding why men and women generally respond so differently to shame and humiliation. "Women are humiliated and shamed as well, and they don't go off on shooting sprees," says Kimmel. "Why not? Because they don't feel entitled to be in power. [For men], it's *humiliation plus entitlement*. It's the idea that 'I don't feel empowered, but I should.'"

This is the rallying cry of the men's rights movement: men have been robbed—of jobs, dignity, sex, and so on—and need to take back what's rightfully theirs (especially from the women who have "stolen" it). This attitude is weaponized into homicidal misogyny in the desperately sad and often vicious "incel" community, where "involuntarily celibate" men congregate in online forums like Reddit and post bitterly about how their ugliness has doomed them to a life without sex. When they're not cheering each other on to suicide (because "hope is for idiots"), they workshop ideas on how to take violent revenge on the women (a.k.a. "Stacys") who refuse to have sex with them. The Stacys aren't just rejecting these men, they are denying their basic human rights. This isn't just empty talk in some dark corner of the internet: since 2014, self-proclaimed incels (including Elliot Rodger) have carried out two mass shootings in North America, with the explicit aim of punishing the Stacys and the "Chads" (the attractive and successful men who get to have sex with Stacys).

———

Men's violence against women is an epidemic, and its prevalence in private and in public means there is no place where women can be truly safe. But men's violence against men—predominantly in public—is also perpetrated at staggering levels. When it comes to general violent crime (murder, assault, bullying, bashing), boys and men are both the primary victims and the primary perpetrators of these crimes. In this maelstrom of competition and violence, men and boys become keenly aware of their position in the pecking order. Here we have the answer to the Atwood riddle at the end of chapter 3. *The self-consciousness and fear that men feel toward other men is the reason they are so afraid of women laughing at them*: being humiliated by a woman means being emasculated, revealed as weak, and made vulnerable to the ridicule, control, and violence of other men.

Of course, under patriarchy nothing represents weakness like being a girl. The reality of men's lives has changed dramatically over the past century, but the primary rule of masculinity hasn't. "No sissy stuff. You can never do anything that even remotely hints at femininity," says Kimmel. "Your masculinity is the relentless repudiation of the feminine. That's rule number one. Everything else is an elaboration of that." The way men prove they're not a sissy is by obeying three other rules: be a big deal, be a "sturdy oak" (a.k.a. boys don't cry), and give 'em hell (show everyone how brave you are by taking risks). Essentially, being a man means *not* being in any way like a woman.

The pressure for boys and men to prove they're not "girls" is the jet fuel for misogyny. Rejecting, criticizing, and policing femininity—and girls and women—is not just something some men do. Misogyny is a ghost in the machine of our culture: it is what makes men and women alike believe that women are not as competent, trustworthy, reliable, or authoritative as men, and that women are better suited to caregiving roles than jobs that require clear thinking and decision-making. Misogyny shapes the opinions and beliefs of men and women alike, to varying degrees, because misogyny isn't a personality flaw, as Allan Johnson writes, but "part of patriarchal culture. We're like fish swimming in a sea laced with it, and we can't breathe without passing it through our gills. Misogyny infuses into our cells and becomes part of who we are, because by the time we know enough to reject it, it's too late."[8]

The training to reject anything perceived as feminine starts young. Boys are expected to disconnect from their mothers—lest they become a "mama's boy"—and identify with their fathers. Then, in order to be strong, they must disconnect from their own sense of pain or distress, lest they be bullied by other boys (or girls) for being weak. First and foremost, though, they must prove that they are not a girl. Family therapist and expert on masculinity Terrence Real saw this in his own three-year-old son, Alexander, a flamboyant boy who loved dressing up, especially as the "good witch" Barbie. One day, when his older brother had some friends over, Alexander came whooshing down the stairs in his "cherished paraphernalia—white dress, silver wand, and matching tiara [and] struck a magnificent pose for the kids." The boys looked up, and said nothing. They knew better than to ridicule Alexander, but their stares said it all: *You are not to do this.* "The medium that message was broadcast in was a potent emotion: *shame.* At three, Alexander was learning the rules." Real sensed his own face burning red as Alexander "turned heel, threw off the dress, jammed into a pair of jeans and, as casually as he could, joined the group as they retired downstairs to work on their swords, knives, and guns. That dress has never been touched again."

Moments of "induction" like this are what Real calls the "normal traumatization of boys."[9] "The way we 'turn boys into men' is through injury," he writes. "We pull them away from their own expressiveness, from their feelings, from sensitivity to others. The very phrase 'Be a man' means suck it up and keep going. Disconnection is not fallout from traditional masculinity. Disconnection *is* masculinity."[10] In this model of manhood, there is no society. It's every man for himself, dog eat dog.

When your identity and power rest on rejecting femininity, misogyny can be worn like a coat of armor. The more boys openly hold women and femininity in contempt, the less likely they'll be pegged as "sissies" or "fags." Australian novelist Tim Winton hears boys talking like this every day. "Some of it makes you want to hug them. Some of it makes you want to cry. Some of it makes you ashamed to be a male. Especially the stuff they feel entitled or obliged to say about girls and women." In their unguarded moments, Winton says, these boys are "lovely...dreamy, vulnerable," but these qualities are being "shamed out of them" every day. "There's a constant pressure to enlist, to pull on the uniform of misogyny and join the Shithead Army that enforces and polices sexism," Winton said in a 2018 speech. "Boys and men are so routinely expected to betray their better natures, to smother their consciences, to renounce the best of themselves and submit to something low and mean. As if there's only...one valid interpretation of the part, the role, if you like."[11]

Kimmel explains: "We've constructed an idea of masculinity that [sets] individual autonomy as the highest goal. So you hate those parts of yourself that aren't autonomous; that aren't individual. And then you see this living embodiment out in front of you—a woman—who embodies all the qualities you so hate in yourself. They are the ones who have these qualities, you hate those qualities, and therefore you hate them, and you get angry at them for eliciting those very qualities from you. *You make me weak in the knees, you make me feel these things that I didn't want to feel—love and tenderness and all of that stuff. I hate you for it.*"

Bruce, a white man in his forties, says he's struggled his whole life against this straitjacket of masculinity. "I've kind of spent a lot of my life feeling disappointed that I never stepped on a grenade, or stood in front of a wall of bullets and saved somebody," he says. Bruce has two grown children who no longer speak to him because of the violence he used against their mother. Slaps, mostly, but also rage: shouting down the house, smashing things. "I threw myself against walls, I punched walls, and I also—it's really hard to say—I...I did attack my ex-wife. In the beginning it happened a couple of times a year. By the end, it was happening weekly." Since his wife left him thirteen years ago, Bruce has spent hundreds of hours in therapy rooms, trying to vanquish what he calls "the monster in the basement." "It really, really profoundly sucks to be terrified of your own thoughts and terrified of your own behavior," he says.

Bruce was taught to be terrified of his emotions when he was a little boy. "The earliest memory I have is of being in the backyard and starting to cry. I ran into the house, into my bedroom, and closed the door. I didn't want my dad to hear me crying, because I had a pretty good idea of what was going to happen next," he says. "When he came into my bedroom and yelled at me not to cry, I remember thinking, *Can't you tell that you're making it worse?* He said, 'I'll give you something to cry about,' smacked me, and left. I remember deciding that I was never going to cry in front of him again." Bruce took his pent-up sadness to school, where he "spent a lot of time crying, until the teachers told me you're not supposed to cry. This was the 1980s, and boys don't cry. It was a very simple lesson I was supposed to learn, and I learned it."

Bruce's father was a diplomat who was "tremendously successful at doing things to promote peace in the world." Within the four walls of the family home, however, he was "terrifying." Retreating into his teenage universe, Bruce became obsessed by computers, and was determined to be the next Steve Jobs. In this private world, he cast himself as the hero: a true believer in justice and good deeds, who would prove to the world he was better than everyone else. Later, as he became bigger, and his father grew older, Bruce got his first taste for the power of violence. "I hit him back," he says. "That was a delightful powerful feeling that I was profoundly ashamed of. My desperate need to not admit to that made it harder to manage later on, when I started being violent toward my wife."

When Bruce was nineteen, he fell for a woman who'd moved to the city to flee her own violent father. Before long, when Bruce felt he was being disrespected, he resorted to violence. "She said something that offended me. I didn't like that, and I wanted to bring the situation under control. I don't actually have my own memory of what happened next, but she claims I slapped her in the face, and I believe her. Back then, though, I was angry with her for some time for suggesting that I had done this horrible thing. The idea that I had done that was so profoundly offensive to me. But I believe her now."

When Bruce's girlfriend announced soon afterward that she was going to leave him, Bruce spontaneously burst into tears. He says that when she challenged him to at least get angry and "prove he cared," he obliged. "On that occasion, I worked up to it, and ended up raising my voice. It came more naturally after that."

Once they had children together, Bruce says he was determined to make it work, no matter how bad it got. "I was trapped in the relationship because I was never going to abandon my kids. My father had got a divorce and had kids afterwards, and I was never going to repeat the things he had done."

Bruce doesn't relate to the idea that underlying all domestic abuse is a basic disrespect or contempt for women. "Being told I hated women did not help at all." His major problem, he says, is that he had no idea how to properly express his emotions. "If I was lost and happy, then I was in awe of the mystery of woman, but if I was lost and unhappy, then my very limited vocabulary could lead me relatively quickly to taking control and using the tools that I had."

For a while, Bruce used this lack of emotional vocabulary as a kind of power. "If you've only got two modes of communicating with someone—one of which is a polite request, the other being violence—the polite request *is* the threat of violence. And so you can then maintain the self-image of a person who is unfailingly polite, while everyone responds very quickly and actively to everything you ask for."

When I spoke to Bruce in 2016, his second marriage was "on the rocks," he was still terrified of his own violence, and was having suicidal thoughts. In the three years since, however, things have turned around. With the support of a "team" of therapists ("I'm extremely fortunate to be able to afford a team!"), Bruce has been able to return to work, and has developed the ability to lose his composure without becoming violent. "I might cry or raise my voice, but the days of violent and threatening behavior seem to be over, although I'll remain on guard against them for the rest of my life," he says. "And the second marriage is getting stronger every week."

———————

Patriarchy trains into men a deep, shame-ridden urge to put women in their place, and to prevent them from exposing male tenderness. This power over women has always had an erotic quality, but never has it been exploited and transmitted as it is today. Through pornography, capitalism has turned the erotic charge of female subordination into a multibillion-dollar industry.

The past twenty years have seen hardcore porn—particularly "gonzo porn," in which there is no storyline—go mainstream. Extreme and inhumane sex acts such as gagging, ejaculating on a woman's face, and double penetration are now considered unremarkable, and in a lot of pornography, aggression is now the default setting. Porn actor Anthony Hardwood told sex educator Maree Crabbe that this modern porn is worlds apart from what he was making back in the mid-1990s. "When I started, it was like, very lovey-dovey sex, not tough like 'gonzo,'" said Hardwood. "After three years they wanted to get more energy, more rough. They do...one girl with, you know, like four guys and they just take over and destroy her... It's like we want to kill the girl on set." Another veteran porn actor, Nina Hartley, told Crabbe, "In the last ten years, there's been an increase in what I would call the aggression that we see on camera."[12]

Not all porn is degrading to women, but a great deal of it is. As the Australian Institute of Family Studies (a federal research body) found, "the most dominant, popular, and accessible pornography contains messages and behaviors about sex, gender, power, and pleasure that are *deeply* problematic. Physical aggression (slapping, choking, gagging, hair pulling) and verbal aggression such as name-calling, predominantly done by men to their female partners, permeate pornographic content. In addition, this aggression often accompanies sexual interaction that is nonreciprocal (e.g., oral sex) and where consent is assumed rather than negotiated."[13] Choking—which police see as a red flag for domestic homicide—is a common feature in hardcore porn. "Women are choked with anything from a penis to a fist to the point of gagging, and in some cases almost passing out," writes Gail Dines, professor emerita of sociology and women's studies at Wheelock College in Boston. "The victim obviously can't speak during these acts because she is choking, so it is typically not until the end of the scene that she says, often in a hoarse voice, how much she 'loved it.' Meanwhile, she looks exhausted, upset, and—in some cases—distraught."[14] In a recent study of the top fifty most popular pornographic videos, 88 percent of scenes were found to include physical aggression (acts like gagging, slapping, or choking), and 94 percent of that was directed at women.[15] "In almost every instance," adds Crabbe, "women were portrayed as though they either didn't mind or liked the aggression."[16]

What's even more telling is the result of another study, which found that the rate of physical aggression in mainstream pornography was as low as 1.9 percent.[17] What accounted for the difference? The researcher defined aggression as something that was clearly intended to harm and was resisted by the female performer. But that's just the point: women in pornography *don't* resist their degradation. As the narrative goes, they know they've been bad and deserve to be punished. As Dines documents in her landmark book *Pornland*, a lot of modern porn creates a fantasy world for men in which women are turned on by their own degradation: they deserve to be abused, they want to be punished, and there's no limit to what they're willing to accept. This fantasy sex, she says, "looks more like sexual assault than making love."[18] Male performers, too, are commonly reduced to patriarchal caricatures: "Men in porn are depicted as soulless, unfeeling, amoral life-support systems for erect penises who are entitled to use women in any way they want."[19]

This kind of porn is everywhere, available to adults and children alike. The average age at which boys start watching porn is eleven, and 94 percent of kids will see porn before they turn eighteen.[20] For many—especially young—people, porn is fundamentally changing the way they have sex. The Children's Commissioner for England has reported "frequent accounts of both boys' and girls' expectations of sex being drawn from the pornography they had seen. We also found compelling evidence that too many boys believe that they have an absolute entitlement to sex at any time, in any place, in any way and with whomever they wish. Equally worryingly, we heard that too often, girls feel they have no alternative but to submit to boys' demands, regardless of their own wishes."[21]

Research is inconclusive on whether there is a direct link between men's and boys' viewing of hardcore porn and their committing sexual violence against women. Nevertheless, data from rape and sexual assault centers like the Gold Coast Center Against Sexual Violence in Australia show that, in the past five years, the severity of sexual violence they are dealing with has increased exponentially.[22]

Director Di McLeod told the Problem with Porn conference in 2016 that sexual injuries that were once uncommon are now an everyday story involving women of varied ages and diverse backgrounds. Increasingly, these injuries are requiring treatment from emergency departments on the Gold Coast; in the previous five years, the center had seen a 56 percent increase in referrals from emergency departments. "These levels of physical and sexual violence are bordering on and including behavior that would meet the criminal code definition of torture." It was common, said McLeod, for victims to report that the partner who had savagely abused them was also a regular consumer of pornography.

If we can agree that seeing uncritical portrayals of violence, racism, and sexism have an impact on our cultural norms—and should therefore be closely monitored and perhaps regulated—then surely there is something to be said about what happens to men and boys who frequently masturbate to the sight of women being aggressively used sexually (sometimes to the point of tears and vomiting), when all the while those women are portrayed as *liking* it. Though we hope to reduce domestic abuse by changing young people's views on misogyny and sexism, the endless wave of misogynistic porn is a heavy tide to swim against.

––––––––––

We say we want men to be more compassionate, more open, more vulnerable. But do we really want that? Do heterosexual women find vulnerability sexy? Are we ready to accept men into conversations about gender that have largely, for the past fifty years, been our sanctuary *away* from men?

Women have good reason to be wary of male converts. Too often, men say all the right things about rejecting patriarchy, but fail to do any work on themselves. However, many other men—some of whom spend whole careers dedicated to analyzing their own privilege and advocating for women and children—find themselves relegated to the fringes by a small faction of feminists who are, in the words of feminist writer bell hooks, "anti-male."[23] Often, these are women who have been seriously harmed and traumatized by men's violence. They are victims and survivors of child abuse, rape, and domestic abuse, and they have channeled their fear of and revulsion to men into a vengeful fury. Their fury may be legitimate, or at the very least understandable, but it warps the debate.

Outside the realm of gender politics, in bedrooms across Australia, we are deeply confused about how we want men to behave. The truth is that many women struggle to feel compassion for men's vulnerability. Here's bell hooks again, from her stunningly brave book *The Will to Change*: "Most women do not want to deal with male pain if it interferes with the satisfaction of female desire. When the feminist movement led to men's liberation, including male exploration of 'feelings,' some women mocked male emotional expression with the same disgust and contempt as sexist men. Despite all the feminist longing for men of feeling, when men worked to get in touch with feelings, no one really wanted to reward them. In feminist circles men who wanted to change were often labeled narcissistic or needy. Individual men who expressed feelings were often seen as attention seekers, patriarchal manipulators trying to steal the stage with their drama."[24]

I know I've struggled with this. When my husband tells me how stressed and tired he feels, or wants to talk about problems in our relationship, part of me can feel repulsed. I want to tell him to just suck it up and deal (and sometimes, to my shame, that *is* what I tell him). If he's in a difficult place emotionally, I'll happily talk about it for hours. But if it's a chronic problem—especially one that has anything to do with a failure on my part—it can really push my buttons. Once, when he cried during an argument, I accused him of using his emotions to manipulate me. Deep down, beneath my wall of defense, I knew that wasn't true. But part of me wants my husband to always be my rock: the one who supports *me* when I feel afraid or distressed, not the other way round.

None of this is coherent, of course, because the traits I most love in him are his emotional tenderness, the way he is moved by art and literature, and how he can sometimes explain what I'm feeling better than I can. bell hooks gets the tension exactly right when she explains this knee-jerk response as the result of women's own patriarchal training. Men's pain—especially in relationships—sounds to us "like an indictment of female failure. Since sexist norms have taught us that loving is our task whether in our role as mothers or lovers or friends, if men say they are not loved, then we are at fault; we are to blame."[25] This sense of failure for women is a major trigger for shame—an unbearable feeling we desperately want to go away. How much room, then, can we allow for men to be truly vulnerable?

In her TED talk on shame, Brené Brown talks about the moment she realized that in her four years researching shame and vulnerability, she hadn't thought to consider its impact on men. Brown said subsequent research had shown her that "men are often pressured to open up and talk about their feelings, and criticized for being emotionally walled-off; but if they get too real, they are met with revulsion." When this realization dawned on her, she exclaimed aloud, "Holy shit! I am the patriarchy!"[26]

Patriarchy is not just a system populated by men; it's one we've all been raised in. As women, we have to do our own work to reject and replace the faulty norms patriarchy has seeded in us. However, acknowledging that women have their own work to do doesn't mean for one second that it's the job of women to fix abusive men. Only men can fix men. As the feminist author Laurie Penny tweeted, "Men's healing should not have to come at the price of women's pain, ever... I know too many women who have worn themselves out trying to understand the men who hurt, harassed, and abused them, believing that love and empathy would cure their hatred. If that was all it took, we'd have a better world."[27]

Nor is it enough for men simply to "get in touch with their feelings" and learn to be more vulnerable. Some of the most abusive men could sit and talk about their feelings all day long—and will demand that their partners put aside their own needs and pay full attention.

The unifying trait among abusers is a radioactive sense of entitlement. The animating force behind their violence is the belief that their feelings are more important than those of their partners and children. Confronted with feelings of discomfort or shame, abusive men will do whatever it takes to avoid those emotions and move to a feeling of power. When this combines with a sense of entitlement to women's bodies, and the patriarchal belief that women should put aside their own needs (for comfort, safety, and independence) in order to meet the needs of men, the outcome can be catastrophic.

Male entitlement afflicts almost all men, in different ways and to varying degrees. However, to many men, those feelings of entitlement are undetectable. In fact, many would deny feeling entitled at all. The belief some men have that their needs must take priority is so deeply entrenched it is almost invisible to them, and thus very hard to shift. Also, as Michael Kimmel noted earlier, men often feel individually powerless; they feel they live at the whim of their bosses, their partners, or their children. The core of patriarchal masculinity is not power, as Kimmel points out, but the feeling of being *entitled* to power. But how do you show an abusive man who believes himself to be powerless—as many abusive men do—that he is actually acting from a position of entitlement?

This is the fundamental problem facing us when we talk about ending men's violence against women. As the stalwart Australian feminist Eva Cox said at a public event on the #MeToo movement, "The question is not 'how do we stop that man from doing that to us?' but 'how do we stop men feeling like they're *entitled* to?' We have to start looking at what we are doing to little boys to make them feel entitled. We need to sit down and start addressing the social problem, because we are still the second sex."[28] It's not enough for men to reconnect with their feelings. A society of newly realized, emotionally sensitive men who still have raging senses of entitlement—and who expect women to prioritize their newfound feelings—sounds like a dystopia worthy of a Margaret Atwood novel. Until men reckon with their overblown sense of entitlement, they cannot reach emotional maturity, and there can be no solution to domestic abuse. So what does it look like for an abusive man to do this?

It took Rob Sanasi, the reformed abuser we met in chapter 1, months of intensive therapy before he was able to make anything resembling real and lasting change. At first, he tried to use his therapy to manipulate Deb. "He was saying things every woman in this situation has longed to hear," she says, "like, 'I'm wrong, I've treated you badly, I'm so sorry for what I've done to you.' So I'd start getting hopeful. But then he'd slip in: 'I want to make up for it, Deb. So if you would just quit that job and come home, I want to now make up for all the years we've lost.'" Across from Deb at their kitchen table, Rob nods sheepishly. "Sneaky, sneaky stuff," he says.

When Deb refused to quit, Rob became increasingly desperate. "He tried many different tactics to regain control of me," Deb recalls. "Like threatening to kill himself. He really escalated. It was very intense." But every time Rob tried a different tactic, Deb called him on it. Eventually, he realized it was all or nothing. His counselor had been trying to get him to take responsibility for his abuse and to develop some empathy for Deb. To do this, Rob had to go back to the roots of his need for control.

Rob grew up around domestic abuse, fighting, bullying, and neglect. "Every night I went to sleep to massive, massive fights." When he was a little boy, his mother used to go out and not come back for hours, leaving four-year-old Rob at home alone with his younger brother. "When the sun would go down, I used to think, *Oh shit, she may never be home again.*" Feeling completely out of control at home, Rob tried to control everything outside it. "Even through my schooling life I had control over friends, over relationships. I always controlled my environment."

Deb interrupts: "I've heard you say, Rob, too, that you had an attitude that everyone was there to serve you. Do you remember?"

Rob laughs awkwardly. "Yeah, and I don't even know where that came from."

At no stage did his counselor let Rob use his childhood as an excuse: being accountable came first. Slowly, Rob started to get some perspective. Instead of blaming Deb for his abuse, he began to see that she had nothing to do with it at all. "To anyone looking in from outside, it would have looked like we were having marriage problems and fighting a lot. But *we* weren't fighting—it was just *me* fighting Deb." Rob started to realize that he wasn't the powerful man he thought he was; he was actually deeply insecure. "When you're insecure, you want to control something so you don't feel insecure anymore," he says. "But to try and control someone else—another human being—just doesn't work, 'cause we're not built for that."

As I listened to this, I thought of all the women I'd spoken to who'd stayed with their partner, believing he could change, but who ended up getting drawn further into the abuse. Deb was a counselor, and she'd read a lot about domestic abuse, so she must have known that Rob's chances of reform were extremely slim. What was it that made her believe he would change?

"I was very suspicious, because I was reading the statistics, and I also heard that a lot of men go to counseling so their wife will, you know, settle down. So I was really just observing, and going, *Is this change real, or is it just another manipulation?* Because everyone I was speaking to in the field was sort of rolling their eyes and saying, 'Nah, it doesn't happen, very rare, don't get your hopes up.' And I was like, 'Well, I get that, but if only 5 percent of men actually change, what does that change look like?'"

Then one day, Deb felt Rob start to change. "I can actually pinpoint an actual day when I felt the control stop, when I felt those claws come out of me. Rob stopped focusing on me and started to take responsibility that *this has nothing to do with Deb—I need to leave her be and stop harassing the poor woman. I just need to deal with my stuff and let her recover from me.*" It was a pivotal day for Rob, too. "I went into the bedroom and I think I cried for, like, four hours," says Rob. "And literally from that day, all the work—all the counseling, all the memories, everything that had been done—kind of hit a peak, and it was like a volcano that just erupted."

Relinquishing control, however, was only the first phase. Next Rob had to relinquish his overblown sense of entitlement.

When Deb finally felt safe in the relationship, she sank into a post-traumatic state. "All of a sudden I would start crying and I couldn't stop," she says, "and then a door would slam and I would be hypervigilant." Some days Deb would be "extremely angry" with Rob and need him to get away from her, and on others she would feel vulnerable and need him to hold her. Rob had to learn that no matter what Deb did, or how unfair things seemed, her needs had to come first. "I think the biggest thing I learned is *it's not all about me.* As Deb said, you know, she needed a lot of support, and that support might have been just for me to get lost. For a two-year period I just denied myself. Even if I thought she did something that was a bit irrational, and wasn't really the way it should've gone, I would not speak up. I just knew that it was not my time to even have an opinion, you know. That sounds a bit weird, but I almost decided to deny myself any rights. And I think that was really good, for me, because it totally went against [what I'd done] my whole life—my upbringing, my behaviors. Not only did I have to stop [controlling], but I had to do the opposite of what I was doing: I had to think of other people, I had to think of Deb, I had to think of the kids, I had to think of other friends who I'd always, I suppose, used to get what I wanted."

"Rob went from a person that was quite narcissistic, that didn't have empathy, to a person that did," says Deb. "It was kind of like suddenly he had eyes to see, *Oh my gosh, I've actually hurt quite a few people.* Empathy is not just comprehending that, but actually *feeling* that. He really had empathy for me, whereas before he didn't care about anything else other than himself." Deb describes Rob's process as being "like a twelve-step program." Rob says, "I started to get memories about different people that I hadn't done really bad things to, but in my heart I knew I didn't treat them right. And so I called some of them up, and they were like, 'Holy cow, I can't believe that's you saying this.' I spent two years apologizing to people."

Today, Rob is someone men come to for informal advice when their relationships are falling apart. "Usually the only time I've seen guys start to realize anything at all is when they've just about lost it all," says Rob. "I've never had any guy come to me and say, you know what, I'm really doing the wrong thing, and I want my relationship to be better. It's always like a country song, you know—*my wife's gone, the car's gone, the kid's gone, the dog's gone*—you could write a song about it. And they're all the same. And *I* was the same; I'm no better. I'm exactly like that, or was.

"I think they think like I did, you know: *What if I do all this work and then my wife still leaves me?* Yeah, that still may happen," says Rob, "but you know what? The best thing about coming through this journey... I think there are three good things. Number one, it stops any more pain going to your wife. Number two, if you have children, it will hopefully stop them from passing that on and going through counseling themselves. Number three is you get to wake up in the morning yourself and be free."

———

That is just one story about one couple. For other men, the journey is a lot rougher.

"Brendan" says the only thing that could ever stop his abuse was jail. "I needed to be locked away. She needed protection, and I needed protection from myself."[29] Brendan was sentenced to more than twelve years for attempting to murder his wife. If he hadn't been jailed, he says, he would have killed her. Nothing had stopped him before. Multiple intervention orders, short stints in prison: he wasn't bothered by any of it, and he just returned to torturing his wife as soon as he was released. "Men who commit domestic violence, something is broken inside," he says.

Brendan can't even remember why he started abusing his wife. He had never hit a woman before. "But once I had, that was it. The switch was flicked." His abuse didn't come in a rage; rather, "it was just cold-blooded revenge." It became like an addiction he couldn't shake, and ruined not only the lives of his wife and children, but also his own life; by the time he was planning to murder his wife, he was also planning to kill himself.

In jail Brendan found himself surrounded by extreme violence, and he was desperate to get out. He signed up for a behavior change program, hoping that it would get him early parole. For some reason, though, Brendan didn't end up being one of those guys who just do it for the piece of paper. He actually listened, and started to understand why he'd become an abusive man. "That course taught me all [the] things I should have already known," he says. Out of jail now, Brendan says he's lucky his children stuck by him. "I have a good life now—even though I don't deserve it. But how much better would it have been, how much better would we all have been, if I had never taken that first punch? Or, at the very least, been locked away for a long time, the first time."

––––––––

For many women, the idea of their abusive partner attempting anything like this is unimaginable. Worse still, often women will be persuaded not to leave by a man who is "willing to change," only to find that he has no intention of changing. By the time that becomes obvious, it may be much harder for her to leave.

"The proportion of men that get really nonviolent—they're small," says Rodney Vlais. "But they're so inspiring. This very small percentage of violent men are actually working toward understanding their privilege and their gender power—way beyond what most men are willing to do in our society. That is the beginning of a social movement. If those men can do it, then surely all of us men can do it."

Domestic abuse is, first and foremost, a tragedy for the victim—but it is also a tragedy for the perpetrator. Most abusive men were once tender little boys, vulnerable and shy, who just wanted to love and be loved.

That boy didn't dream about abusing women when he grew up. He didn't dream of becoming a violent father. Yet so many boys grow up to do both. As abusive men, they use power to inflict misery and violence on their lovers and children, but they do not necessarily *feel* powerful themselves. These are not the raging patriarchs of old, granted their every wish by the women and children who fear them, and vaunted by society. Modern perpetrators of domestic abuse are often miserable creatures, unable to love or be loved, and so wracked with secret shame that their only defense is to construct a grandiose narcissism behind which they can hide. Something has to interrupt the process that transforms tender boys into violent men.

Prevention campaigns that use slogans such as "real men don't hit women," "man up," and "be the hero" don't actually model an alternative to patriarchal masculinity; they simply reinforce the existing one. "Prevention campaigns present us with men defined by the stereotypically masculine attributes of success (strength, money, power) who say they don't hit women," writes Michael Salter, the expert on gendered violence we heard from in chapter 3. "The message is clear: keep our tough competitive masculinity, but abandon gendered violence."[30]

Symbolic gestures, like "taking an oath" against violence, are similarly pointless. As men's educator Danny Blay once told me, the vast majority of perpetrators he's worked with say they are staunchly opposed to men's violence against women. These messages simply don't work. Salter writes, "Violent men often don't understand where their violence comes from and don't know how to stop. Men who have engaged in violence and abuse toward women are often deeply ashamed of their conduct. It's unclear how further shaming will produce a change in their behavior, and it may inhibit them from seeking treatment and support."[31]

When abusive men feel powerless and afraid, they use violence to dispel their fear and return to a feeling of power. No amount of condemning their violence is going to persuade them to act otherwise. Instead, as Salter writes, they need to be shown the way back to *non*violence. They need to be shown, as Rob discovered on his long recovery from abusiveness, that taking the path of nonviolence leads to a better and more successful life. "Nonviolence is not simply the absence of violence," writes Salter. "Nonviolence is the presence of characteristics that oppose violence—like care, patience, or compassion. Rather than idolizing 'real men' who don't hit women, prevention campaigns could be valuing the other kinds of choices boys and men make, such as caring for others, supporting those in need, and working for the collective good."[32] Casting perpetrators out as "irrevocably tainted" only compounds their shame, and potentially makes them all the more dangerous.

Ultimately, to stop domestic abuse, we need to do more than teach men to respect women. We need to teach men to respect other men, to give each other space and permission to live fully embodied, emotional lives—and we need women to allow that to happen, too. But achieving this will require men to take a hard look at their own sense of entitlement, a subject that can make even the staunchest feminist ally bristle.

Patriarchy sells men the lie that in order to be "real men" they must kill off their emotional intelligence, their intuition, and their empathy when they are young, so they may vie for power in the *real* world, where success is measured by what you can control. This is the lie that is killing women and men alike.

Women are at risk from the homicidal force of men's humiliated fury: on the street, when they dare to walk outside at night, but especially in their homes, from the people they love the most. But men are dying from this, too. Picture the destructive force of male shame as having two extreme poles: at one end, men react by attacking others, and at the other, they attack themselves. There are men who would rather die than say a word about their emotional pain. They are victims of the same patriarchal system. Among other factors, a deep fear of revealing emotional weakness and stunted emotional development are driving record numbers of men to commit suicide. In the United States, suicide rates have increased 30 percent since the end of the twentieth century.[33] In 2017 alone, the Centers for Disease Control recorded 47,173 suicides—70 percent of them white men.[34]

The need to address the destructive force of patriarchy and male shame is stark and urgent—for women *and* men.

And for the children they are raising.

6.
Children

There is no greater agony than bearing an untold story inside you.
MAYA ANGELOU, *I KNOW WHY THE CAGED BIRD SINGS*

In the cool blue light of a cold October morning, fifteen-year-old "Carly" stands shivering with her school friends on the train platform. She's nervous. She's been planning this moment for days. As the train approaches, she drops a hint that she's about to run away, gives one of them her phone—*just in case he's using it to track me*, she thinks—and quietly takes one of their tap-and-go travel cards, so police won't be able to trace her when she taps off. Minutes later, she's on a train heading away from her school. After the morning rush of students, Carly shrinks into a corner, tucking her chin to her chest to avoid security cameras. At every stop, her heart races. *Do the police already know where I am? How long before he finds me?*

When Carly gets on that train, it has been more than a year since the police last caught her running away from her father. She was fourteen then, in a car with her mother and eleven-year-old brother, "Zac." They had been on the run for nine months, fleeing a Family Court order that not only granted Carly's father, "John," sole custody, but also prohibited her and Zac from making any contact whatsoever with their mother. During the years before this order was issued, Carly's mother, "Erin"—whose story of financial abuse we detailed in chapter 2—had tried to shield her children from their father's violence. Finally, in 2012, blunt advice from her doctor gave her the push she needed to leave. In front of their screaming children, John had choked Erin so hard her eyes had rolled back in her head. "If you don't leave," her doctor warned, "you're as bad as he is."

So she did, but she was still terrified. John had threatened that if she left, he would hunt her down like a dog and shoot her. Seeing that she needed protection from him, a magistrate issued an intervention order.

Soon thereafter, John applied to the Family Court for visitation. Despite the intervention order, the advice from Erin's family lawyer was blunt: consent, or risk losing custody of your children. Her evidence of abuse would not be enough to argue for full custody, and besides, she should "stop playing the victim" and get over it. Against her better instincts, Erin consented to visits. But when both children refused to see or even speak to their father, Erin felt she had no choice but to support them and breach the orders.

Then John made another application—this time for sole custody. When the Family Court assigned a social worker to interview each family member and write a report for the court, both children refused to be interviewed with their father. Their position was supported by their counselor, who told the court such a meeting might well be "harmful." The children's treating psychiatrist had even stronger words: he predicted that a change in custody would cause them "grave psychological damage." In that same report, he described Erin as an "intelligent, thoughtful person, with a secure attachment style, a high level of empathy and relational skills, and a high level of self-awareness/insight."

The kids had a laundry list of reasons why they were afraid of their dad. He had choked their mother in front of them, held a knife to her throat, thrown Zac across the room, and put their cat in the dryer—with the dryer *on*—to torment them. Then there were other things that were just as frightening but harder to explain: the temper tantrums he'd throw, where he'd smash things around the house. The weird paranoia he had that Erin was poisoning his food. The little "evil" smile he wore while he tormented them. The times he would walk around the house saying he wanted to die.

Carly and Zac explained this to the court-appointed social worker, but he paid scant attention to their concerns. Instead, in his family report, it was Erin's motivations that were questioned and *her* parenting that was criticized. The social worker recommended that Zac be ordered to live with his father for three months and have no communication during that period with his mother. This was supposedly a "preventative measure": if Zac were to live only with his mother, there was a risk that, because he bore a strong physical resemblance to his father, she might eventually reject him.

In 2014, two months before the scheduled custody hearing and without Erin's knowledge, the Family Court suddenly held an interim hearing and issued temporary orders for John to have sole custody. "I was not represented, not notified, and no reasons were given [for the change in custody], because it was only an interim hearing," says Erin. The orders were inexplicably severe. "I was to have no contact with the kids, despite there being an AVO [apprehended violence order] in place. I couldn't even ask about their welfare." Erin thinks the court might have issued this sudden interim order because the independent children's lawyer (ICL, a representative for children in family law hearings) told the court she had "absconded" when she and the kids went away for the school holidays.

The interim order directed federal police to collect the children from their mother and deliver them to their father. For Erin, though, that was not an option: Carly had threatened to kill herself if she was made to live with him. "I was asked by my children to protect them. So we fled," says Erin.

When the police finally caught up with Erin and her kids nine months later, they had run out of money and were on their way to the nearest

Children's Court to seek help. The night before, Carly had finished writing a protest letter. Erin handed the letter to the police and asked them to read it.

My name is Carly, and I am scared of my dad. I have seen him in a rage throw my brother across the room. He has held a knife to my mother's throat telling her how easy it would be to cut it...and the court has given me to him.

I have tried to tell *all* the legal people involved how scared he makes me but I am too young for anyone to listen. Why am I not allowed to help decide what happens to me? I feel like I'm screaming in a sound-proof room because my voice has been stolen from me... At what point do I become old enough to have a voice? At what point will those with the power choose to let me be heard?

I need someone to hear my voice and understand that all I want is a life without fear. The only person to listen to me is my mom. She believes me when I tell her I am scared and keeps me safe, but they will jail her for listening to me... I need your help.

That afternoon, police drove Erin and her kids to a nearby town, where Erin would later go before a magistrate on criminal charges of falsifying the children's passport applications—a charge that carries a maximum sentence of ten years. There was one last chance to say goodbye, and then the distraught children were taken away.

"When I was separated from Mom at the police station, I spent, like, six hours inconsolable on the floor, along with my brother," says Carly. When their father arrived, he told them how much he had missed them. The kids were unmoved. "My brother and I were both like, 'No, we're not going anywhere. We hate you! You hurt us, you hurt Mom! We don't want to be with someone like you!'" Carly says. "This went on for a good half-hour, and then a policeman came up and essentially threatened to remove me and my brother to the car by force."

For the next two months, Carly and Zac refused to live with their father and stayed with friends instead. They only agreed to move in with him when he promised to help them see their mother: an easy promise to make, because it was virtually impossible to keep. They now lived several hundred miles away, so for Erin to see them, she would have to travel interstate to a contact center, where her visit would be short and supervised, at a cost of more than $100. This would be impractical for most people, but it was inconceivable for Erin, who at that point was so broke that she was sleeping in her car and showering in public bathrooms, surviving on just a few dollars a day and the kindness of friends. The only way she could imagine being with her children again was to play the long game: go back to university, study law, represent herself in the Family Court, and get them back for good.

In the meantime, the court process rolled on. The new orders forbade Carly and her brother from contacting their mother, and their father forbade them from contacting their maternal relatives (and even threatened their grandfather with legal action should he try to contact them again). "That ruined me," Carly told me by phone. "I love my mom's parents. Dad's parents are weird; they're not nice. But my grandma and grandpa on my mom's side are really involved, they take pride in all my achievements."

Quarantined from her mother's family, Carly decided she had no choice but to try to make peace with her father. "For a while there I wanted to believe he was the great person he says he is. I was just going along with everything, because I knew if I argued, there would be a really, really big issue." But as the months progressed, Carly began to feel more and more like her father's prisoner. "He was always asking, 'Where are you going? Who are you going with?' but not in a protective way: in a possessive, sort of aggressive way. There was only one time I was out alone with my friend.

She was like, 'I'm surprised your dad's not here this time.'" Living with her father made Carly so anxious that she often couldn't go to class.

In October 2016, Carly wrote a letter to Robyn Cotterell-Jones, a veteran advocate for victims' rights, based hundreds of miles away. "I am extremely unhappy living with my father and I fear for my safety," she began.

> There is a frightening history of family violence committed against my mother, my brother, and myself by my abusive father. Yet the court finds him a fit parent... I'm so frightened that I never fail to lock my door whenever I enter my room... No one should feel like this in an environment where they are meant to feel nurtured and supported.
>
> I don't understand why I have been denied access to my own family. I have been denied my own mother. This is not justice—this is not an outcome beneficial to me or to my brother. I can't stay here any longer. I am so afraid here. No one should be forced to live in so much fear. Please help me.

Two days later, just over a year after police had returned her to her father, Carly got ready to run again. She decided it was too risky to take her younger brother. The night before she left, she sat him down to explain what she was about to do. "I tried to tell him I was going, but that I'd never abandon him and I'd come back and talk to him and everything. As I approached the subject, he just burst into tears and said, 'I don't want to be here, Carly, I want to kill myself! I don't want to be with Dad—I miss Mom.'

"And he's twelve!" Carly exclaims. "No twelve-year-old should think about killing themselves!"

As she got off the train, Carly felt as though a huge weight had lifted. A short bus ride brought her to the offices of the Victims of Crime Assistance League, an advocacy group Carly and her mother had contacted just before the police caught up with them in 2015. There to greet her was a surprised Robyn Cotterell-Jones, its executive director and founder (Carly's letter hadn't arrived yet). She ushered Carly inside and told her that as a mandatory reporter she had to call child protection. Soon after that, Cotterell-Jones called me.

A prominent figure in victim advocacy, Robyn Cotterell-Jones is a legend, known for her commitment to helping victims of crime find hope and courage. We'd spoken about heinous cases of child abuse in the past, but I'd never heard her this upset. "What are we doing to our children, Jess?" she said, her voice shaking. "This is just madness. I've been working on this issue for twenty-five years, and it's only gotten worse. I feel like a failure."

———

The kids growing up with domestic abuse live on your street and go to your local school. They return home each day to houses where they feel defenseless and afraid, or where it is their job to protect their mother and siblings. They know all the best places to hide and how to make themselves disappear when the yelling starts. They hold their mother while she cries, and they help her wash off the blood; they comfort and hush their siblings; they call police to beg for help. They are recruited as spies. They blame themselves—and get blamed—for the violence, and they fantasize about hurting or killing their parents. They beg their mother to leave, because one day "he's gonna kill her." They see their parents come home from the hospital and carry on like everything is normal. They watch their father get arrested. They *know* the violence is their own fault and that if they can just find a way to be good enough, to do or say the right thing, it will stop. Deep down, many are also terrified that when they grow up, they too will turn into abusers or end up marrying one.

There is little reliable data on how many children live with domestic abuse; it's simply not officially measured. A study done in 2006, based on a nationally representative sample, estimated that in the United States, 15.5 million children live in households where partner violence occurred at least once in the past year, and seven million lived with severe violence.[1]

Children trapped in abusive environments have to develop their own strategies to survive—not just physically, but psychologically as well. As Judith Herman writes, these children "must find a way to preserve a sense of trust in people who are untrustworthy, safety in a situation that is unsafe, control in a situation that is terrifyingly unpredictable, power in a situation of helplessness."[2] These children can become master tacticians, with senses fine-tuned to the onset of violence and danger.

These are the children we refer to as "witnesses" who've been "exposed" to domestic abuse. Such language does gross injustice to their experience. These children are not bystanders. They are victims in their own right, with needs, fears, and loyalties independent of those of their abused parent. This is a fact recognized in American law: in some states, exposure to domestic violence is now considered a form of child abuse.[3] When children experience domestic abuse, we know that they are also much more likely to be physically or sexually abused themselves. Domestic abuse co-occurs with approximately 55 percent of physical abuse, and 40 percent of sexual abuse against children.[4] That's not to mention the many instances in which a female victim becomes abusive toward her children—because she yearns to feel some kind of power; becomes addicted to drink and/or drugs; or believes that if she disciplines her children harshly, it will shield them from getting worse from the abuser.

As a society, we still haven't really grappled with the impact domestic abuse is having on children. In news reports, children often get only a cursory mention, as though they are mere extensions of their parents. Many journalists balk at interviewing kids regarding trauma, believing they don't have the skills for it. Those who do make the effort can find themselves rebuffed by advocates, who fear that even adolescents are too immature and vulnerable to speak for themselves and who regard journalists as untrustworthy. This caution is understandable. Children do need to be protected from insensitive or predatory journalists; they should be interviewed only if they are safe, supported, and guaranteed that they will not be identified. Journalists who interview traumatized children need to take extra time, be more sensitive, and seek advice from experts on how to avoid retraumatizing them. However, there are many child survivors who *want* to tell their story and who are distressed that the adult world denies them their right to do so. Instead of assuming that we know what's best for young people, why don't we ask *them*, "Do you want to tell your story?"

For kids like Carly, this silencing is patently dangerous. The family law system too often treats kids as little more than parental property and domestic abuse as an adults-only affair that is resolved once the parents separate. Within this system, children are given very limited opportunities to be heard. Even when they bravely offer stark, detailed testimony to psychologists and lawyers, they can end up having their words twisted in court and are too often dismissed as unreliable witnesses. "It's like wading out into the middle of an ocean; you can see a big wave coming, and you know it's going to crash over your head," explains Carly, describing the court process. "I'd tell my ICL [independent children's lawyer] that I didn't want anything to do with my dad, that my dad is abusive, and then in court she was like, 'There are a few minor problems, but otherwise things are going very well.'" If we as a community don't make an effort to listen to children, why should we expect our justice system to be any different?

The silencing of children still vexes Australian author Ruth Clare, now in her late thirties, who grew up dodging her father's sadism after he returned from Vietnam a damaged and violent man. She remembers how invisible her trauma was to the adults around her, no matter what she did to try to get them to hear her. "I cannot think of a single time during my childhood when I felt my views were heard, considered, or taken seriously," she writes. When Ruth was thirteen, she woke late one night to her mother's cries for help. She climbed out of bed and followed the noises to the kitchen, where she found her mother pinned to the ground beneath her father. When Ruth tried to intervene, her father threw her across the room, and threatened to scoop out her mother's eyeballs with the cap of his beer bottle. Police arrived after Ruth bravely ran next door to get help, and though her mother refused to press charges, Ruth persuaded her to seek protection in a refuge. In the back seat of the police car on the way to the refuge, Ruth waited for the officers to ask her and her brother what had happened. "Instead, they asked what grades we were in and the name of our budgie [bird]," she writes. "It felt like they were showing us what we were expected to do. Act normal. Put it behind us. Not dwell." Instead of feeling comforted by this distraction, Ruth took it as proof that aside from emergencies, police would be of no real help. "My problems were my problems and it was up to me to figure out how to deal with them," she writes. "The story they didn't want to hear now felt unspeakable; by association I felt unspeakable, too."[5]

Listening to children is a matter of national urgency. Self-harm among ten- to fourteen-year-old girls in the United States has nearly tripled since 2009.[6] Even worse is the fact that kids aren't just self-harming: in increasing numbers, they are killing themselves. Since 2007, the suicide rate for girls aged ten to fourteen has risen by 13 percent.[7]

As Australia's National Children's Commissioner, Megan Mitchell, reported in 2017, domestic violence—across all cultures—is a significant risk factor for youth suicide.[8] In the words of one police officer she consulted, "Every child who suicided in the last twelve months came from a domestic violence family."[9] These are the children we think we're protecting with distractions about pets and school. The fact is that *we* can't handle the truth.

In this chapter, you will read testimonies both from children and from adults who grew up with domestic abuse. First, though, let's take a look at the inner lives of children who are literally unable to speak for themselves.

Infants

If it's hard for us adults to put ourselves in the shoes of children, it's virtually impossible for us to imagine what it's like to be a baby. Despite the fact we've all been one, infants appear to us like aliens: emotional whirlwinds that shit, piss, and scream with abandon and whose inner worlds seem wholly inscrutable. Do they even have inner lives? Aside from a handful of people on Earth who claim they can remember their first few years, most of us have no recollection of being a baby; our lasting memories don't start being encoded until we're around three-and-a-half years old.

Perhaps that's why infants are often dismissed as blissfully oblivious, containing only enough consciousness to discern when they are hungry, tired, or hurt. New parents who are victims of domestic abuse are sometimes comforted by this notion, relieved that at least their babies are too young to see or understand the violence going on around them.

But this view of infants, though tenacious and widespread, is utterly obsolete. Over the past thirty years, there has been a revolution in the way we understand babies. In her book *The Philosophical Baby*, Professor Alison Gopnik—a philosopher and child psychologist—refutes the notion that babies are "primitive grown-ups gradually attaining our perfection and complexity." Instead, she says, infants resemble an entirely different form of *Homo sapiens*, with minds that are "equally complex and powerful."[10] This may seem hard to believe. After all, infants can sometimes barely land their eyes on one object before being distracted by something else. However, Gopnik shows that while adult attention operates like a "spotlight," babies and young children have "lantern consciousness"—not so good for focusing on a single thing, but marvelous for casting light around and absorbing information from a range of sources simultaneously. What psychologists and neuroscientists have come to understand is that babies "not only learn more, but imagine more, care more, and experience more than we would ever have thought possible."[11] They can even—at least for a few months—remember specific events. They are not, in other words, oblivious blobs of instinct and emotion.

Wendy Bunston works with infants exposed to family violence. With her no-nonsense approach, Bunston has spent the last twenty-five years preaching the science which shows that babies are highly attuned to violent environments. Infants don't just float along blithely, she argues; rather, they are like sensory sponges, soaking up every interaction in a constant effort to learn strategies of adaptation and survival. In a violent home, the abuser is a clear source of threat and danger, but to an infant so may be an abused caregiver. If that caregiver is routinely afraid or unavailable, the child soon learns that their caregiver will not be able to protect them. In the groups Bunston runs for infants and mothers, she has seen babies reach for facilitators instead of their mothers, sensing that the facilitator is more available to them and more reliable. Imagine being unable to walk or talk (or even crawl) and *knowing* that the one person on whom you are utterly dependent for your survival cannot protect you. That is the terror of a preverbal child growing up with domestic abuse.

When infants are regularly denied the safety of emotional connection, they enter a heightened survival mode. The infant's brain is bombarded with chemicals designed to manage fear. Over time, if this continues, the nascent pathways developing in the infant's brain will begin to reflect the chaos of the environment. As Bunston and Sketchley write, the fearful infant's brain "will build restricted pathways that serve the purpose of survival."[12] Living in such an environment can put infants on a lifelong hair trigger, their brains trained to react to the slightest hint of perceived danger. Thus the primitive, fear-processing part of the brain, the amygdala, responds to stimuli before the rational parts of the brain have a chance to discern whether the perceived threat is real or not.

Because scared infants are physically unable to hide—a skill that older children in abusive households later become expert in—they may have no choice but to hide within themselves. Emma Gierschick, who was abused in pregnancy and during her child's infancy, gives a compelling portrayal of this state. "I have absolutely no photos of [name redacted] smiling at all in the first twenty months of her life—and I just thought I had an unanimated, quiet, withdrawn child who would look startled, with big wide eyes, most of the time, [and] who didn't smile. She rarely cried, but also didn't engage much and certainly never laughed or giggled with happiness or joy." Sometime after Emma left her violent partner, she realized this behavior wasn't normal. "I discovered what a giggly, energetic bundle of mess, noise, and mischief I have, who is always very 'busy' and loves dancing, singing, and laughing. She wakes with a smile on her face now or a giggle."[13]

Social worker Robyn Lamb, who has worked in the Child Protection Unit at Westmead Hospital, Sydney, for more than thirty years, says parents commonly misread their children. Lamb says the kids described by parents as being "so good" for being quiet and not crying when their parents leave the room are actually her most alarming cases. "Because that's not what a normal child does. A normal child cries, they want someone to come, they want attention, they don't like being left alone," she tells me, as we tour the children's unit. "But these kids learn *I don't get responded to if I cry*, or *I get responded to with violence.*"

As the Child Grows

As children seek to protect themselves in a violent home, they become behavioral detectives. "Children in an abusive environment develop extraordinary abilities to scan for warning signs of attack," writes Judith Herman. "They become minutely attuned to their abusers' inner states... They learn to recognize subtle changes in facial expression, voice, and body language as signals of anger, sexual arousal, intoxication, or dissociation."[14]

"Finley" is nine years old ("going on forty-one," says his mom) and a keen gamer. He lived with his father's violence until his parents separated a year ago. Finley says that when his dad lived with them, he learned to read his face like "an algorithm": "There'd be an expression of dead silence," he says matter-of-factly, "and then he'd go off." Finley had to rely on this algorithm because the rules his father applied were petty and arbitrary, and enforced at a moment's notice. "It was really random. If the sky wasn't blue enough, he'd get angry… [The rules would] be valid for ten seconds, and you'd be abiding by them, but then the new rule would state that you're doing something wrong, just so he could get mad at you."

When he was "bored," Finley's father would devise new ways to terrorize his children. Once, he smashed a plate in the face of Finley's little brother, landing him in the emergency room. One particular favorite was a threat to take Finley to the doctors, where he said Finley would have hot pipes stuck up his nose. One day, with no explanation, Finley's father stopped talking to the family. He stonewalled his wife and children for two whole years, menacing the house with his silent, brooding presence. Over time, Finley became so hypersensitive to the quality of his father's presence, he could *feel* when his father had gotten home even before he heard him.

"Michele," now fifty-four, says she too spent her childhood on high alert. "I have no memory at all of ever feeling safe at home," she says. "Ever. When my father was in the house, there was this constant state of hypervigilance, trying to work out what he was going to do and when he was going to do it." Her childhood was "Dickensian" in its unrelenting misery; all of her conscious memories are of violence, or the threat of it. "One of Dad's favorite tantrums was to hurl his plate of food at my mother if he felt it wasn't good enough," she remembers. "One morning I happened to be standing behind my mother when the plate was sent flying through the air. Mom ducked, and the plate broke across my back. I panicked and bolted out the back door. I got to the end of the block before my dad caught me.

Picking me up, he said, 'I'm sorry, I didn't mean to hit you. I was aiming for your mother.'" Michele was eight years old.

As we sit together on her sofa, one particularly vivid memory surfaces. Michele and her siblings were sitting in the living room watching television one night, while her mom and dad screamed at each other behind the closed kitchen door. After a while, she and her brother went into the kitchen to intervene. They found their dad sitting on their mother's head, "bouncing up and down." "My brother and I were just going, 'Get off, get off, you're gonna kill her!' And he was laughing. He had his golf shoes on, and he had just been kicking her, kicking her, kicking her in the legs. Her legs were like jelly. She had blood all over her legs." Michele's father got up, walked into the living room, and sat next to his children as though nothing had happened. "We just sat there pretending it wasn't going on. It's like you're complicit."

In a home that never felt safe, Michele could discern the precise quality of footfall that foretold escalating danger, and learned how to read her father's expressions like tea leaves. "I could literally tell by my father's face whether he was going to be beating my mother up that night."

This kind of hypervigilance is something we usually associate with combat veterans, as a hallmark of post-traumatic stress. It's a habit acquired both in training and in combat zones, where soldiers must be alert to everything from a sudden acrid smell to a person who looks like they don't belong. Every time a potential threat arises, a survival response triggers in the brain, motivating the soldier to act defensively—a reaction that can be the difference between living and dying. Having worked in the Middle East as a foreign correspondent, I have a real problem with journalists describing a scene in a suburb as being "like a war zone." But in the case of children experiencing domestic abuse, this comparison isn't just warranted, it's a scientific fact. Children raised amid domestic abuse exhibit the same hypervigilance as veterans exposed to combat.

This astonishing connection was made in 2011 by a team led by Professor Eamon McCrory at University College London.[15] For many years, brain scans conducted on combat veterans had shown heightened responses to potential threats in two areas of the brain: the anterior insula (the part that processes emotional and physical pain) and the amygdala (the tiny almond-shaped part that mediates our fear responses). The UCL researchers conducted brain scans on forty-three children (twenty who'd grown up with domestic abuse and twenty-three who hadn't) while showing them a series of angry faces. As the children looked at these faces, researchers watched their brains process the memories and emotions associated with them. The researchers saw a familiar response: the brains of abused children lit up in the exact same places as the combat veterans' brains had. Here, the authors concluded, was "hard evidence" that domestic abuse conditions children to be hyperaware of potential threats.

Although hypervigilance may serve both soldiers and children well in a high-threat environment, it can be exhausting in everyday life, and highly distressing. Like combat veterans, child victims of domestic abuse also report recurring nightmares and flashbacks. In Finley's most vivid dream, he stands frozen to the spot as he watches his family home burn down in front of him. Twelve-year-old "Harley" has regular waking flashbacks of his dad's violence. Sometimes they happen at school, other times at home: he can never be sure when they'll come. In these flashbacks, he sees his father pushing his mom down the stairs and hitting and kicking her. Then he sees what his mom looks like afterward. "It feels like it's happening at that moment," he says quietly. "It makes me feel really upset and...defenseless."

Trapped in an atmosphere of ever-present threat and fear, children living with violence become masters of the strategic art of survival. "Anna" was still in diapers when she learned it was futile for her to try to protect her mother. "I remember getting out of bed, and because I'd never experienced violence before, I said 'Stop!' And my dad turned around and belted me. I flew and hit the door. My mom came and put me back to bed, and I didn't understand what was going on. After that, I knew to stay out of the way as much as possible." From when she was little, Anna, now thirty-four, knew she had to find a way to survive at home until she was old enough to survive on her own. For Anna, surviving meant literally treating her father as an enemy combatant. "It's funny," she says, "because Dad fed me all those books on the art of war, and I took it to heart. Trying to survive that household, it was war. I used everything that I could." As Anna became a teenager, she assumed the role of daddy's little helper, running regular missions to her father's bar fridge in order to get him drunk so he would fall asleep faster. When he was asleep, she would sneak out the window, run into the city, fake her way into nightclubs, and have sex with men three times her age. "I was sleeping with adults by the time I was fourteen." Like so many kids who grow up with violence, Anna mapped the house for all the best places to hide. "I found hidey-holes on the top of the garage, in the bottom of the linen closet, in a side closet near the dryer, and a crawlspace under the house. The yelling would start, and I would hide. But I would also hide as practice. It was a deadly serious game. Because if you were found you didn't know what was coming. So my sister and I would play it as though our lives depended on it."

Surviving a violent home isn't just about protecting the body: it's also about protecting the mind. Renowned child-trauma clinician Bruce Perry says children often report going to a "different place," imagining themselves as superheroes, or standing outside the experience as though they're watching a movie they've been cast in.[16] "Will" is nine years old and the eldest of four. Like Finley, his parents separated around a year ago, and now he and his siblings are court-ordered to stay with their dad every second weekend. When his dad flies into a rage, Will tries to pretend he's somewhere else. "It's hard to start thinking and to start believing that you're in another spot when something really bad has just happened. But it happens. I guess I can say I have an active imagination," he says with a smile. In his bedroom, Will tries to think about "everything that's good." "Sometimes I go into my bedroom and get a sheet of blue paper and pretend I [am] at the beach, or at Wet'n'Wild." Will's younger brother "Adrian" is six, and is "all about violence." Adrian has been diagnosed with several behavioral issues and regularly attacks Will and his two sisters, "Anwen" and "Ivy." Because Adrian is the hardest to control, he bears the brunt of his father's rage. Adrian comes up with his own scenarios to pretend the experience away. "When our brother learned the word 'guard,' he called our dad the prison guard," says Will, laughing. "He was like, 'We gotta break out of prison! We're not bad guys, the prison guard has picked the wrong people!' I have an overactive imagination like him, so I'm like, 'Yeah, we gotta break out of prison!'"

For some children, the need to change their reality—or outright deny it—becomes so powerful that it leads them to dissociate. As a very young child, survivor and now advocate Olga Trujillo experienced some of the worst domestic abuse I've ever heard described. When she was three, she burst into her parents' bedroom to find her father about to rape her mother. When she grabbed his arm and tried to pull him off, her father hit her across the face and said he would teach her what happened to little girls who didn't respect their fathers. Right there, in front of her mother, he pinned three-year-old Olga to the floor and raped her. Olga looked over in panic as her mother half-heartedly told him to stop, and then "went blank." "She had gone away in her head," writes Olga, in her blistering memoir *The Sum of My Parts*. Olga then felt her own mind get "fuzzier and fuzzier" until her panic subsided, she went still, and then felt herself leave her body. "It was a very strange sensation to me," she writes, "almost like splitting into two little girls. My hands felt weird, and I noticed that I had more fingers than I should. Each hand split and formed into two separate hands. While I could still feel the pain Popi was inflicting, it was fading and becoming more distant. At last, I split off my mind and floated up to the ceiling, where I watched in safety."[17] Throughout her childhood, Olga was raped and beaten repeatedly by her father. Before she turned ten, he pimped her out to his friends—with her mother's cooperation—supposedly for money to pay the rent, which he then spent on himself. Olga describes dissociation as a "superpower" and a highly effective survival technique that "allows an individual enduring hopeless circumstances to preserve some areas of healthy functioning."[18] Dissociating, says Olga, helps children keep trauma at a distance, until it's safe enough for them to confront what they've experienced.

Children unable to escape their reality through fantasy or dissociation must find other ways to make sense of it. Some may be quite clear in blaming their abusive parent (or both parents); others may join the abusive parent in blaming the victim (as abusers often encourage their children to do). Commonly, however, children will make excuses for their parents and blame themselves. These children search themselves for what they've done to make their parents fight and may even become convinced that their very birth was a curse and the cause of every bad thing that happens to the family.

"I used to think, *How have I caused this, what have I done wrong?*" says Finley. Rescinding blame has been an essential—and hard-won—part of Finley's recovery. "Now I know that it's completely not my fault," he says. "I don't need anyone to tell me." But in Judith Herman's compelling interpretation, his instinct to assume blame was not just childish and wrongheaded, it was a key element in his psychic defense. As Herman explains, the abused child:

> must find a way to preserve hope and meaning. The alternative is utter despair, something no child can bear. Inevitably the child concludes that her innate badness is the cause. The child seizes upon this explanation early and clings to it tenaciously, for it enables her to preserve a sense of meaning, hope, and power. If she is bad, then

her parents are good. If she is bad, then she can try to be good. If, somehow, she has brought this fate upon herself, then somehow she has the power to change it. If she has driven her parents to mistreat her, then, if only she tries hard enough, she may someday earn their forgiveness and finally win the protection and care she so desperately needs.[19]

In believing themselves to be at fault, children actually create what they need in an otherwise helpless situation: a sense of agency.

Sometimes assuming blame is not something the children do themselves; instead, it is foisted on them by the family. When Michele first contacted me, she introduced her story with some trepidation, explaining that although her mother was a victim of her father's abuse, she was also incredibly cruel toward Michele. "My teenage years are just a mess of memories of Dad beating up Mom; of Dad screaming at me; of Mom screaming that it was my fault, and of knowing—deep in my bones—how wrong it all was."

Michele's mother would beat her children with the handle of a feather duster, using such force that their legs would be covered in bruises. When Michele's father was home, her mother—"who didn't have an ounce of assertiveness in her"—insisted on the children's absolute obedience to him, and punished Michele if she ever talked back. But when he wasn't home, she would draw her children into rituals of resistance, doing things that would have greatly angered her husband had he been home to see them. A favorite transgression was to smoke cigarettes—something Michele's father despised—and to make her kid smoke too. "I got my first cigarette from my mother when I was ten years old," says Michele.

After her father was violent, which was often, Michele's mother would not only attack her daughter for having a temper just like her father's, but she would also deny that the assault had occurred. "You know when people talk about gaslighting?" says Michele. "Mom's a master of gaslighting. Something that literally just happened, she would tell you it didn't happen." To maintain her grip on reality, Michele became obsessive about journaling. To this day, she second-guesses whether things that happen right in front of her have actually happened.

When Michele was seventeen, her father brutally attacked her for the first time—after years of her mother promising he never would. "My dad was six foot five and possibly twice my weight. Standing over the top of me, he brought the full power of his height and weight into a punch." As she tried to escape, he punched Michele repeatedly in the stomach until she let go of the door handle and collapsed onto the floor. "I sat there cowering, in total shock that I was now his punching bag. As verbally abusive as he had been toward me, I never thought he would ever beat me up." In the hallway, her mother stood and watched. "I just thought, *Fuck. I have memories of myself as a five- or six-year-old standing between you and Dad to stop him from hitting you, and you just stood there and watched that happen.*" The next day Michele was so devastated she couldn't get out of bed. Around midday her mother walked into her room and told her to "stop being such a drama queen" and come downstairs, because she was hurting her father's feelings. "She made me get out of bed, sit at the kitchen table and drink a cup of coffee with him. My dad cracked jokes and I had to pretend all was okay with the world." That's when Michele realized that what her mother had said her whole life was not true. "Her narrative had always been that she stayed with him because of us. But in that moment at the kitchen table, I realized, 'You are not with this man because of your children. You're here for you.'"

Most mothers do try their best to protect their children, but that doesn't necessarily stop them becoming a target of their *child's* violence. This is especially common after the abuser has left and the mother is trying to rebuild a stable life with her children. For some families, leaving the abuser can be the end of one ordeal and the beginning of another.

For the first few years after "Liz" left her abusive husband, her family home was safe. There were, however, a couple of incidents that made her nervous. On one occasion, one of her sons, "Blake," went through the rubbish to find a receipt of what she'd spent and quizzed her on it—a repeat of his father's behavior. Then, a couple of weeks later, Blake assaulted "his younger sister—held her up by her neck against the wall," says Liz. "But he was still pretty normal with me, and he was getting good results at school. There was no build-up, no nasty talk." Then one night, after Liz asked Blake twice to do the dishes, he punched her in the face with brutal force. "It came from nowhere," she says. Liz felt she had no choice but to call the police. "They turned up within ten minutes. He was taken out straight away and put in the paddy wagon. The punch had split right through my face. The police said, 'I can see the inside of your mouth from the side of your face—that was one hell of a punch.' I've got permanent scarring from it, and it's still numb." In the aftermath of the attack, Blake showed no remorse. "He turned around to the lawyer and said, 'Oh well, I could have hit her harder.' I think he thought he'd get away with it." Liz says friends and teachers judged her harshly for calling the police. "I had people turn to me saying, 'How could you call the police on your son?' 'Poor Blake,' they said, 'he'll have a criminal record.' One of them—a teacher, in fact—said, 'You should have punched him back.' But it wouldn't have done him any favors to not get the police involved. What if he did that to his girlfriend?"

Eddie Gallagher is a child counselor who has specialized in child-to-parent abuse since the 1990s, when it was virtually unmentionable. He's worked with almost five hundred families. "Some violent children come from loving homes," he says, "and have well-adjusted siblings who love their parents. But the most common pattern is a boy abusing a sole mother post-domestic-violence." This pattern accounts for half of the families he's seen, and 70 percent of the violent children have been boys. Apart from the gender element, there's little rhyme or reason to why some children imitate the behavior of their abusive parent and others don't. "Within the same family...you can have three kids who have all seen Dad be violent toward Mom. One kid is very responsible; you could say they've been 'parentified'—they're caring, responsible, and protective toward Mom and the other brothers and sisters. You've got another kid who is anxious and withdrawn, and then a third kid who's angry, lashing out and showing behavior very similar to Dad. Kids with different personalities can have very different responses to the same exposure."

It can be just as difficult, says Gallagher, to predict whether a child in a domestic abuse setting will identify and ally himself—sometimes herself—with the father:

> Some of the worst and most impossible boys to work with are 100 percent on Dad's side, and excuse Dad's violence, and might even say they hate their mom and want to go and live with Dad. And they often do go and live with the dad when they're in their teenage years. Then there's the absolute opposite extreme: I see lots of kids who will tell me that their father's a shit, they don't want anything to do with him, men should never hit women, Dad's a scumbag—and yet they're still copying his behavior. The outlook's a lot better for them, and it's much easier to work with them in counseling, as you can imagine, but they can still be copying his behavior.

Gallagher has worked with violent kids as young as six, and says it can be difficult to tell whether a violent and reactive phase that starts when the child is as young as three will simply fade out or become an ongoing pattern of behavior. "What I think is really significant and underestimated is the continued influence that some of these guys have, even without a lot of contact," he says. "Kids who are exposed to their father putting their mother down or being verbally abusive—that can have an enormous impact, even without direct exposure to the violence. They don't have to see Dad hit Mom for them to end up being violent toward their mother, because a big part of it is losing respect." A child who has grown up seeing his or her mother constantly belittled and in a "weaker" position can thus have an implicitly derogatory view of her. Attachment to the perpetrator is also a pretty good survival mechanism: if you side with him against your mother, you are less likely to be victimized.

There is much to say about child-to-parent abuse, especially about the children who retaliate after years of abuse or in self-defense. In these cases, the abusive parent may get police involved and, based on a single incident, succeed in taking out an intervention order against the child who has long been the victim of the parent's violence. In the most tragic cases, the victimized child ends up killing the abuser. In Australia, in September 2016, a seventeen-year-old boy stabbed his violent stepfather to death after he saw him strangling his seven-year-old sister. The night of the killing, the stepfather was drunk and had already twice tried to choke the boy's fifteen-year-old brother, who has cerebral palsy. When the boy saw him strangling his little sister, he ran into his bedroom, grabbed his "Bear Grylls" knife, and ran at his stepfather, stabbing him in the chest twenty-five times. When he stopped, he cried out in horror, "Oh my god, what have I done, I'm sorry!" He was given a three-year suspended sentence.[20]

Whereas boys are more likely to adopt the behavior of the abusive parent (usually the father), girls are more likely to internalize the narrative of the victim—even when it's their mother who is violent. "Every night, he would get home from work and she would just start yelling at him about whatever," says eighteen-year-old "Frankie," describing the violence her mother inflicted on her father. "Dad doesn't really fight back—if he's getting yelled at about stuff he doesn't care about, he ignores it. And because Mom realized that yelling wasn't getting her anywhere, she started hitting him and stuff. She never used weapons on him, like the stuff she used on my brother and [me], but she would just hit him. I think she tried to burn him at one stage, too, because she was cooking dinner and the oven was on, and she grabbed his arm and put it on the oven."

Frankie's father left two years later, and though he brought up the abuse in the custody dispute that followed, care of Frankie and her brother was granted to her mother. Frankie didn't hear from her father for years. In the meantime, her mother found two new targets for her abuse. "The first week [after the separation] was really bad, because she no longer had him to hurt. She was obviously upset too, because she'd just lost her husband." Frankie says she was violently abused by her mother at least once a week. "She would choke me a lot, so there'd be times when I couldn't breathe. I'm trying to tell her that I couldn't breathe, and she still wouldn't stop." One afternoon, Frankie came home from school to find her mother holding a knife to her brother's throat. "He grabbed it and threw it across the room, and she just kept punching him and shit. I was, like, probably only about ten, just watching it like, *What the fuck?*—I didn't know what to do. I was scared, and I didn't want my brother to get hurt, but, like, if I stepped in, she'd hurt me."

When she was in high school, Frankie got together with her first boyfriend. He was in the year above her. "I dealt with a lot of depression, so I pushed him away a lot. So he thought I didn't love him. He didn't like that. He would hit me and push me against walls and stuff. It was my first relationship. I'm like, *I don't know what I'm doing!*" After three months, Frankie put her foot down and broke up with him. A year later, she got together with another guy, this time from another school. She lost her virginity to him when he raped her. "Then he got his friend to do the same thing to me. Two guys in one week. It was my first sexual experience. After that, I didn't want to date at all."

About a month before we spoke, the ex-boyfriend who had raped her turned up out of the blue and accosted Frankie at work. "He cornered me and started talking to me. Then he somehow got my phone number—he must have got it from a mutual friend or something—so I got home to all these text messages from him." In his messages, he said he liked how nervous and anxious she had looked. In fact, he thought it was funny. "What really got to me was his last message: *I hope when your boyfriend fucks you, you think of me.* That's what kind of tipped me over."

Days later, Frankie tried to kill herself. While recovering in the hospital, she spent a lot of time piecing together the events of her life, trying to figure out how they had brought her to this point. Something dawned on her. "I was drawn to guys that were similar to Mom," she says. "The way that some of the guys treated me was the way my mom would treat my dad. That was a big insight for me."

This kind of insight has the potential to change a young person's trajectory. Eddie Gallagher's experience makes him wary of drawing any straight line from family history to a child growing up to become either a victim or an abuser. "It's a dangerous assumption, and it's not true," he says. "I ran men's groups for over twenty years, and I met close to a thousand abusive men over that time. A fair number of them grew up in violent homes; probably half were exposed to domestic abuse or had been abused themselves. But a lot of them hadn't."

Joe, now in his thirties, feared for a long time that he would end up like his violent father. "When I eventually realized I was my own person, thanks largely to my mom and some amazing friends, it was a huge relief," he says. "I've been with my partner for ten years now, and it's proven to me that I'm the antithesis of my father. Every couple has to work on their relationship, and I'm not saying ours is perfect by any means, but we're honest, open, we communicate our feelings—something I didn't do a lot for the first twenty years of my life—and now we have a two-year-old daughter. She's the best— attitude, cheeky—I love her. Having a kid is something I would never have considered if I thought I would be like my father."

It's a fear that still haunts nine-year-old Finley. "It's actually a nightmare, almost," he says. "Sometimes I'll think I'm just like my dad. The way I act, I have to be careful—if I'm gonna say something mean or critique someone, I'll have to say it in a nice way, not just snap at them... I don't want to become like my dad. I want to have a happy relationship with anyone that I am with."

Two years after I first interviewed Frankie, I got back in touch with her to see how she was doing. She was in a newish relationship with a man twenty-eight years older, and they were running a photography business together. "This guy has been through a lot of bad things in life, and he convinced me I needed to move in with him," she told me over email. "Stupid me, thinking I could 'fix' someone, went along with it. He made me feel like I had no other option." Once Frankie said yes to moving in, "everything else became harder and harder to say no to." That's when he turned. "He never physically abused me, but he did emotionally, and that hurts just as much." Frankie had been trying to leave him for a month, but every time she tried he would threaten to kill himself. Her therapist had helped her to understand that if he harmed himself, that wouldn't be her fault, but she still felt a kind of guilt that made her too frightened to leave. "The reason I'm telling you this story," she wrote, "is because I feel it all relates back to my childhood and the love, or lack of love, I saw around me. Normal scares me because it's something I'm not used to and it all feels false. I feel like I deserve these bad situations and blame myself for putting [myself] in them." Frankie was candid: her need to black out what was happening had become so strong, she was dosing herself with a varying cocktail of cocaine, marijuana, MDMA, and prescription meds virtually every day, "just to cope." That was alarming to hear, but what she wrote next was worse: "After I send you this email, I'm going to delete it, as the guy goes through my phone and I don't want him finding this."

When the Child Runs Away

When Carly ran away from her father in 2016, she joined a global population of homeless kids. In the United States each year, around 550,000
unaccompanied youth experience homelessness for a week or longer, and
around half of them do not have shelter. They sleep outside, in cars, under
bridges, in churches, and other places humans are not supposed to sleep.[21]

When Anna ran away from home at fifteen, she was bounced from shelter to shelter and ended up sleeping outside in the dead of winter. Her sudden
homelessness was triggered by a terrifying episode of violence. After a huge
argument with Anna's father, her mother and sister fled and left her alone in the
house with him. She ran upstairs and hid behind a door, listening as he threw
knives around the kitchen, bellowing that he would "salt the earth" where he and
Anna's mom had planted a vegetable garden. Then he said he was going to get his
gun—and if Anna ran he would kill her. She waited until he was at the other side
of the house and made a run for it. For that entire night, she sat, freezing cold, on
her youth group leader's doorstep. "His dad opened the door the next morning
and fell over me. They had me stay for about two weeks." After that, she was
moved on to a youth refuge, which was "incredibly violent." The extreme conditions she endured while homeless were shocking to Anna. "Even though my
situation was violent, I was still incredibly privileged. I went to a private school
and had lived in incredible wealth." Anna ended up at a YWCA with mostly
older, pensioned women, before her mother got some money together for her to
live in a housing unit. Anna was a freshman in high school. "I bounced through
a couple of schools at that point, then quit school for half a year... Sometimes I
was home, sometimes I would sleep out in the street."

The Child Adapts

There's no question that growing up in a violent home makes it more likely
that a child will become either a victim or a perpetrator of domestic abuse

themselves, will turn to criminality as they grow older, or will suffer significant physical and mental issues related to their trauma. Nevertheless, not every child who grows up with domestic abuse is condemned to suffer the impact for life. A review of 118 studies on children exposed to domestic abuse found that more than one-third were doing just as well, or better, than children from nonviolent homes.[22] The distinguishing factor here is a mystery: Was it that they had one teacher who believed in their potential? A close friend who gave them a sense of security? A neighbor who provided a safe place to escape?

Many children, however, are not so lucky. For them, life becomes a confused mixture of symptoms, both psychological and physical, that seriously impede their capacity to care for themselves and trust others. They can spend years searching for a way to explain how they feel, often experimenting with prescription cocktails that improve things for a while, until they wind up feeling worse. No drug will heal their wound; even when they may appear to be coping on the surface, the original wound festers, untreated, until something comes along to tear it open and start the bleeding afresh.

After years of wondering if she was bipolar like her father, Anna was recently diagnosed with a condition that finally made sense to her: complex post-traumatic stress disorder (C-PTSD). It took a suicide attempt for her to seek help. "You know, child abuse and domestic violence [are] really common, so I thought I should be able to get on with this by myself. I spent a lot of time unsure why everyone else seemed to do things so easily. *Why can't I take a shower? Why can't I just fucking brush my teeth?* I wondered why I'd react so strongly to things other people let slide, why relationships with people I cared about would inevitably break down, and why I couldn't get the treatment I needed."

In the hospital after her suicide attempt, doctors told her that she was smart enough to know she'd have needed double the dose to kill herself, and then discharged her. "They were right," says Anna. "I didn't want to kill myself. It was a cry for help." Staff gave her a contact number for a psychiatrist—"only because I asked for it"—who had a six-week waiting list. Anna was on edge every day, thinking constantly about suicide. "Suddenly I decided that I would use my skills and try and help myself. I began ringing different psychologists and psychiatrists and saying, 'This is what I'm going through, tell me how you would help me.' I would sit there and listen, and then I would say, 'Thank you very much, goodbye,' until I found three I thought might be on the money. And I paid for sessions with all three of them." Anna got lucky with the last one on her list. "She was the first person who talked about childhood developmental trauma and C-PTSD. I'd never heard those terms before. As soon as I left her office I started googling, and then I realized what she was trying to say to me."

Complex PTSD, also known as *childhood developmental trauma*, was first conceptualized in the early 1990s by two of the world's leading child trauma specialists, Judith Herman and fellow Boston psychiatrist Bessel van der Kolk. The notion of trauma as a profound disruption to life and behavior had only been officially recognized about a decade earlier. In 1980, traits that rendered many Vietnam War veterans pariahs—drug and alcohol abuse, chronic unemployment, homelessness, violence—were finally recognized as symptoms of a new condition: PTSD. The diagnosis was simple: a person who had responded to a traumatic event with intense fear, helplessness, or horror then went on to reexperience the trauma over and again, through vivid recollections, nightmares, dissociative flashbacks, and hallucinations. People with PTSD would become, among other things, hypervigilant, easily angered, irritable, and pathologically detached from other people, and often had little hope for the future.

PTSD became an official "condition" with one simple occurrence: it was published in the third edition of the *Diagnostic and Statistical Manual of Mental Disorders* (*DSM-III*). As soon as PTSD became an official diagnosis, it was applied to an enormous range of people who had suffered trauma, including children who had grown up with domestic abuse. However, the childhood abuse survivors Herman and van der Kolk were seeing did not fit the PTSD diagnosis. Their trauma stemmed from ongoing abuse that was usually perpetrated by someone they trusted. Although they shared several symptoms with sufferers of PTSD—hypervigilance and flash-backs, for example—they had a laundry list of extra symptoms. As van der Kolk explained, his clients were needy, reckless, clingy, angry, despairing, chronically ashamed, or suicidal. They had severe problems trusting other people, frequently self-harmed, had trouble remembering large sections of their childhood, and often felt utterly disengaged or disembodied. They also shared a familiar script: that they were innately unlovable and their loneliness was so intense nobody could possibly understand how it felt. They were often chronic oversharers, divulging the most intimate details to virtual strangers, and they suffered a raft of physical health problems, from fibromyalgia and irritable bowel syndrome to headaches and back pain. No single diagnosis could describe their condition; instead, they were diagnosed with a mixed bag of PTSD, bipolar disorder, depression, and especially borderline personality disorder.

Seeing the enormous harm misdiagnosis was doing to their patients, van der Kolk and Herman proposed a new diagnosis that made sense of their symptoms: "complex PTSD," or the rather clunky "DESNOS (Diagnosis of Extreme Stress, Not Otherwise Specified)." As van der Kolk writes, this new condition included the physiological and emotional responses common to PTSD, such as hypervigilance and flashbacks, but complex PTSD was very different, because at its core it was a condition caused by betrayal.

Children with complex trauma "develop a view of the world that incor-porates their betrayal and hurt. They anticipate and expect the trauma to recur and respond with hyperactivity, aggression, defeat, or freeze responses to minor stresses." Faced with reminders of their trauma or other stressful triggers, they tend to become "confused, dissociated, and disoriented." Because they are conditioned to expect betrayal, they "easily misinterpret events" as signaling a return of trauma and helplessness: a worldview that causes them to be "constantly on guard, frightened and over-reactive." Because they have lost any belief in being looked after and kept safe, they organize their relationships around the expectation of being abandoned or victimized. "This is expressed as excessive clinging," he writes, "compliance, oppositional defiance and distrustful behavior, and they may be preoccupied with retribution and revenge."[23] Because they feel they can't rely on anyone, they are suspicious of others and have problems with intimacy, which results in social isolation. They are, wrote van der Kolk, often literally out of touch with their feelings and have no language to describe their internal states.

Common symptoms of complex PTSD are:

- distrust
- suicidal thoughts
- episodes of feeling detached from one's body or mental processes
- isolation, guilt, shame, or a feeling of being totally different from other people
- helplessness and feeling hopeless
- self-harm, self-mutilation
- alcoholism or substance abuse.[24]

By the early 1990s, the concept of complex PTSD had gained so much credibility that the American Psychiatric Association asked van der Kolk to examine its validity as a psychiatric diagnosis, in preparation for the fourth edition of the *DSM* in 2000. After reviewing hundreds of studies, the DSM-IV committee voted nineteen to two in favor of inclusion in the upcoming manual—but it never made it in. As the proposal was passed up the decision-making chain, it drew criticism from the *DSM*'s most powerful stakeholders. They were uncomfortable with the way the symptoms of C-PTSD overlapped with those of so many other disorders. For van der Kolk and Herman, this was precisely the point: their patients needed to be treated for the one common condition they actually had—C-PTSD—not a pastiche of inaccurate conditions and disorders, each with its own medication and treatment schedules. But neither van der Kolk nor Herman anticipated how fiercely the establishment would defend these conditions. At stake was millions of dollars in research funding and, because C-PTSD is not treated with medication, the potential for an untold loss of profits to the pharmaceutical industry. Introducing a new diagnosis of C-PTSD threatened nothing short of a revolution in how millions of trauma survivors would be treated: with therapy rather than medication.

Today, there is still no official disorder in the *DSM* to describe the full range of symptoms and behaviors experienced by children and adults who have lived through prolonged trauma. "Because they often are shut down, suspicious, or aggressive, they now receive pseudoscientific diagnoses such as 'oppositional defiant disorder,' meaning 'This kid hates my guts and won't do anything I tell him to do,' or 'disruptive mood regulation disorder,' meaning he has temper tantrums," notes van der Kolk in his bestselling book *The Body Keeps the Score*. Before they reach their twenties, he writes, many patients have accumulated a collection of impressive but meaningless labels and, if they receive treatment for those conditions, it usually consists of whatever ranks as the trendy method of the moment: medications, behavioral modification, exposure therapy, and so on. "These rarely work," writes van der Kolk, "and often cause more damage."[25]

When people with C-PTSD finally get diagnosed, it can be a huge turning point in their lives—a feeling they have been "seen." "I felt overwhelming relief when I finally got a diagnosis of C-PTSD," says Anna. She has been receiving specialized therapy for complex PTSD "on and off" for three years now, but the struggle to overcome the symptoms may be lifelong. "C-PTSD divorces you from your ability to create emotional bonds. In relationships, I'm constantly waiting for the other person to betray me, because my parents—who I loved more than anything in the world—betrayed me constantly. It's not just that trust has been broken with the parents and within the self, but with your relationship to the universe. It's your whole schemata, and you can't get it back. But you *can* work on it."

C-PTSD is not a disorder in the classic sense of the word. It is an identity that has formed around defense and survival, a genius adaptation by the child to survive physically and psychologically. The trouble is that once these children are safe, the tactics and beliefs they employed to survive become severely maladaptive. A trick such as dissociation—mentally disappearing during a trauma—is a brilliant survival tactic. But if you dissociate when you're at school, at work, or crossing the road, it's no longer serving you as a survival tactic; now it's putting you in danger. However, people with C-PTSD can become very attached to their survival mechanisms, no matter how maladaptive they are. After all, those mechanisms kept them alive in times of chronic threat.

Anna says the need for people across various systems to understand C-PTSD is urgent. "Failing to treat the effects of trauma dooms women and their children to lives through a glass darkly: you escape the violence, but the lens of trauma never leaves you and your descendants. The fight against domestic violence doesn't end when we flee the house in the middle of the night."

———

Halfway through work on this chapter, I received a voice message from Carly's godfather, who was letting her stay with them after she fled her father's home and went to Newcastle. "Today, an order was issued through the Family Court to have Carly returned [to her father]," he said. "We're expecting police and a really ugly scene."

Two months earlier, not long after she had run away, Carly's father, John, had applied for a court order to have her forcibly returned. This had now been issued by the Family Court, with police directed to "find and recover the child" and to "stop and search any vehicle, vessel, or aircraft and to enter and search any premises or place."

I spoke to Carly the next morning. She said that after seeing the court order, she'd spent the night in tears and had barely slept. She would be safe until 4:00 p.m., she said, which was when the order would take effect. I asked what she would do when the police arrived. "I'll just stand my ground and tell them my story, and invite them in for a cup of tea," she said. "That's basically it."

The next day, Carly's godfather called again. "At about 9:00 a.m., a paddy wagon came up my driveway," he told me. "Three police officers came to my door in full uniform, guns on their belts, all male, and said they had a recovery order for Carly." They informed him that John was waiting at the police station to collect her.

Carly's godfather immediately called his partner, who was out with Carly. He told her she had to take Carly to the police. Not knowing what else to do, she drove Carly to the nearest station. When she got out of the car, Carly locked herself in and threatened to self-harm if police forced her to go inside. After her godfather's partner explained the situation to an officer inside, "he recommended that she take Carly to the hospital to have a mental health intervention."

The emergency triage notes for Carly say she was diagnosed with "Adjustment Reaction Disorder with Depressive Features" and "Significant Risk of Intentional Self Harm." She was referred to a locked ward, where she received a second mental health assessment. The psychologist noted that Carly "presented as an intelligent, mature fifteen-year-old. Her distress appeared genuine, no calculated attempts to manipulate the assessment were perceived." The assessment also noted that if Carly was forced to return to her father, she would try to kill herself; that she had stashed a razor blade in her bedroom, and if she couldn't do it that way she would look for drugs to overdose on.

Carly was kept in the hospital for almost three weeks. When she was ready to be released, her father—who still had sole parental responsibility—refused to let her stay with relatives. Carly was forced to find accommodation in a refuge. The rules were harsh: she wasn't allowed to stay there during the day, so she had to spend daylight hours in the library or sitting in the local food court. For the four months she lived in the refuge, and despite asking for schoolwork, she received no schooling. She went through all of this without mental health support, and alone; by court order, she was still prohibited from speaking to her mother.

That was two years ago. Since then, life for Carly has changed dramatically. Now seventeen, she is no longer subject to the whims of the Family Court and is back living with her mother. Despite failing freshman year (the year she ran away), she is now in a college preparatory course, where she is at the top of a class of more than two hundred students.

Unfortunately, the Family Court story hasn't ended for her brother, Zac. Now fifteen, he still lives with his father. He hasn't seen his mother in four years, and the last time he saw Carly was the night before she ran away. As I sit here writing, in front of me is a drawing with a love heart at the center. It's a picture Zac drew for Erin when they were at the police station, after they were intercepted in 2015. In a child's writing at the bottom of the page, it says, "Don't stop trying, Mom."

7.

When Women Use Violence

Once she got me to a place where she could see that I wouldn't talk back or question her...this was when the physical stuff started. Just a slap or shove to start with, and then that slowly increased to full-blown and terribly violent and repeated beatings, often in front of the children, and often with leather straps, fists, knees, kicking, kitchen utensils. She would tell the children, "This is what happens when you don't do as you are told or if you upset Mommy"... She forbade contact with family and friends... I was allowed no money... I felt trapped and alone, frightened and very intimidated. I felt it was important to stay there to protect my children. The hardest part of all this was—and still is—that no one believes or accepts that domestic violence against men exists.

SURVIVOR[1]

On the first floor of the Southport courthouse, there is barely a spare chair. It's quiet, save for the whispering of those leaving the two courtrooms, shaking, steady, exhausted, relieved, crying. Against the back wall sits one work-bronzed man, his T-shirt bearing fierce animals long-faded, with his head craned back, mouth open wide, lightly snoring. Beside him, an impeccably dressed woman waits patiently in a tight blue business dress and strappy suede heels. People wait hours before being called. Occasionally, the torpor is broken by the voice of a clerk over the loudspeaker; dozens of glazed eyes focus, register an unfamiliar name, and glaze over again. Knee to knee, the seated stare at the floor or their phones, waiting to be called in for a restraining order hearing or a criminal trial. Behind two closed doors, in a "safe room" secured from the public and staffed by support workers, women wracked with fear and anxiety also wait. For them, boredom would be sweet relief.

However, not all the women here are applying for protection. In Court Four, a woman who looks about forty-something, with lank blond hair and desperate eyes, leans into her lawyer's ear, giving incessant instructions and weeping. As the magistrate reads aloud the details of her case, the woman shakes her head, pleads with her lawyer. She is accused of verbal abuse and of threatening physical harm and suicide. At the other end of the bench sits an older man with gray, stringy remnants of long, curly hair, his eyes resigned and exhausted. He's seeking protection from this woman, his daughter. He wants her evicted from his apartment and responsibility for her care transferred to the state. She is almost inconsolable.

"I yell more than I hit, because I'm stressed," she insists, crying. "I'm not violent—I've got cerebral palsy on one side!" It may be a frontal lobe brain injury that makes her like this, the court hears; that may also explain her three distinct personalities and itinerant lifestyle. Her father wants her to get help; he can no longer manage. He's cared for her since she was fourteen, after a childhood spent in a string of foster homes. "He promised he'd always look after me!" she wails.

The magistrate, a no-nonsense woman with a stern demeanor, listens patiently to the woman's outbursts, then issues a protection order. She'll have a short grace period to collect money and essentials, then she will be forbidden to come within 100 feet of her father's home. The magistrate sets out provisions for crisis accommodation to keep her off the street—for now, at least. The final condition of the restraining order is explicit: the respondent must not commit domestic violence. If she breaches this order, she can end up in jail. With that, the crying, quivering young woman joins a significant minority: women who've had protection orders issued *against* them.

This was what I was trying to examine. What did domestic abuse look like when it was being perpetrated by women? And how often did that really happen?

On the subject of women's violence, I was determined to build my conclusions from the ground up. What if the gender narrative on domestic violence *was* narrow and out of date? Could it be possible that, as men's rights groups insist, women's violence is minimized and ignored because it doesn't fit the feminist narrative? If I was to write anything worthwhile on women's violence, I would need to put all my prior understanding aside and come at the issue with fresh eyes.

———

"Patrick" arrived at my front door with a zip-locked bag of farm-bought cherries and a bottle of port. In large wire-rimmed glasses and a checked flannelette shirt, he looked like someone who found the city to be a fast and foreign place. He was visibly nervous. Patrick had agreed to this interview on one condition: that his family not be identified, for the protection of both his ex-wife and their three children. His twenty-five-year marriage had ended with him being forced into early retirement, too damaged by his wife's abuse to keep working. Recently he was diagnosed with posttraumatic stress disorder (PTSD).

The first act of physical abuse Patrick could remember by his wife was when he walked in on her violently shaking their infant son, who would not stop crying. Weeks later, she advanced on Patrick with a knife in the kitchen. "This is really dumb," he says, "but when she put it away, I just carried on like nothing had happened." Although Patrick doesn't remember fearing for his own safety, he *was* afraid for his children. That's why he stayed. "It was my greatest vulnerability," he says, "and my wife exploited it to the full. 'Do this or I will take the children and go'—this mantra was repeated several times a day, reinforced by draft letters from solicitors setting out her demands." Her temper was as volcanic as it was unpredictable. Sometimes she would seethe in silence for hours on end. Other times she would hurl objects; once, when a vase smashed above his shoulder, glass shards cascaded onto their youngest daughter, who was sitting at his feet. "That was the worst," Patrick recalls. When he turned up to work one day with a black eye, his boss asked, "Did you forget to duck?"

Patrick says he was not "entirely blameless." On two occasions, he struck his wife: once when he momentarily grabbed her by the throat, and a second time when he struck her almost by accident, during what he now recognizes was his first major panic attack. As Patrick recalled this history of violence, I watched him oscillate between downplaying the effect of her abuse and going quiet and remote, as if the true extent of his ordeal was something he was still coming to terms with. It was as though, in the telling of it, the magnitude of his experience was becoming all the more real.

In chronic abuse, incidents are just fragments: they rarely give precise shape to the whole. It's the *atmosphere* victims live in that keeps them in a state of high alert. Over time, this climate of constant abuse and threat can end up shredding the nervous system. "The circumstances were always changing," says Patrick, "and I was always trying to adapt. I found it harder and harder to keep up." Toward the end of the marriage, Patrick was so exhausted he had to find places to nap at work. "After I'd finish a class, I couldn't walk all the way back to the staff room. I'd go halfway, to the common room, and I'd literally go to sleep on some chairs." He began to take his frustration out on his students, which ended up being a factor that led to his early retirement. "If a kid did the wrong thing in the classroom, I'd go off," he says. "To do that with high school seniors is just crazy."

Patrick didn't make a formal report to police: not because he didn't think he'd be believed, but because he worried about the consequences for his wife. (When he finally did discuss the abuse with police, he received a "sympathetic hearing.") When he looks back on the relationship now, Patrick can see why he stayed. "Fear became the dominant emotion, and the desire to protect. I would do anything to attempt to protect my children and even my wife. I hesitated to go to the police because of the impact it would have on my wife and her career."

Most of what we know about male victims of domestic violence comes via anecdotal reports from men like Patrick. There is little credible research on female perpetrators. This is not a feminist conspiracy; it's a matter of priority. Male victims of women's violence rarely flee the relationship fearing for their lives, and they are almost never killed. However, we do have a few excellent studies on female perpetration that portray a vivid picture of how abuse is experienced by male victims such as "Karl":

I remember one night when she got really out of control. I had accidentally left the toilet seat up before going to bed. Well, when she went in to use the bathroom, she fell into the toilet. She started yelling and screaming and stomping around the apartment. Then she came into the bedroom. I was pretending to be asleep, but I could see her shadow. She had something in her hands, raised above her head. I figured it was a wooden spoon or a rolling pin or something like that because she had hit me with those before. So I waited until she came around to my side of the bed, then rolled over to the other side. When I turned back over, I saw that she had stuck two of the biggest steak knives into the bed up to the handles exactly where I had been lying. I grabbed my pants, ran out of the apartment, and jumped into the car. She followed me, screaming, and jumped on the hood. I reversed the car and she fell off. Then I drove away. Later, when I called her, I told her, "If I have to live like this, I don't want to live."[2]

In this same study, "Ben" said he became so convinced he deserved his wife's abuse that he gave her permission to do it. "She would say, 'I am so pissed off that I want you to let me be violent to you.' I would get down on my knees so she could slap me or hit me in the head. And she would do whatever. She would pull hair. She would pinch me hard until I bruised. She would kick me in the balls... Scratching. Hitting. Slapping in the face."[3] Six out of the twelve men in this study reported hitting their wives back in self-defense, usually with one slap or a punch. But this raised a new fear: that his wife would call the police on *him*.

Although we can see some elements of coercive control in the accounts of male victims, there is typically one element missing: fear. This is the linchpin of coercive control, what robs the victim of their sense of self. An abusive woman may raise a kind of fear in a male victim (one that may center on what she might do to the children, for example), but rarely does this fear become the kind of deep, existential terror that engulfs female victims of coercive control.

Still, while it is extremely rare for men to be subject to coercive control, it's certainly not unheard of. The diary extracts of a white, middle-aged professional known as "NH," featured in a study by British sociology professor Jacquelyn Allen-Collinson,[4] portray the chilling, unmistakable hallmarks of coercive control. Written over two years in the life of his twenty-year marriage, NH "initially composed the entries in the third person, finding it too emotionally charged and embarrassing to write in the first." One reads:

He closes the bedroom door slightly in order to get undressed. His wife interprets this as slamming the door in her face... She delivers a full-force blow to his face... His vision becomes blurred. He pleads to her to stop. She hits him again. He goes down to the kitchen, hoping that she will calm down. She is there immediately. She pushes him into a corner and takes a kitchen knife with an 8[-inch] blade from the block. She is now holding this over-arm, above him, threatening to stick it in him.

The abuse from NH's wife is not just physically violent, but also degrading:

He finishes work by 11:30. Phew. Rings three times from the office and twice from the [cell phone] to see if he can bring anything home in preparation for Christmas. She tells him off for having been at work. He brings home the turkey but gets into trouble because there is not the right stuffing at the butcher's. Once home, she tells him to "get out of the house" until 17:30, when her parents are coming round. How does this fit with him never doing anything to help? He sits in the car on the common for three hours, getting more cold and more tired. What a way to spend Christmas Eve, he thinks.

She is also seen to "induce debility and exhaustion":

She will often come into his bedroom after he has gone to bed (sometimes after he has gone to sleep) for "a chat." This is often acrimonious and intrusive and sometimes lasts until 2:00 in the morning.

The abuse that NH suffers renders him traumatized and exhausted:

She picks herself up and fists him in the face. He goes upstairs to get out of the way. She follows, scratches, pokes, thumps, and what he hates most now, puts both of her hands inside his mouth and pulls it open further than it will naturally go. By midnight he has a blood blister on the inside of his upper lip, a black eye, and scratches to his face. By 3:00 a.m. she wakes him to complain of her "blindness" as a result of hitting her head on the sofa. She is violent with him again and he goes to sleep on the floor in the next room in only his dressing gown. He hears the 5:00 news on the radio before he falls asleep. She wakes him again at 7:15. He has had five hours sleep; his face is stinging and he has to go and face an audience of 1,000. He cries on his way to work. He *hates* his life.

Why did NH—a "physically fit, well-built, and muscular man"—not retaliate or defend himself? Collinson suggests a range of reasons. For a start, his father had raised him to abhor physical violence, especially the most "deplorable" kind: violence against women. NH also knew that if he showed anger, his wife would only attack him harder, or worse, accuse *him* of being the violent one. This was a claim she made frequently:

He holds his arms up against his chest to defend himself. She loses her balance and falls back, hitting her head on the sofa. She accuses him of hitting her. This is significant as he is now [deemed to be] the violent party in the relationship. He has been waiting for this moment—that she will injure herself as a result of him defending himself and then he will become the guilty one. Throughout the rest of the evening, she is saying that he is the violent one in the relationship or at best he is as violent as her.

NH stayed with his coercive controller for twenty years. Why? For a reason common to male *and* female victims: he was afraid his abuser would harm their children.

There are many factors that differentiate the experiences of male and female victims. Primary among them is that male victims generally have the financial resources to leave, and they are not usually afraid of being killed. Nevertheless, just like women, they will hide the abuse from themselves with a set of similar rationalizations: they believe they can "fix" her, for example, and will excuse her behavior as the result of substance abuse or mental illness. Just as it is for women, the process of recognizing that they are victims of domestic abuse can be achingly slow and personally devastating.

These are terrible cases of domestic abuse, but anecdotal research can only tell us so much. Do these stories reflect what women's violence *commonly* looks like? At what rate do women perpetrate violence against men?

Finding reliable answers to these questions is incredibly difficult. The study of domestic abuse is broadly divided into two camps: "family conflict" researchers on one side, and "violence against women" (VAW) researchers on the other. Family conflict researchers—many of whom recoil at being labeled "anti-feminist"—insist that in the home women are just as violent as men. They have credible statistics to prove this, as we'll see. In the other camp—in fierce opposition—are a disparate group of VAW researchers: feminist scholars, domestic violence workers, police, and medical personnel. They regard claims of "gender symmetry" as rubbish and insist that perpetrators are overwhelmingly men. They too have credible and persuasive statistics.

What's especially bewildering about this academic feud is that on both sides are respected experts who have come to reasonable conclusions based on reasonable data. In fact, if we were to judge by statistics alone, we'd have to say that *both* sides are right. But they can't be, because the realities they claim to describe are—on the surface at least—utterly contradictory.

Consider for a minute the claim by family conflict researchers that within intimate relationships women are as violent as men. How could this be true? Outside the home, where acts of violence are more reliably measured, men are the heavyweight champions of assault: they outperform women by a rate of at least nine to one.[5] Why would such a clear distinction suddenly disappear when the violence is behind closed doors? In addition, if women's violence is such a real and present threat to men, how has it remained a secret for so long? Despite what some men's rights activists believe, feminists don't *actually* run the world, and are thus unlikely to have orchestrated a global conspiracy of silence. Chances are, if women were attacking their intimate partners at the same rate as men, we would have heard about it...a *lot*.

So where does this idea of "gender symmetry" come from? Like so many of our modern ideas about domestic violence, we can trace this idea back to the 1970s—specifically, 1975. This was a time when public violence was at the front of the American mind: men in their thousands were returning from Vietnam damaged or dangerously disturbed, assassinations and terrorism seemed almost commonplace, and right-wingers were eagerly stoking paranoia about crime. What still wasn't being talked about, though, was the *private* violence in millions of American homes. There was almost no research on domestic violence in the mid-1970s; the entire oeuvre could be read in a single afternoon. But two New Hampshire sociologists, Richard Gelles and Murray Straus, had a hunch. Much of this public violence, they believed, had its origins in violent American homes. To test their theory—and against the strong advice of their academic peers—Gelles and Straus conducted the first nationwide survey on family violence. The surveyors they dispatched asked 2,143 randomly selected individuals a simple question: In the past twelve months, have you used violence to settle disputes with your partner and, if so, exactly what kind of violence was used?

The results were surprisingly candid and sensationally grim: "With the exception of the police and the military," the authors found, "the family is perhaps the most violent social group, and the home the most violent social setting, in our society."[6] In the previous year, 16 percent of American couples had experienced violence, as had 28 percent over the course of their marriage. To the enormous surprise of Gelles and Straus, the victims were not predominantly women. In fact, the numbers of men and women who said they had experienced violence in their current relationship were almost equal (12 percent of women and 11.6 percent of men). When they narrowed that field to those who had experienced *severe* violence, they again found almost equivalent numbers, only this time women were even *more* culpable than men: 4.6 percent of men had experienced severe violence, compared to 3.8 percent of women. In the 51 percent of relationships that featured a primary aggressor, the result split virtually down the middle: 27 percent men, 24 percent women.[7]

This was not what Gelles and Straus expected to find, but it did echo the findings of a small study Gelles had conducted in 1972. In this limited sample (of eighty informal interviews), he had found that "the eruption of conjugal violence occurs with equal frequency among both husbands and wives."[8] This early study recorded statements from women explaining why they had used violence against their husbands. Said one, "He would just yell and yell—not really yelling, just talk loudly. And I couldn't say anything because he kept talking. So I'd swing." Said another, "I spent all that time by myself and sometimes the kids would get on my nerves...so when I got mad I hit him." A third openly admitted, "I probably had no reason to get angry with him...but it was such a bore... He was such a rotten lover anyway. So I'd yell at him and hit him to stir him up."[9]

Despite the statistics indicating that women were as violent as men, Gelles and Straus were quick to add caveats. It was still men who exhibited the highest degree of dangerous behavior: the kind that would leave women injured, hospitalized, or dead. Women were also, they noted, less likely to have enough money to leave the relationship. It was also possible, they added, that some women were using violence in self-defense (they estimated that the vast majority of husbands who experienced severe violence were probably also being violent toward their wives).

In 1977, their colleague Suzanne Steinmetz released a different interpretation of their findings. Her short, incendiary paper created a deep chasm in domestic violence research. "Battered husband syndrome" was the first paper to claim that within American families there were as many battered husbands as there were wives—a fact Steinmetz claimed had been hidden beneath a "cloak of secrecy" by journalists and researchers guilty of "selective inattention."[10] This was no dispassionate academic treatise. It was an unabashed polemic, and that's how it was received. The reaction was fast and furious, ranging from attempts to block Steinmetz's academic career to accusations of fraud. VAW researchers were both incensed and amused, quipping that her paper suffered from "battered data syndrome."

Despite widespread condemnation, Steinmetz's secret society of battered husbands did not sink back into obscurity. Instead, battered husband syndrome became the founding text of the gender symmetry argument and spawned a field of researchers dedicated to proving that domestic violence was an equal-opportunity crime. As Straus writes, the more empirical evidence he gathered on women's violence, the more he was persuaded that Steinmetz was right. When both he and Gelles—once towering figures in domestic violence research—also began arguing in support of gender symmetry, they too were shunned. "Bomb threats were phoned in to conference centers and buildings where we were scheduled to present," they claimed. "Invitations to conferences dwindled and dried up... Advocacy literature and feminist writing would cite our research, but not attribute it to us. All three of us became 'nonpersons' among domestic violence advocates."[11]

For years, Steinmetz, Gelles, and Straus pursued the notion of gender symmetry in virtual isolation. Today, a growing number of academics and more than a hundred empirical studies show that when it comes to intimate partner violence, women are just as violent as men. Data from these studies is legitimate and, as Gelles points out, even quoted by the domestic violence sector—when the data refer to female victims.

So is there really a vast cohort of abused men? Are these the men who, after suffering for so long in silence, are now seeking protection? The answer depends on how you define *domestic violence*. When it comes to the statistics on women's violence, the devil is not in the details, but rather in the way those details are collected and presented.

To get a good look at this devil, we need to do a little academic detective work. Almost all the studies that "prove" women are as violent as men get their data via an instrument known as the Conflict Tactics Scale, or CTS. It's the survey instrument Gelles and Straus used in their first study back in 1975, and it is still in wide use today. It asks respondents to answer a series of questions: Does violence occur in their relationship? How frequently does it occur? What does it look like?

What we must ask is this: What exactly do these surveys measure, and how do they measure it? How does the CTS yield statistics that show equal levels of domestic violence by men and women?

Let's run a hypothetical experiment. Say you're sitting at home and there's a knock at the door. When you open it, the strangers on your step are not trying to sell you something or convert you to a religion. Instead, they want to come into your house and ask you incredibly intimate questions about your relationship—all in the name of research, of course. You've just finished the last season of *Game of Thrones* and are at loose ends, so you invite them in. The researchers take a seat in your living room and bring out their clipboards. If they are using the boilerplate CTS survey—the one devised by Gelles and Straus—they will start like this: "No matter how well a couple gets along, there are times when they disagree, get annoyed with the other person, want different things from each other, or just have spats or fights because they're in a bad mood, are tired, or for some other reason. Couples also have many different ways of trying to settle their differences. This is a list of things that might happen when you have differences."[12]

Stop right there, say the critics. Michael Kimmel, one of the world's leading experts on masculinity and domestic violence, argues that from the start the survey errs in framing domestic violence as an argument that gets out of control. As we have seen, the most dangerous form of domestic violence—coercive control—is not about losing one's temper, and it doesn't occur as the result of a fight. Rather, it's a pattern of behavior, in which abusers manufacture conflict (while using a dizzying array of other methods) to confuse and dominate their partners. A tally of one-off incidents—slaps, shoves, threats—cannot capture the subtle pattern of cruelty common to coercive control. Even among less controlling abusers—the insecure reactors—conflict is still something they largely manufacture.

But let's get back to your living room. The researcher wants to know if, during the past twelve months, either of you has used force to "settle your differences" and, if so, what kind of force you used. The CTS ranks forceful acts on a scale of severity. At the least severe end is "saying something to spite your partner"; further up the scale is slapping; higher still is kicking, biting, or hitting with a fist; above that is hitting or trying to hit your partner with something. The most severe acts involve threats or attacks with a knife or a gun. You have something to confess: A couple of months ago, you bit your partner. The surveyor nods and notes your violent act on the survey. But when you try to explain why you did it, the pen goes still. They're not interested in why. Their job is to record and rank each incident according to severity. Context is irrelevant.

For many scholars and statisticians, this is a big problem. When it comes to domestic abuse, they argue, context isn't just another data point. If you don't include why a violent incident happened, what impact it had, and what role violence plays in the abusive dynamic, then the overall picture is missing. Without context, for example, the CTS gives equal weight to a kick that barely leaves a bruise and to a kick that causes traumatic brain injury. The kick that is intended to mean "leave me alone" is registered as equal to a kick that means "if you try to leave the house again, I'll break all your ribs."

"This false equivalence," cautions University of Southern California psychology professor Gayla Margolin, means that "a woman's hardest punches, which might be laughed at by her husband, would count as 'husband abuse' based on actions alone." If her husband struck her and broke her jaw, his punch would receive an equal ranking.[13] There is another, related distortion. "Those who have perpetrated several violent 'acts' (no matter how serious) and those who have reported committing a single act (no matter how trivial) are both defined as 'violent,'" write VAW scholars Russell and Rebecca Dobash.[14] A woman who tries but fails to hit her partner will be recorded as "violent"—just as he will if he beats her unconscious. According to the CTS, this relationship consists of one violent woman and one violent man in a situation of *mutual* violence.

It's easy to see how such a method can produce misleading results, but family conflict researchers are not worried by this. That's not because they're sloppy. It's because their research focuses on how couples resolve arguments: calmly or violently? From the family conflict viewpoint, both the man and woman in our examples chose violence. Even if one of them had a greater impact, both are culpable, because both used violence.

For Kimmel, this is an abstract academic perspective, utterly disconnected from human experience. "Who initiates the violence," he writes, "the relative size and strength of the people involved, and the nature of the relationship all will surely shape the experience of the violence—but not the scores on the CTS."[15] This is the fatal flaw in family conflict research. Family conflict researchers did concede one point early on: that it was important to know whether one partner was acting in self-defense. In 1985, for their second national survey on family violence, Gelles, Straus, and Steinmetz added a question about who had initiated the physical conflict. This produced another result that shocked many experts: women had initiated the violence at virtually equal rates to men.[16] Again, the data contradicted the long list of established studies showing that women mostly use violence in self-defense.

This is another statistic that requires unpacking. Cast your mind back to the case of Jasmine and Nelson in chapter 1. Nelson's dominance over Jasmine was established over many years, but on the CTS, forcing Jasmine to sleep in the car would not register as violence. In fact, if Nelson hadn't used violence in the past twelve months, he would not show up as violent at all. If, however, Jasmine finally snapped and brandished a knife when he tried to banish her to the car, she would be recorded as having *initiated* violence. Following the rules of an incident-based survey, there would have been only one act of violence, committed by one perpetrator: Jasmine. What's more, if she threatened Nelson with a knife, Jasmine would have committed an act of severe violence. Despite enduring years of physical and psychological abuse, she would be classified as a "violent" woman—a perpetrator of domestic violence—and Nelson would be recorded as her victim.

The CTS has been enormously successful in alerting society to the high frequency of violence that occurs in conflicts between lovers and spouses. Nevertheless, as Kimmel says, incident-based surveys like the CTS do not paint an accurate picture of domestic violence. "Imagine simply observing that death rates soared for men between ages nineteen and thirty during a period of a few years, without explaining that a country has declared war," says Kimmel. "Context matters."[17]

The message is plain: Data alone cannot accurately portray the complex nature of women's violence. The fact remains, however, that a large number of women in these surveys do admit to using violence in their relationships. How do we explain this?

Penn State sociologist Michael Johnson is one of the world's leading thinkers on domestic violence. In the early 1990s, Johnson was puzzling over the contradictory positions of family conflict researchers and VAW scholars. "How," he wrote, "did we come to have two groups of renowned scholars presenting ostensibly credible evidence for their obviously contradictory positions regarding the simplest possible question about partner violence: 'Who does it?'"[18] So Johnson ran his own experiment. He took every empirical study on domestic violence that used the CTS (showing equal or near-equal perpetration by men and women) and compared them to the statistics from police, hospitals, and women's shelters (showing predominantly male perpetration). The difference between the two datasets, said Johnson, was "dramatic." Compared to the CTS, the agency statistics showed male violence that was more frequent, more severe, escalated over time, and was rarely equal to any violence used by their female partners.

Johnson had a light-bulb moment: it wasn't that one side was right and the other wrong. Both datasets were legitimate, but these two groups of researchers were simply looking at fundamentally different kinds of violence.

Family conflict researchers, through their surveys, were identifying what Johnson called "situational couple violence." This is the most common type of domestic violence, the kind that erupts out of frustration or the need to stop or win an argument. Commonly the violence is mild and either isolated or sporadic. For some, however, "situational violence" does warrant a call to police; for others it can become a dangerous and escalating

pattern which may even lead to homicide. Nevertheless, even in relationships where the violence is dangerous or distressing, there generally isn't
one partner totally dominating the other; instead, it's a type of reactive violence that really does stem from low emotional intelligence and poor anger
management. Generally, the absence of a severe power imbalance is why, in
situations of situational violence, it is not a life-threatening act to leave the
relationship. Situational violence usually ends when the relationship does
(unless the violence can be addressed while the couple is still together).

Though Johnson accepted that women are just as likely as men to be the
aggressors in situational couple violence, he emphasized that the *impact* of
this violence is still distinctly gendered. "Men do more serious damage," he
explained, "and their violence is more likely to introduce fear into a relationship and to get the authorities involved."[19] Family conflict researchers agree,
especially since it shows up in their own data: in the 1985 survey, 3 percent
of females sustained injuries that needed medical attention, compared to
0.4 percent of male victims.[20]

The other kind of domestic violence—the kind that dominates the statistics collected by police, hospitals, and shelters—is what Johnson calls
"intimate terrorism" (more commonly referred to as coercive control). As
we saw in chapter 1, this is the kind of domestic violence that exhausted
and terrified women described when they started fleeing to the first wom-
en's refuges in the 1970s. Today, when the domestic violence sector says
"domestic violence," they are usually not including or even thinking about
situational couple violence. They deal primarily with coercive control:
abuse from which women and children need ongoing protection, even
long after they have left. Coercive control dominates police and hospital
data precisely because it inspires the kind of violence and fear "that leads
victims to turn to such agencies for help," writes Johnson. "Thus, researchers who work with such agency data see violence that is primarily male in
perpetration."[21]

As we've seen, coercive control is not a product of frustration or poor anger management skills. It is a systematic campaign—either strategic or instinctive—by one person to dominate and control a partner, enforced with the threat of physical and often sexual violence. Intimate terrorists are almost exclusively men, but Johnson acknowledges there are rare exceptions (like NH, whose account we read earlier).

"I've worked with men who are being terrorized by their partners," says Johnson, "and the pattern looks very much like the pattern that is perpetrated by men against female partners. One man I worked with was married to a police officer, who terrorized him in all the same ways that male intimate terrorists terrorize their female partners. She used her weapons, she beat him, she threatened him. He couldn't go to the police because the police were all her buddies. He had children, so he couldn't escape without leaving the children with this intimate terrorist. So he was struggling with all the dilemmas that female victims of intimate terrorism struggle with. But," he adds, "I want to emphasize that the vast majority of this happens, in hetero relationships, from men to women."[22] This cannot be stressed strongly enough: coercive control is a particular kind of violence that is almost always perpetrated by men against women.

When distinguishing between intimate terrorism (coercive control) and situational violence, something else occurred to Johnson. Few women living with an intimate terrorist would agree to answer a stranger's detailed list of questions about violence in her relationship. Sure enough, when he checked the number of respondents who refused to answer the National Family Violence Survey, the percentage was high, over 40 percent. Within that group of nonresponders, Johnson concluded, are the vast majority of victims of intimate terrorism.

Johnson had figured out how both research groups could be right and wrong at the same time: "[VAW] researchers using agency data cite FBI statistics that men are the violent ones in intimate relationships, while [family conflict researchers] using survey data can show that women are as violent as men. In fact, they are talking about two completely different phenomena—intimate terrorism and situational couple violence—but both are using the same term—domestic violence—to describe what they study."[23] Another researcher, the clinical psychologist Neil Frude, who belongs to neither camp, describes the difference between male and female violence like this: "[B]oth husbands and wives may be said to be 'aggressive,' but many more husbands are 'violent.'"[24]

So if we can agree that a significant percentage of women are using violence in relationships—and not just in self-defense—why don't we hear more about this from the domestic violence sector? Because a hit is not a hit, says Di Mangan, who spent many years at the helm of a statewide helpline. "There is dysfunctionality within families, and there are gradients of that," says Mangan. "Some of that leads to mutual combat... But there is a big difference when you can have a fight, walk out of the room, and know you're not going to be king-hit [knocked out with a single blow]."

Mangan is adamant: Women's violence may cause distress to men in abusive relationships, but men are almost never in danger of being killed. That is the key difference, she says. The sector is overflowing with women who are facing very real threats of homicide, who have been tortured nearly to death, who are living with traumatic brain injury, who have been made homeless as a result of the violence of men.

For advocates like Mangan, domestic violence involves the imposition of a system of power and control held in place by violence or the threat of violence. Anything else is, well, something else.

————

Back at the domestic violence court, everybody wants to help but nobody wants to talk. The two magistrates politely decline my interview requests.

Court support staff—though generous with their time and happy to show me around—can't speak on the record.

Up the road from the court, lawyers and prosecutors mingle with court-goers at Verdict Espresso, a classic low-rent café that sells hot snacks and pastries in fluorescent colors to weary patrons seated at aluminum tables festooned with pots of tiny fake flowers. Down this street winds a worker ant–trail of suited men and women, taking lattes and cappuccinos back to the dozens of criminal defense offices that surround the court. Every other door on this street is emblazoned with a double-barreled name and bullet-pointed lists of legal services that range from family law to traffic infringements. Many are no-frills shop fronts, in which lawyers usher clients into windowless rooms and seat them on pine furniture direct from a factory outlet. This is exactly what I'm looking for: lawyers too busy with quick-and-dirty cases to have any interest—or investment—in the red-hot gender politics of domestic violence.

In the foyer of one such office, Howden Saggers Lawyers, I meet Dave Garrett, a solemn criminal defense lawyer. Around a third of Garrett's work is related to domestic abuse, mostly protection order breaches, for which he represents both men and women. "Everybody thinks males are the main perpetrators," he says, "but it's very balanced." Garrett has one female client on his books when we talk (a woman in her sixties who has been violent toward her stepmother). Another client is a one-armed man accused of strangling his female partner. It's fair to say that Garrett has a varied caseload.

Among his female respondents, I ask, does he notice any common characteristics? "It's more of a one-off heated incident," he says. Unlike his male clients, the women aren't likely to be accused of prolonged violence.

Garrett's experience squares with Australian data from Women's Legal Service NSW, which shows that the majority (68 percent) of protection applications taken out against their female clients related to a single incident. Only 6.1 percent of the women they represented in 2010, for example, were accused of a prolonged pattern of violence. The most common violence alleged was a threat (47.6 percent), followed by physical violence (39.8 percent). Physical violence was punching and slapping (66.7 percent) or scratching and biting (23 percent each). As the study noted, bites were almost always on the arm or hand—an injury most likely to come from women defending themselves against an attack (particularly a headlock or strangulation).[25]

Once women are named on protection orders, I ask, what kind of breaches do they generally commit? "They would be more of a low-level, technical breach," says Garrett, "sending emails or text messages that are prohibited by the order. Unfortunately, guys are more likely to breach an order physically." This is one of the most significant differences between male and female perpetration: an abusive man who has been left is far more likely to violently stalk his ex-partner than an abusive woman.

"Most women are engaged in 'expressive' violence—tension builds, bang! Shit flies everywhere, they feel better," says Mark Walters, who manages a phone counseling service for men. "It's typically a 'push-away' motion. 'Piss off, you're a hopeless lover,' all that. It's all horrible, all hurtful. But the intention is to drive him away." The men perpetrating coercive control, in contrast, are using what Walters calls "instrumental" violence. "Instrumental violence means, you get up in the morning and you start to plan ways to stuff the other person up. I'm hiding your keys, messing with your phone, letting air out of your tires—anything to stop you getting to work. The message these perpetrators constantly send their victims is, 'You're mine, you can't get away. If you try to run away, I'll come and get you.'"

Overwhelmingly, the male callers to Walters's phone service aren't victims; they're usually dealing with their own anger or violence. Still, the vast majority—"probably 90 percent"—of male callers introduce themselves as the victim. "By the end of the call," says Walters, "only 10 percent [of men] still hold that perspective." I ask Walters, of that 10 percent, how many describe situations of intimate terrorism? "That is as rare as hen's teeth," he says. "You ask them about fear—like, 'Did you have to leave your job?' No. 'Okay, so what have you had to change to keep yourself safe?' 'Oh, well, not a lot.' It's a different lived experience. I'm not trying to minimize it. But when we ask, 'What do you need in terms of protection?' they generally say something like, 'I just need her to fucking stop.' There just aren't the same vulnerabilities." The exception to this rule is men with physical and intellectual disabilities, who are at much greater risk. "Often, exploitative women will be taking their [disability payments], or using them as a drug mule, or for housing," he says.

Walters commonly sees perpetrators attempting to present themselves as victims. "Just the other day in court, there was a guy who had the child, and he was sending [his partner] harassing texts throughout the day. His defense was that, when he opened the door, she had a raised baseball bat; that's why he punched her in the face and dropped her to the ground. That's what he was trying to tell the magistrate was reasonable force in response to her. Now we've got to look at the pattern over time—he was harassing her, he had her child, he put her into a state of fear. She knew he was combat-trained and he'd returned from Afghanistan." Perpetrators can be particularly adept at using selective evidence to frame their victims. "Men will bring to court little video clips, strategic moments, when she's picked up the knife and she's swinging it around and looks horrible, dangerous, frightening. But what happened before that, and what happened after? Yes, she picked up a knife—that was the only way she could get you to step back or move out of her space!" Walters is keen to stress that it's not as simple as saying all women are princesses and only men are villains. "There are challenging, complex, difficult women and there are vulnerable men," he says. But in terms of serious harm, "overwhelmingly, women are the victims."

Defense lawyer Kathleen Simpson also specializes in domestic violence. She's only ever seen one man she would describe as "scared." "He was waiting to go into court," she says, "and he was obviously traumatized. It was to the point where one of the support staff said, 'Oh, I wish we had a men's room for him to go to.' But that's one case out of a whole history of working in domestic violence."

———

The stock image of the "true" victim—a passive, usually white, recipient of an abuser's blows—is who judges expect to see in their courtrooms. If they are faced with a woman who has fought back, some judges (especially those with poor comprehension of domestic abuse) can struggle to see her as a "victim."

In the majority of Simpson's cases, women's violence is what she labels "reactive," and what Johnson and others call "violent resistance." Violent resisters are almost exclusively women. They retaliate against a violent and dominating partner because they want revenge, they feel the need to stand up for themselves, or they hope it will stop the abuse.

Too often, though, when women use violent resistance, they become— in the eyes of untrained police and judicial officers—just as guilty as their abusers. Such was the case for "Olivia." After she violently resisted an attack by her partner, "John," she became the subject of what's called a "cross-application," in which both partners apply for restraining orders against each other. What's incredible about this case is that in one court proceeding, Olivia looks just as guilty as John; in the next hearing, she is clearly the victim. What's the difference? Two separate police reports.[26]

The first police report is a summary of the incident, which police submitted to the court with their application for protection orders against both Olivia and John:

Parties have been arguing with each other over the last two days. Yesterday both parties had assaulted each other. Tonight, around 5.30 p.m., further assaults took place by both parties. [John] assaulted [Olivia] by throwing her against [a] wall, choking and hitting her. [Olivia] assaulted [John] by scratching him severely all over his body. Both parties charged with assault.

In court, Olivia consented to the protection order, which stipulated that she must not intimidate, stalk, assault, molest, harass, threaten, or otherwise interfere with John for twelve months. If Olivia breached the order, she could be fined or jailed.

A second police report painted a starkly different picture of the same incident. This report was a charge sheet for offenses allegedly perpetrated by John, and it was submitted for a separate hearing, in which police were charging both Olivia and John for offenses related to the incident. Here we see what actually happened that night:

[John] punched [Olivia] with his fist onto her left kidney area. [He then] commenced walking out of the bedroom, while he was doing so he punched the door causing damage to it. [He] woke the children and made them scream.

[Olivia] ran toward [John] and grabbed him by his collar of his shirt and she...scratched him at this time. [Olivia] said, "Why do you do this, why do the children have to put up with this? I am sick of you smashing my stuff, and how do you like it?" [Olivia] walked up toward the stereo and pushed her foot on it, causing it to crack.

[John] grabbed [Olivia] with his two hands onto her shoulders and threw her to the ground. [John] had a tight grip [on Olivia's] neck causing her to not breath[e]. [John] released [her] neck and stepped away from [her].

[Olivia] got up from the ground and said, "Are you trying to kill me?" [and verbally] abused [John].

[John] said, "Fuck you, you['re] dead." He grabbed [Olivia] and threw her onto the ground. He pushed [her] head back and forth onto the ground, while this was occurring [Olivia] was swinging her hands at him to protect herself.

[John] leaned over [Olivia's] body and started to head butt her onto the head area...[Olivia] sustained lumps and bruises to her head and ear...[John] said, "If DoCS take my kids, you['re] a dead cunt," and "get off the floor you fucker." At this stage [Olivia] was vomiting blood from her mouth area and could not get up from the floor. [John] tried to wipe off the blood from the floor. He said, "Get up like nothing has happened, get onto the lounge." [Olivia] had trouble getting up from the ground. [John] grabbed a blanket and placed it onto [Olivia's] head and later placed his hands over [her] mouth.

[Olivia] tried to release herself from [John], while this was happening [Olivia] bit his finger for him to let go. [John] was screaming for [Olivia] to get her mouth of[f] his finger....

In her analysis of these two reports, Professor Jane Wangmann observes that the second, more detailed account reveals many things the first does not: John uses violence that is more serious and aggressive, and the violence Olivia uses against him is clearly being exercised in response to his attacks. But that's not all. We can deduce that this is not a one-time occurrence, because the reports show Olivia is angry that John is attacking her again and that their children are again being forced to see his violence. As Wangmann writes: "I present Olivia and John's story—not for the numerous questions it raises about the police response—but rather for the way it illustrates that in order to understand the nature of domestic violence, we need to know more than simply 'who did what to whom' and 'how many times' before [we deploy] labels such as 'domestic violence,' 'perpetrator,' and 'victim.'"

————

So why, when police are better trained than ever to understand domestic violence, are the arrest rates for women increasing? It comes down to a change in policy that was introduced in the 1980s, first in the United States, which removed police discretion concerning domestic abuse: if an assault occurred, they had to make an arrest. This was supposed to be a win for victims. Finally, abusive men would be held accountable!

Of course, it wasn't that simple. After mandatory arrest policies were introduced, an unprecedented number of women started being arrested for domestic violence (DV) offenses. In some areas, the rate of arrest for men even went down: in Sacramento, while the arrest of women shot up by 91 percent from 1991 to 1996, the arrest of men *fell* 7 percent.[27] Anne O'Dell, who worked on thousands of cases of domestic violence with the San Diego Police Department, says mandatory arrest policies had a dramatic influence on her colleagues: "Officers would often state they were afraid to *not* make an arrest in DV situations." For police under pressure to arrest someone, female victims were an easier "get" than their male abusers. As one probation officer explains: "The women are more likely to admit what they did, like they'll say, 'Yeah, I stabbed him! But this is why.' The men, a lot of times, will not even admit that they struck her unless you say, 'Well, then how did she end up with a broken nose?' Even then, the men still sometimes don't admit it, even when you have the facts right there."[28]

That's what happened to Crystallee Crain, a resident of Oakland, California, in 2016. Crain had just emerged from her bathroom, where she had been washing blood off her face, when she found herself facing seven police officers. Her ex-husband—who had just finished brutally beating her—had been in the living room telling his version of the story to police, who turned up after being called by the neighbors. The police confronted Crain, having been convinced by her husband that she was the primary aggressor. Standing there in her bedroom, her body covered in bruises under her pajamas, Crain was handcuffed and arrested. She readily admitted that she had tried to defend herself. "I was sure," she later wrote, "that my battered body would be enough evidence."[29] But instead of being protected and having her injuries seen to, Crain was arrested under California's mandatory arrest policy. Police refused to allow her to change out of her pajamas and put her in the back of the patrol car. With her wrists bleeding from handcuffs that were too tight, Crain started having a panic attack; from the front seats, the officers made fun of her and told her to stop crying. When Crain was booked into Santa Rita Jail, she was shaking so hard it took three tries to fingerprint her. Police then placed her in a holding cell for fifteen hours; so battered was her body, she could hardly bear to sit on the concrete bench, and so had to lie on the floor. When she was released the next day, Crain returned home and gingerly removed her clothes. She counted thirty-four bruises on her body. Crain published this story online under a pseudonym, but for this book, she wants to be named for the first time. She wants readers to understand that this experience left her forever changed, that she has "lost a spark that was once there."

Survivor advocate Rosemary O'Malley remembers a typical case. "Neighbors called police out. The male partner was in the driveway to meet them, and she was also standing in the driveway. Police warned her, because she was incoherent, she looked like she was drunk and she was threatening them. They said, 'If we have to come back, we're arresting you and taking you away,' and then they left." For some reason, one of the police decided to go back. When they returned to the house five minutes later, the man had the woman on the ground in the driveway and was banging her head on the concrete. "She wasn't drunk," says O'Malley, "she was actually concussed, because that's what he'd been doing before they'd arrived."

Mistaking concussion for intoxication is not uncommon. When someone is concussed, they can exhibit all the signs of being drunk: incoherent speech, confusion, memory loss, a dazed or vacant stare, and—the symptom that so often leads police to mistake victims for perpetrators—irritability and aggression.

In this case, police didn't end up arresting the woman, but it could easily have been different. "Quite often when women are arrested, it's been a complete misinterpretation," says O'Malley. "I don't say that it's willful... When police go to an incident, they see just one scene in a movie. The problem is, they don't look at the whole movie."

———————

On my last day at the specialist domestic violence court, I was on my way to talk to local police about female perpetrators. Then I got an email: the meeting was canceled. There had been a serious incident—"DV-related"— and no officers would be available to talk to me.

I felt ill. There was only one kind of incident that could be.

Over the next couple of hours, the news started coming through. A woman, Teresa Bradford, had been killed that morning in a suburb fifteen miles out of town. Her ex-husband had also been found dead in the house. Their four children were home when he murdered their mother and killed himself.

I drove out to the scene with no sense of what I was even looking for; I just needed to be there. On the highway, my eyes stung with tears. I felt stupid and angry at myself for spending so much time looking at women's violence. I clenched the wheel, raging silently at all the murderous men with their pathetic nihilism and their raging entitlement. *His children were in the house, for fuck's sake! Fuck, fuck, fuck. Another woman murdered.*

Obeying the GPS, I turned off to Pimpama, a rural township on the motorway between the Gold Coast and Brisbane in Queensland. Everything here was brand-new—a Mirvac dreamscape of identikit houses for young families and up-and-comers. The unforgiving Australian sun beat down on new saplings, planted equidistant along the nature strip. A solitary man was leaf-blowing his driveway. The only other sign of life was a flash of blue and red lights.

Up ahead was a miniature police town. With no trees to shelter under, forensic investigators were shaded from the punitive heat by temporary awnings. There was no point hanging around to ask questions. "As soon as it's DV-related, the police just clam up," said a reporter leaning against a television van at the end of the street. She was the picture of commercial television: silky straight blond hair pulled into a tight ponytail, a bright-orange fitted dress. "What is it with the Gold Coast?" I asked, honestly hoping she could tell me why, in just sixteen months, five men here had killed their female partners. "I know," she replied, "it must be something in the water. Or the heat." We exchanged pleasantries for a little longer and I told her I was writing a book. As I got back in my car to leave, she called out, "Good luck with the book," and then paused. "People always ask, 'Why didn't she just leave?' People need to understand why."

Teresa Bradford *did* leave. When her ex-husband, David, attacked her a few months earlier, she went to the police, expecting protection. The attack had been severe: David had punched her until she passed out; when she came to, he was choking her, saying he was going to cut her up. It was also premeditated. David arrived at the house that afternoon with a box of tools—duct tape, rope, clear piping, box cutter—that he'd bought a week earlier. When Teresa's brother helped her clean up afterward, he also found knives and axes hidden around the house, "mostly in the bedroom where he was trying to get her to go." David Bradford was arrested for choking, deprivation of liberty, assault occasioning bodily harm, and domestic-violence-related common assault. But despite police imploring that he be kept behind bars, the specialist domestic violence magistrate was persuaded by Bradford's defense lawyer to release him on bail due to his "fragile mental state." After all, Bradford had no prior criminal convictions, and there were no independent witnesses to the attack. Strofield—a knowledgeable magistrate on domestic abuse—made a terrible error that day. Bradford had been charged with strangulation, a known risk factor for future homicide. Magistrate Strofield did not take this red flag seriously enough.

When that news got out, women's groups called for him to be removed from the bench. I might have joined them, had I not been sitting in Magistrate Strofield's courtroom just the day before, watching the effort he put into getting things right. His close attention to the defendant's history of violence. The care he gave his decisions. His empathy for victims. His no-nonsense approach to perpetrators. His decision to release David Bradford on bail was a terrible error by an otherwise fair magistrate.

Two weeks after he was released on bail, David broke into Teresa's house early in the morning, stabbed her to death in her bedroom, and then killed himself. It is nearly impossible to find a case in which a female perpetrator has done this to a man she has victimized.

———

This is an inarguable fact: When women kill their intimate partners, they are almost always killing a perpetrator. A review by the New South Wales Domestic Violence Death Review team in Australia found that, in the decade to 2010, twenty-eight out of the twenty-nine men who were killed by their female partner were themselves violent perpetrators. You won't hear about this inconvenient truth from men's groups like One in Three, who misuse the data on domestic homicides to make it sound like dozens of male victims are being killed every year. That group's website states: "Seventy-five males were killed in domestic homicide incidents between

2012–14. This equates to one death every ten days." This is nothing short of rank propaganda. There is nothing comparable about male and female victims of domestic homicide in heterosexual relationships. When women commit intimate partner homicide against men, they almost always do it after suffering years of abuse. In the vast majority of cases, women kill because they can think of no other way to be safe. Further proof of this comes from the United States where, in the 1970s, the domestic homicide rate for men and women was roughly the same: around a thousand per year.[30] Since refuges were introduced, however, there has been a significant drop in domestic homicides: not in the number of women being killed, but the number of *men*. Between 1976 and 2002, the number of male perpetrators killed by female victims went down by *69 percent*.[31] In a bizarre twist, the introduction of women's refuges in America—an innovation intended to save the lives of women—has actually done more to save the lives of the men who terrorize them.

The gender gap in domestic homicide is crucial. Men almost never have to flee the house with only the clothes on their back and the change in their pockets. They don't jump every time they hear a creak in the floor or a tree branch scratch the window. They don't need shelters to protect them from vengeful exes. The standard hallmarks of a female victim's experience do not apply, for one simple reason: male victims of female perpetrators are almost never at risk of being killed.

———

There is nothing controversial about the fact that male victims of domestic abuse need help and advice on how to recover from abuse. But it's very hard for the domestic violence sector to prioritize a cohort of victims who are generally not facing life-threatening abuse. Which raises a pointed question: If men's rights groups are so concerned about male victims, why don't they set up their own shelters?

There are some in the domestic violence sector who make time for male victims. Paula Mudd manages a women's refuge, which in its first year had to turn away fifty women who needed a bed—twice as many as they were able to shelter. But even when the shelter is full, Mudd has a totally open approach. "You knock on my door, I will help you to the best of my ability. I don't care if you're male, female, transgender." I'm curious, given that perpetrators often claim to be victims, how does she tell the difference? "I say, 'Where's your responsibility in this? You must have responsibility.' [Perpetrators] don't take ownership. As soon as they don't take ownership, you know we've got a perpetrator." Mostly, the few inquiries Mudd receives from men are not for refuge, but for help to explain an intervention order, or just to talk. "A lot of men thank me for believing them. Even if they know I can't help them, the main thing is I'm listening to them. I think they want validation a lot of the time—*yes, I'm a male victim of domestic violence, and I'm not making this up.*"

———

The last word on women's violence should go to the legendary Ellen Pence, who spent her life advocating for victims and changed the way the world understood domestic violence. At one of her last public lectures before her death in 2012, Pence told the crowd she wanted to get an unqualified statement on the record. "I think women are very, very capable of being violent," she began. "If you look at our history, women participated in the saddest, sickest ways in slavery. We told [our boys] we would turn a blind eye to what they wanted to do with African American women who had first been captured, and then enslaved. And then we'd let those men take advantage of those women, use those women, rape those women...and we didn't do much about it. We in fact escaped much of men's violence because we let some other woman take it for us," she said. "Women are capable of abusing power. We've done it throughout the centuries, and we continue to do it in many ways." For too long, said Pence, the domestic violence sector had dodged the issue of women's violence and had lost credibility: "We kept saying it didn't exist, and now all this stuff is coming forward that of course it exists. We cannot act like every time a woman does something aggressive, it's because a man made her do it. We have our own aggression, and so we have to say, yes, women have the capacity to and will use violence."

As Pence rightly says, it is a big mistake to ignore the topic of women's violence. When we relegate women's violence to a footnote—or claim it doesn't happen at all—we leave a vacuum for men's rights groups to fill with disinformation.

Here is the story, simply put. When it comes to family conflict and domestic hostility in heterosexual relationships, women are just as capable of being physically and psychologically abusive as men, and can cause serious distress and even trauma to their male partners. But when it comes to coercive control—the most dangerous form of domestic abuse, suffered by 60 to 80 percent of women who seek help—women make up an extremely small minority of perpetrators.

Domestic abuse *is* gendered. In its most dangerous form—the kind that leads most commonly to homicide—it is a crime perpetrated by men against women.

8.

State of Emergency

The legal system is designed to protect men from the superior power of the state but not to protect women or children from the superior power of men.

JUDITH LEWIS HERMAN, *TRAUMA AND RECOVERY*

The moment Nicole Lee realized she was about to die, she didn't see her life flash before her eyes. "In the last moment of your life, it's fucking terror. Absolute, pure terror." Her husband was driving wildly, faster and faster and faster down the freeway, screaming, "I'm gonna crash the fucking car! I'll fucking kill both of us! We're both gonna fucking die!" As terror engulfed her, one thought hammered over and over in her mind: "This is how it ends, and I hope it's quick. I hope it doesn't hurt. I hope I die straightaway."

That was in 2012. Nicole had been living underground for eight years. Leaving "Greg" wasn't an option. He wasn't just her husband and her son's father, he was her caregiver. Nicole can't walk; she injured her spinal cord when she was a kid. "You're told your whole life, being disabled, *It's going to take someone really special to want to love you, to take on a person like you.* That played into the abuse once it started. I'd think, *At least he wants to be with me.*" For eight years, the man she'd once loved, whom she relied on to help her shower and look after her kids—the man who, to the outside world, looked like a devoted caregiver—had been intent on destroying her. "You're belit-tled, beaten, raped, told you're worthless and useless. You slowly become isolated from everyone. Then the gaslighting—'They're gonna take the kids from you,' 'You're not capable of doing this on your own,' 'You can't survive by yourself, you'll kill yourself.' You think to yourself, *I'm going crazy, I'm mad!* But you're going crazy because you're coping with that happening to you over and over and over."

The day Greg almost killed her, Nicole weighed 84 pounds and had been diagnosed with severe anorexia as well as bipolar disorder with bor-derline personality traits. She had no previous history of mental illness; in fact, her symptoms were a reaction to Greg's violence. "The system tells you the violence is happening because of your mental health," says Nicole indignantly. "No, my mental health is suffering because of the violence." Like so many women living underground, Nicole was "checking out" in her mind. "When you're starving, you can't think. If I can't think, I don't have to acknowledge what's going on. I don't have to *feel* what's going on. I can just be completely outside of my body. I couldn't control anything else around me, but I could control what I ate." It may sound counterintuitive, but for Nicole, anorexia was a survival tactic. Being hospitalized was the only way to escape, even if just for a while.

"I'd go in there and I'd be safe. I could sleep, I'd be okay—for a little bit—before they sent me back home again." Four months after Greg's attack on the freeway, Nicole became so dangerously underweight that she had to be admitted to a long-term anorexia ward. There, Nicole told staff she was being raped and abused by her husband on a regular basis. The mental health nurse gave her pamphlets.

Greg had been raping Nicole since their son was six weeks old, sleeping in a bassinet beside their bed. From then, "he was just on me constantly, every night. I'd be pushing him away, *leave me alone, will you just fuck off, fuck off,* until eventually the pushing away wasn't enough." Nicole initially blamed herself: with a new baby, she hadn't felt like having sex. "I thought, *Okay, I need to initiate sex, that's how I stop this. I'll just be more proactive!* So I did my wifely duty, and [later] that night he raped me. The next day I was like, *How fucking dare you—you said it was because you never got sex! You got sex, and you still raped me!* Then he'd cry and apologize, saying, 'I'm a filthy human being, I'm disgusting, I hate myself, I wish I could stop.' And then I'd feel bad." Over time, though, Greg stopped apologizing. "It went from 'I'm a bad person' to 'You *made* me do it—if you weren't so fucking crazy, if you didn't make my life so goddamn hard, I wouldn't do this to you.'"

At the hospital, in a routine family therapy session, the therapist told Nicole and Greg to look into each other's eyes. "Now," he asked Nicole, "why don't you trust Greg?" Nicole refused to say: "He knows why." When the therapist pressed Nicole, Greg interrupted. "Oh," he said matter-of-factly, "it's because I rape her in her sleep sometimes." "The therapist was like, 'What do you mean?'" says Nicole. "And he was like, 'What am I supposed to do? I've got needs!' He could not understand why the therapist said, 'But that's a crime! You shouldn't be doing that!' He was like, 'What the fuck would you know? She never wants to have sex!'" Greg then became so threatening the therapist had to call security.

A few days later, Nicole's treatment team offered to call the police and get her into a refuge. "But at no point did anyone say, 'We can help you go to a refuge, and we can get your kids, too.'" To Nicole, it was clear that leaving the relationship would mean losing her boys. "I'm in the hospital with a tube up my nose. I'm refusing to eat. Who's going to believe *me*? 'No way,' I said. 'I can't go. I will never see my children again, and I cannot do that to them. I cannot leave them.'"

There are critical moments in the trajectory of a woman's life underground. When—even for a moment—her private abuse becomes public, she sees other people seeing it and seeing *her*. In a rare moment of clarity, the fog shrouding the underground clears enough for her to get some perspective and see the danger she's in. She senses, but dares not believe, the possibility of an alternative future. These moments must be seized immediately. If they are missed, her belief that nobody can help her is confirmed. The fog closes back in, and she slips underground again, where the abuse continues, unseen.

This was one of those moments. When Nicole refused to call police or go to a refuge, the hospital could have called in a family violence caseworker to talk to her, to allay her fears, to develop a safety plan. But they didn't. "Nobody sat down with me to say, 'You're not going to lose your children, you will be okay, we'll put supports in place.'" The medical team responsible for her well-being instead discharged her into the care of a man who had admitted to raping her in her sleep. For Nicole, this was confirmation that nobody could pull her out of this trap. Worse still, it made her doubt her own mind. "When nobody takes action, you start to disbelieve what's going on in your own head. You're thinking, *Maybe it's not as bad as I think it is. They don't seem to be too worried about it—they've sent me home to him.*"

Within two weeks, Nicole—still dangerously underweight—collapsed on the kitchen floor and passed out. When she woke up, Greg was anally raping her. "It was fucking painful. I just laid there and cried. I was completely broken. I was just thinking to myself, *No one's called for help! What's going on here?* That's the main thing that really, really got to me." As Nicole lay there crying on the kitchen floor, Greg sneered at her and said, "Think of this as your motivation to eat. If you didn't pass out, I wouldn't have done it."

Nicole managed to survive for another year. While she was in the hospital, Greg had sold the house *she* owned; he'd come with the estate agent into the anorexia ward to get her signature. Because he'd already put a deposit on a new house—with money they didn't have—Nicole felt she had no choice but to sign and sell. In the new house, a year after she was sent home from the hospital, Nicole tried to kill herself. "I couldn't stand living in the relationship anymore, and I knew I couldn't survive on my own. So I thought, *I just need to get rid of me. I'm the problem.*"

When Greg found her unconscious on the kitchen floor, he just rolled her onto her back and walked away. "His words afterward were, 'Why would I call an ambulance for *you*? Why would I *bother*? When your heart stops beating, I'll call an ambulance.'" When Nicole's sixteen-year-old son got paramedics to come to the house, Greg refused to assist; he wouldn't even show them Nicole's Medicare card.

When she regained consciousness in the hospital the next day, a doctor asked Nicole why she did it. "It just poured out of me: 'He's raped me four times this week, I can't fucking do this anymore, I do not want to live anymore.'" When Nicole again refused to go to a refuge, the hospital called Greg to come get her.

This time, however, was different. Somebody at the hospital had called child protection. "That was the change," says Nicole. When the child protection workers arrived at the house, they confronted Greg about what Nicole had said. Greg was blithe: *Yeah, so what?* After ushering the two kids away for a private chat, the workers came back into the room and told Greg his kids had just told them they were afraid of him. Greg told them to get out of his house. Then the police arrived. "The police stepped in and said, 'We can't let this man back into your house. You cannot protect yourself, so we have to,'" says Nicole. "I was petrified. I was begging them, 'You can't do this, he's my caregiver. You can't take him away.' And they said, 'No, you don't see this right, but one day you will.' And they were so right. They didn't take the decision of leaving off me—they took it off *him*. They forced him outside the house. It was the best thing anybody ever did for me."

However, Nicole's ordeal didn't end there. With Greg gone, she was alone with her two children and no care. "I don't think I slept the first week. I was scared. I needed help, and there was no one. I couldn't get my back door open to feed my dogs, I couldn't get my kids to school, I couldn't even shower myself." Nicole was ready to go back to court to ask that the protection order be lifted so Greg could come back to the house. "I [didn't] know what else to do. The thing I was so afraid of—of not surviving—was coming true. But it didn't have to. All I needed was support."

It was eight weeks before someone thought to refer Nicole to a disability service. "When my child protection worker approached them, they were like, 'Oh yeah, we've got a disability family violence initiative package, which is twelve weeks of funding. What does she need? Does she need someone to come in right now?'" A caseworker came and helped her to get groceries and clean the house, fixed the back door, and put in a dishwasher. "That's when things changed. I had the energy to get up and get the kids to school. It was like, *Okay, maybe I can be here by myself, if someone's here to help me.* It wasn't the family violence sector that helped me—it was the disability sector."

Then, just as Nicole was getting her life back together, she was drawn back into Greg's web of abuse—this time through the legal system. Even after he was charged with nine counts of rape, Greg was allowed to contest both the intervention order and the child protection order in court. "The Children's Court should have just said, 'Look, this is a losing battle, you're never going to win this, sir, I'm granting child protection their order.' Not, 'Oh, he's entitled to his due process.'" Nicole had to attend four separate court dates, including one in which Greg was due to contest his intervention order *from prison*, after he jumped bail. "I'm down at [the] court, and I'm waiting, waiting, waiting, and someone comes out and says, 'I'm sorry, Nicole, we're going to have to adjourn today; we can't unload prisoners because downstairs is flooded.' I'm like, *Oh, okay*, and then, *Oh shit—you're sending him here from prison to contest an intervention order? He was going to be in that courtroom?* I felt sick. I was getting dragged through this process because this man in prison was stomping his feet. It's control—it all comes back to control."

Eventually, because Greg had openly admitted to raping Nicole, he had no choice but to plead guilty to all nine counts, as well as assault and breaching an intervention order. "It wasn't because he was remorseful," she explains. "It wasn't to save me a trial, it was to save him time in prison." Greg was imprisoned for two years and six months.

Today, the fierce woman sitting across from me in a wheelchair—with crimson red hair, tattoos on her arms and hands, and big glasses—is not only thriving with her two sons, she's in a loving relationship, and just ran as an independent in her local state election.

It's stunning to think that so much of Nicole's pain and suffering could easily have been avoided. There were so many opportunities for professionals to intervene. Like many women underground, Nicole reached out for help several times, but was placed back in danger by professionals who should—and need to—know better.

———

As we've seen, reliable data on domestic abuse can be hard to find. What happens underground is almost impossible to quantify, because domestic abuse is largely hidden from view, and women are often under threat to keep it that way. Whatever statistics we have are just an indication, showing only what we've been able to measure. An Ohio State University study found that 81 percent of women who have been abused at the hands of their partners and seek help have suffered a head injury[1]—but how many women sustain traumatic brain injuries, from being hit or strangled, and never think to seek help? How many women simply live with the personality changes, the depression and anxiety, the difficulty in concentrating, the headaches and fatigue? How many women start to believe that these symptoms prove they really *are* crazy, like he says?

Most of what happens underground is never measured. There are no statistics for the number of women in this country who are maimed, forced into hiding, or begging on street corners, or sleeping in their cars. No one counts how many women leave their partners but remain locked in a feverish routine of survival, in which every decision is weighed against an unpredictable threat.

What we *can* measure—more or less—is domestic homicide. This data tells us that 16 percent of America's homicides are due to intimate partner violence,[2] and that four men kill their current or former partner every day.[3] Police data, too, shows that domestic abuse is one of America's most serious law-and-order problems: every forty seconds, police are called out to a domestic incident. In fact, domestic abuse is the number-one reason people call police for help.[4] Now, as you digest those statistics, consider that only 25 *percent* of domestic assaults are reported to police.[5] Imagine if they were all reported.

Just because women choose not to call the police doesn't mean they're not seeking help. Many call domestic violence helplines for advice, emergency accommodation, or just to tell someone what's happening, so at least *somebody* knows. These helplines act as a gateway: they assist women to develop safety plans, place them in crisis accommodations, and refer them to the support they need (interpreters, legal aid, housing, and so on). For women in remote areas, helpline operators can even book flights to get them out. Sometimes the abuser is so dangerous, women have to be urgently flown out of their *country*.

The calls to these helplines can be harrowing. At Safe Steps, I listened to a counselor respond to a woman stuck on a farm with her small children. Her husband was about to be released from jail and she was desperate to get away before he got home, but didn't have a car. When the counselor asked if there was anyone who could help, the woman replied flatly that there was not a single person she could call. Safe Steps sent her a taxi, got her into crisis accommodations, and gave her vouchers for food and groceries. I'll never forget how desolate and afraid she sounded, or the sound of her children playing and crying in the background. These are the kind of unadulterated accounts that helplines hear hundreds of times a day. It's what makes helplines perhaps the best—and most underrated—source of information about what domestic abuse really looks like.

When Safe Steps gets a call, the counselors keep an ear out for serious risk factors: strangulation, use of a weapon, threats to kill, sexual assault, stalking. When these factors are reported, they record them. Their data provides a nuanced answer to the question, "Is domestic abuse getting better or worse?" It shows that in the past few years the violence *has* been getting worse: violent incidents are happening more frequently and becoming more severe.

Some readers may think this increase can be explained by women's greater willingness to report. There *are* more women reporting: in just one month in 2017, Safe Steps received 10,293 calls, a staggering 70 percent increase over the previous year.[6] Nevertheless, increased reporting doesn't account for what the data shows. The women calling are reporting greater levels of risk than ever before. In total, 67 percent of the women who called Safe Steps in 2016–2017 were in need of immediate protection,[7] up from 58 percent in 2014–2015.[8]

Rosemary O'Malley, director of a domestic violence prevention center, backs this up. "The severity and complexity we're seeing has definitely increased over the last five years. It's different from what we've seen previously. There's something else going on. What's coming out of the shadows, especially with these new women who are reporting, is stuff we've never seen before: sexual and physical violence that's really tantamount to torture. So that's kind of terrifying."

In 2015, Annette Gillespie, then the head of Safe Steps, predicted a backlash from perpetrators. "Anytime the status quo is challenged," she says, "there is always resistance—especially from those under the most pressure to change. We're saying to men with the propensity for violence: 'We don't accept the way you do things anymore—you've got to change.' It's like a woman moving on and finding a new boyfriend. Society is saying,

'We prefer these men over here, and the way they act.' So the resistance [from perpetrators] is, 'Nobody's going to tell me what I can or can't do in my home, or with my family, with my children.'"

Men have never had less control in society than they do now, argues Gillespie, and that's why they are exerting power more firmly within their relationships. "It's the only place they can safely have control, where they can be king of the castle. It's their domain."

———————

Julie Oberin heads up the peak advocacy body WESNET and runs a women's refuge. Her workers used to quiz every woman coming into the refuge on whether her partner was tech-savvy. "If she said he wouldn't have a clue, we wouldn't worry too much about" stalking and cybermonitoring. Now, though, they don't even bother asking. "You don't have to be tech-savvy anymore. It's so simple now—you can just YouTube instructions. Easy to buy and install, easy to use."

With WESNET, Oberin has pioneered research and training on high-tech stalking, bringing experts out to train and raise awareness with local lawyers, police, service providers, and public servants. She says the severity and frequency of tech stalking has "really escalated." The week before I spoke to her, she got a call from a refuge where a worker had just seen a perpetrator running along the alley behind the refuge. He was clearly looking for his ex, who was inside. He wasn't supposed to know where she was, and the refuge's address was secret. "That's a tracking device," says Oberin. "Sometimes they're not perfectly accurate, so they end up in the wrong street. I told her, you have to eliminate whether it's the car or the phone. I would leave the car behind and go somewhere in some other vehicle and see if he finds you. If he does, it's the phone."

Technology-facilitated abuse has become so ubiquitous that refuges and domestic violence services are teaming up with specialist risk and safety assessors trained to detect concealed devices and apps, which can even be hidden in a child's favorite toy. One such risk and safety assessor is Nic Shaw, a former correctional officer and supervisor.

"Anytime they have a woman coming into [a] refuge, they'll get us to come out and assess the devices," says Shaw, who now works for the private risk and safety business Protective Group. At one of the refuges Protective Group partners with, 80 to 85 percent of the women who come in are being tracked in some way. When they're hidden in a car, tracking devices are almost invisible to the untrained eye: one device Shaw recovered looks like the car's cigarette lighter; others look like a small battery and can be fixed under the hood. "I can go on eBay right now and buy a tracking device for $10, and they're accurate to within thirty to one hundred feet. In five years' time I'll be able to buy one for $5 that's accurate to within a foot."

Most commonly, though, a perpetrator tracks his partner through her phone. "For $45 per month, you can see everything on someone's phone, including stuff that's been deleted. You can also see encrypted messages, because the encryption only happens when the message is being sent; once it's actually received, it's no longer encrypted." Shaw says this kind of surveillance usually starts *before* the perpetrator becomes overtly abusive: it's an early foray into control.

———

Women don't just leave domestic abuse. They journey away from it, step by step. There is no straight path out: it's a game of chutes and ladders, and women can slip back underground just when they're about to escape. This means that any potential escape route requires attention and support.

Calling police is one of the most fraught decisions a woman can make. She may think she knows how to manage this man better than anyone, but once police arrive, the situation is out of her hands. She can't control what the police will say or do, and she has to surrender to a system that she may not trust. Everything is up for grabs: *What if they don't take me seriously? What if Child Protection takes the kids? What if he punishes me for calling? What if the police just make things worse?* When police show up at the front door—whether they're responding to a call from her, a terrified child, or an alarmed neighbor—the surface of the underground suddenly cracks open and the world above comes flooding in.

It doesn't matter if it's the first time police have intervened or if they've come so many times they're on a first-name basis with the household. The moment they arrive, the perpetrator is no longer the most powerful person in the room. What police do and say next is critical.

If a woman is lucky, she'll get a cop like Genelle Warne. Warne and her team pay regular visits to women at risk, including women still in violent relationships, and keep a close eye on their partners. It's a strategy that's saving lives. In one instance, Warne made a routine follow-up call to a woman who'd come into the station to make a complaint about her boyfriend. During this call, Warne managed to convince the woman to talk about the torture to which her boyfriend had been subjecting her. She confided in Warne that over the past six years, he had forced her to commit sex acts on his friends, carved a game of tic-tac-toe into her back, and burnt skin off her arms with a hair iron. "I said to her, 'You're going to be dead if you don't leave. He's going to kill you.'" Warne managed to persuade the woman to leave, and her abuser was charged with twenty-seven offenses. Since then, Warne has stayed in touch with the woman and, after two years of regular encouragement, finally convinced her to see a counselor. The day of her first appointment, Warne dropped her off and picked her up.

There are police officers like Warne across the country. They are the cops who give out their personal phone numbers, who tell victims to call anytime—day or night—if they need help. They're the cops who will come to the station when they're off duty to take a statement, because they know that by the time their next shift starts, the victim may have had a change of heart. They're the cops who know that victims of extreme trauma often can't provide the neat chronologies they need for their reports, so they work around it. They know the perpetrator will try to manipulate them and how vital it is to resist. Most importantly, they don't make their protection contingent on the woman's willingness to leave or even cooperate: their first priority is to do whatever they can to make sure the woman is safe, even if she tries to resist.

Sadly, though, this brand of protective policing is not the norm. Despite the introduction of domestic violence training, pro-arrest policies, and other strict protocols, victims still commonly report that police don't take their fears seriously, that they speak to women disrespectfully, that they side with the perpetrator, and that they don't follow up or arrest the perpetrator for breaching a restraining order. In one study of sixty-five survivors of family violence, law professor Heather Douglas found that the majority of women who had sought help from police found the response inconsistent at best.[9] Most reported a lack of interest and understanding, and many felt that police didn't take them seriously, even when there were protection orders in place. "I hate to use the term, but I feel I'm just getting 'cock-blocked' everywhere," said Susan, one of the survivors in Douglas's study. She was being threatened and had reported many protection-order breaches to police, but couldn't get the police to do any follow-up. "I said to this [police officer] this morning...you guys have ignored every single complaint I [have] made for the last six months and they're just getting worse. His behavior is escalating. What's it going to take for me to be noticed? Do I have to show up here black and blue?"

Douglas's study found that even when women and children were at high risk, police sometimes failed to take the situation seriously. "One woman talked about how she was hiding out in the bedroom with the kids," says Douglas. "Her ex-husband had come around really drunk and irate, and was trying to get into the house. She'd changed the locks, and he used so much force trying to get in that his key was broken in the door. Then he was under the house, banging on the floor of her bedroom. By the time the police came, two hours later, he'd fallen asleep under the house. The police said, 'Oh, it's all right…you're safe right now.' There's a damaged lock, she's got recordings of him threatening to kill her, and they don't follow up. That's pretty bad."

Women were also aghast at police siding with the perpetrator. One reported that after her partner had assaulted her, a female police officer told her, "Look, I've had a talk with him… He says he feels very nagged in the relationship, and you really need to think about whether you're putting too much pressure on him." The woman did end up getting her partner charged with assault, but with little help from police: she took her own photos and got her own medical report.[10] She had the means and time to do that. A lot of women don't.

———————

Often, the stories with the worst endings are not blockbuster horror stories, but catalogs of negligence, laziness, and procedural error. These are perhaps the most important cases for us to grapple with.

Just after midnight on February 8, 2014, Norman Paskin called police to report that there was a man inside the house of his neighbor, Kelly Thompson, who shouldn't be there. For more than two hours, Norman had seen his former neighbor, Wayne Wood, drive past Kelly's house repeatedly in his white van. He knew something was up: in the past month he'd seen Wayne at the house several times with a police escort, removing items from the garage. That night, when Norman saw Wayne park his van some distance away and approach Kelly's house on foot, Norman called the police and told the junior constable on duty that he suspected there might be an intervention order against the man now inside Kelly's house.[11]

A call about Kelly Thompson's address should have raised immediate red flags to the local authorities. Over the previous thirty-nine days, Kelly had called her local police station thirty-eight times. She had first come to police attention just a few weeks earlier: Wayne had attempted to choke her, and when she managed to escape, he had chased her down the street in his car. A passing driver, Steven Hall, saw a distressed woman walking quickly down the street and had the presence of mind to stop and ask if she was okay. "Not really," Kelly replied. "My partner tried to strangle me." As Kelly was talking to Steven, Wayne swerved his car around and trapped her between Steven's car and his own, then started shouting at Steven to "get the fuck out of here." As Wayne raved and yelled, Kelly leaned into the passenger window and whispered her address to Steven's girlfriend, and asked her to call the police.

At around 8:50 p.m., emergency services relayed these details to the police station:

Female versus male in a vehicle. The female asked the complainant to call the police for her. The complainant's not involved. She's stated her partner's tried to strangle her. The male came around in a vehicle. He told the complainant to leave.

Dispatching a car, the police radio operator said it was "just a domestic." When the two constables arrived at the house, Kelly looked "a bit disheveled, like she had been crying or very upset." Police separated the couple to question them. Wayne, "upset" but "calm," told his story: they'd had an argument over business, and he had just been trying to get Kelly to come back to the house after she walked off saying the relationship was over. The police appeared to accept that this was just a lover's tiff. As one of the attending constables later testified, "He wasn't violent toward us at all and he didn't seem violent toward her" and "none of them had any injuries on them." Kelly refused to explain what had happened, insisting that she wouldn't say anything until their business partner (who was on the way to the house) arrived. Instead of waiting, though, the two constables simply advised Wayne to stay somewhere else for the night "to allow both parties to calm down" and told Kelly that if she wanted to take out an intervention order, she could apply for one.

It's police policy to gather statements from all available witnesses, but the constables did not interview Steven Hall or his girlfriend, who had called the police. If they had, they would have heard how Kelly looked and sounded when she disclosed being choked, and learned of her whispered request to call police—a clear indication that she was frightened of Wayne. They would also have had witness testimony about Wayne's erratic driving and his attempt to pin Kelly between the two cars—something that would likely have warranted an investigation into separate charges and cast a very different light on Wayne's story. All of these missed opportunities, and the laziness of the constables' response, set off a chain reaction that would tragically compromise the police response over the coming weeks, until the night Norman Paskin called to report that Wayne was inside Kelly's house.

When the constables returned to the station, they did what all police do after a family violence incident: they filled out a form. Police following up on this incident would need the information on this form to tell them the victim's level of risk, the kind of support she may need, and whether the perpetrator was likely to reoffend. The constables wrote up the incident exactly as Wayne described it: as an issue regarding "relationship breakdown and business problems." Kelly was described as "not fearful," despite her clear refusal to speak about the incident in Wayne's presence. With no mention of the choking—a known red flag for future homicide—the matter was classified as a low-risk case. Another constable reviewed the information, which the two attending members had assessed as "minor in nature" and "unlikely" to present any future risk. That constable followed every protocol to the letter: Kelly was referred to a family violence service and, after he called and left a message on her phone, the incident was marked as complete. Kelly didn't return the call.

Meanwhile, although Kelly had made it clear the relationship was over, Wayne became more controlling. At a local pool competition a week later, Kelly complained to a friend that Wayne wouldn't even let her go to the toilet without him. Afraid that Wayne's behavior was escalating, Kelly asked her brother Patrick to come and get her. When Patrick arrived, Wayne confronted him: "What, are you here to belt me?" "No," said Patrick, "I am here to take my sister—she doesn't want to be with you."

Two days later, Kelly applied for a restraining order. "He tried to strangle me 1/1/2014," she wrote on her application. In notes taken by the intervention order registrar, Kelly said, "He is jealous and possessive, and I don't believe he will leave me alone, and I fear he may kill me." Given how serious the threat was, the courts granted her an interim order immediately, and the order was faxed to police. Over the next five days, Kelly—too afraid to return home until the order was served—called the station ten times to ask when the order would be served. It took five days, a delay that almost certainly wouldn't have occurred had police applied for the order on Kelly's behalf.

Within a week, Wayne had breached the order, approaching Kelly when she was out to dinner with friends. Kelly reported the incident, and police called Wayne into the station for questioning. However, despite Wayne admitting that he had breached the order, police did not charge him, telling him only that he might be summoned to court later. There is no ambiguity in police protocols: breaching an intervention order is a criminal offense, and breaches—no matter how small—are to be strictly enforced. Yet even when Wayne breached it a second time, he was not arrested. Kelly confided in a friend that police had told her it took "ten breaches" before they could arrest someone for breaching an intervention order.

While Kelly's status in the police files remained as low-risk, Wayne was calling police repeatedly to accompany him to collect property from the house. This kind of controlling behavior should have rung alarm bells, as assistant police commissioner, Luke Cornelius, would later testify: "I would've expected this issue to be the subject of some discussion back at the station."[12] Meanwhile, Wayne was stalking Kelly's friends and hiding in her backyard. According to one friend, Kelly had called police to report that he was lurking outside the house and showed up everywhere she went. "She told the police that on numerous occasions," they said. There is *no* police record of Kelly reporting any of these breaches.

On February 8—the day neighbor Norman Paskin called the police— Wayne attended a reunion of friends. He was not drinking but was sweating profusely and looked "devastated." To one friend, he said he was going to "do [kill] the business partners [who had ripped him off], Kelly, and then himself." To another, he said, "I will get her, you know." Wayne couldn't read or write, and because the business had failed, he had no choice but to go on welfare. "I've lost everything," he said.

While Wayne was at the reunion, Kelly was at lunch with a friend and his wife. They urged her to stay with them, and offered to help her move so that Wayne wouldn't find her. Kelly agreed, but said she needed to go home and do a couple of things first. She was also worried about her beloved dog, Roxie.

That night, Norman was out late, tending his garden, when Wayne walked straight past him "without any kind of acknowledgment." Norman thought he must be drunk: Wayne was staggering, "seemed unaware of the things around him," and was staring intently at Kelly's house. After he drove around the area a few more times, Wayne parked his car at the end of the street around midnight and walked over to the house. Norman asked his wife to text Kelly, so she messaged: "Hi Kelly, It's Sheryl your neighbor. Norman has noticed that Wayne has driven past the house a few times. Is everything OK?" When Kelly didn't respond, Norman called the police. As he was on the phone to the junior constable, Sheryl saw the en-suite light at Kelly's house switch on, and the silhouette of Wayne's bald head in the window.

On the phone, Norman was struggling to get the police to take him seriously. Despite him saying that he thought there was an intervention order in place, the constable dismissed his concerns, explaining that the police escorts he'd seen at Kelly's house could have been supervising a simple property dispute. He asked Norman: "Can you do me a massive favor, pal, and keep an eye on the address? If the circumstances change, you notice anything untoward, or if you hear any yelling or screaming coming from that particular address, please do not hesitate calling back and I'll send a van around."

Three days later, after receiving a missing persons report from Wayne's brother, Gavin, police went to Kelly's house. They found her car in the driveway and could hear a dog barking inside. Forcing their way in, they went up to Kelly's bedroom and found two bodies. Kelly had been stabbed with a hunting knife, and Wayne was found kneeling on the bedroom floor, with a rope attached to the bedpost tied around his neck. There were two kitchen knives beside Kelly's bed, and a third in the top drawer of her bedside table.

In his testimony to the coroner, Assistant Commissioner Cornelius was contrite, conceding to a laundry list of police failures in the lead-up to Kelly Thompson's murder. The failure to dispatch police to Kelly's house the night she was murdered was "a very significant oversight." Police should have waited for Kelly's business partner to arrive during that first crucial callout, and they should have interviewed the driver to whom she disclosed the choking, Steven Hall. It was clear there was a story to be told, he said, and the attending police had "a duty to inquire." Leaving out the strangulation report on the form was "a critical omission," and the fact that local police still relied on fax machines for receiving intervention orders was akin to "using a carrier pigeon." By agreeing to escort Wayne on several occasions to pick up property from Kelly's house, police may have been used as "an instrument of family violence," he added.

In his findings, the coroner said that Kelly took "all the right steps." She was obviously in fear for her life. As her mother, Wendy Thompson, told the inquest panel, "I knew she was fearful, but the thought of the depth of her fear as to need three knives close to her bed shocked me." The coroner stopped short of finding police responsible for Kelly's death, attributing that blame solely to Wayne. Even if police had responded to the call from Kelly's neighbor, he said, it's unlikely they would have been able to save her. Her mom had a different response: "Had [police] responded, or shown him there were consequences for breaching those orders early on, Kelly would be alive today."[13]

––––––––––

Murders that follow police negligence can trigger significant changes in police protocol, as happened in Kelly Thompson's case. But protocols don't fix culture. Culture is stubborn, especially in a hypermasculine environment such as policing. The toxic attitudes are embedded within the police forces of every state like a noxious weed. Despite all the positive changes to police policies and protocols, women are still experiencing the same old victim-blaming attitudes. As one study from 2016 noted, "despite policy changes toward greater victim support and offender accountability, the next generation of law enforcement professionals still share[s] some of the attitudes and beliefs of their predecessors who operated in the early days of the women's movement (in the 1970s)."[14]

A joint study by the American Civil Liberties Union, the City University of New York, and the University of Miami,[15] which surveyed nine hundred advocates, attorneys, and service providers on police responses to domestic abuse and sexual assault, found that police responses were more or less split down the middle between "very" or "somewhat" helpful (57 percent), and "a little" or "not at all" (47 percent). Predictably, respondents reported that some police had pretty limited notions of how "real" victims looked and behaved: "Police are reluctant to believe women when they are being abused, especially if they are women of color, poor women, under the influence of substances, or have mental health problems. The police seem very taken by the idea of 'good victims' vs. 'bad victims.' If a victim has tried to defend herself, has had to call the police many times on the same partner, is drunk, on drugs, disoriented from abuse, or uses profane language, the police are much less likely to believe her and treat her fairly... In order to be a 'good victim,' a victim needs to not be angry or defend herself but also to present as a 'good woman.'"

Unsurprisingly, the experiences of LGBTQI victims were characterized by disrespect. As one respondent described, police attending same-sex incidents would ask questions such as "Who's the wife here?" and "So you two are just roommates, right?"

Perhaps the starkest insight into police attitudes I've seen, however, came from within the police force itself.[16] The Australian survey was about general police attitudes toward victims of crime; without direct prompting, the vast majority of the 204 participants raised the topic of intimate partner violence. The results were disturbing. "On the whole," the authors wrote, genuine "victims of family violence existed for officers only on a purely hypothetical plane, drowned out for the most part by a steady procession of impostors, liars, and time-wasters, presenting what were regarded as highly suspect claims to victim status."[17] Even where there was evidence of a physical assault, some police were still frustrated at having to respond to it:

You're an adult, do it yourself... [I]f you think he's going to hit you, then leave. Don't stay around and call us and expect us to come and kick him out of your house and do something proactive about it… That's the most frustrating part about it… I refuse to regard them as a victim when they've got a say in what actually happens to themselves.

Urban station, Senior Officer, six years[18]

Many emphasized that only a few domestic incidents were even legitimate:

They're just unhappy with their lives and expect you to sort it out for them, and the majority of times there's no assault…99 domestics out of 100 are just someone's husband yelling at the wife and vice versa.

Urban station, Senior Officer, eight years[19]

The frustration directed at women "refusing to help themselves" was a common theme:

When you go to some domestic which you've been to fifty times before, you've done everything you can for this person, they refuse to do anything to help themselves… You do what you have to do and what you procedurally have to and probably nothing more.

Urban station, Sergeant, nine years[20]

There is no excuse for victim-blaming, but as the authors of the study make clear, these comments from police must be understood in the context of the enormous amount of family violence they deal with. The magnitude of what police are confronting cannot be captured in cold statistics. Here is one day's schedule from just one local police area "on no special day in particular":

6 a.m.: We are called to a house where a man has beaten his girlfriend up by punching her in the stomach. Both were drinking all night and he is extremely violent and unpredictable when we get there.

10:30 a.m.: We go to an incident where a man had gone to his ex-girlfriend's house and tried to abduct her. She escapes and runs into her bedroom where he follows her and then blocks her in. A friend comes to help her out and the ex-boyfriend punches this guy in the face. The woman escapes as her ex-boyfriend threatens to kill her.

1 p.m.: We respond to a neighbor's call to police because of screams of distress in the house next door. We arrive to find a couple arguing and the male having thrown furniture and plates around the house and at the victim. A small child was there, saw the whole thing, and was crying and distressed.

3 p.m.: We go to a house and find a man who was previously arrested for breaching his intervention order and bail conditions. He was breaching those conditions again. Another trip to the Court.

8 p.m.: We find a man who was wanted for assaulting his girlfriend. When we try to arrest him at his mother's house, he assaults both our police officers and we find he had also bashed his mother.

11 p.m.: We go to a house where a 14-year-old girl has held a knife to her mother's throat as she was not happy about her mother's treatment of her.

4 a.m.: We respond to a neighbor's call about hearing screaming and glass breaking. We send two divvy [police] vans. When we get there, we hear the glass smashing and a woman screaming. We find a large pool of blood and broken glass everywhere. We find a woman lying on a bed with a cut on her arm. We try to arrest the man who starts to fight my two people and we wrestle him for five minutes until we are able to handcuff him and take him [in].[21]

Every day, police face a state of emergency that threatens to overwhelm them. The domestic violence calls they receive are both the most tedious of duties and the most dangerous. They turn up to some of the most fraught and confrontational scenes imaginable. They deal with victims who, under the disorienting effects of abuse, are terrified of their partner one day and in love with them the next. They attend houses where both parents are out of their minds on drugs or drink, their kids crawling around on filthy floors. They have to pick apart two opposing stories in the heat of the moment, under enormous pressure to get it right. They are threatened with guns. At the end of it all, there is a Sisyphean pile of paperwork to complete.

It seems clear that many in the police want domestic violence to be something it's not: a discernible crime, like a home invasion or a drug deal, with a clear victim and a clear perpetrator. They want the "gotcha" moment, and they resent anyone who gets in the way of that—especially the victim. As one constable said, "The system works as long as the victim abides by it. Like...getting an intervention order, that will work if the victim reports the breaches, but they never do, and when they do, then they change their mind... It's very frustrating; you just get sick of it. I think, 'Don't call me, I don't want to be involved until you're willing to actually use the service that we provide.'"

Police with attitudes like this need to make friends with reality. Domestic abuse is not just a crime. In fact, there may be no discernible crime committed at all. Victims need police to protect them, to understand that domestic abuse is a complex pattern of behavior that generally escalates over time and is perpetrated by men who may be just as skilled at manipulating police as they are at manipulating their partners. Victims need police to accept that they may not be what police want them to be: the damsel in distress willing to do whatever police say. Each victim has complicated links to the perpetrator and has to weigh each action against his reaction. They are often operating within conditions of extreme trauma, and may, in the moment police arrive, be bound to their perpetrator by love, loyalty, and children.

Some police really get this. As one senior sergeant explained, "Family violence is...a love or hate thing, [police officers] are either fine to do it or they hate it. Because it's a gray area and it's not that fun like it is to go and catch a crook... It's not as black and white."

Law professor Heather Douglas says police need to start attending domestic violence incidents with the primary goal of protecting the victim, no matter how many times the victim has called or how uncooperative they might be. "You want to get police understanding that women will leave eventually, probably, but they may not be ready today. So how do you make them safe? ...I think the training is telling them to think that way, but most still revert back to the easy, incident-based, 'beyond reasonable doubt' approach."

———

Considering the scale and stubbornness of these issues, many countries have pursued an entirely new model of policing that, if implemented in North America, would revolutionize the way women report domestic abuse. To see this radical change in action, we need to turn our attention south—specifically, to Argentina.

Here's the backstory: In the 1980s, as Argentina emerged from a brutal military dictatorship, newly elected democratic governments faced an enormous trust deficit when it came to law and order. Women—who had experienced severe forms of gendered violence—didn't trust the police. The military police "were the ones who abducted them, raped them, tortured them," says Professor Kerry Carrington, head of Queensland University of Technology's school of justice. "You know *The Handmaid's Tale*? That's based [partly] on Argentina, where young women were kept in captivity, made to have babies for officers, and then had their babies stolen."

Needing a new approach, Argentina looked to Brazil, where women had been similarly brutalized by the state. Brazil had introduced a new model of policing: *delegacia da mulher* ("police stations for women"). These new police stations looked nothing like the old ones: they were brightly painted converted houses, located in the heart of the *barrios* (neighborhoods). Most importantly, they were led—and mostly staffed—by female police officers.

Argentina introduced its first police station for women in 1985, and today in Buenos Aires alone there are 128 *comisarías de la mujer y la familia* ("police stations for women and children"), staffed by around 2,300 police. They have all the powers of regular police—they conduct investigations, make arrests—but that's where the comparison ends. Their structure is completely different—they report to the police minister via their own Commissioner for Women's Police, not the head of the common police— and their mission is different, too. Their primary purpose is not to enforce the law; it's to protect the victims.

"The police there are completely guided by what the woman wants to do," says Carrington, who spent three months with the women's police in Argentina. "They will listen to her story, and investigate and prosecute—if the woman chooses to do that. Whatever they do, it's always at the woman's instigation, because they know that intervening is not always the solution. They prefer to empower and prevent. They never turn a woman away, and they never take their power away from her, which is what abusers do." Sometimes they will help a woman apply for a protection order. Other times, she may want them to kick her abuser out of her house. Or she might just want them to talk to him. "It's not driven by punitiveness," says Carrington. "It's driven by what works." No matter is too trivial: they are there to listen and protect, not to decide whether a law has been broken.

The stations are designed to be inviting. Instead of walking into a hard, gray waiting room, women enter a living room hung with paintings, where they are welcomed. If the woman has kids with her, she can leave them with a worker who will look after them in a playroom while she is interviewed by police. Crucially, all the services she needs—lawyers, social workers, psychologists—are under the same roof, and police will also help her to get medical and financial aid. Instead of having to contact several different agencies, as most women in other countries do, they can get everything they need in one place.

Furthermore, the women's police don't just wait for victims to come to them: they go out and find them. "They go to hospitals, and if there's a woman who looks like she's been beaten, they'll go and ask her about it. They even stand outside churches when the congregations come out on Sunday and hand out flyers to women that read 'domestic violence is a crime,' saying, 'If you ever want to talk.' They're just amazing—they're not frightened of the local minister. They know where the pockets of resistance are." The women's police even organized a public march to end violence against women, which drew a massive crowd of about seventy thousand people. This community outreach is a big part of their power. "They form incredible links with the community. At Christmas time, they get in their police cars and take donated toys to children in the *barrio*. They have roving units that go to remote and rural areas of the province of Buenos Aires to hand out information. When you drive in a women's police car it's an amazing feeling—everyone's waving and saying hello. They don't do that to other police."

Women don't report domestic abuse to police for many reasons: they think it's too trivial, they're ashamed, they're afraid their children will be removed, or they don't trust police to act in their best interests. Nevertheless, getting police involved early can be the best kind of protection a woman can have. Studies have found that although women are afraid that calling the police will make the perpetrator escalate, the opposite is true. A decade-long study from the United States, in which each victim was interviewed six times over three years, found that perpetrators were 89 percent less likely to reoffend after police were called.[22] The longer women delay reporting, the more dangerous their relationship may become, and the harder it is for them to leave. Only 11 percent of perpetrators kill their victim within the first year.[23] Getting women to report early is critical for preventing future homicide.

That's where the women's police are making a difference. A five-year study from Brazil—which compared two groups of 2,074 *barrios* with comparable sociodemographic characteristics—found that the homicide rate for all women dropped by 17 percent. The result was much better for young women in metropolitan areas, aged fifteen to twenty-four: the domestic homicide rate for these women went down by 50 percent.[24]

Across the world, women's police stations are becoming increasingly popular. There are now 485 in Brazil, and the model has spread not only to Argentina, but also to Bolivia, Ecuador, Ghana, India, Kosovo, Liberia, Nicaragua, Peru, the Philippines, Sierra Leone, South Africa, Uganda, and

Uruguay. In 2011, a UN Women evaluation found that in Latin America, women's police stations enhanced women's access to justice; increased the likelihood of conviction; and gave women greater access to other services such as counseling, health, legal, financial, and social support. The stations were also incredibly well received by the communities: of those surveyed, 77 percent in Brazil, 77 percent in Nicaragua, 64 percent in Ecuador, and 57 percent in Peru believed they had reduced violence against women.[25] This was also having a ripple effect in terms of advocacy: victims who'd been helped by women's police, and educated on their rights, were more committed to helping other women leave domestic violence and to pursue their abusers through the courts.

"We have a structural problem: around 85 to 90 percent of sworn officers [in the United States] are men, whereas the vast majority of victims are women," says Carrington. It's a statistical imbalance that has remained unchanged for more than twenty years.[26] "That structural problem is not going to be fixed by just telling women to report. They're not going to do it. You need to have a completely different culture—a completely different mechanism." For Carrington, it's a no-brainer—and as she points out, it wouldn't even cost that much. "They don't have to be police stations. They don't need cells, so you can convert houses, units, churches, community halls—there's all sorts of ways you can do it... Women's police stations have taken off around the world because they're cost-effective, they're on the front line, and they're really solving that structural issue of women not wanting to report to male police."

———

Many women who are dominated and controlled underground don't report because they think that without proof of physical violence, the police won't help them. Sadly, often they're right. In the United States, coercive control is not a crime. Laws empower police to arrest for discrete acts of violence, but not for an ongoing pattern of controlling behavior (aside from violent threats and stalking). In other words, the U.S. justice system still responds according to what sociologist Evan Stark calls the "men's definition of violence." This is a fundamental disconnect. Governments funnel millions into awareness campaigns, emphasizing that domestic violence is not just physical. Report domestic violence, women are told: it's a crime. But if we don't treat coercive control as a criminal offense, is domestic violence *really* a crime?

For many women, it's not the physical abuse, but the prolonged domination that ruins their lives. In a 2014 survey of UK victims, 94 percent said that the coercive control was the worst part of what they suffered.[27] These women now have laws recognizing that harm: in a world first, England and Wales outlawed coercive control in 2015 and made it punishable by up to five years in jail. Police, trained to focus on specific incidents, have been slow to apply the new law; a 2016 report recorded only fifty-nine convictions in the first eight months. Nonetheless, it signals the beginning of a paradigm shift. Since the laws were introduced, men have been convicted for patterns of behavior that include confiscating or destroying their partner's mobile phone; demanding that they eat certain foods or sleep on the floor; prohibiting them from working; deleting all male contacts from their social media; and threatening or actually committing self-harm to prevent them from leaving.

Criminalizing coercive control is not a new idea, and there are many in the legal and domestic violence sectors who oppose it. They have legitimate concerns, particularly that an untrained police force will mistake victims for primary aggressors; police will find it too difficult to prove; and that it will be used disproportionately against minorities. Across the UK to date, though, those fears have not materialized: the vast majority of offenders convicted, for example, have been male, and there is no evidence that minorities are being disproportionately targeted for prosecution.[28]

In Scotland, new coercive control laws (which went into effect in April 2019) are being hailed as the "gold standard." The women's sector played a central role in drafting the Scottish legislation, and it shows. Not only is the legislation sophisticated and nuanced, it is also backed by an impressive countrywide education program, led in part by the domestic abuse charity Women's Aid. Fourteen thousand police officers and staff have received first-responder training designed to help them recognize the "seemingly innocuous actions" that constitute coercive control. A further thousand officers have had more intensive training; they are the domestic abuse "champions" working on the front lines to lend support to police and embed long-term cultural change. But the education doesn't stop with police: the domestic abuse charity Women's Aid is being funded by the Justice Department to train Scotland's judges and sheriffs on the impacts of coercive control on adult *and* child victims, and on how it will be prosecuted. "This new offense is groundbreaking," said Gillian MacDonald, crime and protection lead for Police Scotland. "For the first time, it will allow us to investigate and report the full circumstances of an abusive relationship." Laws and police-force training are not going to magically reform Scotland into a feminist utopia, but they may empower those within the force who want to do more to protect victims but feel limited by what they can charge.

The Scottish law requires the prosecutor to demonstrate that there was a pattern of abusive behaviors: that is, two or more incidents of abuse that a reasonable person would think of as causing the victim/survivor to suffer physical or psychological harm (including fear, alarm, and distress). These include classic signs of coercive control:

- Isolating a person from friends and family
- Depriving them of basic needs
- Monitoring them through online communications tools or spyware
- Taking wages and benefits

- Threats to reveal or publish personal information
- Threats to harm a child
- Threats to hurt or kill
- Threats to harm a pet
- Criminal damage (such as destruction of property)

The Scottish laws go even further to include other complex, difficult issues that are essential for our justice system to grapple with, including forcing (or coercing) the victim to take part in criminal activity (e.g., shoplifting), or abuse/neglect of the children in order to encourage self-blame and prevent disclosure to authorities.

The list is not prescriptive, because authorities understand that coercive controllers tailor their abuse to their particular victims. The distinct behaviors can be quite different from one relationship to the next, even if the overarching architecture of coercive control is repeated time and again.

Detective Superintendent Gordon McCreadie, the former national police lead for domestic abuse in Scotland, says the genius of the Scottish legislation is that all of the harms are included under the one charge. Physical, sexual, psychological, control, threats, surveillance, and so on are all considered equal. Importantly, there needn't be *any* physical or sexual violence present for a charge to be brought. Also, critically, the law does not make a distinction between those who *intended* to cause physical or psychological harm and those who were reckless as to whether the behavior would cause harm. That speaks to what we know about perpetrators: that some use coercive control instrumentally, as a modus operandi in all of their relationships, whereas others recreate the same techniques of coercive control spontaneously, almost unconsciously. Whether it is instrumental or instinctive does not matter to the victim, however: the harm is the same.

When the new laws were announced in 2019, Marsha Scott, the chief executive of Scottish Women's Aid, was thrilled. Together with survivors, legislators, police, and the prosecutor's office, she and her team had sweated over the legislation for more than four years, wrestling it through several drafts, until it was a law she believed would work for victims. Upon its launch, she said, "We think this new law has the power to transform Scotland."

When I spoke to her several months later, she was still buoyant, but was also quick to point out that the laws hadn't been a magic fix for the justice system. "We are seeing a very mixed bag at the moment in terms of response," she said from Scotland. "It would probably be surprising if that were different."

Reservations aside, the law has already exceeded her expectations. A few weeks after it came into effect, the Women's Aid helpline received a call from a woman who had been reporting to the police for "a long time." The police were always sympathetic—"they'd say, 'We understand, it's awful, it's abuse, but it's not criminal in Scotland until the new bill comes through.'" After the bill came into force, the woman went back to the police. "And they were like, *Yeah, all right—it's time!* The guy pled guilty," says Scott, "she got a two-year nonharassment order, and she said she hasn't felt this safe in years." Nevertheless, says Scott, the police response is still very inconsistent. "We can have one woman report coercive control, and she'll have police say, 'Yep, we'll help you gather evidence, we'll charge it, and pass it on to the crown (prosecutor).' And then in the same police area—they obviously receive the same training—another police officer will say, 'That's not illegal, that's just a bad relationship.'"

When police do take women's reports seriously and refer cases to the prosecutor, the job of proving coercive control in court is nowhere near as hard as people had feared. In fact, it's actually *easier* to prove domestic abuse now, compared to when courts could only hear evidence about specific incidents. "That's because it's a 'course of conduct' offense," says Scott, "and this can be proved in court using an enormous range of evidence like women's phones and all kinds of elements of everyday life which were not admissible as evidence before."

It didn't take long for the Scottish courts to record a conviction. Within a month of the bill passing, a Glasgow man, William James Murdoch, was convicted for a number of new offenses under the act, including harassing his wife with abusive phone calls and breaching the peace. Murdoch was sentenced to a community payback order with fourteen months' supervision and two hundred hours of unpaid work and was placed on a two-year intervention order. In November, fifty-four-year-old Kevin Skelton was jailed for eighteen months for a variety of offenses, including threatening to kill his wife of twenty-nine years and threatening to set fire to the house. As the court heard, Skelton's wife had, on one occasion, been so afraid of him that she barricaded herself in a room. Outside the door, he sharpened knives and other implements, and attempted to force his way in. He had seized her mobile phone and disconnected the landline to stop her calling for help. "The penny seems to have dropped for the prosecutors," says Scott. "I was speaking to a prosecutor a couple of months ago, and he *loves* this legislation, because he can [bring] so much more evidence into the court than he ever could before. He can also go for a higher sentence, because when you hear all of the evidence of the relationship, it's very difficult for anyone not to be horrified and not to see the harm. Whereas before, you could only talk about the fact that he slapped her, but not that he restricted her everyday movements, and so on."

The most innovative and radical feature of this bill, according to Scott, is the inclusion of children. "We didn't get everything that we wanted with this, but we got a great improvement: that children can be harmed by domestic abuse even if they are not present and they don't see or hear it. [It rests on the fact that] a reasonable person, when they hear all the facts, would say that that perpetrator's behavior is likely to be harmful to children in the family."

Perhaps the most important question to answer, however, is this: Do women actually want these new laws? Are the laws working for them? "For forty years, women and children have been saying that the emotional and psychological violence is the most traumatic, the most difficult to recover from, the most minimized by the system," says Scott. "Now we're hearing women and children say, 'Oh my God, the police asked me questions about what I really care about.' The law we have in Scotland now actually prosecutes what hurts people. It actually prosecutes domestic abuse, not just an assault. Even if we do nothing else with this bill, what we have already done is say, 'What you've been telling us matters.'"

For too long, women have been left to protect themselves and their families from men intent on destroying everything they love and cherish. Why should coercive control—the most dangerous kind of domestic abuse—be invisible to the criminal justice system? It's not good enough to wait for the bruises to appear: we know controlling behaviors are red flags for future homicide. Scotland has set an example for the world to follow.

9.

Through the Looking Glass

Women will be told by Child Protection, it's absolutely critical that your child have no contact with the [abusive] father, otherwise we'll remove the child from you. Then the next week, they're told in the Family Court it's absolutely critical that this child has contact with the father.

FIONA McCORMACK, VICTIM ADVOCATE

"Harry" is nine years old. If you were to ask him what he likes, he'd probably tell you his favorite drink is milk (through a flavored straw) and that he loves to sing songs from his favorite movies. If you were to ask him what he's afraid of, he might tell you he's scared of his dad. He's not shy about it: he's told doctors and police and psychologists that his dad has punched and slapped him, and gets really angry and swears at him, and that he never wants to see his dad again. His younger sister has also said she doesn't want to see her dad.

Harry knows that a court has ordered him to see his dad every second weekend. He feels sick every time he has to go and often tries to hide. Once he hid under his bed with his toy sword and shield and "built forts with escape routes and everything" so his dad couldn't get him. Another time he saw his dad coming to get him after school, and he ran, past the McDonald's and into a stranger's front yard, where he hid behind the flowers and used the mobile phone his mom gave him to call the police.

He whispered to the operator that he was being "chased down" by his dad, and that Harry was scared of him because his dad had hurt him before. Harry did his best to remember what street he was on and how the street name was spelled. When a kindly policeman came on the line, Harry said he was hiding in front of a red brick house with a chimney and lots of flowers and trees in the yard. He'd come out for police, but nobody else. The policeman asked if he could see a police car on the street. Harry's voice brightened. "I can hear them!"

The next time Harry saw the police was four months later, and they were chasing him down a busy street. Amateur video shows Harry running jaggedly, the fluorescent yellow soles of his sneakers slapping the wet pavement as he dodges passers-by. He's fast and light, with the stop-and-go footwork of a midfielder. He makes a sharp right-hand turn toward a building, runs up a set of steps and slows, seeming unsure. He yanks himself away from a man who's grabbed his arm; Harry's uncle, running alongside the pursuing police, tells the man to leave his nephew alone. Harry runs through the sliding doors of the entranceway and over the gleaming tiles, weaving deftly around a courier before darting past the elevators to the end of the foyer, where he hits a dead end. He turns, clutching his arm and breathing heavily, and stares defiantly at his uncle and a policewoman as they stride toward him. Then the video cuts out.

Police were chasing Harry on that cold morning in 2016 because a judge had told them to. When Harry had stubbornly refused to enter the courthouse with his mother and sister, Harry's mother says the judge announced he was not about to be held to ransom by a child and ordered the police to deliver Harry by force.

Harry was afraid because he suspected the judge would order him and his sister to live with his father, "Justin," who had applied for custody. According to his father's affidavit, Harry's mother, "Ginger," was the one making Harry afraid of him. In his application for sole custody, he added a striking request: that the kids have no contact whatsoever with their mother for six months. After that, he'd be prepared to let them spend limited time with her—as long as it was professionally supervised.

Harry's mother was also fighting for sole custody. Both kids had consistently said—to her, to family and friends, to doctors, to the police and mental health professionals—that they were afraid of their father and they did not want to see him.

There had been fear in the marriage, too; that's why Ginger left. "It was all about control," she says. Justin's abuse bore many of the hallmarks of coercive control: he controlled the finances and made her ask for money; he made her give up her job to support his business; he constantly called her names, both in private and in public; he was aggressive toward her dog; and he made terrifying asides, such as "in my job I could hide a dead body." Ginger stayed in this atmosphere of fear and threat because, after Harry was born, Justin agreed to take anger management classes. Then, during her second pregnancy, when he viciously abused her in front of Harry, she decided to leave. "I was sick of being controlled, but also, I didn't know where it was going to go. Was he going to snap one day?" After she left, Ginger was horrified to find her ex-husband treating Harry the same way he used to treat her.

I met Ginger in 2016. She looked drawn and pale, as though every last tear had been wrung out of her. Her final orders would be handed down that Friday, and she was terrified of what might happen. As we were leaving, Ginger handed me a stack of documents and asked me to "please read them." On top of the pile was a letter in a child's handwriting. "Dear the corte," it read, "I do not want to go to dads place why are you not doing anything I DONT WANT TO GO TO DAD!!! He swears at me he hit me he yells at me like I am going to explod. I have told lots of people why are they not listening I am not happy at dads I am scared at dads I get torchered at dad I do not want to go. Why are you making me go? Wold you like to live there?" It was signed "Harry."

A custody evaluator for the court had interviewed the family and assessed the allegations. Though she described the father as a "physically imposing" figure, she believed his story, which was that Harry had been taught to fear his dad by his mother.

That Friday outside the courthouse, nine-year-old Harry was brought into the court by four police officers. He was persuaded to go with them when they promised they were there to help. When they got inside, Harry realized that the help they'd promised was not for him, it was for the court. To get him into the childcare room, police had to pick him up kicking and screaming and carry him in by force.

Upstairs, the judge handed down his final orders. He dismissed Harry's disclosures of physical and verbal abuse, despite the evidence provided by police, Harry's doctor, his school counselor, and two emergency calls Harry had made about his father. The matter was "plainly urgent," he said. Though the children might be "devastated" by a move to their father, whom they barely knew, leaving them with their mother "would effectively remove the father from their lives."[1] He granted sole custody to the father and, as Justin had requested, prohibited Ginger from communicating in any way with her children for six months (aside from some supervised time on her daughter's birthday and on Christmas Day). After that, she could see them for two hours every weekend, which would have to be professionally supervised for six weeks, at Ginger's expense.

Ginger called me from the court that morning. "They've taken the children," she said, sobbing. "I never believed this could actually happen... We're going up to say goodbye to them now."

When Ginger and her parents approached the childcare room, they were intercepted by the custody evaluator and the independent children's lawyer (ICL, the person appointed by the court to represent the best interests of the children). Both had argued in favor of the father's application for sole custody. Blocking Ginger and her parents from entering the room, they said Harry was still very distressed and it wasn't in his best interest for them to say goodbye. All Ginger could think to say was, "You people are evil, plain evil." When they were instructed to leave, Ginger walked around the waiting room in disbelief, yelling out, "Goodbye, Harry, goodbye, Mia!"

When women leave the underground, they choose to leave an abusive partner, but the choice to end the abuse is not in their hands. If the perpetrator is hell-bent on maintaining control, they don't need the victim in physical proximity: they can control them through the system. The courts and child support services can all become another weapon in their armory. For women with children, however, no system is as punishing—or as dangerous—as the family law system.

In the years I've spent investigating family law, I've heard countless stories like Harry's and Ginger's: Mother alleges abuse, father claims she has alienated the children, court believes the father, mother loses the children. It's a narrative being played out across the Western world, in North America, Australia, the UK: stories from across these legal systems are virtually identical.

Survivors say that entering the family law system is like walking "through the looking glass" and entering an alternate reality where everything is upside down. In this parallel universe, the survivor is no longer someone who needs help to protect her children; she is the one her children need to be protected from. When I first started hearing these stories, it took me a long time—and a lot of research—to accept that they were part of a pattern, but it soon became clear that these weren't just the experiences of an unlucky few. Reports dating back twenty years[2] show that the family law system has repeatedly failed to detect and comprehend domestic abuse and the impact it has on children. In these studies, countless survivors (mostly mothers and children) speak of being disbelieved and belittled in the family law system—even by their own lawyers. Time and again, the same narrative repeats: despite repeated disclosures of abuse, children are ordered to have contact or even live with their alleged abuser.

This phenomenon is also pronounced in American family law courts. In 2018, Congress passed a resolution stating that "abusive parents are often granted custody or unprotected parenting time by courts, placing children at ongoing risk,"[3] and urging family law courts to prioritize child safety in custody decisions.

Given all we know about domestic abuse and its impact on child development, how is this happening?

Sometimes it has to do with how some survivors present in court. When survivors are fighting for custody of their children, they are already at a significant disadvantage. After enduring years of trauma and abuse, they may be disoriented and anxious. They are terrified that their children will be ordered to see or live with someone they regard as dangerous. When they're asked to recall details of the abuse (sometimes years after it happened), their telling of it may sound chaotic, because trauma typically disrupts the way we process memory. Tragically, this can undermine their credibility as witnesses and even make them look like unfit parents. As Professor Kelsey Hegarty explains, in contrast to survivors, "the father [perpetrator] may present as calm and rational...in these cases the father's version of events is more likely to be believed, and he will likely present as the better parent."[4] Even if a survivor presents well, her evidence can sound implausible because, as we've seen, many of the signature traits of domestic abuse and child abuse are counterintuitive. It doesn't make sense that someone who seems like a hard-working family man could be play-ing sadistic mind games with his wife and children. It doesn't make sense that, having escaped, a survivor may go out of her way to encourage the abuser's relationship with their child, and then suddenly apply for a no-contact order. Nor is it "logical" that child victims may still love their abuser and show no fear in his presence, or that a child may disclose abuse to one person, then deny it to another. None of this makes sense—unless you understand the dynamics of domestic abuse.

Of course, even its most ardent critics don't think the family law system has it easy. Custody cases can be wickedly complex, especially when one or both parents is alleging abuse. These are not straightforward decisions, and they require great skill and understanding to get right.

Such skill and understanding, however, appear to be dangerously inconsistent in family law systems across the world. Domestic abuse is core business for family law courts, and yet there's little to no mandated training on domestic abuse for family law judges, lawyers, or judicial staff.[5] Today, despite numerous attempts to make the system safer for children, moth-ers who seek no-contact orders on the grounds of abuse are still routinely warned by their lawyers that they risk being viewed as a hostile parent, which could cause them to lose custody of their child altogether. If the per-petrator has a record of violent offending, that *may* persuade the court to prohibit contact. However, as we've seen, perpetrators aren't usually that obvious; they can often present as decent, high-functioning people.

Until the mid-1990s, it was "extremely rare" for a mother to lose care of her children for alleging, say, child sexual abuse. But when I interviewed Professor Patrick Parkinson, former chair of the Family Law Council (an advisory body to the Australian federal attorney-general), he told me that this result was becoming more common. "I've noticed more and more cases where the court's been persuaded, usually by an expert report writer (cus-tody evaluator), that the abuse hasn't happened, they've switched the care from the mother to the father, and have cut off all contact with the mother, which is the most draconian remedy imaginable," he said. "I'm seriously worried about this trend... I think it is based on a certainty about what has occurred which is not [always] justified by a serious examination of the facts." This dynamic is so entrenched, said Parkinson, that "some lawyers now tell their clients, 'If you make these allegations, you risk losing the care of your child.'" This same dynamic is also being reported in family law systems in the UK and North America.

Protective parents who present allegations of domestic abuse and ask for no-contact orders *are* at risk of losing custody of their kids. To prevent that from happening, lawyers may push them to sign consent orders (custody arrangements that are negotiated outside the courtroom and agreed to by both parties), even when those orders will put children at risk.

This was a trap that ensnared one mother, "Tina," and her now-adult daughter, whom I'll call "Lucy." When Lucy was eight, she learned about her "no-no zones" in a personal development class and then told her school counselor that her father was touching her in ways she didn't like. "It suddenly clicked with me at eight years old that the things that were happening in my household shouldn't be happening," said Lucy. She'd never thought to say anything before, because she thought it was part of a "special father–daughter bond": "I wasn't supposed to speak about it because it would ruin the secret."

Tina had left Lucy's father when Lucy was a baby, after enduring severe abuse. "It was very violent," Tina says. "He'd lay into me while I was holding my daughter, he'd force himself on me constantly, and I didn't have any access to money. He had control over all cards, all money, all finances." When she left, Lucy's father vowed revenge. "He told me that if I left him, he would make my life miserable in any way, shape, or form... And he did. He did that and more." When the school told her of her daughter's disclosure, Tina went back to the Family Court to stop contact with the father altogether. To get an independent assessment of the allegations, the judge requested that a custody evaluator prepare a report.

Custody evaluators are used routinely in complex custody cases where abuse is alleged, and their opinions are hugely influential. They are usually child psychiatrists, psychologists, or social workers who are regarded by judges as honest and independent witnesses, particularly because they're usually selected and paid for by both parents. At the judge's request, the evaluator is contracted to write a family report, which will likely become the most important piece of evidence in the case.

To prepare a report, a custody evaluator will consider evidence from child protection, police, and schools, and may interview friends and relatives. They then interview each immediate family member and observe how the parents and children interact. The report describes the family dynamic and the psychology, background, and behavior of each family member; it assesses any allegations that have been made and finishes with recommendations for the judge to consider on how best to allocate custody. It's in these reports that children can have their concerns put before the court. There is little other way for them to be heard—children do not get to testify.

The pool of single experts is shallow. "In any given city there may be only five or six experts prepared to do these reports at all," says Professor Parkinson. "They are cross-examined, sometimes fiercely, by lawyers. That's not a pleasant experience for any doctor to go through." Parkinson says this small group of professionals exerts huge influence over custody decisions, mainly due to the "hierarchy" of expertise in the Family Court. "The gods of the Family Court are psychiatrists," he says. "At the bottom [of the hierarchy] there are social workers... Police officers have slightly more credibility, and psychologists more credibility again." But nothing matches the power of the psychiatrists.

The family law system doesn't require single experts to do specific family violence training; being a psychiatrist is considered expertise enough. The problem is that psychiatrists are, by and large, poorly trained on family violence: a 2018 study—the first of its kind—found that almost half of Australian psychiatrists had received less than two hours training.[6]

After Tina was interviewed by the single expert—we'll call him Dr. X— she felt sure that he would convey her daughter's allegations and concerns to the court. "This report writer shook our hands, looked my daughter and myself in the eyes, and he said, 'We will help you.'" But when Tina received the report, she could barely believe what she was reading. "They painted him as gold and made me look crazy, psychotic." In his report, Dr. X observed that when Lucy was interviewed alone, she became tearful talking about her father touching her private parts, reported that her father often slept next to her, and that she had woken up one morning feeling "all sticky." To test Lucy's allegations, Dr. X interviewed her with her father present. Without warning, he asked her point-blank whether she was worried about her father touching her in a bad way. When Lucy refused to answer, Dr. X asked the question again. Lucy avoided the question and instead became angry at her father for "letting her cat die." Dr. X concluded that although Lucy's defiance was a very difficult situation for the father, he "appeared to have managed the situation extremely well."

Lucy, then eighteen, recalled this interview as she sat across from me at her mother's table. "It's unnerving," she said, with an edge of indignation. "Like, when Dad's sitting in the room, you don't want to tell, because he's the one who's doing it! And he's sitting there staring at you the whole time, monitoring what you're saying."

Although Lucy had told Dr. X the same things she told her school counselor, Dr. X concluded that it was highly unlikely Lucy had been a victim of abuse. Instead, she'd made allegations against her father because she'd felt pressured to reject him by her "anxious" and "over-protective" mother, who was possibly suffering from psychosis—an assessment he made with no psychometric testing or evaluation. In the final section of his report,

Dr. X made recommendations to the judge. Despite Lucy requesting no contact with her father, he concluded that she had a "close, loving relationship with him." This, wrote Dr. X, was the view of her father, who said she enjoyed her time with him, and it had also been confirmed by a church elder. Given that Lucy was "benefiting greatly" from their relationship, Dr. X recommended she continue to spend regular weekends and half the school holidays with her father. Tina's attitude toward the father was "unhelpful," however, and she should get counseling to help her support Lucy's relationship with him. If Tina continued to press these "spurious" abuse allegations, Lucy should be ordered to live full-time with her father, and Tina should receive close psychological assessment.

Dr. X's assessment was diametrically opposed to the Family Court judgment handed down seven years earlier. In 2000, Justice Graham Mullane had found that Lucy's father had used her as a "hostage in a power play with the mother" and she needed to be "protected from exposure to [his] controlling and abusive behavior." Several pages of his judgment detail the history of physical, emotional, and psychological violence perpetrated against Tina, and he noted a "whole pattern of factual material that leads the Court to conclude that the father is a controlling and abusive man." (In Dr. X's report, the history of domestic abuse was all but eliminated; a passing reference was made to a relationship that was "long, convoluted, and strained.")

With Dr. X's definitive report against her, Tina was panicked. She thought about running, or hiding Lucy with relatives, but in the end felt cornered. Feeling she had no choice—that she might lose custody altogether if she fought it—Tina consented to Lucy staying overnight at her father's house once a week. "I will never forget the first time we had to drop her back to him. I felt physically sick, watching how distressed she was. I didn't know if she was going to vomit or wet her pants," says Tina. "She was terrified—absolute, sheer terror."

Lucy was scared into silence for years. "I shut down and pretended nothing was happening." In the years that followed, the abuse escalated. "It went from being Daddy's little secret, to just full-on...just awful abuse," she told me, tripping over her words. "It became very violent, and if I wouldn't comply, it was brought up that I wasn't allowed to speak about it [by the court], so maybe I should just shut up and let it happen, and no one would believe me anyway." Lucy spoke matter-of-factly, with an edge of derision. "It did come to the stage where he was in fact having sex with me, and I got my period quite young, so it was scary to the point where I didn't even know if I'd come home pregnant." In considering whether to tell someone, it wasn't just the court's reaction Lucy was worried about. "Dad threatened that if I did bring it up again, he'd start hurting members of my family. Mum had a new partner at the time who was a father figure to me," says Lucy. "Dad said he knew where he worked, and that [if I told] he wouldn't come home one day." Eventually, when she was thirteen, Lucy's father relinquished his custody claim, without warning or explanation. Lucy says she thinks it's because she was old enough to be believed.

It's taken years for Lucy to feel safe again. "It's hard to learn how to be a normal human being after that. Coming out of such an abusive situation, being put back into a decent environment, you don't know how to deal with it. And the trauma doesn't stop, so you're still having the nightmares and reliving it daily." Lucy is incensed that the Family Court was able to wield so much power over her life. "The fact that I had to be sent back and abused... That was something that they could have stopped. Now I've been asked if I want to go back and finish the report with the police. I'm like, what's the point? Are they going to listen? I still don't have any more evidence than I did back then."

––––––––––

Despite the proliferation of stories like Tina and Lucy's, the popular belief remains that it is *fathers* who are discriminated against in the family law system, not mothers. This is a powerful narrative that fathers' rights groups have been cultivating for decades. Stories about distressed fathers who've lost access to their children are legion. Typically, stories like this have two villains: the Family Court, supposedly in the thrall of the feminist lobby; and vindictive mothers, who will apparently do and say anything to stop a father seeing his children.

However, research shows that false allegations in custody battles are at least as likely (if not more likely) to be made by fathers. One of the most thorough, and thus most cited, studies to date comes out of Canada.[7] In 1998, a Canadian parliamentary committee heard testimony from men's groups and various professionals claiming that abuse allegations were the "weapon of choice" for scorned mothers and that "only 15 percent of allegations made in divorce cases were likely true."[8] That same year, a nationwide study told a different story. In a review of thousands of child protection cases, it was found that fabricated abuse allegations were rare (around 4 percent). In custody disputes, that rate rose to 12 percent (with "neglect" the most common false report). Within that 12 percent, it was noncustodial parents (typically fathers) who made them most frequently (43 percent). Neighbors and relatives were next in line (19 percent), and then custodial parents, who were usually mothers (14 percent). False allegations from a child were almost unheard of (2 percent). "This indicates," the lead author later concluded, "that the problem of deliberate fabrication by noncustodial parents (largely fathers) is more prevalent than deliberate fabrications of abuse by custodial parents (largely mothers) and their children."[9]

Within Australia's Family Court, opinions on false allegations differ significantly. In 2013, retiring Justice David Collier said mothers were increasingly fabricating child sexual-abuse allegations to stop fathers seeing their children. "I'm satisfied," he told Fairfax, "that a number of people who have appeared before me have known that is one of the ways of completely shutting husbands out of the child's life."[10] Privately, a retired Family Court justice told me Collier's comments were "unfortunate," and another said that in his experience it was "uncommon" for parents to raise false abuse allegations.

That's not to say that some fathers aren't unfairly treated in the courts and prevented from seeing their children. There are desperately sad stories of fathers who, in the face of a determined and manipulative partner, have had to forfeit their claims to custody and even visitation. Some fathers have also tried and failed to get the family law system to protect their children from an abusive mother, although these stories are far less common.

––––––––

There is a word that's commonly used to describe so-called hostile parents: *alienators*, a reference to the theory of parental alienation. For parents accused of domestic abuse or child sexual abuse, parental alienation has become a go-to counterclaim: deny the abuse and instead allege that the other parent has alienated the children against them. This is a particularly powerful defense when the children themselves have made the allegations. As the theory would have it, alienated children have been so influenced by the parent's lies that they may even think they were abused when really they weren't. *Alienation* is a controversial term, so it's not always referred to explicitly. Instead, the concept may be presented with related terms: *enmeshment, brainwashing,* or *parentification.*

The notion of parental alienation first gained currency in the 1980s, when it was put forward as a "syndrome" by the American child psychiatrist Richard Gardner. His theory had a clear target: spiteful mothers who alleged child abuse in custody disputes to punish ex-husbands and ensure that the mothers got custody of the children. Gardner identified several symptoms in children suffering from what he dubbed "parental alienation syndrome" (PAS): using foul language against the rejected parent, insisting that they alone came up with the allegations (a type he called "the independent thinker"), and supporting and protecting the "innocent" parent. Gardner claimed that PAS was especially prominent in custody cases involving allegations of child sexual abuse. The vast majority of these allegations (90 percent), he claimed, were fabricated.

Gardner's cure for PAS was radical: force the children away from the alienating parent (usually the mother) and place them with the alleged abuser (usually the father). He also recommended severing contact between mother and child for months at a time, in order to "deprogram" the child; he even encouraged jail time for mothers who persisted with abuse allegations. Despite presenting no statistical evidence to prove his theory, Gardner became the guru of child-custody evaluations in the United States. He testified in more than four hundred court cases, and PAS also became popular with family lawyers across the United Kingdom, Canada, and Australia.

Gardner invented parental alienation syndrome in the mid-1980s, when society was reeling over what seemed like a sudden epidemic of child sexual abuse. In just ten years, reports of child sexual abuse had risen eighteen-fold.[11] What made the logic behind PAS especially incoherent was the fact that while Gardner claimed that 90 percent of sexual abuse allegations in custody cases were false, he also claimed that adult–child sexual relations were "ubiquitous."[12] In his view, however, sex between adults and children was not problematic: the problem was the way society reacted to it. In his 1992 book *True and False Allegations of Child Sex Abuse*,[13] Gardner condemned what he called "sex-abuse hysteria," and outlined his staunch opposition to society's "overly moralistic" and punitive approach to pedophilia: "It is because our society overreacts to it that children suffer."[14] Gardner also advised therapists treating child sexual-abuse victims to work with the whole family to help older children "appreciate that sexual encounters between an adult and a child are not universally considered to be reprehensible acts."[15] As for any mother raising the abuse in court to stop contact between a father and a child, she too should be helped to appreciate that such child–adult sexual encounters are common.[16] The father, in contrast, should be reassured that "there is a certain amount of pedophilia in all of us"; however, in these modern, puritanical times, he must "learn to control himself if he is to protect himself from the Draconian punishments meted out to those in our society who act out their pedophilic impulses."[17]

Reading Gardner's extensive—and disturbing—literature on child abuse, one conclusion looms large: he devised parental alienation syndrome to hide child sexual abuse from the eyes of the law.

———————

Gardner stood by his theories until his violent suicide in 2003. By then, PAS had been discredited as a "syndrome" and disavowed by psychiatric associations.[18] To devote so much attention to this deeply flawed individual may seem a distraction. I wish it were, but Gardner's arguments have clearly had a significant influence on how our system responds to allegations of child abuse.

Diagnosing parental alienation syndrome is no longer permitted in most courts.[19] However, referring simply to "parental alienation" (without diagnosing it as a syndrome) is still widely accepted.

When divorce turns bitter, parents don't always spare children from the vitriol. However, kids are generally pretty resilient, and it takes a lot to turn them against a beloved parent. Indeed, clinical research has shown that even when parents engage in "indoctrinating behaviors," only a small proportion of children end up turning against the other parent. When it does happen, it's a horrific experience for the innocent parent.

Nevertheless, the way the family law system currently responds to so-called "alienation" is alarming. Gardner's "cure"—severing contact between "alienating" mothers and their children, sometimes for months— is still being written into parenting orders, despite what we know about the harm done to children when they are separated from their primary attachment figure. Remember Ginger and her two children, at the opening of this chapter? She was prohibited from contacting them for six months. Her crime? Apparently she had alienated her children against their father. Ginger is just one of many mothers to have lost custody on the basis of alienation.

————————

The first I ever heard of this phenomenon was during a phone call one rainy afternoon, when I spoke to a woman I've called "Sandra." She told me about her battle to protect her children and herself from domestic abuse, about how she'd walked in on her ex-husband being indecent with her children, and how she had then believed them when they later made sexual abuse allegations against him. When she presented these allegations to the Family Court, she said, a judge decided that she had alienated her children from their father and, as a result, removed them from her custody and ordered them to live with their father. We spoke for two hours and, though I was intrigued, I didn't really believe what she was saying. I promised to look into the story, but I did wonder if Sandra was just a mother's version of a father's rights activist, spinning her story for a certain effect.

Then I read the judgment.

In 2014, a judge ordered that Sandra's two children—both under the age of nine—be removed from her care.[20] This followed Sandra supporting both children's allegations of sexual abuse against their father, "Robert," based on statements made by both children, "Tim" and "Sally." Sally had made the same statements to her maternal grandparents, the police, child protection services, and a counselor: she'd been asked to "rub" and "look at" her father's "private parts." Child Protection had also intervened in the proceedings, finding that the father was a risk of sexual harm to one or both children. In an extraordinary departure from standard procedure, Justice Margaret Cleary issued the parenting orders in an after-hours ex parte hearing (meaning the parties to the case, including Sandra and child protection services, weren't present). Ex parte hearings are justified when there is an immediate risk of harm or flight—neither of which was believed to be a factor in this case. Unlike regular hearings, it was held in secret and was not audio-recorded, on the advice of the custody evaluator who had assessed the family for the court (the same custody evaluator who assessed Tina and Lucy). It's clear the judge based her orders on the findings in Dr. X's report.

The judgment cited the following rationale from Dr. X: "I don't believe the sexual abuse on balance is likely to have occurred. This has been more the anxiety of the mother which has been projected onto the children. I believe the only alternative now is for the children to be placed with the father. I recommend this happen immediately and without notice."

The following day, without warning, Sandra's two young children were fetched from class and told they were going home early. "The day the children were taken," Sandra recalls, "I had gone to the school and talked very briefly to the school principal to say, just as a heads-up, we now have a final trial date, and that Child Protection had recently filed an affidavit with the Family Court, advising it believed one or both children were at risk of sexual harm in their father's care." What happened next was devastating.

"Within an hour and a half of getting home, the principal rang, saying the most shocking thing had happened—almost as soon as I had left, two officers arrived and presented court orders that the children were to be immediately removed to go and live with their father." Sandra was "gutted." "I just couldn't believe it... Why didn't they at least involve the [Child Protection] department?"

When Sandra received the orders, she discovered she was prohibited from seeing or even speaking to her children for the next two weeks. Following that, her access would be restricted to a couple of hours every fortnight and monitored by a supervisor, which would cost Sandra $65 an hour. When Sandra made an urgent application to challenge the decision, the judge refused to hear it, because "it would not afford the other parties procedural fairness."

On appeal, the full court said that Sandra had been "denied procedural fairness," and it was not "necessarily persuaded there was sufficient justification for making orders which removed the children from the mother's care without giving the mother the opportunity to be heard. Moreover, there were apparently unresolved concerns about the risk of abuse of the children by the father."[21] Nonetheless, the court left the children with the father, citing a future hearing scheduled more than a month away.

After the final trial, the court went to the extraordinary length of adding a clause prohibiting Sandra from showing anybody (besides her lawyer) documents relating to her case. By connecting with others who were involved in this case, I was able to review the documents for just a few hours. One of the documents I trawled through was a signed affidavit from the children's head teacher, written after the children were removed. Attached to it was a letter he had sent to Child Protection, detailing his "great concern" over the "extraordinary set of events" that occurred the day the children were handed to their father. "In my opinion [as an educator of young children for over twenty years]," he wrote, "the process was ill-conceived, poorly executed, and traumatic to the children in the extreme." When they saw their father, "both of the children appeared to stop and freeze." When they were told they'd be living with their father, the little girl "took a small step backwards [and asked] for how long? It was the look of extreme concern that troubled me most of all," he wrote. "This young child appeared very frightened at the prospect of spending an indefinite period of time with her father." In summary, he wrote, "The look of betrayal I received from the children when they first saw their father waiting for them was very disconcerting. I hope I have not permanently damaged the children's trust in me."

Three other letters attached to the affidavit, written by the children's teachers, observed changes in the children that had occurred after they were ordered to live with their father. The little boy, Tim, had changed from "bright, happy, and bubbly" to "inward and withdrawn," his eyes "constantly vacant and emotionally unresponsive." His younger sister, Sally, had withdrawn from friendships, and appeared to be a "very sad and insecure little girl." On several occasions, she arrived at school crying and upset, and seemed "lost and fragile." Her behavior had changed markedly: she had begun saying mean things to other children and telling on them "a great deal for insignificant things." "This not only breaks my heart to be witnessing," wrote one of her teachers, "but I believe it is worrying and worth reporting on a professional level as well."

In the final hearing, the court ordered the children into the care of their father, again favoring the expert evidence of Dr. X. Six months after the children were removed from Sandra, Robert moved them to another school.

Sandra says she still can't believe the court would tear the children away from their primary attachment figure when there was no evidence that she or her parents were a threat to them. "We are all that my daughter has ever known, because [my husband Robert] left when she was five weeks old," she says, adding that Robert had had a mix of unsupervised and supervised visits since that time. "I now have to pay a supervisor to monitor my visits with the children... [In the single expert report] it says I'm a capable, caring parent: no psychosis, no mental illness, no personality issues, not a threat to the children. So why are we being supervised? What risk are the children being protected from?" Fighting the orders was sending Sandra into bankruptcy: four years in the Family Court had cost her more than half a million dollars.

On the afternoon I spent with Sandra discussing her case, we spoke for four hours straight, barely moving to turn on a light when the birdsong rose to a cacophony and the sky darkened, leaving us in a dim room.

She described how she had twice caught Robert in the bath playing with his erect penis while his legs were wrapped around Tim, and explained that that was one of the main reasons she left him the following year. She told me that Robert became abusive toward her when she stopped earning the family income and discovered his porn addiction, around the time she was seven months pregnant with Sally. Once she'd separated from him, he threatened to kill the dog and smash the windows to get back into the house. In previous hearings, the judge excluded from consideration the two-year restraining order against Robert on the basis that it was "historical." Sandra recalled with a chill his threat to see her "homeless, penniless, childless."

As my interview with Sandra was winding up, her father, "Richard," who lives with her mother upstairs, invited me to stay for dinner. I was mindful of keeping a professional distance, but it felt rude to refuse. As his wife, "Charlotte," prepared the meal, Richard sat with me in the living room and told me about the first time his granddaughter disclosed to him. "We were sitting on our veranda, and our little granddaughter...came across to Grandma and me, and said to me, 'Grandpa,'—and I won't use his [Robert's] name—'asked me to rub his privates.' I was taken aback and said to her, 'And what did you do?' And she said, 'I said, "No,"' upon which I said words along the lines of, 'That's good, because that's not nice.'" Richard had seen Robert's inappropriate behavior with his own eyes, and recalled with a look of disgust suggestive comments he'd heard him make to Sally.

In the Family Court orders, Richard and Charlotte were also prohibited from seeing or speaking to the children—for *five months*. No reasons were given for imposing these AVO-like conditions. "One wonders what one has done to be made to feel like a criminal," Richard said hoarsely. "On one of the phone calls—after a phone call to their mother was eventually allowed—the kids asked, 'Are Grandpa and Grandma still there?' And they wanted to know could they please speak with Grandpa and Grandma? And of course, if we're going to follow the court orders—which any law-abiding citizen really has to do—then you can't speak." When Sally turned four, he was prohibited from wishing her a happy birthday, so he played "Happy Birthday" on his trumpet to her over the phone.

I first met Sandra's family in the winter of 2015. The children are now ten and fourteen. Last year, nearly four years after he was ordered to live with his father, Tim returned to live with his mother full time. When he came back to her, Tim told Sandra he had confronted his father, saying "I don't want my little sister to be raped." Robert had then texted Sandra, saying Tim "does not want to be here, I can't get through to him, can you collect him...as soon as suits please." Tim remembers seeing Sally, who would be staying with her father, sobbing at the front door. Months after coming home, Tim revealed to Sandra that he had tried to bargain for his little sister. "I told Dad, if you have to keep someone, keep me and let her go." He described how he planned his escape soon after they went to live with their father, and how Tim's best friend had promised to bring him food and let him live in his backyard. When Robert found out his son wanted to leave, he reminded Tim, "You told Dr. X you wanted to live with me." Tim replied, "Dr. X is a liar."

Nothing makes domestic abuse or child abuse disappear faster than an allegation of alienation. A 2019 study by Joan Meier from George Washington University found that when mothers allege child abuse in family court, they lose custody of their child a third of the time. But when the father uses "parental alienation" as a defense, and the courts accept that the mother is an alienator, they lose custody in 73 percent of cases.[22]

Family lawyers know this, and they know which evaluator will give them a report to suit their client. This was made clear in research done by Griffith University criminologist Samantha Jeffries. As one lawyer explained to her, "When I worked in private practice, we would look for report writers who don't report on the violence because that was in our client's [the perpetra-tor's] interest."[23] I wanted to find out exactly how these custody evaluators did their assessments, so I decided to seek a few of them out.

I met child psychiatrist Christopher Rikard-Bell in 2015 in his office. Generous with his time, he sat with me for more than an hour. Rikard-Bell is one of the Family Court's most prolific evaluators: as he explained, in the past twenty-five years he's probably evaluated around two thousand families. He said his regular caseload featured the narrow group of "highly conflicted" cases in which allegations of abuse are often made. Speaking specifically about allegations of child sexual abuse, his "guesstimate" was that these comprised about 1 percent of the court's cases. To be clear, I asked him: "Okay, just so I know that we're not talking about a specific subset of child sexual abuse allegations, but the whole set of allegations equals about 1 percent?"

"I think so, yes."

As we sat down, I mentioned the comments made by Justice Collier, regarding his belief that mothers were increasingly fabricating child sexual-abuse allegations. "I don't think it's just a simple case of mothers making up allegations," he replied, explaining that what he sees most are overprotec-tive parents, anxious about letting children out of their sight, who end up questioning their children and—when they get "unclear answers"—often "develop their own illusion of validity about abuse." When I asked him how often he saw children under twelve making up or exaggerating allegations of abuse, he said, "I think in the Family Court—in this very severe, highly acrimonious group, where parents are making allegations against each other through their children—that there are a lot of false allegations."

I pressed him to tell me roughly what percentage of allegations were unfounded. What about child sexual abuse, for example? "In my experi-ence, about 90 percent are unfounded, in this very narrow, small group that are highly conflicted," he said matter-of-factly. "So there is still sexual abuse and physical abuse that comes through, but a lot of the people who end up in the Family Court are highly motivated people, and highly competent people, so they're a different group from, say, the lower courts, or the Children's Court."

That figure—90 percent—sounded eerily familiar. A few days later, I met another custody evaluator, child psychiatrist Carolyn Quadrio, who has spent much of her four decades in psychiatry working with survivors of child abuse and family violence. When I put Rikard-Bell's estimate to her, she was astonished. "Gardner...also suggested it was 90 percent false allegations," she replied. "He produced no data at all, no facts; he just said this was what he believed." Conversely, she added, the research shows that "something like 80 to 90 percent [of allegations] have a reasonable foundation to them when they're investigated."[24]

Given Rikard-Bell's alarming and unorthodox view on the rate of false allegations, how did he go about assessing claims of abuse? "One cannot just depend on what the child's statements are," he explained. "Often this is seen as the gold standard for trying to decide whether abuse has occurred [in other courts], whereas in the Family Court, one has to be cautious about just accepting at face value a child's statements." This was, he said, because often children are interrogated by the anxious parent, and are at an age where they are not aware of what facts are and will say whatever is necessary to please their parent. So how reliable are children's disclosures, I asked; are they more easily led or suggestible than adults? "Very easily," he said. Children up to the age of seven or eight are at a "magical stage of thinking," he said; they believe in Santa Claus and fantasy, and their main aim is to please the parent. Then, up to the age of thirteen, children are able to report facts better, but are still "very much under the influence of their parents."

Sitting with Quadrio in her practice, I asked whether anxious questioning could lead a child to a false belief that they'd been abused. It was possible to implant false memories, she said, but the likely success of that would depend on what kind of memory you were trying to implant.

In one famous experiment, participants were given—and wound up believing—a false memory that as a child they got lost in a shopping mall and were crying for "Mom."[25] But, said Quadrio, implanting a false memory about getting lost in a shopping mall wasn't the same as fooling a child into believing they had been abused. "Compare that with persuading a child that when you were in the bath last Saturday, Daddy put his finger inside your vagina," she said. "If you're going to implant a false memory, I don't think they're equally easy to implant."

So, if a child's disclosure wasn't enough on its own, how did Rikard-Bell test the allegation? "There is no particular test that says a child has been abused or not. So one has to look at a situation [including reports from authorities like police and Child Protection], form a view, and then develop on balance of probabilities is it likely that abuse has occurred or not." One way to do this, he said, was to interview the child and the alleged abuser together, and, after a few broad questions about whether anything "uncomfortable" has occurred, raise the allegations to see how they both react. "If abuse has occurred, generally there's an awkwardness, and some representation of that difficulty between the child and the parent," he said. "If there is no substantial sign of abuse generally one can tell if a child and a parent [have] a good rapport, and the child's relaxed. Or if the child's frightened, it gives you strong information. Often parents are confused about what's been alleged against them. It's important to allow that conversation to occur between the child and the parent, so there can be some clarification for them, and that's often helpful during the assessment." I asked Rikard-Bell if this could be traumatic for a child, especially if the allegations were true.

"That's always a concern," he said, "and in other jurisdictions it's probably not always wise to interview a perpetrator and a victim... However, allegations of abuse [are] a big problem in the Family Court, but the actual rate of abuse is far different from [that in] the Children's Court, so one cannot presume that abuse has occurred. Just as much damage can occur to children by denying a relationship with a healthy parent as it can be by perhaps exposing a child to a parent who may have victimized them."

When I related this method to Quadrio, she was taken aback. "No, I don't think that's appropriate," she said, screwing up her face. "I think that has to be done by forensic interviewers. That has to be properly recorded. It would be hopeless for me to ask those questions and then write the report saying this, that, and the other happened. I'd have to have a video of it, preferably have somebody else around." The Family Court does not require or advise expert report writers to record their sessions, and interviewees are forbidden from taping them. The only proof of what occurs in these interviews is what's in the report writer's notes and the report itself.

In assessing whether a parent was likely to have perpetrated abuse, Rikard-Bell explained, one could look for certain traits. "People who are more likely to abuse children are people who have substantial personality disturbance. So often you get a history where a person has had a very traumatized childhood themselves, and often they've had a very troubled youth, and then they've had a lot of problems with the law, and often they have significant antisocial or behavioral problems."

After these interviews were broadcast on radio in 2015,[26] I received dozens of emails, including one from a man who identified himself as a police officer and psychologist working in Child Protection, who asked not to be named. "This is a very important story," he wrote, "one that deeply troubles many practitioners working on the ground in Child Protection. All too often we see very sophisticated manipulation skills being employed by child sex offenders [CSOs]. This is reflected in the scholarship indicating that less than 1 percent of CSOs are convicted of their crimes." In future stories, he wrote, "it may be instructive to speak with practitioners who have extensive experience assessing and treating child sex offenders."

So I decided to run Rikard-Bell's theories and methods by one of the leading experts on child sexual abuse, Emeritus Professor Kim Oates. "It would be really good if there was a sort of abuser test, wouldn't it?" said Dr. Oates, when I asked him if it was possible to profile a perpetrator. "The public stereotype of the sexual abuser is sometimes an unsavory-looking character in a corner in a raincoat. He's nothing like that. People who sexually abuse can be model citizens. They can be highly respected in their communities, in their profession, in their jobs, within their families. It's a very hidden thing. There's certainly no clear type." Some perpetrators do exhibit other criminal behavior—"violence, robberies, that sort of thing"— but the majority are just "ordinary, respectable people." "That's why people have such difficulty believing children. 'How could that person possibly be [an abuser]? He's a really nice guy.'" Oates also trashed the idea that you could identify abuse by observing how a child behaves with the accused parent. "A sexually abused child may relate well to the parent or the person who's done it. Some might avoid them. Some might enjoy being with them at times—they can get pleasure from being made to feel really important. They'll often get presents and bribes." Children who were less self-assured were particularly vulnerable, he said, because their abusers made them feel valued. "That's terrible for the child, because the child grows up feeling they're of value in a sexual way."

During our interview, I asked Rikard-Bell whether he had specific expertise in child sexual abuse. "As part of training as a child psychiatrist, one is exposed to all forms of potential adversity that could influence a child's development," he said, "and sexual abuse is one of those. So I guess the training that I would have had is exposure [through clinical work] to the various ranges of trauma that children can experience, not specifically sexual abuse, but sexual abuse is one of those areas of abuse."

In the judgments I had read, I said, there were references to terms such as *parentification* and *brainwashing*. Where did these theories come from?

And which child sexual abuse experts did he refer to when he was forming an opinion on a case?

"It's a very difficult area to get objective information and to carry out controlled trials," he replied, "so the scientific literature is really a combination of looking at very experienced, well-regarded people in the field, and looking at their opinions and their experience. Often it's really looking at eminent people," he said. Anyone in particular? "Well, there are various people who've looked at various syndromes, so Gardner, for example, looked at parental alienation syndrome, and there's been a lot of debate about the use and misuse of parental alienation syndrome. But clinically often we see children who have become distanced from the other parent under influence, and so develop a degree of alienation. I think that's a useful concept in some circumstances, but it's sometimes over-used and misused. The term *parentification* originally came from one of the earliest children's therapists, Salvador Minuchin, who talked about seeing children being parentified and taking care of the parent, rather than parents taking care of the child, and that's often a dynamic you see in particularly older...children who are worried about their parent—they start to become parentified."

I asked him if he thought that Gardner's theories had been unfairly maligned. "I think he's very relevant," Rikard-Bell replied, "but I think that one needs to specifically not just throw out that term *parental alienation syndrome*, one needs to actually describe what one is seeing clinically, and then talk about the degrees of alienation which Richard Gardner talked about; I think that that's useful, where there's mild, moderate, or severe, and that may lead to an appropriate response from the court."

When I later emailed Rikard-Bell to ask if he ever referred to parental alienation syndrome by name in his reports, he replied, "I refer to alienation if it specifically occurs and describe it but I avoid using [the] PAS label even though it is often useful as it has now come under such scrutiny that it often creates more debate than is helpful... Richard Gardner's suggestions are

useful as a guide [and] PAS is useful to have [as] some background literature to refer to. [However], it is worth noting that PAS is not a diagnosis;
that has been one of the major criticisms, as it is sometimes used in a way
that infers it is a diagnosis, which it is not."

When I asked Justice John Faulks, deputy chief of the Family Court of
Australia, if the court had minimum standards for single experts, he scoffed
and said my question was "misconceived." "It isn't a question of minimum
standards. If you're getting a crown on your teeth you wouldn't go to a
carpenter." Justice Faulks said all experts had to demonstrate their relative
expertise to give an opinion.

But if a psychiatrist has no formal training in the dynamics of child sexual
abuse or family violence, isn't that *exactly* like getting a carpenter to do your
dental work? If you haven't specifically studied the counterintuitive traits
of family violence and child sexual abuse, how can you claim expertise on
that subject—such that you can provide expert evidence in court? I put this
question to Justice Faulks: In cases specifically involving allegations of sexual
abuse, for example, would there be minimum standards of training or specialist expertise? Justice Faulks was irate. "Weren't you listening when I spoke,
ma'am?" After some confusion and back and forth, Faulks said, "You might
say that the minimum qualification would be that the person is qualified as a
psychologist or a psychiatrist. Or in some case...as a social worker."

This lack of specific expertise is a concern for at least one judge working
in the family law system. In his 2013 paper on assessing allegations of child
sexual abuse, federal magistrate Matthew Myers wrote, "Those delivering
'expert evidence'...rarely have the training, knowledge and skills needed to
do this type of work adequately."[27]

————————

Disputes that reach the Family Court can seriously test participants'
capacity to fight for their children. It can be physically and emotionally

exhausting, it can be extremely expensive, and it can require a massive amount of case-building and documentation of assessments and reports that can themselves cost thousands of dollars. For some parents, the ability to protect their children will depend on whether they can afford to. If resources run dry, or when avenues for appeal are blocked, children have virtually no choice but to obey court orders. There is no formal process to review a child's well-being after parenting orders are made; there is no process that assesses whether that child is safe with the parent they've been ordered to visit or live with. For a child ordered into the care of an abusive parent, this lack of oversight can be diabolical.

"Alex" was six when he was removed from the care of his mother, "Emily," and ordered to live with his father, after Emily raised sexual abuse allegations in the Family Court. This order was made despite the judge's own acknowledgment that the father's two former wives had also accused him of sexually abusing their young children. "That one decision the judge made ruined my whole childhood," says Alex, who was fourteen when we spoke in 2015. For as long as he could remember, Alex's father subjected him to regular physical and emotional abuse. It happened so often, he said, it was hard to single out individual memories. "One time, I was brushing my teeth, and he just walked in the door and slapped me really hard across the face, for no reason." Alex said he tried "again and again" to tell people what was happening, but nobody would believe him. "I was too small."

In 2013, Alex breached the court order and ran away to his mother, threatening to kill himself if he was forced to go back. When his father filed recovery orders, the judge requested that another custody evaluator assess Alex's allegations. The single expert was Dr. X, the same expert chosen to assess Sandra and Tina's cases. Dr. X concluded that Alex's "suicidal feelings" were stress-related and that he didn't believe Alex really wanted to die. He recommended that the judge return Alex to his father and that, to help father and son reconnect emotionally, Alex should not contact his mother for a month. If Alex fled again, "the mother should be held responsible and incarcerated." On Dr. X's advice, the judge issued a recovery order mandating the police to return Alex to his father and suspending contact between Alex and his mother for a month. "I wondered, *How could this even happen to me?*" said Alex. "No one was listening to me—at school or anywhere—so you get this really bad feeling, that no one can help you except yourself."

The next morning, instead of going to school, Alex rode the train to his older brother's house. They went to the police. "There was a very, very good police officer who said he would do anything he could...but he couldn't do anything," said Alex. Police records show that at 8.30 p.m., Alex's father arrived at the station with a recovery order. "They actually dragged me to the police car, put me in, and drove me back to my dad's house," says Alex. Every day for the next three days, Alex ran away to the police, and each time they had to return him to his dad. "The Family Court, they overrule everyone," he said. "Even the police—the police!—couldn't protect me."

Two weeks later, Alex fled again to the police, and made allegations of physical abuse. This time, they applied for a provisional AVO to protect Alex from his father. A child protection report recorded Alex "shaking and crying when discussing living with his father."

With the case set to go back to the Family Court, child protection officers needed to find somewhere else for Alex to live in the meantime. He wanted to stay with his maternal grandmother, but his father, who had sole parental responsibility, refused. When Alex rejected his father's suggestion to stay with a family friend, the father said Alex, then thirteen, could stay in a refuge for two months, adding, "That might give Alex some time to have a think about things."

"For that whole two months, I couldn't speak to my brother or my mom—no phone calls, no nothing," said Alex. Back in the Family Court, Child Protection filed an intervention, seeking orders for Alex to live with his mother. "Finally there was another court order made that I get to live with my mom," said Alex, "and I've been living with my mom happily ever since." It's been four years since I interviewed Alex. He's since turned eighteen, and tragically, his story does not have a happy ending. He has been diagnosed with PTSD, a condition his psychiatrist says stems from the "harrowing and protracted" abuse from his father, and from being separated from his mother when he was six years old. Alex suffers "traumatic flashbacks, anxiety attacks, difficulties with memory and concentration, and dissociative episodes where he loses time." So severe are these symptoms, Alex is unable to study, let alone work, and likely won't be able to do either for several years. Instead of looking forward to being an independent adult, Alex is now applying for a disability support pension.

In 2015, then fourteen-year-old Alex told me he had started a support group for other children who were being forced to live with parents they feared. He was determined to campaign for the rights of children to be heard in the court process. "I really, really don't want children to get taken away from their mothers or fathers and given to the abusers," he said. "I'm doing this so their childhood doesn't get destroyed like mine did."

When domestic abuse victims say going through Family Court is like walking through the looking glass, I believe them. In all my time as a reporter, I have never felt so disturbed and disoriented as I did when I was investigating the family law system. It's like parts of this system exist in a parallel universe—one in which we don't understand domestic abuse and the impact it has on children.

"Until they sort out the Family Court, people should stop telling women to leave," said one barrister I spoke to, "Nikki," who stayed in a violent relationship herself for ten years after she first saw her husband hit her child. She knew just how unsafe the Family Court could be for victims of abuse, and how hard it would be to prevent her husband getting access, so she stayed in the marriage as a "supervisor." "It was the only way I felt I could protect my son."

If you're a parent making a genuine allegation of abuse in the Family Court, you could be lucky: your judge may understand family violence, your evaluator may be trained to recognize it, and your lawyer might believe you. For many domestic abuse survivors, though, the reality is that they will be dragged through the courts for years after they've left their abuser and will be free of the ordeal only after the courts rule that their children are old enough to decide for themselves. Overwhelmingly, the people who contact me about their cases are mothers, but I've also heard from a handful of fathers who had solid evidence they were abused in their marriage and were met with similarly unprofessional assessments by single experts and disbelief from the bench.

I want to put a sharper point on this. The family law system is ruining the lives of vulnerable children—kids like Carly, Jess, Tim, Sally, and Alex— who will spend the rest of their lives dealing with the legacy of their trauma. However, these decisions can have even more tragic consequences. According to the Center for Judicial Excellence in the United States, at least ninety-eight children over the past decade have been killed by a parent or parental figure who was given unsupervised contact by a family court. Nothing can take back the extraordinary harm that has already been done, but we *can* act now to make sure no other child is ordered to live with a parent they fear.

Harry and Mia, whose story opened this chapter, were returned to live with their mother after their father relinquished custody. When I asked Harry what he thought about the Family Court, he said, "I think [the] Family Court is terrible, and it shouldn't be a real thing, because children shouldn't be put with their abusive parent. You can't accuse the one parent who isn't doing anything wrong and basically steal their children and give them to an abuser." To other kids who were being ordered to live with a parent they were afraid of, he had one last thing to say: "Don't give up. Keep trying."

10.

Dadirri

Dadirri is inner, deep listening and quiet, still awareness... In our Aboriginal way, we learned to listen from our earliest days. We could not live good and useful lives unless we listened... We learned by watching and listening, waiting and then acting. Our people have passed on this way of listening for over 40,000 years. We have learned to speak the white man's language. We have listened to what he had to say. This learning and listening should go both ways... We are hoping people will come closer. We keep on longing for the things that we have always hoped for—respect and understanding.

MIRIAM-ROSE UNGUNMERR-BAUMANN, ABORIGINAL
ELDER, ARTIST, AND EDUCATOR, NAUIYU (DALY RIVER)

Humankind has not woven the web of life. We are but one thread within it. Whatever we do to the web, we do to ourselves. All things are bound together. All things connect.

CHIEF SEATTLE, ANCESTRAL LEADER OF THE SUQUAMISH TRIBE, 1854

It was a winter's night in the "Bronx," and the Night Patrol van was doing what it always did: picking up kids wandering the streets late at night. Some were too scared to go home because of the drinking and fighting there; others ran around outside because there was no room inside to sleep.

The only unusual thing about the van that night was the famous white man sitting in it. In a long-sleeved orange patrol shirt, then-Australian prime minister Malcolm Turnbull was looking out the window, seeing firsthand what young kids in this remote town got up to after dark.

His was the first visit from a prime minister in more than thirty-five years. After all this time, it had suddenly become unavoidable: in the summer, the town of over three thousand people in the Northern Territory had become a household name when nightmarish headlines announced that in this place, an adult man had raped a three-year-old girl. Even more horrifying was the fact it wasn't unforeseen: family and police had been begging community services to protect the little girl since she was eleven weeks old. So severe were the toddler's injuries that it was reported she had to be put in an induced coma and flown to a capital city for treatment. By the time Turnbull was being driven into the Bronx, fifteen kids had been removed from their families.

With Turnbull in the van that night was Fiona, who was the acting CEO of the local Aboriginal organization. "I didn't tell him we were taking him down there, and I didn't tell any of the cops. I just said, 'Oh, we'll take you on a night tour with the Night Patrol and you can get some photo opportunities.'" As the van drove into the notoriously rough area, Fiona turned to the prime minister, and said, "Oh, look where we are! This area's the Bronx, Malcolm, and look over there—that's the house where the little girl got raped." As they approached the house, Fiona asked the driver to slow down. "I made him look," she says. "Made him see it."

Turnbull was visibly shaken and distressed. "I don't want your tears, Malcolm," Fiona told him. "I want your answers."

———

Fiona's arrival in this tiny town in central Australia was something of a fluke. "I put 'remote' into a job search on CareerOne, and the first job that came up was something that had been advertised for six months. Nobody wanted it." The position was for a family violence educator at the town's women's refuge. Fiona wrote an application then and there, and two weeks later packed up her three-bedroom house in Tasmania and flew to remote central Australia with little more than a toddler on her hip.

People told her she was crazy. Moving away from Tasmania meant leaving the one state where a magistrate had given her the equivalent of a lifetime protection order against her horrifically violent ex-partner. But Fiona says she had to get out. "I just got fucking jack of it, basically. I thought, *If I don't shift this, I'm gonna be a victim for the rest of my life.*"

Moving to one of the most violent towns in Australia may seem an unlikely choice for someone who had just survived some of the most terrifying violence imaginable, but Fiona needed to do something with all the trauma and the ugliness she'd experienced. "I thought there must be something I can offer to women who are some of the most violated and abused women in Australia." Sitting on her deck late one night, drenched in the sweat of another summer heat wave, Fiona told me her story.

She'd been with Cameron (not his real name) for six months when she knew she wanted to leave. When he took control of her finances and wouldn't let her use her key-cards, she knew it was domestic abuse. She'd been working in women's services for half her life, and she'd seen this pattern play out time and again. She also knew from experience that she was dealing with someone she couldn't just up and leave. "He was a very, very, very dangerous man," says Fiona. "I'm an Aboriginal woman, and he was an Aboriginal man, and basically he used a technique of never leaving me alone. He surrounded me with male family members all the time, especially when he wasn't present." Twice she tried to get away, and both times he tracked her down and sexually assaulted her. "The consequences of leaving just weren't worth it."

The first time Cameron physically attacked her, police responded and drew their guns on him. "But then they just looked at it and went, *Oh, it's just Aboriginals fighting*, so they put a gun on me." An Aboriginal Legal Service worker shouted at police to stop: "She hasn't done anything, I've been here the whole time—he's the perpetrator, get him!"

The next attack on Fiona was unbelievably vicious. "It was a forty-five-minute sustained attack: I was threatened with weapons, slashed, kicked down flights of stairs, punched through a solid wooden door, and, just to be really nice to me, he kicked me in between the legs," she says, then recites a shocking list of injuries: "two skull fractures, broken wrist, broken cheekbone, broken eye socket, lost four teeth, broken ribs, broken fingers, broken toes." As Fiona was trying to get away, Cameron slashed her back with a thirty-centimeter carving knife.

This time the police, responding to a call from the neighbors, took Fiona seriously. Cameron was charged with and later convicted of six offenses, including grievous bodily harm and assault with a deadly weapon.

Fiona was so relieved when it came time for sentencing, as she was sure he'd get jail time and that she would be able to get away from him. "Imagine my horror, then," she says, "when he got let off." In court, she sat aghast as Cameron charmed the magistrate and feigned confusion. "He played the magistrate like a fiddle, and the magistrate bought it." Cameron was let off with a good behavior bond. He walked out of court and stormed over to Fiona, who was standing on the sidewalk. Right there, in front of family violence support workers on the front steps of the court, Cameron knocked Fiona out cold.

He wasn't jailed for that either. All Fiona could do was get a restraining order against him. But that too was easy for Cameron to get around: he just forced her to move with him to another state, where the restraining order wasn't valid. "I think we lived in like five states over five years."

Fiona's situation is still so precarious that we've decided not to share the rest of the details here. Suffice to say, hers is one of the most incredible survival stories I've ever heard. Fiona's tactical ingenuity was the only thing that kept her and her daughter alive. When they finally escaped, her ex-partner was deemed so dangerous that police moved them from safe house to safe house, where they would occasionally share a roof with criminal witnesses under police protection.

The housing estate she and her two-year-old daughter were eventually placed in was so dilapidated that it barely functioned as even basic shelter: "It had no front windows in the lounge room, and no curtains. We didn't have anything. I just remember lying on the floor, in the middle of a Tasmanian winter, with no bedding, no electricity, no heating, no curtains, and with the wind just howling in through these boarded-up windows. And I was too petrified to move, because everything I saw outside those windows was him coming to kill us."

For two years, Fiona toughed it out. During that time, as she tried to work through her extreme trauma to care for her traumatized little girl, she also had a full-time job just dealing with the family violence services that were managing her case. "At the height of it, I had twenty-seven different services engaged. They would just ring one after the other, and say they'd been referred by another service I was with, and that they'd need to take some notes on my case, so could I tell them what had happened? I was just continually having to talk about it."

Some of these service workers subjected Fiona to practices that were not only culturally insensitive, but downright bizarre. One day, while she was in the kitchen making tea, family violence workers cut a lock of her daughter's hair, intending to make it into a Christmas gift as a present for Fiona. When she saw what they were doing, she felt a surge of fear go through her. "In Aboriginal culture—and particularly the culture my daughter comes from—cutting someone's hair and taking it is a sign that you're gonna use magic on them," Fiona explains. "But you try explaining to white family violence practitioners the fear you have that he might get hold of your child's hair. They would just say to you, 'Don't be so ridiculous.'"

After two years living at the housing estate, Fiona was done. Even though she knew she'd lose the protection of her lifetime order, she knew she had to reinvent her life. When she saw the position in the remote Australian town advertised online, she jumped on it.

In 2011, when she and her daughter landed in central Australia, the town they had moved to had the highest rate of domestic assault in the entire Northern Territory, and a murder rate thirty times higher than the United States. It was practically designed for alcoholism: ten liquor stores catered to a population of fewer than three thousand people. Extreme violence in the town was so ordinary that brutal street fights were a regular occurrence. The women's refuge was doing a heroic job with scant resources, but although it affected virtually everybody in town, family violence was not something that was being talked about. "The very first thing I did when I arrived," says Fiona, "was I started talking to a lot of people, going, 'You have a very high tolerance level to violence in this community. Do you realize that?'" In the former gold-mining town, there were signs in the street announcing how many days it had been since the last mining accident. Fiona would ask people: "Where's the sign up in town saying it's been 0 days since a woman got knocked around?"

She hadn't come all this way to go softly. "I basically did whatever I could do in that community," she says. "I think I was just exploding with post-traumatic growth." Fiona trained everyone in sight: the Royal Flying Doctors, all the staff at the local hospital, the police and service providers. Her singular focus was on changing whatever she could to better protect women and children. For instance, when she saw female assault victims being taunted by their perpetrator's relatives in the hospital waiting room, she agitated to set up a separate trauma space for those women.

"We just kept driving it from every conceivable angle," she says. The refuge even brought an Aboriginal comedian into town "to give the community a pressure release." In a community that was being deformed by violence, there was no point in looking at family violence in isolation. So Fiona set about educating people on lateral violence and talking openly about the tension between the black and white people in town. "The things that were completely useless were things like 'the cycle of violence,' because you've got communities who are in crisis constantly—there's no honeymoon period for them."

Fiona never considered herself off duty. One day, during a massive street brawl that involved more than a hundred people, she drove up the middle of it shouting, "Women's refuge peacekeeper—come on all you kids, jump in the back!" and drove the kids back to her house to make pancakes until the fighting stopped. On top of all this, she had a caseload of up to forty women, and she designed what would become an award-winning family violence education program called No More Now! "It was relentless."

Fiona was also determined to break the taboo on talking about family violence. To start this, she did something deceptively simple: she printed a run of purple T-shirts, emblazoned with the number of the women's refuge and the slogan "No More Violence." "We started distributing them for free in the community, and they just went off. Then the men came to me and said, 'You know those shirts you got for women? Where's our shirts?'" So I did a run of them for men—black T-shirts—and then we did kids, and pretty soon we had bandannas and this and that. My philosophy was, it's really difficult to talk about this issue in the community, but everyone's concerned about it. You gotta make people wear the problem and make it visible to generate the discussion."

Talking about it was only the beginning, though. The violence Fiona was dealing with in the town was extreme. She saw babies that had been sexually abused. She saw women who had been attacked with knives and machetes, who had injuries from bottle stabbings and slashings, severe burns, and choke holds, and hair ripped out of their heads. At the women's refuge, very young girls who had been sexually assaulted would ring the buzzer.

Police in town commonly treated female victims like criminals. Even women with severe head injuries would be driven to the refuge in the back of a paddy wagon and "unceremoniously dumped" on the doorstep. "It was just a horrible, horrible situation," says Fiona.

You'd think that Fiona's own extreme trauma would have been compounded by witnessing such atrocities, but that wasn't the case. "I don't quite know how to explain this," she says, "but I just got inspired by that community and how resilient and culturally loyal those women are. So much of the response to those women had been anti-cultural. It was an honor to sit with those women and say, 'How do we deal with this better?'"

By the time the prime minister visited in the winter of 2018, Fiona was in no mood to hold back. Just prior to taking him on a tour to the Bronx, she was at a buffet dinner with him and some of the area's Traditional Owners. Turnbull looked tired; he was already facing the stirrings of a leadership challenge that would soon end his prime ministership. "I think Malcolm was also just shell-shocked by what he'd seen," says Fiona. "At dinner, he came over and said, 'Can I sit with you, Fiona?' And he sat down with his buffet plate, looked at me, and said, 'Can you tell me what's really going on here? I need to understand what's going on here.'" Fiona was typically direct. "You have to deal with the poverty and inequity here by investing in the town and the region," she replied. A short time later, the government announced a multimillion-dollar funding deal to boost the local economy.

Fiona cackles when she talks about it now. "Never underestimate how effective black women can be. Most people are just looking for what the answer is, and they're looking for something that's a win-win. Now they've got $60 million for that region. Let's hope a good amount of that is used to protect women and children."

Still, Fiona isn't under any illusions. She knows First Nations communities need more than just cash to deal with family violence. In the long term, no amount of fiddling with policies and programs is going to be enough. The problem lies at the heart of how Indigenous people are policed and governed—not only in Australia, but also across North America. Just as Biderman's Chart of Coercion describes the tactics and behaviors of domestic violence perpetrators, so too does it describe the systematic abuses these states inflict on Indigenous peoples. Just like victims of domestic violence, Indigenous people today live under constant surveillance, microregulated by police and governmental agencies; they are degraded and disempowered by a system that sees itself as superior; they are physically abused, denied medical treatment, and humiliated by police who are supposed to protect them; they are promised help and assistance from governments that break their promises time and again; and they are made to believe that they are to blame for the abuses that are inflicted on them. In North America, Native Americans are more likely to be killed by police than any other group—even more than African Americans. As Fiona told the Tasmanian premier in his first week of parliament, "The problem with you white fellas is that you've got my people in a domestic violence relationship. Only we can't call the cops on you, because you *are* the cops."

"That's what domestic violence is all about: inequity and abuse of power," she tells me, still sweating in the unbroken heat as midnight draws close. "And where abuses of power thrive—including the state against Aboriginal people—you are going to find violence flourishing in all the wrong places. Unless you address the overall power dynamic with the state, you'll never get it right. When we see equity, we'll see change."

Right now, the prospect of equity—from remote towns in Australia to reservations across North America—feels abstract and elusive. The power imbalance is oppressive, and it's hard to imagine that changing.

———————

After centuries of systematic degradation and trauma, it should be no surprise that First Nations people in Australia and across North America also suffer the worst family violence. In some communities, it is so endemic that the women living there can't imagine a life without violence. On reservations across North America, Native American mothers "talk to their daughters about what to do when they are sexually assaulted; not *if* they are sexually assaulted, but *when*."[1]

The statistics are brutal. Almost 85 percent of Native American and Alaskan women have been subjected to violence in their lifetime. From intimate partners, more than half have experienced physical violence, and two-thirds have experienced psychological aggression. American Indian and Alaska Native women suffer sexual violence more than any other ethnic group;[2] in some counties, the murder rate of Native women is ten times higher than for any other category of women in America.[3]

What is truly scandalous, though, is the number of Native American women that disappear and are barely looked for. In Montana, where they make up just 3 percent of the population, Native American women account for *30 percent* of all missing persons.

In Australia, the statistics are also shocking. Indigenous women are thirty-five times more likely to be hospitalized for family violence–related assaults, and that's just the national average; in some remote areas, it can be more like *eighty* times the average.[4] They are also eleven times more likely to die from their injuries.[5] When they do, their deaths are scarcely mentioned in the press. As Arrente writer and activist Celeste Liddle says, "the death of Aboriginal women is *expected*."[6] This attitude—a hangover from the "doomed race" mythology that fueled brutal systems of colonization—still thrives in North America as well. In the words of Muscogee woman Professor Sarah Deer, "Native people are simply invisible in the United States."[7]

Indigenous women and children are targeted more than any other group, but their abusers are not always Indigenous men. In fact, for Native American women, the likelihood they'll be abused by a Native man is actually relatively low: *90 percent* of female victims are victimized by a non-Native partner.[8] As Professor Deer writes, "This is an anomaly in American criminology. Most violent crime in America is intraracial. In other words, if you are a white victim, your perpetrator is more likely than not to be white; if you are a black victim, your perpetrator is more likely than not to be black."[9] But not if you're a Native American.

When I started researching how First Nations women and children experienced domestic abuse, I knew the basics. Police often don't take women's complaints seriously and fail to properly investigate when they are assaulted or killed. Stories about this are legion, like the "botched investigation" of the death of twenty-five-year-old Kwementyaye Green, a mother of two found dead in a vacant lot in the central Australian town of Tennant Creek in 2013. Even though her de facto partner, Rodney Shannon, was found lying next to her, police developed what the coroner labeled an "irrational preoccupation"[10] with the explanation, provided by Shannon, that Green had stabbed herself.

I remember the moment when I realized how little I knew: I was listening to *Curtain*, a podcast hosted by journalist Amy McQuire and lawyer Martin Hodgson. Hodgson launched into a monologue that left me breathless and enraged. It started with a bold claim: "Not only are the police and services not actively supporting Aboriginal women," he said, "they're actively *punishing* Aboriginal women who even dare to speak out about domestic violence." I suspected hyperbole. But then Hodgson cited a real case:

> Just last year, an Aboriginal woman supporting her daughter con-
> tacted the police to speak about a domestic violence issue that her
> daughter was experiencing. This is precisely what we ask people
> to do: to support one another, to support their loved ones, and to
> contact the police.
>
> This woman would end up in prison. Why? Because when she
> contacted the police and they came to her home—as she requested
> of them—they discovered that there was a warrant of commitment
> [for an outstanding fine], and she was imprisoned for weeks. It
> could have been longer, but luckily someone paid the fine....
>
> What was that warrant for? An unregistered dog. Police placed
> the civil infraction of an unregistered dog ahead of the lives of two
> Aboriginal women, did not address the issue of domestic vio-
> lence, and instead imprisoned an innocent Aboriginal woman at
> Melaleuca women's prison because she dared try to seek help for
> her daughter.[11]

I couldn't believe what I'd just heard. Arresting and jailing women for unpaid (and unrelated) fines *after they had actually called police for protection*?

I needed proof that this police response was a pattern of "punishment," so I called Hodgson. As a lawyer, Hodgson works *pro bono* not only for victims of domestic violence, but also for vulnerable people all over the world: from Australians falsely accused of terrorism overseas to African Americans facing execution for crimes they didn't commit (such as the case of Rodney Reed, who has been on death row since 1988, and who many believe to be innocent). Hodgson does all this from his home above a garage on the south coast of New South Wales, supporting himself the way he did when studying law: writing late at night for car and motorcycle magazines.

When we speak, he's still tired from the night before, when he slept in his car outside a local Indigenous woman's house. He was there not as a warning to her abuser, but to the police. "This is a very common example of what happens to Aboriginal women in particular," he explains. "Often women will make a report, and then the police will turn up, and before they do anything about the DV [domestic violence], they're asking everyone for bloody identification. Of course, someone will have outstanding fines, so they'll be trying to drag them away. It's an inflamed situation, because often teenage sons wanna protect their mom, but are really in no position to do that."

In the case of the woman whose house he slept outside, "the stepson is sixteen and has some outstanding fines. So the mom is very scared of going to the police, because as has happened in the past, if she rings the police for help, they'll do nothing for her and they'll drag her son away." The stepson's fines are for "the most petty stuff imaginable—shoplifting's the worst of it." It's even worse for this particular woman, explains Hodgson; police now see her as a "troublemaker" because after she reports her abuser, she can't follow through with taking him to court "for her own reasons." The man abusing her is an ice [crystal methamphetamine] user, and "when the ice hits town, she's at risk, and she can't call the police." This woman is in a terrible bind: she's a mother to several children, she's illiterate, and she's quite financially dependent on her abuser. "And of course because he has a job and he's not Indigenous, the police take his side and become de facto abusers, as far as I'm concerned," says Hodgson.

The reason Hodgson spent the night in his car is because this woman did call the police, and they told her they wouldn't come if she was going to kick up a fuss about them taking her son away. "So she's in a no-win situation," explains Hodgson. "Technically, she can't house someone who's wanted, which is a completely abusive, manipulative thing on the police's behalf. Go and catch him if you're any good at your job, he's not home most of the day." Hodgson slept in his car outside her house as a warning to police: It would be easier for them to drive past than to come in and hassle her. "I like the fact the cops know I won't back down, because half the time it's the only thing that stops them doing what they really want to do. If they see my car parked out in front of someone's place, it's better to just keep driving. That's why me sleeping in the car out front works."

Hodgson says he spends half the time protecting his clients from perpetrators and half the time protecting them from police. It's hard to imagine a worse response from the state than what he describes. When a woman underground reports her abuse, she not only needs protection and support, but also someone to challenge her abuser's worldview. She needs someone to tell her it's not her fault, that she is not a bad person—that, in fact, asking for help is an act of courage. When she gets none of this, and instead gets arrested for something as petty as an unpaid fine, her shame is supercharged by the humiliation of her arrest and the degradation of being incarcerated. After this additional trauma, it's much less likely she'll seek help from the system again.

The situation for Native American women—especially those living on reservations—*should* be different. Indian tribes have a kind of sovereignty on their reservations; they have their own police and they run their own courts, with their own judges and prosecutors. But that sovereignty is severely limited by the power of the state.

Since 1978, many perpetrators of domestic abuse on reservations have been protected by a ruling from the highest court in the country. Until 2013, non-Native offenders were gifted virtual immunity by the Supreme Court decision *Oliphant v. Suquamish Indian Tribe* (1978), which ruled that on their reservations, tribes did not have criminal jurisdiction over non-Indian perpetrators. This meant that if tribal police were called to a domestic violence incident, and found that an offender was not Native, they would have no authority to remove or charge him, and would have to call for city or county backup (which would seldom arrive). James Kilbourne, a prosecutor on Cherokee territory, outlined how abjectly racist this was when he commented to the *Wall Street Journal*, "Where else do you ask: How bad is the crime, what color are the victims, and what color are the defendants? ...We would not allow this anywhere else except Indian country."[12]

Now think back to that earlier statistic: more than 90 percent of Native women who've suffered violence from a partner have been victimized by a non-Native offender. Why this anomaly? As Assistant Professor Andrea Smith explains, "non-Native perpetrators often seek out a reservation place because they know they can inflict violence without much happening to them." On average, according to the U.S. Census, more than three-quarters of people living on reservations are non-Native.

Marcus Dominic Wells, a reservation chairman, described to a U.S. Senate Committee what happened to one tribal member when she called police for help:

> BIA [Bureau of Indian Affairs] responded and could not remove the non-Indian. The county would not respond. Officers managed to control the situation and left the residence. Hours later, the officer responded a second time. Things had escalated. The woman, in self-defense, had pulled a knife in an effort to protect herself and her children. The BIA officer removed her and she was booked for the offense. Her children were taken by social services. Where is the justice?[13]

The only way a non-Native perpetrator could be prosecuted was if the U.S. Attorney's office—often hundreds of miles away—could be persuaded to investigate. It took a lot to persuade them. The perpetrator had to have caused serious bodily injury: i.e., something that was life-threatening or caused extreme physical pain, disfigurement, or serious impairment. The emphasis was entirely on the severity of the injury and the likelihood that the perpetrator could be prosecuted, not on the risk the perpetrators posed to their victims. Of the assault matters referred to the U.S. Attorney from 2005 to 2009, fewer than half were prosecuted (as of 2017, the Department of Justice was still refusing to prosecute a third of cases referred from Indian country).

This was all supposed to change in 2013. That year, then-President Barack Obama signed the reauthorization of the Violence Against Women Act (VAWA), which appeared to overturn *Oliphant v. Suquamish* by giving tribes the power to prosecute non-Indian perpetrators of domestic abuse. Before the signing, Diane Millich, a survivor from the Southern Ute Indian Tribe in Colorado, stood in traditional dress at a lectern adorned with the presidential seal and told her story. In the 1980s, when she was twenty-six, she had fallen in love with a white man, who had then moved in with her on the reservation. The violence he subjected her to was extreme—"more than one hundred incidents of being slapped, kicked, punched, and living in horrific terror"—and for years it went unpunished. After one beating, as the *New York Times* reported, he even called the local sheriff himself to prove there was nothing that would stop him. He wasn't arrested until he showed up with a gun at her office, at the Federal Bureau of Land Management, and shot a coworker who tried to protect her. As Millich said at the ceremony, "[i]f the bill being signed today were law when I was married, it would have allowed my tribe to arrest and prosecute my abuser."

To date, these new regulations have empowered at least eighteen tribes to prosecute non-Native perpetrators. The cultural impact of this is seismic;

women who spent years *knowing* that no law stood between them and their abusive partners are now starting to report in larger numbers. "We have always known that non-Indians can come onto our lands and they can beat, rape, and murder us, and there is nothing we can do about it," says Lisa Brunner, a survivor of intergenerational domestic abuse from the White Earth Ojibwe Nation. "Now, our tribal officers have jurisdiction for the first time to do something about certain crimes. But it is just the first sliver of the full moon that we need to protect us."[14]

Brunner is talking about the severe limitations placed on these new powers, which cover only physical violence between two intimate partners. For other crimes commonly committed by abusers—threats and intimidation, destruction of property, hurting a pet, even abusing a child—tribal police still have no power to intervene. As Pascua Yaqui Attorney General Alfred Urbina told Vice News, "We've had about four or five cases that we had to dismiss because they involved things like trespassing, disorderly conduct, and...did not involve an actual assault. The offenders in those cases ended up reoffending and physically assaulting the victim a few months later, after we had dismissed the case for that reason."[15] In a cruel twist, tribal police responding to domestic violence calls (the most dangerous of all calls) have little to no protection against a perpetrator threatening or assaulting them, because they cannot legally respond to such acts.

Professor Deer has worked with survivors of sexual violence for more than twenty-five years and was instrumental in getting the changes made to the VAWA in 2013. "It was hard enough to get the jurisdictional fix that we did get... If we had to take on all these other issues as well, it would definitely not have happened." Deer is determined to change this, however, and is demanding that in the next phase of VAWA implementation—held up by partisan squabbling since 2019—all powers be returned to the tribes, particularly the power to prosecute crimes against children. "We are going to fight for that."

Still, not all tribes can take advantage of these new powers. To prosecute non-Indian offenders, tribes need to meet several special requirements; they must recruit non-Indians as jury members and provide public defenders, a costly task for tribes that are often woefully under-resourced. As Vice News reports, this might be possible for the Pascua Yaqui community, near Tucson, but "for remote nations like the Havasupai Tribe, on the edge of the Grand Canyon, that task might be harder to complete."[16] As of 2018, eighteen of the 570 federally recognized tribes were exercising these new powers. Deer sees it as a work in progress. "A lot of tribes don't want to comply with the law, because it has too many strings attached," says Deer. "Each [tribe] is going to have its own angle on this. I think it's far too early to know for sure what the impact of the law will be long term."

However, changes to the law alone will not solve the problem of domestic abuse against Native American women. Police culture maintains an unofficial policy of "official indifference" to Native American women, says Deer. "There is no support for Native American women in this country, from a structural perspective. The system is broken."

On the other side of the world, in Australia, the state response to Indigenous women is a similarly lethal combination of punishment and indifference. Dr. Hannah McGlade, a Noongar human rights lawyer from Western Australia, has advocated for these women for most of her adult life—from the Australian courts all the way to the United Nations, where she is a member of the permanent Forum on Indigenous Issues.

One woman's story in particular infuriates McGlade. "Did I show you the Tamica Mullaley case in Broome?" she asks. "So many people don't know her story." I interrupt: many people have told me there was a terrible story in Broome (on the coast of Western Australia) a few years back, but no one has been able to tell me the woman's name. "Yes," replies McGlade, "we don't know about Tamica Mullaley, little Charlie, and what they did to Mum. There was no mercy for her."

———————

Over the past five years, I've examined some of the most shocking cases imaginable. I've wept and raged more times than I care to count, but nothing has come close to the anger I felt when I read about what happened to Tamica and her baby Charlie.

A warning to readers: this is a harrowing story. I've done my best to write it as sensitively as possible, including only the necessary details. If you can, please stick with it. Tamica's story happened in Australia, but it bears all the hallmarks of the colonial oppression that persists in both Australia and North America. This is not just a story about one family, in one place. Rather, it is a forensic examination of how racism and prejudice operate to condemn Indigenous women and children.

The story begins on the night of March 19, 2013, at a birthday gathering for Tamica's father, Ted. "We had a little cake that night," says Ted Mullaley, "and then Tamica was going out." Ted speaks clearly, deliberately. He looks like a bush poet or an aging rock-and-roller, with his long mustache, goatee, and wavy gray hair falling to his shoulders. Ted runs a successful trucking business in Broome and—like many Indigenous grandparents—spends most of his free time looking after his beloved grandchildren.

As Tamica was getting ready, she asked Ted if she could leave Charlie, her ten-month-old son, at home with him. "This really upsets me a lot, because I said no," says Ted, "hoping that would make her behave herself and come home at a reasonable time."

Unbeknownst to Ted, trouble was already brewing. Tamica had just come back from Perth, and there were rumors going around town that her new boyfriend, Mervyn Bell, had cheated on her while she was away. He'd already been acting weird that afternoon, when they'd been out drinking with friends. Tamica was building herself up to confront him.

When Tamica arrived at the house, she put Charlie down in the living room to sleep and went outside to hang out with Mervyn and their friends. On the phone from Broome, a coastal town in Western Australia, she tells me what happened next. "I mentioned [the rumors], and he just started being a real asshole." It was getting late, so Tamica decided to walk to a friend's place to pick up a stroller so she could take Charlie home.

Mervyn followed her in his car and then got out and attacked her. "He just went right off, punching me—I tried to get away but he just came up behind me and bashed me more. That's when he really hurt me, and stripped me naked." A nurse from the local hospital was at home when she heard screaming in the street and saw Mervyn bashing Tamica. She ran outside and shouted at Mervyn to leave, and then called the police.

Ted was in bed when his phone rang. It was the nurse: Tamica was sheltering in a carport, naked and badly beaten, wrapped only in a sheet the nurse had given her. Police were on their way. Ted jumped straight out of bed and into his car, desperate to get there before the police did.

As Ted turned onto the street where Tamica was waiting, his heart sank. "I could see the flashing lights coming down to where the house was." Tamica was in a terrible state, crying and covered in blood. "She was yelling at police, 'Go away, nobody wants you here,' but the police kept pushing themselves onto her," says Ted. Police notes say Tamica was calling them "cunts" and telling them to "fuck off." She didn't want the police involved: "I know that police aren't that great in Broome," she explains. "I just wanted to go with Dad, because it was really embarrassing, you know, being naked with blood everywhere. We know a lot of people in Broome, and this was right on one of the main streets."

The police refused to leave. "We were tasked to attend a disturbance," one officer said, "for a woman who had been kicked out of a car and was naked." They needed to know exactly what happened.

The first major question is why they felt they needed to interview

Tamica then and there. She was a victim of assault, seriously injured, in need of urgent medical attention and desperate for the police to leave her alone. As one officer noted, "Tamica had blood surrounding her right eye"[17]—a clear sign that she had suffered significant head trauma. This alone would have made her behavior erratic and her memory faulty. The police had a duty of care to attend to her as a victim first and a witness second.

Furthermore, the police already had a witness: the nurse had given them her account as soon as they arrived. Then, when Ted arrived, he told them who did it—Mervyn Bell. With all this information, why did the police need to harass a clearly traumatized victim of violence for her account?

In Tamica's words: "I was completely battered and bruised, he hit me all over my head and everything. So yeah, I didn't want to talk to police. I just wanted him charged, and for me to get in the car and go home." However, the police insisted that Tamica explain what happened. Feeling distraught and trapped, she spat at one of the officers, Constable Paul Moore. Ted heard Moore say, "That's it," and then he lunged toward Tamica. "Tamica had the baby," says Ted, "and I grabbed the baby off her, gave him to this girl beside me and tried to protect my daughter." It was chaos: Tamica bolted away from the police, who chased her around her father's car, and when she tripped and fell, Moore pinned her to the ground with his knee in her back. "She's screaming out, 'Dad, help me, help me!'" says Ted. "I said to him, 'Let her up—let the woman policeman deal with her.'" When Moore lifted his knee, Tamica jumped up, scrambled into her father's car, and locked all the doors. Police officers surrounded the vehicle and started belting the windows with their batons. "When they eventually smashed the passenger-side window," says Ted, "she jumped out the driver-side door, and then they grabbed her and held her down again, and threw her in the paddy wagon." When Ted asked them what they were doing, police told him they were taking his daughter to jail. "I said, 'You can't, she needs help! Call the ambulance!' And they said, 'Oh, the ambulance won't come.' And I said, 'Well, why not?' And they said, 'Well, it won't.' And I said, 'Well, you've gotta take her to the hospital.'"

The police, who were busy arresting Tamica, didn't take the child into their care. Instead, they told two girls to take the ten-month-old away from the scene. Ted was torn. "I couldn't take Baby with us," he says, "because I had to help Tamica."

When they got to the hospital, Tamica was hysterical and the doctor refused to see her. To Tamica, distressed and disoriented, anyone in authority was a threat. Ted begged her to calm down. As she settled, the doctor said, "I'll give her one last chance." "And lucky he did," says Ted. Tamica had life-threatening injuries: she had a lacerated kidney, her spleen was badly bruised, and she was bleeding internally. "The doctor said if she hadn't gone to hospital, she would've died in her cell."

Once Ted knew Tamica was being looked after, he raced back to pick up Charlie. When he reached the house, he discovered that Bell had returned and taken off with the child. Ted was beside himself. Racing back to the hospital, he found Constable Eoin Carberry, sitting outside the hospital in a patrol car. "I said, 'I need help, he's taken the baby!'" Ted was in a panic: Bell was not Charlie's father, he told Carberry, and he had grave fears that Bell was going to kill the child. Carberry was unmoved. "He said, 'Well, we haven't got any resources,'" Ted remembers. "I said, 'What do you mean?' And he said, 'Well, we're here looking after your daughter, because she's under arrest.'" When Ted implored him to get somebody else to look for Charlie, the officer replied, "How many cars do you think we got?" "And I'll always remember this," says Ted. "He said, 'We've only got two: one's here looking after your daughter, and the other one's back at the station doing business.' Now, I didn't realize then," says Ted, "but I worked out later that the other police back at the station were writing up charges against Tamica for assaulting them, and me, for hindering police. That's all they were doing."

Ted raced down to the Broome police station and reported Charlie's abduction, told them Bell had stolen and was driving one of Ted's cars, and asked police to look for him. Acting Sergeant Darren Connor, on the front desk that night, said Ted came in smelling of alcohol "and who knows what else," that he was aggressive and irrational, and seemed more concerned about his vehicle than his grandchild. There is no evidence to support Connor's claim, as a later inquiry confirmed.[18] "I hadn't had a drink for thirty years!" Ted exclaims. "So that was totally wrong. It was just a way he looked at it: I was just another blackfella, drunk."

Ted then rang emergency services to report the abduction, hoping they might push police to act. "I want someone to take me serious that this guy is going to kill my grandson," he told the operator. The operator said she would contact the sergeant in Broome, and Ted replied, "Will you tell him how important it is? Please."

The operator called the Broome police station and talked to Constable Joel Wright. When she relayed that Mr. Mullaley was "extremely concerned for his grandson," Wright told her that he knew all about Ted and that Ted had "basically obstructed police all night." When the operator asked if Wright would call Ted, he said he'd talk to his supervisor but he didn't know if anyone would contact Ted: he'd already taken up two hours of police time.[19]

After calling emergency services, Ted drove into the bush, thinking Bell might have parked somewhere to hide out for a while. Just as he was getting going, though, he got a flat tire, and had to call a friend to pick him up. Minutes before 3:00 a.m., he received a chilling, garbled text message from Bell: "talk to us I'm putn welfare on da both of use can't Evan look after ur owne gran child . . .???????????? Wat now popo [police] cumn for use… Haha."[20]

Ted went straight back to the Broome police station, hoping that maybe this text could help them locate Bell. When Ted asked Constable

Wright, who was still on the front desk, if they could check where the message had been sent from, Wright told him it would be too expensive—$800—to run a check like that. Ted said he was happy to pay. Wright refused, insisting it would take too long. Ted asked if he could read the text to him, but Wright brushed him off. When Ted said he wasn't happy, Wright said he would have to come back in the morning and see the Aboriginal liaison officer.

Ted's interaction with Constable Wright was recorded on CCTV that night. The state's Corruption and Crime Commission (CCC) inquiry would find that Ted "appeared animated at times and calm at other times" and report that the footage "also shows Wright shaking hands with Mr. Mullaley, who then waved at Wright in a friendly manner as he walked away."[21] But that's not how Wright recorded it. In a report for the Internal Affairs Unit, he said he had found it "challenging to gain information due to E. Mullaley's aggressive and agitated demeanor." The CCC inquiry found no evidence to support this: CCTV showed that Ted would "have sat and provided detailed information for a police statement if asked."[22]

Given how late it was, Ted felt he had no choice but to go home and sleep so he could resume the search for Charlie at first light. As he walked the 100 meters from the police station to his house, he heard a car driving slowly behind him. He turned around to see Constable Wright following him in a patrol car and shining a spotlight on him. "I swore at him and said, 'Don't shine that effing light on me anymore,' or something, and he said, 'And you stop ringing us, too.' They told me not to ring anymore. That's written in all my statements. It's something I'll never forget." According to Constables Wright and Connor, that was not their last contact with Ted that night. What they say happened next defies belief, given how intent Ted had been on finding Charlie and the fact that just an hour earlier he had been willing to pay $800 on the spot to geolocate him. According to the police, however, after Ted returned home, he made another call to the station to tell them everything was fine: he had spoken to Bell, Charlie was safe, and they didn't need to look for him anymore. At 4:15 a.m., Constable Wright updated the file on Charlie's disappearance with a new entry, based on this supposed phone call:

TPC received from Edward Mullaley stating that Mervyn Bell has contacted him and they have had a long and heartfelt conversation. Mullaley states that he no longer has any welfare concerns for the child. He states that Bell loves the child and is caring for him well. Bell explained the evening's events to Mullaley, who now believes that it is good for the child to be with Bell. Bell has arranged to meet Mullaley and transfer custody of the child during the morning (daylight). DCP [Department of Child Protection] advised of development. They have requested that any further updates be provided to the Broome DCP office.[23]

Acting Sergeant Connor (who had earlier described Ted as drunk and aggressive) told the CCC that he was with Wright during this phone call, and that they later discussed it. When I asked Ted if he made this call to Constable Wright, he was emphatic. "No, no, no," he says. "I don't recall that at all. I never felt that Charlie was safe at any time."

What is clear is this: Wright and Connor failed to do the most basic police work on Charlie's abduction. They failed to enter the most basic—and crucial—information in Charlie's file: Bell's violent criminal history and Ted's fears that Bell would hurt or kill the boy. Neither officer filed a missing person report, either. Connor explained this failing by saying he didn't consider Charlie missing because it was common for kids in Indigenous communities to be looked after by multiple family members, and he didn't know that Bell had assaulted Tamica that night. If he really didn't know about the assault, that reveals another catastrophic failure of communication within the Broome police system, because the police's own notes show that Ted told the two officers at the scene of the assault that Mervyn Bell was the perpetrator. He also told police that this same perpetrator had abducted Charlie and that Charlie's life was in grave danger. The only way Connor could maintain his apparent belief that Charlie was just being "looked after" by a member of his extended family is if he paid no heed whatsoever to Ted's reports.

At 6:00 a.m. on March 20, Connor handed the duty desk over to Sergeant William Withers. He says he briefed Withers on what had happened overnight, but Withers has no recollection of any briefing.[24] When he began work that morning, he had no idea that Bell had viciously assaulted Tamica and abducted Charlie, or that Ted had made several reports the night before, including calling for aid.

When Ted returned to the station that morning, he was hoping to hear that police had begun a search for Charlie. "You know, my sister works with child protection, and she says an alert is supposed to blare when a kid goes missing like that. Everyone should swing into action." By that time, ten-month-old Charlie had been missing for more than six hours.

Ted was horrified to find that Broome police hadn't even started to look for Charlie. There were only two roads Bell could have taken out of town: a right turn out of Broome, which would have put him on the road south to Port Hedland; or a left. "I sort of knew he'd gone to the right, toward Port Hedland," says Ted, "because he had phone reception. But they weren't interested in looking either way."

Ted's instincts were right. At 5:45 a.m., Bell pulled into the closed Pardoo Roadhouse, 460 kilometers south of Broome, on the road to Port Hedland. He tried to steal some gas by cutting the hose, and when that didn't work, he drove around until they opened, then filled up and took off without paying. At 6:40 a.m., staff from the Pardoo Roadhouse called the police to report the theft but were told that police didn't attend drive-aways.

As Bell sped away from the roadhouse, a young guy driving behind him called the police to report that a man who'd driven off without paying for fuel was now driving erratically down the highway. Bell's driving was so alarming that a truck driver going the other way also called the police to report him. The Broome police thus missed—or ignored—this chance to locate baby Charlie. "If Broome police had rung Hedland and said, look, we're looking for an 80 series, this color, with this bloke driving it," says Ted, "police would've known that was the car."

Several hours later, Sergeant Withers tasked an officer with calling roadhouses north and south of Broome, which the officer did. Withers also asked him to telephone police stations in both directions. Phone records from the Broome police station indicate that this was not done.

It was 10:00 a.m. before officers went to interview the two women who had been caring for Charlie when he was abducted. At 10:58 a.m., Sergeant Withers called the Police Operations Center in Perth. He told Inspector Trevor Davis that an infant was missing, having been taken by its mother's current partner, and that the Broome police were considering scaling it up to a child abduction scenario. Withers told Davis that the child's grandfather had reported Bell threatening the mother that he would take and kill the child. Davis replied that unless Withers had evidence of these threats—a statement from the mother, for example—there was nothing Perth could do.[25] By that time, Tamica—despite her severe injuries and against doctors' recommendations—had discharged herself from the hospital. She left first thing that morning, right after Ted told her that Charlie had been taken. "I took off from the hospital to go and look for him," she says. In severe pain, she ran two kilometers to a friend's house to borrow his car, then rushed around town, stopping at houses where she thought Bell might have stayed overnight. "By then, most of [the] town knew Charlie was missing, because Dad had rung everyone looking. Everyone was looking for him." Deep down, though, Tamica knew Bell had left town.

Around 11:20 that morning, in Roebourne—some eight hundred kilometers south of Broome—a truck driver who worked for Ted saw a car on the highway that belonged to his boss. Ted hurried back to the Broome police station and reported that Bell had been seen on the road to Karratha, forty kilometers past Roebourne. When police said they would set up a roadblock in Carnarvon—more than six hundred kilometers past Karratha—Ted was furious. "Do you realize how far away Carnarvon is?" he fumed. "I ran amok in the police station actually," he says. "I abused them, to be honest with you."

Ted's sister, who had flown in from Perth that day to help, said, "Let's get out of here." Outside the police station, she rang a homicide detective she knew through her child protection work. On the phone, that detective told her not to talk to anyone else and that he would be on the next flight. "He was absolutely devastated about how they were treating us," says Ted. "He was a helluva nice person. A really, really good policeman."

At 12:57 p.m.—more than thirteen hours after Charlie's abduction was reported—the Broome police finally broadcast an alert about it to all districts. Less than an hour later, as Ted and Tamica were sitting with Broome police personnel, Bell pulled up to the Fortescue Roadhouse in Mardie, 930 kilometers south of Broome, and burst through the front door with a baby in his arms. Yelling Charlie's name, Bell strode toward one of the tables and laid Charlie down on the table in front of Gavin Duff, who was in the middle of his lunch. As Bell hollered for an ambulance, he started trying to resuscitate Charlie. Duff looked at the infant in horror. There was "significant bruising on his body," "a large welt on the side of his head," and "a mark on the center of his chest, where it had started to peel." Bell was worked up, yelling, "Come on, come on," so Duff took over and tried to revive Charlie. When paramedic Gary Harris arrived at the Roadhouse, he put a stethoscope on Charlie to see if he could find a pulse.

But Charlie was dead.

He had been alone with Mervyn Bell for fifteen hours.

Back in Broome, the police told Ted and Tamica that Charlie had been found and was in an ambulance going to Karratha. Ted and Tamica were loading up the car to drive to Karratha when two policemen walked toward them. "They just said bluntly to Tamica, 'Your baby's gone,'" says Ted. "She lost it—ran down the road, rolled in the dirt...."

Five years later, Tamica can barely talk about that moment. "I ran off, crying and screaming, didn't want anyone near me. I ran to the church and was sitting in the church crying."

Tamica's mother, who was going to fly to Broome to be with Tamica, had changed her ticket to Karratha when she heard that baby Charlie had been found. When she got to the Karratha hospital, staff refused to let her see the child's body. It may have been for her own protection. The post mortem revealed devastating injuries to the ten-month-old boy: burns, abrasions, bruising, internal bleeding, and a broken arm and broken leg. His genitals had also been seriously injured.

For Charlie's memorial a few days later, relatives flew in from all around Australia. Ted held Tamica as she sobbed outside the Our Lady Queen of Peace Cathedral. In the memorial program, Tamica wrote a poem for her baby boy, titled "My Child":

So precious, so innocent, not yet knowing what life holds,
Much to learn, much to see, much to hear, much to need.
Loving, wanting, adoring, and demanding.
I love you my child, my second son. I love you my baby, my dear
    Charlie Boy.

———

In 2014, Bell was found guilty of the rape and murder of ten-month-old Charlie Mullaley. "Once in every ten years a crime is so evil it shocks the public," said Justice John McKechnie, as people in the public gallery wept. He sentenced Bell to life imprisonment. Nine months later, in September 2015, Bell killed himself in Casuarina Prison.

Tamica was relieved to hear that Bell was dead. Barely a month later, though, she and her father were back in court. The Broome police—who had charged Tamica with assault and Ted with obstructing police on the night of Charlie's abduction—had decided *not* to drop the charges after Charlie was found murdered. They had pressed those charges, and now they were taking Tamica and Ted to court.

In finding them both guilty, Magistrate Stephen Sharatt said that Tamica had clearly been in control of her senses, because during her scuffles with the police she was worried that her baby would see her bloody and injured. He commended Ted—who freely admitted in court that he had tried to prevent the police from arresting his daughter—on his "candor and honesty," saying, "Rarely do you see such honesty in the witness box." Ted was given a criminal record and a $300 fine. Tamica was given a twelve-month suspended sentence. Magistrate Sharatt said, "If ever there was a time for the court to be merciful, it's this matter today."

Outside the court, Tamica addressed the media, asking why police were more interested in prosecuting her than they had been in searching for her missing baby boy. "They never looked for Charlie at all, and the police need to be accountable for not looking for him," she told reporters. "They could have looked for him and he'd still be alive. It's all wrong, but this is the law and this is how things work."

In April 2016, Western Australia's corruption watchdog investigated the response of Broome police to the abduction of Charlie Mullaley. Although it concluded that several police failures that night had contributed to a delayed and ineffective response, it held that those failures did not justify a finding of serious misconduct. "Whether a more rapid response may have saved Charlie is impossible to know," the report found, "but it is important to recognize that Bell alone was responsible for Charlie's fate."[26] The Mullaley family responded with its own statement:

> There are too many "don't recall" comments and a lot of "notes were not taken" by officers. It is convenient for police not to recall certain matters that we consider crucial and to omit details that should have been included. Ted told them [police] that Charlie was at risk but, as the CCC report states, he was not taken seriously and we have lost our beautiful baby boy.
>
> The big question is: What changes have police made? What happens when the next Aboriginal grandfather walks into the station and reports his grandson missing without any action being taken for hours?[27]

The family's lawyer, George Newhouse, from the National Justice Project, was critical of the CCC investigation. "What astounds me is that in the years since Charlie's death no one has examined the conduct of the WA Police when baby Charlie was alive and under their control," he told *The Sydney Morning Herald.* "It seems obvious that the police should have intervened to protect Charlie when they arrived on the scene, but it appears that the WA Crime and Corruption Commission inquiry totally missed this critical aspect of the case."[28]

Ted only talks about this now because his quest for justice is ongoing. "I knew in my heart that something was wrong. I hate talking about it, actually. I knew. I have to talk about it, to get justice. We don't want to see anyone else go through what we've been through."

———

In both Australia and North America, Indigenous women and children have been assailed by the rage of men for hundreds of years. First came the rage of the colonizers: at their color, their freedom, their sexuality. Then came the humiliated fury of some of their colonized men: at being emasculated, enslaved, and rendered powerless to stop their women and children being taken and raped. For generation after generation, Indigenous women have been expected to absorb these furies and never complain. These men have had one thing in common: they could not tolerate women living free and felt entitled to control them. Today, Indigenous women and children in Australia and North America are more vulnerable to men's violence than any other group.

Despite decades of Indigenous activism on both continents, few of us have ever learned the real history of how our countries were colonized. Most of us who want to learn do so bit by bit, picking up fragments from disparate sources—a book, an interview, a story someone told. Among these fragments, it's rare to read or hear about what white men have done—and are still doing—to Indigenous women and girls. As the renowned expert on Indigenous violence and trauma, Emeritus Professor Judy Atkinson, wrote, "It is now alright to write of the guns and the poisoned flour, the killing of black women and children. It is still taboo to acknowledge the horrific level of sexual violence toward Aboriginal women and girls by white males."[29]

The sexual violence perpetrated by European men against Indigenous women and children weaves an invisible thread through the histories of Australia and North America. To understand violence against Indigenous women today, we need to follow that thread back to the beginning.

————

First, though, let's address a perennial question: Is family violence "cultural"? It has often been claimed, even in our courts, that family violence has always been part of Indigenous cultures, and that women and girls were being brutalized long before the colonizers arrived.

It would be naive to suggest that men's violence against women was alien to Indigenous culture before white people arrived. As Atkinson writes in her landmark book *Trauma Trails*, "Aboriginal societies before Cook were not perfect harmonious groups of people living in paradise... All societies have conflict. All humans have ego, bad behavior, hostility...tensions between generations and gender groups, passions in sexual encounters, and attempts to control others."[30] Indeed, gendered violence is at the heart of one of the most widely told ancient Aboriginal stories: that of the Seven Sisters, who were pursued relentlessly by the bad and lusty shape-shifting sorcerer Wati Nyiru, until they rose into the sky and became the seven stars of the Pleiades. The story of the Seven Sisters is danced, sung, and painted across Australia, and told to Aboriginal girls as a cautionary tale. Ancient myths depicting gendered violence are common to virtually every culture, indicating that men's violence against women has been a constant throughout human history.

However, traditional tales of gendered violence also give us some clue to the status of the women who were subjected to it. As Professor Sarah Deer cites in her book, *The Beginning and End of Rape*, a traditional Ojibwe tale tells of a woman who, after being raped by men from a warring tribe, goes on to become revered by her people as a medicine woman and warrior. As Deer points out, the Ojibwe woman in this story is not defiled, stigmatized, or shamed by her rape, as she would have been in European culture. She is recognized instead for her incredible strength.[31]

Stories aside, what do we know about responses to gendered violence in these cultures before colonization? Quite a lot, as it turns out. Put simply, Native Americans did not devalue women and children nor regard them as the property of men. Unlike European law, which considered the rape of a woman to be a crime against her husband or father (depending on whose property she was at the time), Native Americans broadly categorized rape as a crime against the woman, who had an inviolable right to her bodily integrity. The Lakota culture, for example, held that "the woman owned her body and all the rights that went with it."[32] Other observers from the early years of British colonization attested to the rarity of interpersonal violence in Native American tribes. Said one fur trader, Ephraim Webster, who lived with the Onandaga and Oneida people in 1776: "The Indian have no altercations, and in ten years I have not heard any angry expressions nor seen any degree of passion. They treat their women with respect, even tenderness. They used no ardent spirits. They settled differences amicably."[33]

Webster's testimony is one amongst dozens on the historical record. Given this, why do so many of us believe family violence was cultural for First Nations people? Because in the decades (and even centuries) after European invasion, the lives of these peoples were recorded largely by amateur observers who could not understand what they were seeing, whose perspectives were twisted by racism and prejudice, and many of whom were outright fabricators.

Consider the evidence for the so-called tradition of "bride-capture" in Australia. Bride-capture was considered one of the earliest "proofs" that violence against women was "cultural" in Indigenous communities. As is forensically laid out by historian Liz Conor in *Skin Deep*, this trope was born in 1798, when judge advocate and secretary of the colony David Collins despaired over the "lust and cruelty" inflicted on Aboriginal women by Aboriginal males. Women from enemy tribes were "stupefied with blows," he wrote, until, streaming with blood, the victim was "dragged through the woods by one arm...the lover, or rather the ravisher, is regardless of the stones or broken pieces of trees which may lie in his route, being anxious only to convey his prize sadly to his own party, where a scene ensues too shocking to relate."[34]

The reason Collins couldn't "relate" what happened was because he'd never seen it. His bride-capture story basically amounted to unsubstantiated smut, and its prurience multiplied as the adaptations from his writing proliferated. British newspaper editor Robert Mudie, one of many to cite Collins, added his own rhetorical flourish: "Every marriage...in the neighborhood of Port Jackson...is attended by more violence than the rape of the Sabine women by the Romans."[35] In a geographical dictionary from 1854, Collins again was cited in the category "Races of men in Australia," which read: "The treatment of females in Australia is in the last degree brutal. Wives are not courted or purchased, but are seized upon, stupefied by blows, and then carried off to be the slaves of their unfeeling masters." As Conor explains, such accounts were pure fantasy. "There is no evidence in the colonial archive that Aboriginal men routinely abducted women."[36]

Unsurprisingly, similar rape fantasies were projected onto Native American men, primarily through the "captivity narratives" (one of America's oldest and most influential literary genres) that were wildly popular with American readers in the nineteenth century. These stories generally featured white women taken captive by Native American tribes and Indian men stereotyped as "ruthless rapists with extraordinary sexual appetites." As the political science Professor Stefanie Wickstrom writes, the "white women captives would typically either die heroines resisting Indian sexual advances or be rescued by Euroamerican men."[37] The paranoia and fear stoked by these stories metastasized into virulent hatred toward the Indigenous people and provided the moral cover for settlers to kill them "in the name of civilization and Christianity."[38]

One particularly grisly "account," relayed in Richard Dodge's *The Plains of the Great West and Their Inhabitants*, depicts the "invariable" fate of white women captives:

If she resists at all her clothing is torn off from her person, four pegs are driven into the ground, and her arms and legs, stretched to the utmost, and tied fast to them by thongs. Here, with the howling band dancing and singing around her, she is subjected to violation after violation, outrage after outrage, to every abuse and indignity, until not unfrequently death releases her from suffering.[39]

Most captivity narratives were "apocryphal, and often written by white men,"[40] writes Deer, and "framed with the intent to dehumanize the brutish behavior of Indians, [and yet] there is very little historical documentation of Native men perpetrating rape against white women." As Deer notes, several observers were actually surprised at the *absence* of sexual violence within Native American tribes, especially against captives. Brigadier General James Clinton of the Continental Army told his troops, in 1779, "Bad as the savages are, they never violate the chastity of any women, their prisoners." The Irish-born fur trader, George Croghan, who lived for decades with the Iroquois, similarly testified in the late eighteenth century that rape was abhorred by the Natives: "I have known more than onest thire Councils, order men to be put to Death for Committing Rapes, wh[ich] is a Crime they Despise."[41] Some captivity narratives testified to this, such as that of Mary Rowlandson, a Puritan woman held captive for three months: "By night and day, alone & in company, sleeping all sorts together, and yet not one of them ever offered me the least abuse of unchastity to me in word or action."[42] The function of the bride-capture trope, and of the sexually avaricious Indian, was one and the same: they both served the colonial project of dispossession. As Conor observes, "For the colonizers, these tropes had at least two purposes: they framed all Aboriginal men as brutal perpetrators (undeserving of humanity or sympathy, let alone claims to land), and all Aboriginal women as victims (to be "protected" by the civilized Europeans—very often by removal from their land)."[43] Who would wish for such savage men to live amongst them, and who would therefore oppose their extermination? As writes historian Roxanne Dunbar-Ortiz and Indigenous researcher Dina Gilio-Whitaker, "the implication was that because Europeans were conversely less violent (i.e., civilized) they were more deserving of the land (which was divinely ordained) and thus conquest by any means was necessary."[44] As scholar Andrea Smith notes, the ideology that fueled this was clear and inarguable: "Native women can only be free while under the dominion of white men, and both Native and white women have to be protected from Indian men, rather than from white men."[45] As we will see, the reality—for white and Native women alike—was entirely different.

One story illustrates the tragic irony of this, albeit on a microcosmic scale. Remember Judge Advocate David Collins, the original author of the bride-capture trope? The very year the colonizers arrived in Australia, Collins appears in another historical record concerning domestic violence. In December 1788, Sydney woman Deborah Ellam Herbert appeared in his court to complain about her husband, who had attacked her after their next-door neighbor's pigs overran their vegetable patch. Judge Advocate Collins wasn't as disturbed by *this* man's cruelty: he sentenced *her* to twenty lashes and ordered her to return to her husband.

———

Few anthropologists bothered to study the lives of Australian Aboriginal women (who were generally portrayed as chattel and "no more than domesticated cows"[46]) until the mid-1930s, when anthropologist Phyllis Kaberry went to live with Indigenous groups in the Kimberley. What she revealed overturned "the widespread idea that Aboriginal women are mere drudges, passing a life of monotony and being shamefully mistreated by their husbands."[47] In particular, she showed that intimate relationships were unions of economic interdependence, not male exploitation, in which love and loyalty were primary ("a man would sit for hours by the side of his sick wife, stroking her arm, moving the branches so that they could cast more shade, and fetching her water"). Both parents devoted such care and attention to their children that, according to the Western view at the time, they would be seen as overindulgent. What really set them apart from the colonizers, however, was their balance of power: despite marriages being polygamous and arranged from an early age, women had relative sexual freedom, and even pursued their own affairs. That didn't mean relationships were free from violence, but they didn't generally fit the mold of victim–perpetrator: "I, personally, have seen too many women attack their husbands with a tomahawk or even their own boomerangs, to feel that they are invariably the victims of ill-treatment," wrote Kaberry. "A man may perhaps try to beat his wife if she has not brought in sufficient food, but I never saw a wife stand by in submission to receive punishment for culpable conduct. In the quarrel she might even strike the first blow."[48] Where violence did exist, as was the case in Native American tribes, it generally occurred within a regulated framework of laws, codes, and rituals, and those who broke these laws were called to account and punished.

Perhaps the best proof we have that modern family violence has no specific roots in precolonial Indigenous societies is what we know about the traditional status of Indigenous women. Women in Native American societies had rights that were alien to women in "civilized" Europe. It may surprise readers who believe that patriarchy is *natural* to learn that these Indigenous cultures weren't typically patriarchal. That's because, unlike in Europe, they weren't governed by the principle of "power over," but of "achieving balance in all things."[49] This principle is evident in the native creation stories, in which—unlike the Christian version, which sees Eve created from Adam's rib—men and women emerged at the same time from the womb-like interior of the earth.

As various scholars such as Hilary N. Weaver have documented, many Native societies were *matrilineal*, which meant the children descended from the mother's clan (not the father's), and *matrilocal*, which meant that after the woman was married, her husband moved in with the woman's family.

Although men generally led the tribal councils, in many societies it was the women who chose the leaders. Some could also decide whether or not to go to war: for example, in the Haudenosaunne (also known as the Iroquois), "women held 'veto' power over decisions to go to war," writes Deer, "based on their willingness to provide food for warriors."[50]

Women had rights their European counterparts could not even imagine. Unlike European women, who forfeited their property and legal rights as soon as they were married, Native American women owned most property, including land, animals, and food. They could also divorce their husbands, and if they did—as in the Lakota tribe, for example—they kept the teepee and everything in it, because it already belonged to them. When men were not out hunting, they helped at home, preparing the meals and looking after the children.

Going back through document archives and oral testimonies, Theda Purdue—the most prominent scholar on Cherokee history—has pieced together what precolonial life was like for women in that group. "Men did not dominate women, and women were not subservient to men. Men knew little about the world of women; they had no power over women and no control over women's activities. Women had their own arena of power, and any threat to its integrity jeopardized cosmic order."[51]

Even more pronounced was the status of women among the Iroquois (the federation of the Mohawk, Oneida, Onondaga, Cayuga, Seneca, and Tuscarora nations), whose heartland was in modern-day New York state (and further north, in Canadian Ontario). One Jesuit missionary, Joseph-François Lfitau, who lived among the Iroquois for five years in the early eighteenth century, wrote: "Nothing is more real than this superiority of the women... All real authority is vested in them. The land, the fields, and their harvest all belong to them. They are the souls of the Councils, the arbiters of peace and of war. They have charge of the public treasury. To them are given the slaves. They arrange marriages. The children are their domain, and it is through their blood that the order of succession is transmitted."[52]

Women's equality wasn't the only alien feature of Native American societies. Unlike European societies, in which a person's biological sex dictated their gender, native societies were what we would now call gender-fluid. As the anthropologist Evelyn Blackwood explains, "Individuals possessed a gender identity, but not a corresponding sexual identity, and thus were allowed several options. Sexuality itself was not embedded in Native American gender ideology."[53] Thus, it was not uncommon for women to live as men, and vice versa. As wrote William Roscoe, a fur trader who traveled up the Missouri River: "Woman Chief, a Crow woman who led men into battle, had four wives, and was a respected authority who sat in Crow councils."[54]

In a world where every man, woman, child, and animal was considered sacred, intimate partner violence was a threat to the entire clan. Men who beat their wives "were considered irrational, and his wife had the option of exiling him from her family... Because of his irrationality, [he] was not allowed to own a pipe, hunt, or lead a war party."[55] Not only were men accountable for the way they treated their family—under pain of punishment from the woman's brothers—it was virtually impossible for them to cover it up; communal living meant that nothing could be hidden "behind closed doors."

The depressing contrast for European women is captured in a letter from Abigail Adams to her husband, John Adams, on the eve of the signing of the Declaration of Independence in 1776. Ardently, she implored him to "remember the ladies" in the "new code of laws which I suppose it will be necessary for you to make":

That your Sex are Naturally Tyrannical is a Truth so thoroughly established as to admit of no dispute... Do not put such unlimited power into the hands of the Husbands. Remember all Men would be tyrants if they could. If particular care and attention is not paid to the Ladies we are determined to foment a Rebellion, and will not hold ourselves bound by any Laws in which we have no voice, or Representation.[56]

There was an existing constitution that Abigail could have turned to for inspiration: that of the Iroquois Confederacy. The "Great League of Peace," which included the Mohawks, Oneidas, Onondagas, Cayugas, and Senecas, produced its constitution long before the European invasion. In this document, the position of women is clear and powerful: "The lineal descent of the people of the Five Nations shall run in the female line. Women shall be considered the progenitors of the Nation. They shall own the land and the soil. Men and women shall follow the status of the mother."[57]

Perhaps that is why, when the first wave of nineteenth-century American feminists started to envision a world where women would be equal, they looked to the Iroquois, who lived among them in the state of New York, to imagine what was humanly possible. As writes the feminist historian Sally Roesch Wagner, "They caught a glimpse of the possibility of freedom because they knew women who lived liberated lives, women who had always possessed rights beyond their wildest imaginations: Iroquois women."[58] Indeed, one of the leading feminists of the time, Matilda Gage— described as "one of the most logical, fearless, and scientific writers of her day"—was so taken with the Iroquois treatment of women that she wrote a series of editorials about them in the New York Evening Post. "Never was justice more perfect," she wrote, "never was civilization more higher than under the Matriarchate."[59]

Though their cultures were substantially different, Aboriginal women in Australia had a similar type of sovereignty. Women were largely independent of men: they sourced the vast majority of food, heading off every day with other women and their children to fish, hunt small animals, gather bush foods, and collect other goods such as ocher and medicinal herbs. Men had no say in where the women went or what they did, and while they were out, the women and children ate as much as they needed, bringing back only the surplus to feed the men. That dynamic alone was a significant check on men's power over women: it meant that husbands could not dictate what their wives did during the day and could not punish them by restricting their food. Indeed, as the anthropologist Phyllis Kaberry observed, women actually exercised this power in their intimate relationships. After a struggle, for example, "the wife will pack up her goods and chattels and move to the camp of a relative...till the loss of an economic partner...brings the man to his senses and he attempts a reconciliation."[60] This is why experts like Atkinson resist defining traditional Indigenous culture as "patriarchal." She suggests that a more precise term would be "egalitarian hegemony": a system of male authority balanced "by woman's sovereignty and authority in the social, economic, and spiritual domains."[61]

One thing is clear: the chaotic family violence in Indigenous communities today—supercharged by alcohol and substance abuse—has no background in traditional culture. "If these practices were traditional laws, there would be no Aboriginal society in existence today," Professor Marcia Langton said in a speech in 2016. "If we look at the Indigenous homicide rates, assault and hospitalization rates, incarceration rates, rates of removal of Aboriginal children, we see a rapidly disintegrating society. This is not the society of old."[62]

What I find particularly galling about this debate over cultural violence is that one glaring fact never seems to get mentioned: namely, that domestic abuse as we know it today, in North America and Australia, *does* have a clear cultural heritage—in Britain.

Unlike the ongoing debate over gendered violence in Indigenous cultures, there is no question that domestic abuse in eighteenth- and nineteenth-century England was widespread and that its perpetrators went largely unpunished. In the mid-nineteenth century, abused women in England were dying "in protracted torture, from incessantly repeated brutality," wrote John Stuart Mill and Harriet Taylor in the *Morning Chronicle*, "without ever, except in the fewest and rarest instances, claiming the protection of law."[63] British laws regulating domestic abuse were designed to protect marriage, not women. Perpetrators of serious violence were commonly either exonerated or given a light sentence.

Sadism was not encouraged; men were expected to beat their wives responsibly. In the late 1700s, Francis Buller of Devon, one of the most senior judges in Britain, became known as "Judge Thumb" after reportedly offering this advice: a husband could thrash his wife with impunity provided that he used a stick no bigger than his thumb. Judge Buller's "rule of thumb" never became written law but was cited repeatedly in cases across Britain and the United States.[64]

The courts did, however, have something to say about "wife-beating." In the late 1600s, the prominent English justice Sir Matthew Hale set an important precedent: "For although our law makes the wife subject to her husband," he explained, "still the husband cannot kill her, for that would be murder, nor can he beat her, for the wife can seek the peace."[65] Suing for a breach of the peace was one way a woman could seek redress for her husband's violence (though this was a rare occurrence, compared to the actual prevalence of wife-beating at the time). However, we also have Justice Hale to thank for another crucial legal precedent: the one that gave husbands permission to rape their wives. "The husband cannot be guilty of a rape committed by himself upon his lawful wife," Hale determined, "for by their mutual matrimonial consent and contract the wife hath given up herself in this kind unto her husband, which she cannot retract."[66]

Unlike Native American women, British women had no power to leave their husbands, no matter how cruel or violent their husbands were; until the 1857 Matrimonial Causes Act, divorce could be achieved only by passage of a special (and expensive) act through Parliament (and even after the act was passed, the woman had to prove that her husband had committed "aggravated adultery"—that is, adultery *plus* bigamy, incest, cruelty, sodomy, bestiality, or desertion). If she left without a divorce, she would lose everything, including her children. A husband's wife was his property, and he could do what he liked with her—within "reason."

There is copious research on domestic abuse in Georgian and Victorian England, but perhaps nothing so vivid as the paper produced by the remarkable British feminist Frances Power Cobbe. In 1878, eleven years after the last convict ship left for Australia, Cobbe published *Wife Torture in England*, a devastating report on domestic abuse in the working-class areas of England. Violence against women was so commonplace that the lives of married women were "simply a duration of suffering and subjection to injury and savage treatment," wrote Cobbe, "far worse than that to which the wives of mere savages are used."[67] This treatment wasn't adequately captured by the term *wife-beating*, which conveyed black eyes and bruises; this was the "mere preliminary canter before the race."[68] The violence Cobbe was documenting was so extreme, and characterized by such cruelty, that the only appropriate term for it was "wife-torture."[69]

In the so-called "kicking districts," people were living "lives of hard, ugly, mechanical toil in dark pits and factories, amid the grinding and clanging of engines and the fierce heat of furnaces."[70] But the root cause of domestic abuse, as Cobbe saw it, wasn't drink or overcrowding; such things only exacerbated the violence. The cause, she said, was the attitudes men held toward their wives. "The notion that a man's wife is his PROPERTY, in the sense in which a horse is his property[,] is the fatal root of incalculable evil and misery," she wrote. "Every brutal-minded man, and many a man who in other relations of his life is not brutal, entertains more or less vaguely the notion that his wife is his *thing*, and is ready to ask with indignation (as we read again and again in the police reports) of any one who interferes with his treatment of her, 'May I not do what I will *with my own?*'"[71]

The young were not spared. Child abuse in England was not only endemic, it was endorsed by the state. Poor and orphaned children as young as four were sent to industrial towns to work in dangerous factories, were routinely beaten, and often died. Throughout much of the 1800s, the notion that a child had any rights at all was a foreign concept. The age of consent was twelve (until 1875, when it rose to thirteen), and child prostitutes were a common sight on London streets.

This was the culture that invaded North America in 1607. In 1778, after the newly independent United States refused to take British convicts, Britain took its prisoners to a new colony on a gigantic island that came to be known as Australia.

When the British landed in Jamestown, Native Americans had already been decimated by the European diseases Columbus had brought a century earlier. On the eve of the invasion in 1492, Native Americans had numbered around ten to twelve million (possibly many more), and were grouped into tribes and confederacies that, across the American continent, spoke at least two thousand different languages. In Australia, the land that the British invaders declared *terra nullius*—empty—was home to more than 750,000 people from more than five hundred different groups, united under the complex systems of the Dreaming.

On both continents, First Nations peoples had survived and thrived for thousands of years because they insulated their cultures against the kind of social chaos that engulfed parts of England. Their cosmology recognized that human relationships were fraught, and that maintaining peace within families and between the sexes required dedicated time and effort. "The absolute essence of Aboriginal relationships," writes Atkinson, "was the vibrancy of mediating the conflicts natural to all human associations."[72] The strength of these familial relationships—and the peoples' relationship to the land—was the cultural backbone of precontact Indigenous Australia. "Men and women came together in ceremony...through dance, art, music, theatre, crafts, and storytelling... These were activities of relationship, of making connections, of creating, maintaining, and healing relationships, in which the primary virtues were 'generosity and fair dealing,' and working to 'unite hearts and establish order.'"[73] The "unusually rich" social network of enduring relationships in Aboriginal Australia, for example, so awed the great anthropologist W. E. H. Stanner that he described them as "an intellectual and social achievement of a high order," comparable to the European development of parliamentary government.[74]

Across both continents, the tight-knit systems of Indigenous kin and clan were antithetical—and profoundly challenging—to the atomized, hierarchical society that was about to overrun them.

––––––––

The culture that arrived with the tall ships in Plymouth and in Sydney Cove was both deeply patriarchal and deeply sexist. Europeans considered all women to be naturally inferior, but on this inferior plane there were two categories: the "good" chaste women, who were deserving of male protection; and the whores, who were to be used and abused however men saw fit. As Richard Hughes writes in his study of Australian colonial history, *The Fatal Shore*, domestic abuse was endemic in the Australian colony: "At night, the huts around the stockade would resound with the shrieks of women being thrashed. The forest warden at Longbottom [a farm just outside of modern-day Sydney], a man named Rose tied his wife to a post and gave her fifty lashes with a government cat-o'-nine tails; another settler...stabbed his wife and hung her on a gum tree, with complete impunity."[75] In 1841, the Canadian convict François-Maurice Lepailleur, transported for rebelling against the British and imprisoned at Longbottom, wrote in his diary, "We hear more women crying in the night here than birds singing in the woods during the day."[76] This ubiquitous and unrestrained kind of gendered violence wasn't just a reaction to the colony's harsh conditions. It was a type of violence introduced to Australia like an invasive species. "The sexism of English society was brought to Australia and then amplified by penal conditions," writes Hughes. "The brutalization of women in the colony had gone on so long that it was virtually a social reflex by the end of the 1830s."[77]

There was at least the veneer of civilization in the new Puritan colonies at Plymouth. In 1641, the Puritans enacted the Massachusetts Body of Laws and Liberties—the first laws in the world to outlaw domestic violence— which protected the rights of a married woman to be "free from bodily correction or stripes [lashing] by her husband" unless he was acting in self-defense.[78] Of course, the man of the family was entitled to use violence if his women and children were in need of "correcting"; how would they enter the kingdom of Heaven if they were not shown the right path? The efficacy of these laws is perhaps best judged, however, by the court records: in 169 years, there were only twelve cases of wife abuse (which averages out to about one every fourteen years).

To the men of this culture, Indigenous women were so alien as to be essentially inhuman. Their confident sexuality—sacred and uncoupled from shame—rendered them sex objects in the eyes of many of the invading Europeans. They were deemed naturally promiscuous and perpetually available. In both countries they were stripped of their names: in Australia, they were "black velvet," gins, and lubras; in North America, they were the good princess (who, like Pocahontas, would rescue and be rescued by a captive Christian man) or the whorish squaw (who lived a dirty life of drudgery and discontent). Both types were dehumanized and hypersexualized.

Raping them was no different from taking land or resources: they were simply the spoils of colonization.

In that same British imagination, the unclothed bodies of Native American women were sinful; since their bodies were already violated and impure, there was no moral impediment to stop a man from raping them. There are copious accounts, but among the most moving is the testimony from T'tcetsa, a Lassik woman whose name was Anglicized to Lucy Young, and who was among the countless Indian children abducted and sold as servants to white settlers in the 1800s. In her epic account of rape and colonization, *The Beginning and End of Rape*, Professor Sarah Deer tells her story: "After numerous escapes and recaptures, T'tcetsa was sold to a white trader, Arthur Rutledge, who 'kept her chained at his place because she always ran away.' Rutledge's sexual abuse of T'tcetsa resulted in so many pregnancies and miscarriages that she lost count."[79]

T'tcetsa's rare first-person account was captured by several ethnologists who interviewed her in the early twentieth century: "White people come find us. Want to take us all to Fort Seward. We all scared to dead... I hear people tell 'bout what [Indian] do early days to white man. Nobody ever tell what white man do to [Indian]. That's reason I tell it. That's history. That's truth. I seen it myself."[80]

Deer also quotes Sarah Winemucca, a Paiute leader, who wrote despairingly in 1883, "My people have been so unhappy for a long time they wish now to disincrease, instead of multiply. The mothers are afraid to have more children, for fear they shall have daughters, who are not safe even in their mother's presence." Winemucca herself was subjected to extreme methods of protection by her parents; "her mother and aunt buried her in the dirt and covered her with plants to hide her from violent settlers. 'Oh,' she wrote, 'can any one in this world ever imagine what were my feelings when I was dug up by my poor mother and father?'"[81]

White women participated in the brutalization of Indigenous women and girls: not only did they turn a blind eye to the sexual predations of their husbands and sons, but as "bosses" in the homestead, they could be just as harsh—sometimes more so. "In many cases our women considered white women to be worse than men in their treatment of Aboriginal women," writes Australian historian and activist Jackie Huggins, "particularly in the domestic service field."[82]

In Australia, sexual violence was not limited to outback stations; across the country, the rape and abduction of Aboriginal women and girls became a type of sport. As McGlade writes, the object of "gin sprees" and "gin busting" excursions was "to rape, maim, or kill as many black women as possible."[83] A horrifying sample of this routine brutality was documented by missionary Lancelot Threlkeld, who wrote in 1825 that he had "heard at night the shrieks of [Aboriginal] girls, about eight or nine years of age, taken by force by the vile men of Newcastle."[84]

Accounts of sexual violence are virtually interchangeable between nineteenth-century Australia and America. During the Californian gold rush, when men rushed the Western frontier in a feverish hunt for riches, "white men kidnapped and raped native women with little fear of retribution from legal authorities."[85] California's constitution stated explicitly that a white man could not be convicted of rape on the basis of a Native American's testimony alone. Rape was widespread. Today, the Oliphant v. Suquamish Supreme Court decision that still stands to prevent tribal police from arresting non-Natives for stranger rape means this culture of rape continues in "man camps," the areas that accommodate men working on mining and drilling sites on and around Indian country.

Because the authorities had no interest in prosecuting white men for raping Indigenous women and girls, Indigenous men took it upon themselves to punish the perpetrators under their own laws. The traditional penalty for the crimes of abduction and rape was often death. This in turn set off a terrifying cycle of violence. As Deer writes, "Throughout the nineteenth century, tribal leaders often protested and resisted when women and children were mistreated. Indeed, many tribally-initiated conflicts and 'uprisings' (like the Great Sioux Uprising in 1862) were responses to kidnapping and sexual mistreatment of women."[86]

It would be a shallow reading of history that depicted Indigenous women as passive victims through these invasions. Indigenous women, then and now, adapted to their conditions. As they and their men were banished from traditional hunting grounds, prostitution became a way for women to regain some of their lost economic power: to exchange sex for goods such as flour, sugar, tea, chewing tobacco, or small sums of money. Sometimes this was the only way to support what was left of their groups. As the Australian Eualeyai/Gamilaroi academic Larissa Behrendt writes, "Many Aboriginal women used the 'gin spree' as a source of income."[87] Of course, across the frontier, there were also Aboriginal women who willingly entered into liaisons and relationships with European men, and who may have "actually sought them out either to escape undesired marriage or tribal punishment or to gain access to the many attractive possessions of the Europeans."[88] Indeed, historian Ann McGrath was surprised to hear, during her research into these interracial unions in the Northern Territory in the 1980s, several older Aboriginal women speak "joyfully" of their "longer-term liaisons" with white men.[89] But, as Behrendt is careful to point out, there was no such thing as a simple exercise of choice for Indigenous women: such "relationships took place against a background of continual frontier and sexual violence."[90]

At the end of the nineteenth century in Australia, humanitarians and clergy were so alarmed by the scale of prostitution and violence against Aboriginal women and girls that legislation was devised to bring full-blooded Aboriginal people under government "protection" and force them to live on missions and reserves, segregated from the white community. This was considered an act of kindness—a way to "smooth the dying pillow" of a "doomed race" that was expected to disappear within decades.[91] In some states, mixed-blood Aboriginals could be granted exemptions and allowed to live outside the reserves and among the white community, so long as they surrendered family connections and gave up the right to visit relatives (under threat of jail). Tribal languages were forbidden, culture was outlawed, and even the simplest traditions—like eating bush tucker (wild foods)—became secret acts. Every action was policed to align with standards of whiteness, down to how much grief was "appropriate" at a funeral. "If anyone had wailed," said the white manager at Brewarrina mission, near Bourke, in 1954, "I would have had them thrown out of the cemetery...the Abos must be given an example and made to be like white people."[92]

Within this insidious regime of coercive control, a new kind of violence permeated Indigenous life: gossiping, jealousy, bullying, shaming, exclusion, and feuding. This "lateral violence," explains Associate Professor Richard Frankland, "comes from being colonized, invaded. It comes from being told you are worthless and treated as being worthless for a long period of time. Naturally you don't want to be at the bottom of the pecking order, so you turn on your own."[93]

Native Americans too were moved off their land and onto "Indian Territory" (modern-day Oklahoma), under the notorious governance of President Andrew Jackson. Thousands died on the long journeys away from their homelands, most horrifically on the "Trail of Tears." Jackson had a savage disregard for the Native Americans, saying they had "neither the intelligence, the industry, the moral habits, nor the desire for improvement which are essential to any favorable change in their condition."[94] On the new reservations, it was made extremely difficult for people to hunt and gather food.

In the devastating colonial history of both countries, however, nothing was ever so cruel and destructive as the forced removal of Indigenous children from their families. The separation of Australian Indigenous children from their parents occurred throughout the second half of the nineteenth century, but it didn't become formally administered by the states until around 1910. The policy of forced child removals—later known as the Stolen Generations—was a hammer blow to Aboriginal family life. Over sixty years, up to fifty thousand Indigenous children were abducted from their families. Some children were removed from family situations of neglect and poverty, but as historian Inga Clendinnen explained, maltreatment was not the reason for this policy: "Children were taken on the basis of skin color: a fair child taken, a dark sibling left... Half-caste children were to be removed from their families and taken into protective custody until they forgot black ways, and could be absorbed, at whatever the personal cost, into the dominant community."[95]

Starting in 1879, Native American children too were removed from their families and sent to boarding schools. By the time the boarding schools closed in the mid-twentieth century, more than one hundred thousand children had been forced to attend.

Life for many Native American children removed to boarding schools was brutal and humiliating. So they could be converted to whiteness, they were forbidden from speaking their language and practicing their religion, and were made to march in regimental lines and wear uniforms. "In those days," recalled Lame Deer, a Lakota holy man who was sent to boarding school when he was seven, "the Indian schools were like jails and run along military lines, with roll calls four times a day. We had to stand at attention, or march in step."[96] Sexual abuse was common; at one boarding school in Nebraska, boys were "initiated" by being sexually abused by the priest on their thirteenth birthday.

Walter Littlemoon, also a Lakota man, was abducted from his mother when he was five and taken to a federal boarding school in South Dakota. His memories until then were "good memories...fond memories...we weren't punished [or] treated mean in any way." But one day, a strange car with a small badge on the side saying "U.S. Government" arrived. "I don't know what they told my mother, but she was crying. And then she told me that I had to go with them. She talked to me in Lakota. And that was it."

Littlemoon's boarding school was "almost like a reeducation camp where we were supposed to be turned into something else that we weren't... We were savages. We couldn't learn...and so they had to do these things this way in order for us to learn." It was virtually impossible not to break the rules, as children would be beaten for everything from not shining their shoes to being overheard speaking their own language. "It was just a struggle on a daily basis," Littlemoon told SDBP Radio. "A struggle to be a human being. But we weren't treated that way."[97]

Across Australia and North America, young children were stolen from loving mothers who screamed and sobbed and ran after them. Many of these children were sent to schools and institutions where they were routinely humiliated, forced into menial labor, and sexually and physically abused.[98] They were the kids whose cries in the night were never answered. They were the kids who had to use their wits to survive, as one described: "There was no food, nothing... Sometimes at night we'd cry with hunger. We had to scrounge in the town dump, eating old bread, smashing tomato sauce bottles, licking them."[99] They were the kids who knew which adults to keep away from and which trees to hide in. They were the kids who hid within themselves, floating away to an imaginary place as the white men heaved on top of them, until they were not really *them* anymore.

In traditional Indigenous life, harming a child was a crime that deserved severe punishment. As the anthropologist W. E. H. Stanner observed, young

Aboriginal children were cherished to the extreme: "Aboriginal culture leaves a child virtually untrammeled for five or six years. In infancy, it lies in a smooth, well-rounded coolamon which is airy and unconstraining, and rocks if the child moves to any great extent. A cry brings immediate fondling."[100] As Atkinson writes, "Physical or emotional punishment of a child in the way of Western child-rearing practices of the time was incomprehensible."[101] Children were also venerated in Native American culture, and considered "sacred gifts from the Creator, innately endowed with wisdom."[102] As the Jesuit Le Jeune complained of the Montaignais tribe, "these Barbarians cannot bear to have their children punished, even scolded, not being able to refuse anything to a crying child."[103]

In Australia and North America, it took just a few decades to break traditional child rearing that had developed over millennia and to wreak havoc on future generations of parenting. Speaking at the landmark 1996–1997 national inquiry into the Stolen Generations, *Bringing Them Home*, one mother, who was thirteen when she was removed to Parramatta Girls Home in the 1960s, said: "Another thing that we find hard is giving our children love. Because we never had it. So we don't know how to tell our kids that we love them. All we do is protect them. I can't even cuddle my kids 'cause I never ever got cuddled. The only time was when I was getting raped and that's not what you'd call a cuddle, is it?"[104]

"If you say, 'let us look to the future, all that is in the past' I will say—what effects will there be on a child wrenched from its parents, then subjected to extreme loneliness, extreme abuse, all by order of a democratic state, under the rule of law?" asked historian Inga Clendinnen. "What effect will that grotesque experience have on that child's child? Then tell me that it is over."[105]

———————

This is not a story of *then* and *now*. It is a story from then *until* now; a "trauma trail," as Judy Atkinson calls it. "Through the generations we have seen too much violence, too much pain, too much trauma," writes Atkinson. "It sits on us like a rash on the soul, and it stays in our families and communities to destroy us."[106]

Despite this, in communities that have been wracked by violence and plagued by powerful perpetrators, women and men are devising their own ingenious strategies to achieve peace. Though the strategies discussed in this section are particular to Australia, I include them here because they show the power of Indigenous modes of thinking and what can be achieved when they lead. Native American communities are similarly pioneering some of the best and most successful restorative justice systems in America: a therapeutic form of justice inextricably linked to the values of their cultures. For communities all over the world, there is no one-size-fits-all fix. Indigenous knowledge is key to confronting this seemingly intractable problem.

One of the most startling examples comes from the remote community of Yungngora, in Western Australia's central Kimberley region. In 2017, a group of seven Indigenous women, led by Judy Mulligan, formed a council to enforce bylaws set by elders that outlawed disruptive behavior such as drinking, fighting, and reckless driving. The conditions were strict: after three warnings, offenders would be evicted from the community for three months.

The results were stunning. In twelve months, domestic violence incidents went from six per week to *none*, crime dropped 60 percent, and school attendance—which had been as low as 50 percent—reached around 90 percent. That basic deterrent—temporary exile—was enough to transform behavior. As Senior Sergeant Neville Ripp told *The West Australian*, "People saw [others getting moved on] and thought, *We better stop doing this or we'll be kicked out for three months.* I haven't known this to happen in any of the communities I've worked in. We need to empower these people to take ownership of their own communities...and a lot of people should have a look at Judy's work. They wanted peace, and they're a peaceful community now."[107] Making peace wasn't easy. Judy was threatened and abused at the beginning, but now, she says, people are happy. "I am proud of what I've done. It has to be a safe community, especially for the young ones."[108]

Another impressive example of community-led change is the "No More" campaign, which uses sport as a skeleton key to unlock intractable problems of violence. Spearheaded by broadcaster and former child protection worker Charlie King, a Gurindji man from Alice Springs, the No More campaign rests on a simple premise: men are perpetrating most of the violence, so men should take responsibility for stopping it.

Nevertheless, nothing happens without women. At the core of King's campaign is a commitment to gender equality, not just because it's the right thing to do, but because *it works*. "We think the answer lies in having men and women on the same page committed to doing something to stop the violence," says King, "and to build a strategy that's going to be successful, and owned by them." King told me about the community of Ramingining, home to around eight hundred people in Arnhem Land, a largely Indigenous area at the top of Australia, about three hundred miles from Darwin. "This community was always fighting over football, because the clans were getting even out on the footy field," says King. The fighting wouldn't end with the match: "Someone would get even with them in the street, then it would erupt in the home. It was pretty horrible." A key element in this violence, and other violence triggered by sport, was the humiliation and shame felt by supporters of the losing team. In 2009, clashes on the football field were igniting so much chaos that the Ramingining community banned it outright. After seven years, they called King and asked, "How can we get it back?"

King did what he's done at sporting clubs across Australia: he went and talked to the men about family violence and got them to write a domestic violence action plan (DVAP). "In these plans, we say things like, 'Teach players that this is a game. One team wins, one team doesn't win.' We strike out the word *loser*." Typically, DVAPs declare a club's zero tolerance for domestic abuse (including suspensions for players who offend); educate the players; and use selected matches to declare support for No More, including a "linking of arms" on the field. But every DVAP is unique. In the Ramingining plan, there was a critical element: women. "They're going to be on the board. They're going to be playing the game, and we're going to be supporting them. And the men were like, 'What the hell is going on?'"

Come grand final day, the atmosphere on the field was not combative, but festive. The men danced before the women's team played, and then the women danced when it was the men's turn. Elders spoke before both games, telling the teams they wanted whatever happened on the football field to be left on the field. "It was beautiful—it worked so well," says King. Again, the results were startling. "The police told us three months later that family violence in that community was reduced—have a listen to this, Jess—by 70 percent... Why? Because football became a festival, not a war zone." Local constable Paul Keightley sang the program's praises: "The difference now is absolutely incredible."

The message is clear: when power is placed in the hands of communities, and not just the powerful few, incredible things can happen. Given the deep and abiding legacy of trauma so many Indigenous communities must cope with, it's time for governments around the world to acknowledge that First Nations people are the people best placed to develop their own sophisticated strategies for healing and reducing violence. All they need is for governments and police to stop undermining them, and to start backing them.

11.
Fixing It

We've got so much awareness. We're sick of talking about it. This is not a ribbon, it's not a color, it's not a hashtag.
Just think: How many women and children this year have had to face the last moment of their life? That terror. That moment of going, fucking hell, make it quick. Yeah, you're gonna kill me right now, I get it. But please don't make me suffer.

How can I not do something?
NICOLE LEE, SURVIVOR TURNED CAMPAIGNER

For five years I've closely investigated the phenomenon of domestic abuse, grasping for the perfect combination of words to make you *feel* it so acutely, with such fresh horror, that you will demand—and keep demanding—drastic action from our leaders. I've agonized over how to make these words fierce and definitive enough to convince every politician, judge, and police officer that they must do everything in their power *now* to make sure no perpetrator ever feels comfortable again. But always I have had the crushing sense of futility. The thought of penning yet another "call for action"—one more on the teetering pile—is nauseating.

Even the proposed solutions feel futile. At the heart of our response to domestic abuse—a "national emergency"—is the project to achieve gender equality and change community attitudes, a strategy that could take decades to yield results. Don't get me wrong: the pursuit of gender equality is critically important. Perhaps, when the patriarchy is finally overthrown, domestic abuse will indeed become a thing of the past. In the meantime, though, abusers remain largely out of sight, run systematic campaigns of degradation and terror, and commit acts that regularly escalate to murder.

Why have we tolerated this? Why aren't we confronting perpetrators as our first and most urgent priority? How did we come to accept that until we change attitudes and achieve equality, there's little we can do to stop perpetrators from abusing today, tomorrow, this week, this year?

The United States is a nation famed for courageous responses to public health problems. From thwarting the tobacco industry to criminalizing drunk driving, American governments have shown they are willing to burn political capital to save lives. By doing this, they have achieved results many believed impossible. What would happen if a government were to bring the same zeal to tackling domestic abuse?

———————

It's been almost half a century since feminists opened the first domestic violence shelters. Ever since, they've had to beg for every dollar to keep women safe. The furious words of these women have, in recent years, been stolen by self-serving politicians, who wax lyrical about ending domestic abuse while dabbling with piecemeal initiatives, gutting essential services, and forcing the sector to plead for basic funding.

How this worked in Australia was first made clear to me in 2015. In the suffocating heat of summer, I met with Jocelyn Bignold, the CEO of McAuley Community Services for Women. There was only one twenty-four-hour crisis shelter for domestic violence victims in the state, she told me, and she was in charge of it. As we spoke, Bignold was clearly preoc-cupied. She had good reason to be: as far as she knew, McAuley would have to close in six months' time, on July 1. The immediate threat to her shelter—and many others around the country—was the expected cancella-tion of a funding arrangement called the National Partnership Agreement on Homelessness. "I've got nothing to tell me on paper what the plan is for funding services after the thirtieth of June," said Bignold, her eyes flashing with anger.

That January, as Bignold waited nervously for news, twenty-six-year-old Leila Alavi was working as a hairdressing apprentice and living a new, independent life. Just a few months earlier, she'd left her abusive husband, Mokhtar Hosseiniamrei, after he threatened to kill her and "fix up" her sister and friends. She knew he could do it: he'd already been fetishizing her murder, repeating a routine where he'd pin her to the ground, choke her until she almost lost consciousness, then cover her face with a blanket and jump on her body. Alavi found the strength to flee their home and take out an apprehended violence order. Still afraid Hosseiniamrei would come after her, Alavi started calling domestic violence refuges, looking for a safe place to hide, and found that no room was available—not in Sydney, not even in nearby regional areas. She was given vouchers for a hotel in Kings Cross, but after a few nights on her own, Alavi became scared and went to stay with her sister. After calling up to a dozen refuges a day, Alavi gave up hope that she would find protection and decided to return to work. In the salon that hired her, she was known for being kind and generous: once, when a client with cancer complimented Alavi on her wallet, Alavi emptied it and gave it to the client.[1]

One day, Alavi was in the middle of giving a haircut when her cowork-ers told her that Hosseiniamrei was standing outside. Alavi didn't want there to be any trouble, so she went to talk to him. Hours later, she was found dead in her car in an underground garage, with fifty-six stab wounds to her head, neck, arms, and torso. Speaking later to investigators, Hosseiniamrei explained why he did it: "She broke the contract." In her victim impact statement, Alavi's sister, Marjan Lotfi, said her grief was almost unbearable. "I keep thinking: Why didn't someone help her? Why didn't she receive the protection she needed?"

When it comes to funding shelters and community legal services, governments don't just cry poor, they promote the fiction that if these services receive more funding, others in need will go without. As the economist Richard Denniss explains, making women's groups feel poor is central to the political strategy of people determined to maintain the status quo. They don't just want women's groups to feel poor, he says; they want to make them feel greedy for even *asking*.[2]

Governments—both state and federal—have the money. Withholding it is their choice. Forcing refuges to turn women away is a choice. Making the sector plead for funding is a choice.

However, ending domestic abuse doesn't require just money, it requires conviction and belief. Do we actually believe perpetrators can be stopped—not in generations to come, but right now?

Social problems often seem insurmountable until they're not. In the 1970s, police corruption in Sydney was so brazen that cops could be seen in broad daylight on city streets exchanging paper bags with pimps. Even though this was a common sight from the national broadcaster's headquarters, the journalists there never thought to report on it: police corruption was just the natural way of things. By the late 1990s, however, that had all changed; the Wood Royal Commission named hundreds of dirty cops, who were then purged as the rest of the force was put on notice. Police corruption wasn't magically eradicated, but it was much harder to get away with.

While pimps were handing paper bags to police in Australia's business capital, the citizenry was regularly driving home shitfaced. Drunk driving wasn't a furtive, shameful act: it was done loud and proud, and often in the conviction that one could actually drive *better* with a skinful of wine. When random breath testing (RBT) was introduced in 1982, the backlash was so hostile that clubs refused entry to local politicians, insisting it was an attack on working-class men. But the effect of those RBT units was immediate and undeniable: within two months, fatal road accidents in one state dropped 48 percent.[3]

Like police corruption and drunk driving before it, domestic abuse is a social ill that's been hiding in plain sight for a long time. It seems intractable—just a tragic fact of life—and the broad consensus seems to be that in the short term there's not much we can do to stop it.

It's not that we're not trying. In Australia, we've decided to treat domestic violence as a "public health" issue—in line with the World Health Organization—placing it in the same category as smoking and HIV. We're confronting it on a national scale but, unlike strategies to reduce smoking and HIV, Australia's national plan to reduce domestic abuse is missing one critical element: clear targets. No targets have been set for reducing domestic homicide or the rate of repeat assaults, or even for reducing the number of women and children turned away from crisis accommodation. Indeed, some of the outcomes in the plan are so amorphous it's hard to imagine them ever being achieved, let alone reliably measured. Outcomes such as "Communities are safe and free from violence" and "Relationships are respectful" don't read like serious goals for reducing violence. They read like a wish list for a feminist utopia.

Because success is not measured in actual reductions in violence (despite that being the explicit aim), there is no clear sense of what "reducing domestic violence" would actually look like. For example, progress on that first priority—"Communities are safe and free from violence"—is not measured by reviewing police data or hospitalization rates. Instead, it is measured by surveying and tracking community attitudes. For instance, what percentage of the community understands that control is a form of domestic violence?

This approach—to tackle domestic violence as an attitude problem—was sketched out more than twenty years ago by the American academic Lori Heise. "Violence is an extremely complex phenomenon with deep roots in power imbalances between men and women, gender-role expectations, self-esteem, and social institutions," she wrote in her influential 1994 paper. "As such, it cannot be addressed without confronting the underlying cultural beliefs and social structures that perpetuate violence against women. In many societies women are defined as inferior, and the right to dominate them is considered the essence of maleness itself. Confronting violence thus requires redefining what it means to be male and what it means to be female."[4]

As the theory goes, gender inequality is at the root of domestic violence; ipso facto, gender *equality* is the cure. The way to get there is through changing social attitudes: in sporting clubs, in schools, through the media, and so on. This approach is endorsed by many leading minds on gendered violence. But in measuring something as vital as the safety of our communities, how on earth is surveying people about their attitudes to violence considered adequate? Why is changing community attitudes the central plank of this strategy?

In every interview with experts, I've asked the same question: Why are we prioritizing long-term attitude change when the problem is so dire *right now*? Criminologist and trauma expert Michael Salter agrees there is a jarring disconnect between the horrific reality of domestic abuse and our response to it. "On the one hand we're being told that it's a national emergency, but on the other hand this softly-softly approach increasingly accepts that women who are currently being victimized will continue to be, and that new women will be victimized in the future, and that at some magic point we can bring that to an end," he says. "When you look at other public health issues, like HIV or hepatitis C, you can bet that agencies have a vision of the world where that's stopped. They know what that looks like. How will *we* know when we've got to this point? Are we really aiming for it?"

The mission to transform attitudes toward gender inequality and violence is laudable and will no doubt produce important cultural changes. As a primary strategy for reducing domestic abuse, however, it is horribly inadequate. Why do we accept that it will take decades—possibly generations—to reduce domestic abuse? Why isn't long-term prevention work paired with a relentless focus on doing everything possible to reduce violence *today*? Why do successive governments insist that reducing domestic abuse is a matter of changing attitudes—or, at best, parking the ambulance at the bottom of the cliff? How did public officials decide that surveying community attitudes was the best way to measure whether their strategy to reduce violence was working? When random breath testing was introduced in Australia, did politicians decide that if the majority of men surveyed in bars agreed that drunk driving was a bad idea, the policy would be deemed a success? No, they would have been laughed out of office. The only way to prove that RBT was working was to measure its actual impact: a reduction in road fatalities. Why do we accept anything less when it comes to domestic abuse?

There's another serious problem with this approach: community attitudes *may* reflect public understanding, but they don't reliably predict behavior. Let's say a bunch of policy wonks *had* surveyed men on barstools. How many of those men would tick a box saying that drinking and driving was foolish, then finish their beers and drive home drunk? We all have issues on which we think one way and behave another. I, for one, would happily tell a surveyor that it's terrible to look at your phone right before bed or first thing in the morning, and yet I do it anyway. Psychologists have a term for this: *attitude-behavior inconsistency*. Basically, it means that a stated attitude doesn't necessarily match or predict that person's behavior. As Joan Didion once wrote, "it is possible for people to be the unconscious instruments of values they would strenuously reject on a conscious level."⁵ We see this with perpetrators who condemn violence in one breath and assault their partners in the next. This disconnect is well known to professionals who work with perpetrators; it is just one of many gaps between their stated attitudes and their actual behavior.

There's no question that damaging ideas around gender—more specifically, patriarchy—are at the heart of domestic violence, as this book makes clear. Unfortunately, though, reconfiguring attitudes and behavior is the work of generations. Such work will not prevent women and children from dying tomorrow, next year, or even within the next decade.

Combating public health issues and shifting social behavior requires strong and consistent deterrents and an unwavering focus on pursuit of the objective. Like other public health strategies, Australia's National Plan has three major elements: primary prevention (stopping it before it starts through education in schools and workplaces, awareness campaigns, and promotion of gender equality); secondary prevention (preventing violence from escalating, through initiatives like men's behavior change programs); and tertiary prevention (minimizing the impact of violence, restoring health and safety, and preventing violence from recurring, through the provision of crisis accommodation, counseling, and advocacy, and adequate criminal justice responses to perpetrators).⁶

Primary prevention is the backbone of Australia's National Plan. Let's imagine that by 2022—when the plan is due to deliver on its outcomes—we have made enormous progress on the goal of increasing gender equality and changing attitudes. In fact, let's imagine that by 2022 Australia is ranked number one in the world for gender equality. Undoubtedly, this would be a fantastic outcome. But would it reduce domestic abuse? The evidence on that is unclear, to say the least.

As we read in chapter 5, Nordic countries—world leaders on gender equality—still have shocking rates of domestic abuse. In Iceland, "the best place to be a woman,"[7] domestic abuse seems to be *increasing*, according to Icelandic feminist and anthropology professor Sigríður Dúna Kristmundsdóttir. "Maybe [it's] the anxiety that men are feeling, which can increase violence in the home." Speaking to *SBS Dateline*, she compared men's experience of shifting gender norms to watching a game of soccer they believed their team would win: "Now the position is 3–4, and it's not quite sure if their team wins, or the women's team. So they're very scared and very anxious."[8] What this tells us is that if we succeed in improving gender equality, we may actually see domestic abuse get *worse* in the short term. This means it's urgent that the secondary and tertiary prevention parts of any plan be evidence-based, coordinated, and securely funded.

The fact is that there is no such coordinated approach to domestic violence. "It's been a real scattergun approach, and it changes with each budget cycle," says Lara Fergus, former director of policy and evaluation at Our Watch, the federally funded body assigned to promote primary prevention. "A lot of it has been funding ad hoc programs with limited duration, and with no consistent or coordinated set of objectives across those projects." Individuals and groups are often successful in winning grants for programs in sporting clubs, says Fergus, but often there is no expertise attached to or guiding these programs, and no clear indication of how they will actually reduce violence. "If the bureaucrats and [politicians] decide they like the look of this program, and—dare I say—if they're in 'interesting' [districts], the program gets funded. That's not a way to reduce violence against women."

Fergus says despite all the strong talk from politicians, they're still not willing to do what it takes to reduce violence against women. "There's this sense that you can do these half-baked measures and that it will fly. And it *will* fly—it will fly with the community and the [voters], and that's probably all that matters to a lot of politicians," says Fergus.

What's infuriating—and telling—about this haphazard approach is that we know what it takes to run a successful public health campaign. Take the issue of cigarettes in Australia. Since governments became serious about reducing smoking, Australia has introduced some of the world's toughest smoking laws, rendering cigarettes inconvenient, expensive, and unfashionable. If you get caught smoking in the wrong place, you don't just get a slap on the wrist: in Western Australia, for example, smokers can be fined as much as $2,000.[9] Fines aren't the only deterrent. The federal government has also made smoking prohibitively expensive by ratcheting up the cigarette excise tax year after year; by 2020, a pack of cigarettes is likely to cost more than $45.[10] And governments haven't stopped there: to make cigarette brands homogeneous and unfashionable, the government led by Julia Gillard courageously legislated mandatory plain packaging, making every cigarette pack a drab olive-green, adorned only by a gory and graphic health warning. That world-leading policy change landed it in a multimillion-dollar legal battle with tobacco company Philip Morris, from which the Australian government eventually emerged triumphant.

Some might consider this kind of government intervention over the top, punitive, or even a sign of "creeping socialism," but it's *working*. Smoking rates for Australian men have been halved since the 1980s,[11] and today Australians smoke at a rate of 13 percent, compared to a global average of around 20 percent.[12]

So why aren't we setting measurable goals for reducing domestic abuse? Is the current approach, with its long-range goals, popular with government *because* it avoids accountability?

When I asked Lara Fergus this, she paused. "Initially I resisted [what you were saying]," she said slowly, "and I thought no, we have more of an ideological struggle with primary prevention, because we're talking about gendered drivers and no one wants to hear it. But I do see what you're saying. Holding perpetrators to account, and putting in place the legislative and regulatory mechanisms that will make it impossible for them to continue perpetrating; we haven't taken that as seriously as we should have.

There's a resistance to doing that in a way that there isn't for, say, terrorism offenses. We could do a hell of a lot more."

Most perpetrators of domestic abuse will never be held accountable. There is little reason for them to believe the law will come between them and their victims. By treating domestic abuse like a lesser kind of violent crime, we are not working to change our society at the level that counts.

What would that change look like? What if we placed perpetrators at the center of our prevention efforts? Domestic abuse is fiendishly difficult to measure, but there is one reliable statistic we could target. At least once a week, one perpetrator kills his current or former partner. Why don't we commit to reducing that statistic? When will we see a brave politician step forward and say that, as a nation, we are going to halve the domestic homicide rate?

Let me be clear: to eradicate domestic abuse, we do need to change community attitudes as well as behavior. This means confronting and overturning the prejudices that underpin gender inequality, from unequal pay rates to our gendered responses to shame and anxiety. Teaching kids what respectful relationships look like, and confronting bullying at school, are an essential part of this.

Nevertheless, while these and other programs slowly progress, there are perpetrators out there, today and tomorrow, imposing their regimes of control in homes across the nation, with little in place to stop them. *Can they be stopped?* Most experts I've spoken to say there is no strategy that has definitively reduced domestic abuse, but there is at least one. In the city of High Point, North Carolina—a city where the domestic homicide rate was twice the national average—a dedicated coalition of police, community members, and federal agencies have made it their top priority to stop perpetrators, using a strategy typically deployed against gang violence and gun crime. In just six years, they have achieved the unthinkable: they have more than halved the city's number of domestic homicides.

Why did this strategy work when so many others have failed? Could it work elsewhere around the world?

———————

In February 2012, an extraordinary event took place in High Point.[13] To the uninitiated, it looked like a regular meeting at City Hall, with bright orange chairs packed with the usual mix of local residents, church leaders, and community representatives. What made this meeting extraordinary was the row of twelve men down in the front, shifting uncomfortably in their seats. These men, who avoided eye contact with each other and everyone else in the room, were domestic violence perpetrators. In what was perhaps a world-first, they were about to be called out in public.

Calling the hall to order, Jim Summey stepped up to the microphone and spoke to the men in the front row. "Gentlemen," he said, "you're here this evening because you have been associated through your records with some form of domestic violence. The community is gathering here with law enforcement—we're partners with them—to let you know that domestic violence is wrong, and it's unacceptable."

Summey, an influential local minister, is the leader of High Point Community Against Violence (HPCAV). He is a bear of a man, with a full beard and broad shoulders. "This has nothing to do with your victims," Summey cautioned. "They didn't choose you—we did. But we care about you too. Don't think this is something just to put you down—it's not. It's really an opportunity to lift you up. So take it. We care about you, but it's gotta stop. If you don't, it's gonna be really bad."

Then, one by one, more than two dozen community members— victim advocates, church leaders, bikers, Freemasons—stepped up to the microphone, introduced themselves, and repeated the same message. "I too am against domestic violence," said pastor Sherman Mason, a portly African American man in a gray vest crisscrossed with colorful stripes.

"But if you are for the betterment of your city, I'm for you." Gretta Bush, a middle-aged woman with her hair in a tight bun and pearls around her neck, spoke with direct kindness to the offenders. "HPCAV is a group that connects you with resources in the community. When you leave here tonight, you never have to see us again, if you do not need our help," she said. "But if you do, come with the mindset that *I want to make a change*. We can't do it for you. But we will help, and connect you with resources. We love you, and we respect you—that's why we brought you in tonight."

As the community members cleared the stage, a phalanx of law enforcement officers—from local police and prosecutors to federal agents from the Federal Bureau of Investigation (FBI) and the Bureau of Alcohol, Tobacco, Firearms, and Explosives (ATF)—took their seats in a row overlooking the hall. In the middle of this daunting line-up sat the High Point police chief Jim Fealy. "As the chief of police, I've declared domestic violence our number one public safety threat," Fealy began. "We haven't done a very good job in the past with domestic violence. All that changes tonight: as of tonight, our A-game is on." Fealy made it clear: domestic violence wasn't just hitting, but "pushing, shoving, striking, slapping, intimidating, trespassing, vandalism, burglary, and all the other little games and tricks that domestic violence offenders play on their victims. Any of those actions will trigger actions from us."

Seated next to Fealy was his deputy chief, Marty Sumner, a bespectacled blond with a mild manner and a folksy Southern accent. "My officers, my detectives, will do anything in their power to make a case," he said calmly to the men in the front row. "If we have information that you're abusing your spouse and we don't have a misdemeanor case, we may buy dope from you, we might sell you a handgun, we might reinvestigate a case that was dismissed before and get it reinstated." Sumner wasn't making idle threats. If these men committed even the most minor act of domestic violence, this row of officials would do and use anything they could find to make sure they were punished.

It's what's known as the Al Capone approach, explained district attorney Walt Jones. Capone was once the biggest mobster in Chicago, but police couldn't arrest him, because there were never any witnesses to his crimes. Capone never got prosecuted for his violence, but he did end up dying in prison...as a convicted tax evader. "Starting tomorrow, the folks sitting in front of me are special—special to the prosecutor's office—*if* they choose to reoffend," Jones said. "The status quo no longer exists. We are waiting on you to reoffend. We have the paperwork filled out; we only have to put in the name of the victim and the date." Then a dark-haired, heavyset man with a chiseled jaw introduced himself as Doug Retz, special agent with the FBI. If the local prosecutor couldn't get them on a state crime, he said, the FBI would step in, and would try to make a federal case against them, even if that meant setting them up. "I can pay informants, buy guns, buy dope, all day," he said. "Plenty of resources to do it...So please take the advice, go to these people in the community. I wish you the best of luck." Each official seemed intent on sounding more terrifying than the last. To the would-be fugitives in the front row, U.S. federal marshal John Olson was stern and clear: run, and you'll be caught. "Traditionally you haven't been flagged and you have been able to run to another city, another state, and it's been no big deal. Now that you've been flagged, that ends."

Finally, after each official spelled out exactly how they would ruin these men's lives if the men abused again, it was Chief Fealy's turn. Domestic violence was no longer regarded as a misdemeanor crime, he said. Police now regarded it as High Point's biggest threat to public safety and would treat any incident as a major event. "As of today, you're flagged in our record management system," he said, explaining that if they got stopped for as little as a traffic ticket in a neighboring town, his police officers would know about it. "We're not asking you, we're telling you—control yourselves with your women. That's all we're asking. That's how you avoid us."

The High Point police department had long had a serious problem with domestic violence. "We were spending more than six thousand hours [a year] just on domestic violence calls, not even counting reports for arrest," Sumner explains. Like most police departments across America, High Point had a pro-arrest policy: if any officer had reason to believe an offense had been committed, they were obliged to make an arrest. But that was as far as it went. Domestic violence was mostly treated as a minor crime that just needed to be managed—or so the thinking went until the summer of 2008. In one fortnight, two men—both known offenders—murdered their partners and then killed themselves. To a city of just 100,000 residents, these two murders, so close in time to each other, were a huge shock.

That was a catalytic moment, and Sumner knew he had to seize it. Since 2004, the city had seen sixteen domestic homicides.[14] That made domestic violence the leading cause of homicide in High Point, accounting for one in three murders. When Sumner suggested to Chief Fealy that they devote the next year to reducing domestic violence, Fealy balked. That was like setting the department up for failure, he said. Family violence was just a sad fact of life, something that was "always going on below the surface in any community." Nothing worked. Everyone knew that.

Sumner wasn't deterred. He kept thinking about a paper he'd read, some years back, from a New York criminologist, David Kennedy, who had pitched an entirely new way to police domestic violence. It was based on the strategy that made him famous: "focused deterrence" (or "pulling levers"). Focused deterrence was first introduced in Boston in the 1990s with Operation Ceasefire, a city-wide push against youth gun violence. The strategy hinged on the simple premise that a small group of people commit the majority of violent crimes and their criminal records can be used as leverage to convince them to stop offending. That might not sound particularly radical, but in the 1990s, the popular wisdom was precisely the opposite: it held that you couldn't bargain with violent criminals, because they were fundamentally irrational. Following advice from Kennedy, Boston police identified the most dangerous criminals and sent them a message— delivered by former gang members, church leaders, and other respected locals. It said: *We want you to change, because we care about you, and we will help you change your life, if you let us. But if you insist on continuing your violence, you won't get away with it, and the penalty will be swift and severe.*

The harshest consequences possible would be engineered by a formidable coalition of law enforcement—police, prosecutors, judges, federal agents—who vowed to fast-track trials and request maximum sentences. The impact was not only immediate, but also lasting. Operation Ceasefire achieved a 60 percent reduction in youth homicide and a 25 percent decrease in gun assaults in the following decades. It has also led to reductions in homicides and gun violence all over the country, and is now one of the United States' most celebrated crime reduction strategies. It's even been described as "the only tactic proven to reduce gang violence."[15]

By the early 2000s, Kennedy began to think: if focused deterrence had worked on gun violence and drug-dealing—without fixing the root causes of poverty, racism, and inequality—could it work on domestic violence? In conceiving and proposing this, Kennedy was challenging the fiercely held idea that domestic violence was *predominantly* the crime of "nice guys" with no history of offending. In fact, crime statistics showed that many of the most serious abusers *were* known to police—or to colleagues, neighbors, friends, or family—who could have intervened. The statistics revealed another disturbing fact: in the vast majority of domestic homicides, police had had clear opportunities to act to protect the women who ended up dead. When Sumner dug out the files on the city's seventeen most recent domestic homicides, he found that every single perpetrator had a criminal record. More disturbingly, their abuse had not

been a secret; each of the victims had asked police and advocates for help
before they were killed.

Focused deterrence wasn't going to eradicate all domestic violence in
High Point. There was a cohort of perpetrators who would never show up
on a 10–79 call (the code for domestic violence). Those abusers were, in the
short term, beyond the reach of police. But there was a group of seriously
violent perpetrators, some of whom had abused more than one woman,
who *were* known to police. If these offenders could be stopped, police could
at least do something about the violence they *could* see and also use them
as an example to deter first-time offenders.

When Chief Fealy saw the list of known offenders behind the rash of
domestic homicides, he was persuaded that focused deterrence just might
work. Fealy made a bold call: he publicly vowed to reduce the domestic
homicide rate. He also wanted to see a drop in repeat victimization and
fewer calls involving the same people. Success wouldn't, however, mean a
drop in calls generally. On the contrary, he hoped more victims would feel
encouraged to report.

None of this could happen quickly. It took two years for a working
group of police, academics, prosecutors, victim advocates, and community
members to agree on how the program would be implemented. Digging
deep into the data on offenders, they identified four categories—from
the most violent to first-timers—and came up with strategies to confront
each one.

The A-listers (the city's most violent abusers) were targeted for immediate prosecution. The conviction needn't necessarily be for domestic violence: if a victim was reluctant to testify, police would look for an unrelated
charge against her abuser and, if possible, prosecute him for that instead.
"In one case," explains Sumner, "we had a man with two larceny charges
pending, so we had the prosecutor fast-track those charges and got him
150 days for both charges. Then we told him, 'Hardly nobody goes to jail for

larceny at that level, but you are, because of your domestic violence offense.' That started really sending the message."

D-list offenders were those who had come to the attention of police via a call, but hadn't committed an arrestable offense. They would get a visit from a police officer and a letter that told them they were now being monitored.

If a D-lister was arrested, he became a C-lister. A detective would visit C-listers, either at home or in prison, and would explain the new consequences: longer prison sentences, harsher probation conditions, and so on. This was their chance to realize that consequences would be certain and swift and to make the "rational choice" to stop offending. Their names would be placed on an alert system so that if they offended again, judges would know to impose tougher bail conditions. The victim would also get support: at minimum, contact from a safety planner and a visit from police.

A C-list offender who reoffended was moved to the B-list. They would have to attend a public call-in at City Hall, as the twelve B-list offenders did in February 2012. Each victim, now identified as being at high risk, would be consulted about a letter police would give to the abuser, to make sure it was phrased correctly. Police would also seek out a "proximity informant," such as a neighbor or a friend, to keep an eye on the couple and report signs of trouble.

Before the twelve B-list offenders left City Hall in February, they were handed one of those letters, which spelled out their likely sentence should they offend again. When High Point police contacted their partners to see what happened when those men got home, Sumner said their response was clear. "Oh, he got the message," they told him, "and he didn't like it at all." For these women, the most important element was that it was clear this was being initiated by the city, not by them. As they told Sumner, "That's what had the most impact on him." As for whether these call-ins are basically public shaming, David Kennedy says it's "nearly the opposite." "This type of police response treats them as rational, responsible adults."[16]

A strong justice response is exactly what domestic violence perpetrators least expect. As a later evaluation would find, weak justice responses lead perpetrators to believe they are "immune to consequences" and make the victim feel "incapable of seeking help." When this belief is reinforced for offenders time and again, they feel free to abuse with impunity. As one High Point police officer said, when you "see some [offenders] with eight or nine [protective order] violations against them...you are like, *How can that happen in our court system? How can someone be charged eight or nine times with different victims, not just one victim, and they are still on the street?*"

———————

When the High Point working group was refining its strategy, they considered two nightmarish hypotheticals. The first was that perpetrators might be enraged by the crackdown and take revenge on their victims. The second, as Kennedy described it, was "that he would have her chained in the basement. That would look to us like success, because she [wouldn't be] calling anymore." But Shay Harger, the working group's lead victim advocate, wasn't afraid of the strategy going horribly wrong. "Things were already going horribly wrong," she told me. "We were not even coming close to preventing domestic violence fatalities." Was she worried that victims would be too afraid to report? "No," Harger replied in her North Carolina twang. "She's already not reporting, for any number of reasons, and he's dangerous and unmonitored. At least this way, somebody has eyes on him [and] the community is saying *we're not going to put up with your violence or your bad behavior.*" In the past, Harger said, she had to devise safety plans with women with no clear sense of how the system would deal with the offender. At least now the response would be consistent.

The working group devised six clear goals:

To protect the most vulnerable victims from the most dangerous abusers

To take the burden of addressing abusers from the victims and move it to
the state/police

To focus deterrence, community standards, outreach, and support on the
most dangerous abusers

To counter and avoid the "experiential effect," in which the weak criminal
justice response teaches perpetrators that they can get away with it

To take advantage of opportunities provided by the offender's variety
of offenses (and prosecute on those grounds, if there was no better
option)

To avoid putting victims at additional risk.[17]

To achieve this, service providers and police had to come out of
their isolated silos and cooperate. This result was "stunning," says Susan
Scrupski, a tech entrepreneur and documentary filmmaker who witnessed
it firsthand. "The role High Point Police Department played, particularly
Chief Sumner, in herding cats and negotiating agreements to make a work-
able, effective system was nothing short of heroic." This became the secret
to High Point's success: an interagency working group of police, prosecutors, probation and parole overseers, victim advocates, family services,
social service providers, and community members who would meet every
two weeks and communicate daily to workshop individual cases and discuss how the system was working. "The value of that I can't even quantify,
because there were so many things they figured out and fixed," says Sumner.
"You get the right people at the table regularly enough and you can make
something happen."

Long-term cultural change is important, says Harger, but the act of
calling out domestic violence in public and enforcing consequences for

offenders is a huge cultural change in itself. "In my opinion, psychological and culture change is calling a domestic violence offender into our City Hall and having all of these people say, 'Your violence is unacceptable. She may love you and she may be afraid of you, but we are not. She may feel like she is powerless against you—we are not. This is no longer about her—this is about us and you.' That is very powerful."

––––––

When the High Point program was evaluated in 2017, the results were impressive: intimate partner violence arrests were down by 20 percent, as was the percentage of victims injured. In the six years before the strategy began, from 2002 to 2008, there had been eighteen domestic homicides, averaging three per year; in the decade since, there have been nine, bringing the yearly average to less than one. Of those nine offenders, eight had not previously come to the attention of police, which shows that when High Point police can see and engage offenders, they are able to prevent future homicides. As High Point Police Captain Timothy Ellenberger says, "We feel better about preventing offenders from escalating if we can 'get in front of them.'" More than 2,300 perpetrators have been put on notice and, incredibly, only 16 percent of those have been reported for a repeat assault (in cities using the traditional approach, the recidivism rate is between 45 and 64 percent[18]). "This low reoffense rate indicates that what was previously believed about intimate partner violence—that the violence could not be prevented and the offenders could not be deterred—is, in fact, a myth," says Ellenberger.

The High Point model is already being replicated in other American cities. In South Carolina, the city of Spartanburg—which is three times the size of High Point and saw fourteen domestic homicides in 2015 alone—a program adapted from the one in High Point began in 2017. At the end of the first year, the domestic homicide rate was down to three. Where focused deterrence is applied, domestic homicides drop. That's why the federal U.S. Office on Violence Against Women is providing funding for the High Point model to be replicated in three other cities.[19]

———

The High Point method is just one strategy, and it won't appeal to everybody. I wanted to know if there was any other strategy that was proven to reduce domestic abuse, so I called an Australian crime statistics guru, Don Weatherburn, to see if he'd heard of anything else. As I explained the High Point model to him over the phone, I could virtually hear his attention sharpen. "That's effectively what police in New South Wales are trying to do at the moment. Look at what they're doing in Bourke," he said. "For the first time in years, the domestic violence assault rate has dropped. That's kind of unheard of. You really need to offer the carrot and the stick. If you increase the cost of offending, while at the same time increasing the rewards for *not* offending, you get a better outcome than if you just wave the stick." What he told me about was an American strategy being put to work in the Australian outback—one with fundamental similarities to focused deterrence, but also with distinct and important differences. It offers yet another blueprint for reducing domestic abuse.

———

Home to some twenty-six hundred people, Bourke lies on the banks of the Darling River, at the edge of the Australian outback. In summer, the heat gets so extreme the street tar sticks to your shoes. Then the rains appear, and the dry, barren red becomes lush with green and carpeted by spring wildflowers. Bourke is a troubled town. In 2013, *The Sydney Morning Herald* ran the headline "Bourke tops list: more dangerous than any country in the world."[20] The headline may have been overkill, but it wasn't total fiction: Bourke had the highest rate of domestic violence, assaults, break-ins, and car thefts in the state. If you ranked Bourke's crime statistics, the article warned, this little town had the world's highest per capita crime rate.

Bourke's problems are hardly unique, but they have a particular history. A third of Bourke's population is Indigenous and hail from more than twenty different language groups. Back in the mission days, survivors from dozens of tribal groups were forced to live in missions in and around Bourke, all under the absolute authority of the state Protection Board (much like how the U.S. government moved Native Americans onto reservations and forbade them from leaving without permission). When the missions closed in 1966, many former inhabitants moved to Bourke and formed communities that soon divided along family lines and language groups. As one local described it, generations had been taught that "We don't get on with those people; you stay away from them."[21]

Local elder Alistair Ferguson feels these "legacy issues" in his bones. He grew up in Bourke and saw his community shattered time and again, with families destroyed by violence, kids removed, and parents and children sent to jail—a story that's also familiar on Native reservations across America. All of this was happening in a feedback loop: as one study found, children in Bourke were often out in the streets at night because it felt safer than being at home—but that's when they were committing criminal offenses. Said one community worker: "People say, 'Why don't the police get those kids off the street?' But if you knew where those poor little buggers slept, you wouldn't be saying that."[22] The urge to escape home lives of chaos and violence was also driving young girls into relationships with older men and thereby starting the next cycle of dependency and violence: "The young girls are getting tied up in relationships at an early age and…[when] they say they want out he'll just stand over her," said another community worker. "Next thing they're pregnant…and then it goes from being a small problem to a huge one…and she feels there is no way out."

There was no shortage of government funding in Bourke. Ferguson saw millions of dollars pour into the town for large service providers, but all that money did nothing to improve the crime rate. Dozens of services had been set up, but they worked mostly in isolation, rarely cooperated, and competed for clients.

Back in 2009, Ferguson led a community charge for alcohol restrictions, which substantially reduced the severity of violent assaults. He then turned to working with other community members to find a new approach to lowering Bourke's crime rate, though they didn't know what form that approach should or would take. The answer came when Ferguson discovered a program in the United States that was getting remarkable results. Called "justice reinvestment," this prevention model directed funding away from the endless spending on prisons, and toward services that stop crimes from happening in the first place and prevent people from reoffending. Ironically, this was implemented by Republicans in Texas, a state with the nation's highest incarceration rate. They shelved plans to spend $523 million on 14,000 new prison beds, and instead invested in substance abuse treatment, mental health programs, and support for prisoners after they were released. The results were stunning: parole revocations were cut by 25 percent, and the prison population growth was 90 percent below the projected rate. It saved the state hundreds of millions of dollars, and five years into the program, Texas closed a prison for the first time in its history.[23]

To see if justice reinvestment could work in Bourke, Ferguson invited the not-for-profit group Just Reinvest NSW to a community town-hall meeting. Together they decided to create working groups for three areas: early childhood; children aged eight to eighteen; and the role of men. With the help of philanthropists, they established a central working hub called Maranguka (Ngemba for "caring for others"). In 2015, they devised an innovative strategy, to be led by the newly formed Bourke Tribal Council, chaired by representatives of all twenty-two Indigenous language groups living in Bourke. The new council (a huge achievement in itself; Ferguson calls it a "treaty"), with help from then-Aboriginal and Torres Strait Islander Social Justice Commissioner Mick Gooda, put factional differences and historical grievances aside. To bring young people on board, they set up a council chaired by local kids.

Ferguson was adamant that justice reinvestment wouldn't be merely another program being imposed on the Bourke community—it would be *their* program. Every Indigenous expert I've spoken to says this kind of community-building, beyond its impact on crime, is in itself a powerful way to overcome the dislocation and disempowerment at the core of domestic abuse.

Whereas the High Point program only targeted known abusers, in Bourke the intervention started a lot earlier, with boys and young men at risk of *becoming* perpetrators. As in High Point, though, the Bourke strategy couldn't begin without data. To get a clear picture of how and why young people in Bourke were being arrested and jailed, Maranguka and Just Reinvest had to gather data that had never been collected before. It provided them with a map of what was happening in their town: for instance, the fact that 62 percent of youth offenses were being committed between 6:00 p.m. and 6:00 a.m., and 42 percent on weekends. These were the precise hours that youth services were, of course, closed. With this data, Maranguka could approach youth services and say, "These are the hours we want you to work, and this is why."

———

What the Bourke council was searching for in this data were the "circuit breakers" that would stop boys from being criminalized. At the top of the list was vehicle offenses: Bourke led the state in driving offenses for people aged ten to twenty-five, especially unlicensed driving. The reasons for this were painfully obvious: limited access to registered cars, literacy issues with written driving tests, and not enough licensed drivers to teach them. Here was a basic problem with a straightforward solution. So Maranguka raised money for a car and paid a local to teach young people to drive. When the demand for lessons surged, eight off-duty police officers volunteered as instructors. It's hard to quantify the effect of this on a young Aboriginal person—to have a police officer volunteer to help you, not harass you. But the other effects *can* be quantified: there was a 72 percent drop in the number of people under age twenty-five arrested for unlicensed driving.

Wherever they saw gaps or problems, Maranguka stepped in to fix them. To help students who were violent or disruptive in school, Maranguka teamed up with Bourke High School to run Our Place, which takes young Aboriginal men outside traditional learning environments and teaches them literacy and numeracy through practical work experiences, such as building fences and shearing sheep; and cultural ones, such as making didgeridoos and clapsticks. Some of these students were also appointed to the Youth Council, where they could be the eyes and ears of their community and come up with ways to solve problems affecting their friends and families. After the program was introduced, school attendance for Our Place students rose 25 percent and suspensions dropped 79 percent.

What the Maranguka model had built in from the start was an understanding that no one program or approach would single-handedly reduce either domestic abuse or any of the town's other intractable crimes. "You have to address those underlying causes," says Ferguson, now the founder and executive director of Maranguka Justice Reinvestment, "everything from housing to employment and the limited opportunities in our community. You can't do one thing without the other."

Superintendent Greg Moore is a busy man: he leads the forty-five-person police force in Bourke and looks after the Darling River Local

Area Command, which spans almost 70,000 square miles (roughly the size of North Dakota). Across this gigantic area, there are just 15,600 people, concentrated in five towns. In 2016, all five were in the top fifteen for highest domestic assault rates in the state.[24] "There's not a shift that goes by that the troops aren't getting called out to domestic incidents," says Moore. It's a top priority for Moore—and it's not something he's shy about. "I'm like a broken record on domestic violence. But I don't make any apologies for that—it's had a big impact on our community... We see kids from these families out at night committing offenses or becoming victims themselves."

Though Aboriginal and Torres Strait Islander people make up around a quarter of the population, they perpetrate 90 percent of the violence.[25] Moore refused to take this family violence for granted. "Some people used to say quite distressing things to me, things like, 'Oh, it's just black love.' It's like, 'No, it's not part of your culture, it's a loving culture, and we need to get away from that tolerance that you can do violence to your family.'"

In 2016, inspired by Maranguka, Moore decided that his police officers had to stop doing the same thing each time and expecting a different result. It wasn't enough merely to respond to domestic violence calls; rather, they had to start preventing violence *before* it occurred. Moore had a simple idea: his officers would make house calls to known perpetrators and victims, especially those who were "high risk." He wanted police to do two things: first, check that perpetrators were complying with protection orders, and second—and more radically—assess what could be done to improve their lives.

Like the police in High Point, Moore started with a complex data analysis of known victims and perpetrators, flagging those they saw as high risk. He knew, however, that identifying the most dangerous would require more than raw numbers. "Maybe it's a first-time offender, but often you just get a sense—from your own observations and the risk factors—that this person is an extreme risk, and that maybe this perpetrator isn't going to comply with the orders."

Once he had the data, Moore dispatched his police to do spot checks on families and couples that had domestic violence orders in place, especially those deemed to be high risk. During their visit, police would talk to the victim and the perpetrator to figure out what kind of help they needed—everything from job-seeking aid, to substance abuse and mental health treatment, to assistance with parenting. Then they'd come back to the family with local people or service providers who could help them. To shift away from the old model, Moore had to educate his staff and bring them with him on these visits. "It wasn't about just telling the staff what to do, but *why* we're doing it."

One perpetrator—an alcoholic who regularly beat his wife—was having police called out on him every week. "What we were doing wasn't working," says Moore. So he partnered with a local Aboriginal man, a role model in Bourke, and took him along to the next visit. Sitting with the perpetrator, this man told him straight: "This stuff used to be tolerated, but it's gotta stop. You're on the radar with the local crew, and you've gotta stop belting up Aunty, because it's not on." The pair visited him on several occasions, "and we sort of wore him down a bit. He was a good fella, his triggers were there...he just couldn't handle his [alcohol]." Eventually, the perpetrator agreed to go to a men's group "to have a yarn [talk] about things." The men's group was a Maranguka initiative: a place for men to talk about grief and loss, to focus on healing and to reconnect to country. "Often there's some unresolved trauma or something like that, so it can be a form of group therapy without them even realizing it." When Moore spoke to me, it had been more than a year since police started working with this man. There hadn't been a repeat incident in that whole time.

For Bourke police, this is not just a new operation, it's a revolutionary shift. Moore doesn't want people to wait for problems to arise before they get police involved: "We're encouraging people, once they start identifying that they have some challenges or difficulties, to reach out and make contact." The message is: *We don't want to punish you. We want to protect you.*

————

So what happened to all those service providers, working away in isolation and competition? Maranguka brought them together and got them to cooperate. Unlike the High Point working group, which convenes once a fortnight, Maranguka goes a lot further: they meet almost every weekday. "We have twenty-four-hour check-ins now, with a strong focus on domestic violence," says Ferguson. At 9:30 a.m., Monday to Wednesday, people from Maranguka meet with Bourke police at the Maranguka Hub to discuss any domestic incidents that have occurred in the past twenty-four hours and how best to respond. Does someone need to go and talk to a perpetrator? Do they need help with substance abuse? Mentoring? Employment? What is happening for their partner and children? Each case is talked about in detail and solutions are workshopped. The point is to act early so cases don't end up in court. On Thursdays, the group expands to include all the relevant nongovernmental organizations (NGOs) and government agencies, which, like a triaging medical team, work together to devise the best strategies to help the clients they share. "It's proven to be quite a success," says Ferguson. "We're addressing things almost immediately, instead of allowing them to fester."

————

What has happened in Bourke is nothing short of revolutionary. When I first saw the statistics, I could barely believe what I was reading: by 2017, domestic violence–related assaults in Bourke had decreased by a jaw-dropping 39 percent. Other crimes are also down: drug-related prosecutions (39 percent), driving offenses (34 percent), and non-domestic-violence-related assaults (35 percent).[26] It's no coincidence that Bourke has seen *increases* in other areas: a 31 percent increase in students completing year twelve of their schooling, for example.[27] Indigenous people in Australia and North America have been pleading with governments for decades to let them do what's best for their own people. Bourke is living proof that self-governance—carefully planned, evidence-based, and community-owned—works.

When it comes to domestic violence, there's no question that Bourke Police's Operation Solidarity (combined with the holistic approach of Maranguka) is also working. Across the Darling River Local Area Command, domestic homicides dropped from seven in 2015–16 (when Operation Solidarity began) to zero for the following eighteen months. By 2018, the repeat victimization rate—which had been twice the state average—was also down by a third. Victims have greater trust in police: the number who cooperated with police to pursue legal action is up, from an average of 68 percent in 2016 to 85 percent in 2018. Even with this increased amount of legal action, the conviction rate has remained above the state average, at 75 percent—something Moore attributes to the fact that their prosecutor has been trained to properly understand domestic abuse.

These results are stunning, but Moore isn't content to hang his hat on them. "We're also looking at other measures, like hospital admission rates, domestic violence–related [welfare] payments, and child removals. I think they've only had one child removed in the Bourke LGA [local government area] in the last twelve months, and eight across the whole [Darling River] area. That is historically low."

This didn't require huge government spending. In fact, no extra resources were needed for Operation Solidarity; it was integrated into daily duties. That is the whole point of justice reinvestment: you spend money in the short term to save it in the future. It is estimated that the

Maranguka-initiated changes led to $3.1 million in savings in 2017. If the project can maintain even half of the 2017 results for the next few years, the saving over five years is likely to be $7 million.[28] "Bourke was fairly targeted and identified as one of the most dangerous communities in the world," says Ferguson. "It's not overly ambitious now to think we can become one of the safest communities in the world."

<hr />

The models in High Point and Bourke are exciting, and not just because they have reduced domestic abuse. These programs work because they are community-led; they generate deep collaboration; they see perpetrators as individuals capable of rationality and redemption; and they make victim protection their number-one priority. Whereas traditional systems make victims responsible for protecting themselves, both High Point and Bourke hand that responsibility back to the community and the police. As David Kennedy explains, "We are regularly in the situation in which a woman, whose name we know, is being terrorized by a man, whose name we know... We should not ask her to put herself at further risk: we should make him stop."[29] The High Point model, with its tough criminal justice approach, does not want to see more perpetrators in jail; rather, it wants them to *choose* to stop their abuse and stay free. The message is clear, though: staying free means doing what they have to do to stop their abuse. If they can't make the rational choice to stop abusing, the full force of the law will descend on them, with metaphorical guns blazing.

What is especially promising about these models is the way they center on collaboration. We waste criminally large amounts of money on programs that operate in isolation. So many programs are just tiny drops in the bucket: they're funded to run for a few weeks or months and do little to nothing to ensure that victims and their families return to health and safety. The models in High Point and Bourke don't exist at the whim of political cycles. They are there for the long term, maintained by community ownership, close collaboration, and a common goal. This is not merely good practice for reducing domestic abuse; rather, it is a model for tackling intractable social problems.

Nevertheless, these models are not one-size-fits-all. They are place-based solutions, which means they must be adapted to the unique conditions and situations of each town or city. That takes time. Conflicts must be dealt with, common ground must be established, and strategies must be developed. No doubt there will be many who find fault with the programs in High Point and highlight the challenges of transposing programs from one place to another, from small towns to big cities. My intention in this chapter is not to imply that there's one single silver-bullet solution, nor to suggest that these are the only programs worthy of praise or effort. Courageous people around the world are pushing the boundaries of what's possible and getting remarkable results. If we were to become really serious about ending domestic abuse and actually devoted the resources necessary to do it, the results could be spectacular. It would, in my opinion, be one of the greatest nation-building exercises in history.

For those who still don't believe it's possible to reduce domestic abuse now, consider this. Five years ago, few could have imagined something like #MeToo: a revolution not just against sexual harassment, but against patriarchy itself. Even that disheveled alt-right culture warrior Steve Bannon—a booster of fascists and white supremacists—acknowledges it as the most radical movement of our time. "Time's up on ten thousand years of recorded history," he told Bloomberg CNBC. "This is coming. This is real."[30]

Revolutions are impossible until they are inevitable.

WHO CAN I CALL?

If you or someone you know is experiencing domestic abuse, call the National Domestic Violence Helpline at 1-800-799-7233 or visit www.thehotline.org.

If you need a safety plan—to keep you and any children and/or pets safe while you're in an abusive relationship, preparing to leave, or after you've left—you can call the Domestic Violence Resource Center 24 hours a day: 503-469-8620.

Young people experiencing dating abuse can contact LoveIsRespect.org via its website, by phone at 1-866-331-9474, or by texting "loveis" to 22522. They can also reach BreaktheCycle.org at 202-824-0707.

Native Americans can call StrongHearts, a support line for tribal communities across the United States, at 844-762-8483.

Children looking for help can call Childhelp, the National Child Abuse Hotline, at 1-800-422-4453.

LGBTQI people can call The Northwest Network at 206-568-7777.

If you've experienced rape or incest, call RAINN at 800–656-HOPE.

Immigrants and refugees can call the National Network for Immigrant and Refugee Rights at 1-510-465-1984.

Acknowledgments

To my soul mate, David Hollier: For both of us, writing this book was life-changing, expansive, dark, and sometimes desperate. Nothing about it was easy. But even as "the book" became a burden, you challenged me to strive for philosophical depth and compassion. Your mission to help men live embodied, emotional lives pushed me beyond the easy polemic and motivated me to do the much harder work of trying to *understand*. On the psychology of abusive men, your insights have been invaluable. Your commitment to this project was sometimes astonishing: even when you were shattered by long hours and sleepless nights, you spent the rare, spare hours you had improving these pages, often as our daughter slept in her pram beside you. For the late-night discussions, the weekends sacrificed, the endless housework and solo parenting...for all of our beautiful disasters...I love you, and God Only Knows what I'd be without you.

I began writing this book while trying to become pregnant and finished it with an almost two-year-old daughter, whose wit and charisma thrill us every day. Writing a book with a baby takes an army. To Oma Lynda Hill, for turning up at the drop of a hat, bringing a bag full of random goodies, and staying for days at a time, week after week; to "Grandpa" Richard Hill for his Grandpa Thursdays and grandpa squeezes; to Grandma Susan Davis for her unbending support; to Bear Lorraine Symington, for her selfless mercy missions (especially in the final frenzied weeks); to Auntie Prem and Uncle Dasi, for your magical, healing hospitality: I will be forever grateful for the love and wonder you brought to Stevie during this time, and for the hours you gave me to write. This book could not have happened without you. And to my brother, Joel: Your joyful enthusiasm for my work has given me so much life (plus, you saved my arse when my computer exploded on deadline). Love you, bro.

To Nick Feik at *The Monthly*, who commissioned my first essay on domestic violence: You made everything I wrote better, and I am so grateful for your ongoing support and friendship. Thanks also to Chris Bullock, whose steady hand guided me through two difficult documentaries for *Background Briefing*. Both of you were the solid ground I needed to feel brave. To Aviva Tuffield, the first publisher who recognized that this was a book that needed to be written: You showed saintly patience as I whooshed past deadline after deadline. To my publisher at Black Inc., Chris Feik, and editor Kirstie Innes-Will, your loyalty to this text, your clarity, and your unwavering kindness and support held me together at times when I felt like the book was going to break me. To Meg Gibbons at Sourcebooks, your enthusiasm for this project absolutely blew me away. I can't thank you enough for the way you've taken this book into your heart.

To the survivors: You have taught me so much, not just about abuse, but about love, commitment, and true grit. It's an honor to tell your stories and to know you. To the few I can't name: Your dedication to protecting your children, and to supporting other survivors to protect theirs, is heroic.

I've tapped the minds of many brilliant people over the last few years, but perhaps none so often as Mike Salter, whose blazing intelligence has been a light in the dark on so many occasions. I've also been advised and warmly supported by a legion of fiercely intelligent women, many of whom work on the frontlines: Robyn Cotterell-Jones, Julie Oberin, Magistrate Anne Goldsbrough, Kelsey Hegarty, Kay Schubach, Sherele Moody, Kylie Gray, Susan Scrupski, Moo Watson-Baulch, Tanya Whitehouse, Judy Atkinson, Jenna Price, and the world-changer Rosie Batty.

I was privileged to have people I admire provide vital feedback on several chapters. Respect and gratitude to Hannah McGlade, Paul Daley, Mike Salter, Kristine Ziwica, Eddie Gallagher, Heather Douglas, Liz Conor, Neil Websdale, Martin Hodgson, Amy McQuire, Josephine Cashman, Susan Scrupski, Kay Schubach, Anne Goldsbrough, Julie Oberin, and to my mum, dad, and brother, who also brought their razor-sharp minds to some of the text. To Nikki Stevens, who came up with the title: Thank you for getting it exactly right.

To Gabrielle Kuiper, Monica Attard, and Natasha Mitchell: I can't tell you what it meant for you to back me like you did. To the crowd who supported me on Pozible: You gave me the strength I needed to keep going, and to make this book the best I could make it.

I owe this book to two other influences in my life. Nonna, you made me believe we could keep the bastards honest and that writing was the way to do it. I still can't believe you're gone. You were supposed to live forever. Mark Colvin, you made the world feel epic and taught me that there is always something at stake. People, you said; they are the story. I miss your wisdom and warmth every day. I wish you were here to see this.

Lastly, to Stevie, my Fire Rooster: Your love and spark kept me from sinking into the many dark holes along this path. You are my sunshine.

Notes

NOTES ON MY METHODS

1. Yasmin Khan, "Domestic Violence or Domestic Abuse? Why Terminology Matters," *Women's Agenda*, March 18, 2019, https://womensagenda.com.au/uncategorised /domestic-violence-or-domestic-abuse-why-terminology-matters/.

INTRODUCTION

1. United Nations Office on Drugs and Crime, *Global Study on Homicide: Gender-Related Killing of Women and Girls* (Vienna: UNODC, 2018).
2. Emma E. Fridel and James Alan Fox, "Gender Differences in Patterns and Trends in U.S. Homicide, 1976–2017," *Violence and Gender* 6, no. 1 (March 11, 2019), https://doi. org/10.1089/vio.2019.0005. See also Laura M. Holson, "Murders by Intimate Partners Are on the Rise, Study Finds," *The New York Times*, April 12, 2019, https://www .nytimes.com/2019/04/12/us/domestic-violence-victims.html (1,527 women killed in domestic homicides in 2017).
3. Al Tompkins, "Sexual Assault on College Campuses Often Goes Unpunished, Study Finds," *Poynter*, February 24, 2010, https://www.poynter.org/reporting-editing/2010 /sexual-assault-on-college-campuses-often-goes-unpunished-study-finds.
4. Elliot Rodger, "My Twisted World: The Story of Elliot Rodger," May 2014, https://assets .documentcloud.org/documents/1173619/rodger-manifesto.pdf.
5. Rebecca Solnit, "Listen up, Women Are Telling Their Story Now," *The Guardian*, December 30, 2014, https://www.theguardian.com/news/2014/dec/30/-sp-rebecca -solnit-listen-up-women-are-telling-their-story-now.
6. National Domestic Violence Hotline, https://www.thehotline.org/resources/statistics.
7. Madeleine Carlisle and Melissa Chan, "Here's Why Domestic Violence Kills So Many Women and Children in America," *Time*, October 17, 2019, https://time.com/5702435 /domestic-violence-gun-violence.
8. National Coalition Against Domestic Violence, "CDC National Intimate Partner and Sexual Violence Survey," https://ncadv.org/statistics.
9. Yumiko Aratani, *Homeless Children and Youth: Causes and Consequences*, National Center for Children in Poverty, 2009, http://www.nccp.org/publications/pdf/text_888.pdf.
10. Brian A. Reaves, *Police Response to Domestic Violence, 2006–2015*, Bureau of Justice Statistics, 2017, https://www.bjs.gov/content/pub/pdf/prdv0615.pdf (based on statistic that on

average, American police were notified in 56 percent of the 1.3 million nonfatal domestic violence victimizations between 2006 and 2015 [728,000 notifications annually]).

11. M. C. Black et al., *The National Intimate Partner and Sexual Violence Survey (NISVS): 2010 Summary Report* (Atlanta, GA: National Center for Injury Prevention and Control, Centers for Disease Control and Prevention, 2011).

12. Courtenay E. Cavanaugh et al., "Prevalence and Correlates of Suicidal Behavior among Adult Female Victims of Intimate Partner Violence," *Suicide & Life-Threatening Behavior* 41, no. 4 (2011): 372–83.

13. *Overlooked: Women and Jails in an Era of Reforms*, Vera Institute of Justice, August 2016, https://www.vera.org/publications/overlooked-women-and-jails-report.

14. Family and Youth Services Bureau, *Domestic Violence and Homelessness: Statistics* (2016).

15. Australian Housing and Urban Research Institute, "What Is the Link between Domestic Violence and Homelessness?" (brief, December 5, 2017).

16. Monica Campo and Sarah Tayton, "Domestic and Family Violence in Regional, Rural and Remote Communities," Australian Institute of Family Studies, December 2015, https://aifs.gov.au/cfca/publications/domestic-and-family-violence-regional-rural-and-remote-communities.

17. Gerald T. Hotaling and David Sugarman, "An Analysis of Risk Markers in Husband to Wife Violence: The Current State of Knowledge," *Violence and Victims* 1 (1986): 101–24.

18. "Mum, Two Children Slain in South Australia Farmhouse Horror," News.com.au, June 1, 2016, https://www.news.com.au/national/crime/mum-two-children-slain-in-south-australia-farmhouse-horror/news-story/686435aeb3f9e5397177b8210f975c9f.

19. Evan Stark, *Coercive Control: The Entrapment of Women in Personal Life* (New York: Oxford University Press, 2009), 280.

20. Monica Campo and Sarah Tayton, *Intimate Partner Violence in Lesbian, Gay, Bisexual, Trans, Intersex and Queer Communities: Key Issues,* Australian Institute of Family Studies, December 2015, https://aifs.gov.au/cfca/publications/intimate-partner-violence-lgbtiq-communities.

21. Claire M. Renzetti, *Violent Betrayal: Partner Abuse in Lesbian Relationships* (Lexington, KY: CRVAW Faculty Book Gallery, 1992), 10.

22. Judith Lewis Herman, *Trauma and Recovery* (New York: Basic Books, 1992), 76–77.

1. THE PERPETRATOR'S HANDBOOK

1. Albert D. Biderman, *Communist Patterns of Coercive Interrogation* (April 1955), in Hearings before the Permanent Subcommittee on Investigations of the Committee on Government Operations, U.S. Senate, 84th Congress, 2nd session (June 19, 20, 26, and 27, 1956, Washington, DC).

2. Albert D. Biderman, "Communist Attempts to Elicit False Confessions from Air Force Prisoners of War," *Bulletin of the New York Academy of Medicine* 33, no. 9 (September 1957): 616–25.

3. Biderman, *Communist Techniques of Coercive Interrogation,* n.p.: Office for Social Science Programs, Air Force Personnel and Training Research Center, Air Research and Development Command, 1956, 3.

4. Scott Shane, "U.S. Interrogators Were Taught Chinese Coercion Techniques," *The New York Times*, July 2, 2008, https://www.nytimes.com/2008/07/02/world/americas/02iht-gitmo.1.14167656.html.

5. Diana Russell, *Rape in Marriage* (Bloomington: Indiana University Press, 1990).

6. Amnesty International, *Report on Torture* (January 1, 1973).

7. Judith Lewis Herman, *Trauma and Recovery* (New York: Basic Books, 1992), 74.

8. Herman, *Trauma and Recovery*, 76.

9. Herman, *Trauma and Recovery*, 82–83.

10. Herman, *Trauma and Recovery*, 82.

11. Herman, *Trauma and Recovery*, 82–83.

12. Aussie Banter Facebook page, reposted by Clementine Ford, July 7, 2018, www.facebook.com/clementineford/posts/1775390125871407.

13. Evan Stark, *Coercive Control: The Entrapment of Women in Personal Life* (New York: Oxford University Press, 2009), 197.

14. Stark, *Coercive Control*, 16.

15. Stark, *Coercive Control*, 16.

16. Evan Stark, "Looking beyond Domestic Violence: Policing Coercive Control," *Journal of Police Crisis Negotiations* 12, no. 2 (2012): 199–217.

17. Evan Stark, "A Domestic-Violence Expert on Eric Schneiderman and 'Coercive Control,'" interview by Cari Romm, *The Cut*, May 8, 2018, https://www.thecut.com/2018/05/an-abuse-expert-on-schneiderman-and-coercive-control.html.

18. Albert Biderman, "Communist Patterns of Coercive Interrogation, Appendix," in *Communist Interrogation, Indoctrination, and Exploitation of American Military and Civilian Prisoners*, vols. 74–76 (Washington, DC: U.S. Government Printing Office, 1956), 203.

19. Lundy Bancroft, *Why Does He Do That? Inside the Minds of Angry and Controlling Men* (New York: Berkley Books, 2002), 64–65.

20. P. Cameron, *Relationship Problems and Money: Women Talk about Financial Abuse* (West Melbourne, Australia: WIRE Women's Information, 2014), 25.

21. Biderman, "Communist Patterns of Coercive Interrogation," 203.

22. Evan Stark, "Re-Presenting Battered Women: Coercive Control and the Defense of Liberty," in *Complex Realities and New Issues in a Changing World* (Quebec, Canada: Les Presses de l'Université du Québec, 2012), 13.

23. Stark, *Coercive Control*, 217.

24. Joe Tidy, "Stalkerware: The Software that Spies on Your Partner," BBC News, October 25, 2019, https://www.bbc.com/news/technology-50166147.

25. Isabelle Altman, "A Dispatch Special Report: The Last Step before Murder," Family Justice Center Alliance, April 19, 2017, https://www.cdispatch.com/news/article.asp?aid=56930#.WNRFRA-tbro.email.

26. Survivor testimony in Queensland, Special Taskforce on Domestic and Family Violence, in *Our Journal: A Collection of Personal Thoughts about Domestic Violence* (Brisbane: Queensland Special Taskforce on Domestic and Family Violence, 2015).

27. Nancy Glass et al., "Non-Fatal Strangulation Is an Important Risk Factor for Homicide of Women," *Journal of Emergency Medicine* 35, no. 3 (2007): 329–35.

28. Biderman, *Communist Patterns of Coercive Interrogation*, 203.

29. Herman, *Trauma and Recovery*, 77.

30. John Stuart Mill, *The Subjection of Women* (New York: D. Appleton, 1869), 26.

31. George Orwell, *Nineteen Eighty-Four* (originally published 1949; Boston: Houghton Mifflin Harcourt, 1983), 244.

32. Biderman, *Communist Techniques of Coercive Interrogation*, 16.

33. Herman, *Trauma and Recovery*, 76.

34. A. M. Volant et al., "The Relationship between Family Violence and Animal Abuse: An Australian Study," *Journal of Interpersonal Violence* 3, no. 9 (September 2008): 1277–95.

35. Biderman, "Communist Attempts," 619.

36. Stark, *Coercive Control*, 258.

37. David Livingstone Smith, "The Essence of Evil," *Aeon*, October 24, 2014.

38. Lewis Okun, *Woman Abuse: Facts Replacing Myths* (New York: SUNY Press, 1986), 128.

39. Herman, *Trauma and Recovery*, 83.

2. THE UNDERGROUND

1. Calculated based on the estimated total for women who have experienced coercive control in a report from the Centers for Disease Control and Prevention, *Prevalence and Characteristics of Sexual Violence, Stalking, and Intimate Partner Violence Victimization—National Intimate Partner and Sexual Violence Survey* (2011).

2. WIRE Women's Information submission to the Senate Finance and Public Administration References Committee Inquiry into Domestic Violence in Australia (2014), 6.

3. Kate Campbell, "WA Cop Stephanie Bochorsky Who Saved Two Girls Set Alight by Their Dad Speaks for First Time," *Perth Now*, October 20, 2017.

4. J. E. Snell and Robey A. Rosenwald, "The Wifebeater's Wife: A Study of Family Interaction," *Archives of General Psychiatry* 11, no. 2 (1964): 107–12.

5. Paula J. Caplan, *The Myth of Women's Masochism* (Lincoln, NE: iUniverse, 2005), 36.

6. Glenn Collins, "Women and Masochism: Debate Continues," *The New York Times*, December 2, 1985, https://www.nytimes.com/1985/12/02/style/women-and-masochism-debate-continues.html.

7. Catherine Kirkwood, *Leaving Abusive Partners: From the Scars of Survival to the Wisdom for Change* (London: SAGE, 1993).

8. A. P. Worden and B. E. Carlson, "Attitudes and Beliefs about Domestic Violence: Results of a Public Opinion Survey: II. Beliefs about Causes," *Journal of Interpersonal Violence* 20, no. 10 (2005): 1219–43.

9. Lenore E. Walker, *The Battered Woman* (New York: Harper & Row, 1979), 46.

10. Walker, *The Battered Woman*, 46.

11. Walker, *The Battered Woman*, 46.

12. Walker, *The Battered Woman*, 57.

13. Allan Wade, "Rethinking Stockholm Syndrome" (presentation), October 11, 2015; uploaded to YouTube by the Center for Response Based Practice, www.youtube.com/watch?v=drI4HFJkbCc.

14. Kathryn Westcott, "What Is Stockholm Syndrome?," BBC News, August 22, 2013, https://www.bbc.com/news/magazine-22447726.

15. This analysis draws on the work of Canadian family therapist Allan Wade, and his presentation "Rethinking Stockholm Syndrome," (see note 13) in which he presents his interviews with Kristin Enmark.

16. Terence Mickey, "#13 The Ideal Hostage," *Memory Motel* (podcast), December 6, 2016, https://soundcloud.com/memorymotelpodcast/13-the-ideal-hostage.

17. Wade, "Rethinking Stockholm Syndrome."

18. Wade, "Rethinking Stockholm Syndrome."

19. M. Namnyak et al., "'Stockholm Syndrome': Psychiatric Diagnosis or Urban Myth?" *Acta Psychiatrica Scandinavica* 117 (2008): 4–11.

20. Wade, "Rethinking Stockholm Syndrome."

21. Courtney Michelle Klein, *Combating Intimate Partner Violence through Policing Innovations: Examining High Point, North Carolina's Offender Focused Domestic Violence Initiative* (New York: John Jay College of Criminal Justice, City University of New York, 2014), 6.

22. Paula Reavey and Sam Warner, *New Feminist Stories of Child Sexual Abuse: Sexual Scripts and Dangerous Dialogues* (London: Psychology Press, 2003), 81.

23. E. W. Gondolf and E. R. Fisher, *Battered Women as Survivors: An Alternative to Treating Learned Helplessness* (Lexington, MA: Lexington Books/D.C. Heath, 1988).

24. Lee H. Bowker and Lorie Maurer, "The Medical Treatment of Battered Wives," *Women & Health* 12 (1987): 25–45.

25. Linda Gordon, *Heroes of Their Own Lives: The Politics and History of Family Violence* (Boston: Viking, 1988).

26. Albert D. Biderman, *Communist Patterns of Coercive Interrogation* (April 1955), in Hearings before the Permanent Subcommittee on Investigations of the Committee on Government Operations, U.S. Senate, 84th Congress, 2nd session (June 19, 20, 26, and 27, 1956, Washington, DC).

27. Kirkwood, *Leaving Abusive Partners*, 61.

28. Leslie Morgan Steiner, "Why Domestic Violence Victims Don't Leave," TEDxRainier, November 2012, https://www.ted.com/talks/leslie_morgan_steiner_why_domestic_violence_victims_don_t_leave?language=en.

29. Carol Gilligan, *Making Connections: The Relational Worlds of Adolescent Girls at Emma Willard School* (Cambridge, MA: Harvard University Press, 1990), 25.

30. "An Interview with Carol Gilligan—Restoring Lost Voices," *Phi Delta Kappan*, May 1, 2000, https://www.thefreelibrary.com/An+Interview+with+Carol+Gilligan+-+Restoring+Lost+Voices.-a061971425.

31. Interview with Carol Gilligan, "Fear of Speaking Out Is Holding Girls Back," *Deseret News*, July 6, 1997, https://www.deseret.com/1997/7/6/19322316/fear-of-speaking-out-is-holding-girls-back.

32. Quoted in Francine Prose, "Confident at 11, Confused at 16," *The New York Times*, January 7, 1990, https://www.nytimes.com/1990/01/07/magazine/confident-at-11-confused-at-16.html.

33. Lili Loofbourow, "The Female Price of Male Pleasure," *The Week*, January 25, 2018, https://theweek.com/articles/749978/female-price-male-pleasure.

34. Denis Walsh, quoted in, "It's Good for Women to Suffer the Pain of a Natural Birth, Says Medical Chief," *The Observer*, July 12, 2009, https://www.theguardian.com/lifeandstyle/2009/jul/12/pregnancy-pain-natural-birth-yoga.

35.   Lili Loofbourow, "The Female Price of Male Pleasure."

36.   Steiner, "Why Domestic Violence Victims Don't Leave."

37.   Kathleen J. Ferraro and John M. Johnson, "How Women Experience Battering: The Process of Victimization," *Social Problems* 30, no. 3 (1983): 325–39.

38.   Ali Owens, "Why We Stay: A Deeper Look at Domestic Abuse," *The Huffington Post*, June 6, 2016, https://www.huffpost.com/entry/why-we-stay-a-deeper-look_b_10315292.

39.   Dean A. Dabney, *Crime Types: A Text/Reader* (Alphen aan den Rijn, The Netherlands: Wolters Kluwer Law & Business, 2012), 87.

40.   Julia Baird and Hayley Gleeson, ongoing investigation by ABC News into religion and domestic violence (2017–18).

41.   Judith Lewis Herman, *Trauma and Recovery* (New York: Basic Books, 1992), 87.

42.   George Orwell, *Nineteen Eighty-Four* (originally published 1949; Boston: Houghton Mifflin Harcourt, 1983), 215.

43.   Leigh Goodmark, "When Is a Battered Woman Not a Battered Woman? When She Fights Back," *Yale Journal of Law & Feminism* 20, no. 1 (2008): 75–129.

44.   Francis Bloch and Vijayendra Rao, "Terror as a Bargaining Instrument: A Case Study of Dowry Violence in Rural India," *The American Economic Review* 92, no. 4 (2002): 1029–43.

45.   Sylvia Walby and Jonathan Allen, "Domestic Violence, Sexual Assault and Stalking: Findings from the British Crime Survey," Home Office Research Study 276, Home Office Research, Development and Statistics Directorate, 2004, http://nomsintranet.org.uk/roh /official-documents/HomeOfficeResearchStudy276.pdf.

46.   Jennifer Nixon and Cathy Humphreys, "Marshalling the Evidence: Using Intersectionality in the Domestic Violence Frame," *Social Politics: International Studies in Gender, State and Society* 17, no. 2 (2010): 137–58, 148.

47.   Melissa Lucashenko, "Sinking below Sight: Down and Out in Brisbane and Logan," *Griffith REVIEW* 41 (2013), 53–67, https://www.griffithreview.com/articles/sinking-below-sight.

48.   SBS World News, "Cost of Fleeing Violent Relationship Is $18,000 and 141 Hours, ACTU," SBS News, November 13, 2017, https://www.sbs.com.au/news /cost-of-fleeing-violent-relationship-is-18-000-and-141-hours-actu.

49.   P. Cameron, "Relationship Problems and Money: Women Talk about Financial Abuse," WIRE Women's Information, August 26, 2014, https://www.wire.org.au /relationship-problems-and-money/.

50.   Cameron, "Relationship Problems and Money."

51.   Cameron, "Relationship Problems and Money."

3. ABUSIVE MIND

1.   Heather Douglas and Tanja Stark, *Stories from Survivors: Domestic Violence and Criminal Justice Interventions* (T. C. Beirne School of Law, The University of Queensland, 2010), 23.

2.   John Gottman and Neil Jacobson, *When Men Batter Women: New Insights into Ending Abusive Relationships* (New York: Simon & Schuster, 1998).

3.   Gottman and Jacobson, *When Men Batter Women*, 84.

4.   Gottman and Jacobson, *When Men Batter Women*, 89.

5.   Gottman and Jacobson, *When Men Batter Women*, 90, 92.

6. Gottman and Jacobson, *When Men Batter Women,* 74.

7. Gottman and Jacobson, *When Men Batter Women,* 114–16.

8. Gottman and Jacobson, *When Men Batter Women,* 110.

9. Gottman and Jacobson, *When Men Batter Women,* 93–96.

10. Gottman and Jacobson, *When Men Batter Women,* 86.

11. Gottman and Jacobson, *When Men Batter Women,* 90.

12. Gottman and Jacobson, *When Men Batter Women,* 93.

13. Gottman and Jacobson, *When Men Batter Women,* 38.

14. Gottman and Jacobson, *When Men Batter Women,* 30.

15. Emily Esfahani Smith, "Masters of Love," *The Atlantic,* June 12, 2014, https://www.theatlantic.com/health/archive/2014/06/happily-ever-after/372573.

16. J. C. Babcock et al., "A Second Failure to Replicate the Gottman et al. (1995) Typology of Men Who Abuse Intimate Partners and Possible Reasons Why," *Journal of Family Psychology* 18, no. 2 (1995): 396–400; J. C. Meehan, A. Holtzworth-Munroe, and K. Herron, "Maritally Violent Men's Heart Rate Reactivity to Marital Interactions: A Failure to Replicate the Gottman et al. (1995) Typology," *Journal of Family Psychology* 15, no. 3 (2001): 394–408.

17. A. Holtzworth-Munroe and G. L. Stuart, "Typologies of Male Batterers: Three Subtypes and the Differences among Them," *Psychological Bulletin* 116, no. 3 (1994): 476–97.

18. Data from the Gun Violence Archive, cited in Sam Morris and Guardian US interactive team, "Mass Shooting in the US," *The Guardian,* February 16, 2018, https://www.theguardian.com/us-news/ng-interactive/2017/oct/02/america-mass-shootings-gun-violence.

19. Rebecca Traister, "What Mass Killers Really Have in Common," *New York Magazine,* July 15, 2016, https://www.thecut.com/2016/07/mass-killers-terrorism-domestic-violence.html.

20. Jane Wangmann, *Different Types of Intimate Partner Violence—An Exploration of the Literature* (Domestic Violence Clearinghouse, October 2011), 7.

21. David Gadd and Mary-Louise Corr, "Beyond Typologies: Foregrounding Meaning and Motive in Domestic Violence Perpetration," *Deviant Behavior* 387 (2017): 781–91.

22. Gadd and Corr, "Beyond Typologies," 789.

23. Quoted in Allan J. Tobin and Jennie Dusheck, *Asking about Life* (Belmont, CA: Thomson Brooks/Cole, 2005), 819.

24. Kirsten Tillisch et al., "Structure and Response to Emotional Stimuli as Related to Gut Microbial Profiles in Healthy Women," *Psychosomatic Medicine* 79, no. 8 (October 2017): 905–13.

25. Mark Patrick Taylor et al., "The Relationship between Atmospheric Lead Emissions and Aggressive Crime: An Ecological Study," *Environmental Health* 15, no. 23 (February 2016).

26. Corrine Barraclough, "Domestic Violence: Where Are the Realists?" *The Spectator Australia,* April 12, 2017.

27. Edward W. Gondolf, "Characteristics of Court-Mandated Batterers in Four Cities: Diversity and Dichotomies," *Violence Against Women* 5, no. 11 (1999): 1277–93.

28. S. M. Stith et al., "The Intergenerational Transmission of Spouse Abuse: A Meta-analysis," *Journal of Marriage and the Family* 62, no. 3 (1999): 640–54.

29. Lundy Bancroft, *Why Does He Do That? Inside the Minds of Angry and Controlling Men* (New York: Berkley Books, 2002).

30. Bancroft, *Why Does He Do That?*

31. C. L. Yodanis, "Gender Inequality, Violence against Women, and Fear: A Cross-National Test of the Feminist Theory of Violence against Women," *Journal of Interpersonal Violence* 19, no. 6 (2004): 655–75; L. L. Heise and A. Kotsadam, "Cross-National and Multilevel Correlates of Partner Violence: An Analysis of Data from Population-Based Surveys," *Lancet Global Health* 3, no. 6 (2015): e332–e340.

32. The Hon. Malcolm Turnbull MP, Prime Minister, "Transcript of Joint Press Conference: Women's Safety Package to Stop the Violence," September 24, 2015, https://www .malcolmturnbull.com.au/media/release-womens-safety-package-to-stoptheviolence.

33. James Gilligan, *Violence: Reflections on a National Epidemic* (Vintage Books, 1997), 25.

34. Melanie F. Shepard and Ellen L. Pence, *Coordinating Community Responses to Domestic Violence: Lessons from Duluth and Beyond* (Thousand Oaks, CA: SAGE Publications, 1999), 29.

35. Shepard and Pence, *Coordinating Community Responses to Domestic Violence,* 29.

36. Shepard and Pence, *Coordinating Community Responses to Domestic Violence,* 28.

37. E. Pence and S. Das Dasgupta, *Re-Examining "Battering': Are All Acts of Violence against Intimate Partners the Same?* (Praxis International, June 2006).

38. Margaret Atwood, *Curious Pursuits: Occasional Writing* (London: Hachette UK, 2009), ch. 6, 2.

4. SHAME

1. Neil Websdale, *Familicidal Hearts: The Emotional Styles of 211 Killers* (Cambridge: Oxford University Press, 2010).

2. Lundy Bancroft, *Why Does He Do That? Inside the Minds of Angry and Controlling Men* (New York: Berkley Books, 2002), 151–58.

3. Helen Block Lewis, *Shame and Guilt in Neurosis* (New York: International Universities Press, 1971).

4. Helen Block Lewis, "The Role of Shame in Symptom Formation," in *Emotions and Psychopathology*, ed. M. Clynes and J. Panksepp (Boston: Springer, 1988), 95–106.

5. R. L. Dearing and J. P. Tangney, eds., *Shame in the Therapy Hour* (Washington, DC: American Psychological Association, 2011).

6. James Gilligan, *Violence: Reflections on a National Epidemic* (New York: Vintage Books, 1997), 117.

7. Christian Keysers, "Inside the Mind of a Psychopath—Empathic, but Not Always," *Psychology Today*, July 24, 2013, https://www.psychologytoday.com/us/blog /the-empathic-brain/201307/inside-the-mind-psychopath-empathic-not-always.

8. Katie Heaney, "My Life as a Psychopath," *The Cut*, August 10, 2018, https://www.thecut .com/2018/08/my-life-as-a-psychopath.html.

9. Donald L. Nathanson, *Shame and Pride: Affect, Sex, and the Birth of the Self* (New York: Norton, 1992), 220.

10. Robert Karen, "Shame," *The Atlantic Monthly*, February 1992, 40–70.

11. Peter N. Stearns, *Shame: A Brief History* (Urbana: University of Illinois Press, 2017), 5.

12. The Tomkins Institute, "Nine Affects, Present at Birth, Combine with Life Experience to Form Emotion and Personality," http://www.tomkins.org/what-tomkins-said/introduction/nine-affects-present-at-birth-combine-to-form-emotion-mood-and-personality.

13. D. L. Nathanson, ed., *The Many Faces of Shame* (New York: Guilford Press, 1987), 21.

14. Jim Logan, "For Shame," *The Current* (University of California–Santa Barbara), February 2016, https://www.news.ucsb.edu/2016/016496/shame-pain-evolved-defense.

15. Brené Brown, "Listening to Shame," TED Talk, March 2012, https://www.ted.com/talks/brene_brown_listening_to_shame.

16. Donald L. Nathanson, *Shame and Pride: Affect, Sex, and the Birth of the Self* (New York: W. W. Norton, 1992), 303–78.

17. Helen Lewis, "Shame and the Narcissistic Personality," in *The Many Faces of Shame*, ed. D. L. Nathanson (New York: Guilford Press, 1987), 93–132.

18. Nathanson, *Shame and Pride*, 359.

19. Robert M. Sapolsky, *Behave: The Biology of Humans at Our Best and Worst* (New York: Penguin, 2017), 106.

20. Sapolsky, *Behave*, 106.

21. Sapolsky, *Behave*, 107.

22. Quoted in Jon Ronson, *So You've Been Publicly Shamed* (New York: Riverhead Books, 2015), 6.

23. Penelope Green, "Carefully Smash the Patriarchy," *The New York Times*, March 18, 2019.

24. James Gilligan, "Shame, Guilt, and Violence," *Social Research* 70, no. 4 (2003): 1149–80.

25. Alyssa Toomey, "Nigella Lawson Choking Incident: Photographer Describes Scene as 'So Violent,'" *E! News*, January 9, 2014, https://www.eonline.com/news/497312/nigella-lawson-choking-incident-photographer-describes-scene-as-so-violent.

26. James Gilligan, *Violence: Reflections on a National Epidemic* (New York: Vintage Books, 1997), 111.

27. Judith Graham, *Bulletin #4422, Violence Part 2: Shame and Humiliation* (University of Maine, 2001), https://extension.umaine.edu/publications/4422e/.

28. Germaine Greer, *On Rage* (Melbourne: Melbourne University Press, 2008), 12–13.

29. Michelle Jones, *A Fight about Nothing: Constructions of Domestic Violence* (PhD thesis, University of Adelaide, 2004).

30. Jones, *A Fight about Nothing*, 185.

31. Donald G. Dutton and Susan K. Golant, *The Batterer: A Psychological Profile* (New York: Basic Books, 1995) (e-book).

32. Dutton and Golant, *The Batterer*.

33. Erich Fromm, *The Anatomy of Human Destructiveness* (New York: Henry Holt, 1973), 323.

34. N. S. Websdale, "Of Nuclear Missiles and Love Objects: The Humiliated Fury of Kevin Jones," *Journal of Contemporary Ethnography* 39, no. 4 (2010): 388–420.

35. Websdale, "Of Nuclear Missiles," 410.

36. Websdale, "Of Nuclear Missiles," 413.

37. Jac Brown, "Shame and Domestic Violence: Treatment Perspectives for Perpetrators from Self Psychology and Affect Theory," *Sexual and Relationship Therapy* 19, no. 1 (2004): 39–56.

38. Gilligan, *Violence*, 48.

39. Websdale, "Of Nuclear Missiles," 411.

40. Gilligan, *Violence*, 415.

41. Allan G. Johnson, *The Gender Knot: Unraveling Our Patriarchal Legacy* (Philadelphia, PA: Temple University Press, 2005).

42. Brown, "Listening to Shame."

5. PATRIARCHY

1.   Kathy Caprino, "Renowned Therapist Explains the Crushing Effects of Patriarchy on Men and Women Today," *Forbes*, January 25, 2018, https://www.forbes.com/sites/kathycaprino /2018/01/25/renowned-therapist-explains-the-crushing-effects-of-patriarchy-on-men -and-women-today/#7303e71a2161.

2.   European Union Agency for Fundamental Rights, *Violence against Women: An EU-Wide Survey* (Luxembourg: Publications Office of the European Union, March 5, 2014).

3.   Bureau of Labor Statistics, U.S. Department of Labor, quoted in David Leser, "Women, Men and the Whole Damn Thing," *The Sydney Morning Herald*, February 9, 2018.

4.   David Leser, "Women, Men and the Whole Damn Thing," *The Sydney Morning Herald*, February 9, 2018.

5.   Michael Ian Black, "The Boys Are Not Alright," *The New York Times*, February 21, 2018.

6.   Elise Scott and Elise Pianegonda, "Heterosexual, White Men with Jobs 'Aren't Included in Anything,' Canberra Liberal MLA Says," ABC News, September 21, 2017, https://www.abc.net.au/news/2017-09-20/heterosexual-white-men-are-not -included-in-anything-mla-says/8964916.

7.   Allan G. Johnson, *The Gender Knot: Unraveling Our Patriarchal Legacy* (Philadelphia, PA: Temple University Press, 2005), 5–12.

8.   Johnson, *The Gender Knot*, 64.

9.   Terrence Real, *How Can I Get Through to You?: Closing the Intimacy Gap between Men and Women* (New York: Simon & Schuster, 2010).

10. Real, *How Can I Get Through to You?*, quoted in bell hooks, *The Will to Change: Men, Masculinity and Love* (New York: Simon & Schuster, 2004), 60–61.

11. Tim Winton, "About the Boys: Tim Winton on How Toxic Masculinity Is Shackling Men to Misogyny," *The Guardian*, April 9, 2018, https://www.theguardian.com/books/2018/apr/09 /about-the-boys-tim-winton-on-how-toxic-masculinity-is-shackling-men-to-misogyny.

12. Maree Crabbe and David Corlett, dirs., *Love and Sex in an Age of Pornography* (2013), documentary.

13. A. Armstrong, A. Quadara, A. El-Murr, and J. Latham, *The Effects of Pornography on Children and Young People: An Evidence Scan* (Melbourne: Australian Institute of Family Studies, 2017).

14. Gail Dines, "Choking Women Is All the Rage. It's Branded as Fun, Sexy 'Breath Play,'" *The Guardian*, May 14, 2018, https://www.theguardian.com/commentisfree/2018/may/13 /choking-women-me-too-breath-play.

15. A. J. Brieges et al., "Aggression and Sexual Behavior in Best-Selling Pornography Videos: A Content Analysis Update," *Violence Against Women* 16, no. 10 (October 2010): 1065–85.

16. Maree Crabbe, "Porn as Sex Education: A Cultural Influence We Can No Longer Ignore," *The Guardian*, August 3, 2016, https://www.theguardian.com/commentisfree/2016 /aug/04/porn-as-sex-education-a-cultural-influence-we-can-no-longer-ignore.

17. A. McKee, "The Objectification of Women in Mainstream Pornographic Videos in Australia," *Journal of Sex Research* 42 (2005): 277–90.

18. Gail Dines, *Pornland: How Porn Has Hijacked Our Sexuality* (Boston: Beacon Press, 2010), xxvii.

19. Dines, *Pornland*, xxiv.

20. Fight the New Drug, "Porn Yesterday vs. Porn Today (Infographic)," https://fightthenew drug.org/media/porn-yesterday-today-infographic/.

21. Miranda Horvath et al., *Basically Porn Is Everywhere: A Rapid Evidence Assessment on the Effects that Access and Exposure to Pornography Has on Children and Young People* (London: Office of the Children's Commissioner, 2013).

22. P. Weston, "New Data Shows Gold Coast's Domestic Violence Crisis Being Fueled by Links to Pornography," *Gold Coast Bulletin*, October 7, 2016.

23. bell hooks, *Feminism Is for Everybody: Passionate Politics* (London: Pluto Press, 2000).

24. bell hooks, *The Will to Change: Men, Masculinity, and Love* (New York: Simon & Schuster, 2004), 6–7.

25. hooks, *The Will to Change*, 7.

26. Brené Brown, "Listening to Shame," TED Talk, March 2012, https://www.ted.com/talks /brene_brown_listening_to_shame; Andy Hinds, "Messages of Shame Are Organized around Gender," *The Atlantic*, April 26, 2013.

27. Laurie Penny (2018), https://twitter.com/PennyRed/status/992396816879628289 and https://twitter.com/PennyRed/status/989070547769323520.

28. Steph Harmon, "#MeToo Revelations and Loud, Angry Men: The Feminism Flashpoint of Sydney Writers' Festival," *The Guardian*, May 5, 2018, https://www.theguardian.com /books/2018/may/06/metoo-revelations-and-loud-angry-men-the-feminism-flashpoint -of-sydney-writers-festival.

29. Ann Watson Moore, "Domestic Violence Offender: How I Decided to Kill My Wife," *Gold Coast Bulletin*, November 8, 2018.

30. Michael Salter, "Stopping Domestic Violence Means Rethinking Masculinity," The Ethics Centre, November 25, 2015, https://ethics.org.au/stopping-domestic-violence -means-rethinking-masculinity.

31. Michael Salter, "Real Men Do Hit Women," *Meanjin* (Autumn 2016), https://meanjin .com.au/essays/real-men-do-hit-women.

32. Salter, "Stopping Domestic Violence Means Rethinking Masculinity."

33. Holly Hedegaard, Sally C. Curtin, and Margaret Warner, *Suicide Rates in the United States Continue to Increase* (NCHS Data Brief No. 309, National Center for Health Statistics, 2018), www.cdc.gov/nchs/products/databriefs/db309.htm.

34. S. Rodrick, "All-American Despair," *TIME Magazine*, May 2019.

6. CHILDREN

1. Renee McDonald et al., "Estimating the Number of American Children Living in Partner-Violent Families," *Journal of Family Psychology* 20, no. 1 (2006): 137–42.

2. Judith Lewis Herman, *Trauma and Recovery* (New York: Basic Books, 1997), 96.

3. "State Statutes, Definitions of Child Abuse and Neglect," Child Welfare Information Gateway, 2019, https://www.childwelfare.gov/pubpdfs/define.pdf.

4. Megan Mitchell, "A Life Free from Violence and Fear: A Child's Right" (speech given at 2016 International Congress on Child Abuse and Neglect, August 29, 2016).

5. Ruth Clare, "Seen But Not Heard," *Meanjin* (Summer 2017), https://meanjin.com.au /essays/seen-but-not-heard.

6. M. C. Mercado et al., "Trends in Emergency Department Visits for Nonfatal Self-Inflicted Injuries among Youth Aged 10 to 24 Years in the United States, 2001–2015," *JAMA* 318, no. 19, 1931–1933 (2017).

7. D. A. Ruch et al., "Trends in Suicide among Youth Aged 10 to 19 Years in the United States, 1975 to 2016," *JAMA Netw Open*. 2, no. 5 (2019): e193886.

8. Megan Mitchell, Australian Children's Commissioner, speech at the 13th Australasian Injury Prevention Network Conference, November 13, 2017.

9. Australian Human Rights Commission, *Children's Rights Report* (Sydney: AHRC, 2015), 99.

10. Alison Gopnik, *The Philosophical Baby: What Children's Minds Tell Us about Truth, Love, and the Meaning of Life* (New York: Farrar, Straus and Giroux, 2009), 9.

11. Gopnik, *The Philosophical Baby*, 9.

12. Wendy Bunston and Robyn Sketchley, "Refuge for Babies in Crisis: How Crisis Accommodation Services Can Assist Infants and Their Mothers Affected by Family Violence," Domestic Violence Resource Center, The Royal Children's Hospital, January 2012, 18.

13. Australian Human Rights Commission, *Children's Rights Report*, 155.

14. Herman, *Trauma and Recovery*, 99.

15. Eamon J. McCrory et al., "Heightened Neural Reactivity to Threat in Child Victims of Family Violence," *Current Biology* 21, no. 23 (2011): R947–R948.

16. Bruce D. Perry, "The Neurodevelopmental Impact of Violence in Childhood," in *Textbook of Child and Adolescent Forensic Psychiatry*, ed. D. Schetky and E. P. Benedek (Washington, DC: American Psychiatric Press, 2001), 221–38.

17. Olga Trujillo, *The Sum of My Parts: A Survivor's Story of Dissociative Identity Disorder* (Oakland, CA: New Harbinger, 2011), 18.

18. Olga Trujillo, "DID Starts with Dissociation," *Psychology Today*, June 27, 2011, https://www .psychologytoday.com/hk/blog/the-sum-my-parts/201106/did-starts-dissociation?amp.

19. Herman, *Trauma and Recovery*, 101.

20. Heather McNeill, "Perth Teen Who Stabbed Step-Father to Death Should Not Go to Prison, Court Told," *WAtoday*, February 15, 2018, https://www.watoday.com.au/national /western-australia/perth-teen-who-stabbed-stepfather-to-death-should-not-go-to-prison -court-told-20180215-h0w5fh.html.

21. National Alliance to End Homelessness, Youth and Young Adults online fact sheet, https:// endhomelessness.org/homelessness-in-america/who-experiences-homelessness/youth.

22. K. M. Kitzmann et al., "Child Witnesses to Domestic Violence: A Meta-Analytic Review," *Journal of Consulting and Clinical Psychology* 71, no. 2 (2003): 339–52.

23. Bessel A. van der Kolk, "Developmental Trauma Disorder: Toward a Rational Diagnosis for Children with Complex Trauma Histories," *Psychiatric Annals* 35, no. 5 (2005): 401–8.

24. The Center for Treatment of Anxiety and Mood Disorders, "Complex Trauma Disorder," September 15, 2017, https://centerforanxietydisorders.com/complex-trauma-disorder.

25.   Bessel van der Kolk, *The Body Keeps the Score: Mind, Brain and Body in the Transformation of Trauma* (New York: Penguin, 2014), 157.

7. WHEN WOMEN USE VIOLENCE

1.   *Our Journal: A Collection of Personal Thoughts about Domestic Violence*, from the "Not Now, Not Ever" report by the Queensland Taskforce into Domestic Violence (2015).
2.   T. A. Migliaccio, "Abused Husbands: A Narrative Analysis," *Journal of Family Issues* 23, no. 1 (2002): 26.
3.   Migliaccio, "Abused Husbands," 34.
4.   Jacquelyn Allen-Collinson, "A Marked Man: A Case of Female-Perpetrated Intimate Partner Abuse," *International Journal of Men's Health* 8, no. 1 (2009): 22–40.
5.   Both women and men are more likely to experience violence at the hands of men, with around 95 percent of all victims of violence in Australia reporting a male perpetrator. K. Diemer, *ABS Personal Safety Survey: Additional Analysis on Relationship and Sex of Perpetrator: Documents and Working Papers. Research on Violence against Women and Children* (Melbourne: University of Melbourne, 2015).
6.   Richard J. Gelles and Murray A. Straus, "Violence in the American Family," *Journal of Social Issues* 35, no. 2 (1979), 15.
7.   Gelles and Straus, "Violence in the American Family," 26.
8.   Richard J. Gelles, *The Violent Home: A Study of Physical Aggression between Husbands and Wives* (Beverly Hills, CA: Sage, 1974), 77.
9.   Gelles, *The Violent Home*, 151.
10.   Suzanne K. Steinmetz, "The Battered Husband Syndrome," *Victimology* 2, nos. 3–4 (1977–78): 499–509.
11.   Richard Gelles, "The Missing Persons of Domestic Violence: Battered Men," *The Women's Quarterly* (1999), http://breakingthescience.org/RichardGelles_MissingPersonsOfDV .php.
12.   Murray Straus et al., "The Revised Conflict Tactics Scales (CTS2): Development and Preliminary Psychometric Data," *Journal of Family Issues* 17 (1996): 283.
13.   Gayla Margolin, "The Multiple Forms of Aggression between Marital Partners: How Can We Identify Them?" *Journal of Marital and Family Therapy* 13 (1987): 77–84.
14.   Russell P. Dobash and Rebecca E. Dobash, "Women's Violence in Intimate Relationships: Working on a Puzzle," *British Journal of Criminology* 44 (2004): 324–49.
15.   Michael Kimmel, *Misframing Men: The Politics of Contemporary Masculinities* (New Brunswick, NJ: Rutgers University Press, 2010), 106.
16.   A. Tomison, "Exploring Family Violence: Links between Child Maltreatment and Domestic Violence," NCPC Issues no. 13, Australian Institute of Family Studies (June 2000).
17.   Michael Kimmel, *The Gender of Desire: Essays on Male Sexuality* (Albany, NY: SUNY Press, 2012), 204.
18.   Michael P. Johnson, *A Typology of Domestic Violence: Intimate Terrorism, Violent Resistance, and Situational Couple Violence* (Boston: Northeastern University Press, 2008), 17.

19. Theodora Ooms, "A Sociologist's Perspective on Domestic Violence: A Conversation with Michael Johnson, Ph.D.," from the May 2006 conference sponsored by CLASP and NCSL: Building Bridges: Marriage, Fatherhood, and Domestic Violence.

20. J. E. Stets and M. A. Strauss, "Gender Differences in Reporting Marital Violence and Its Medical and Psychological Consequences," in *Physical Violence in American Families: Risk Factors and Adaptations to Violence in 8145 Families*, ed. M. A. Strauss and Richard Gelles (New Brunswick, NJ: Transaction Press, 1990), 151–66.

21. In Ooms, "A Sociologist's Perspective."

22. Michael P. Johnson, *Types of Domestic Violence: Research Evidence*, YouTube video, November 13, 2013, https://www.youtube.com/watch?v=QEVsfkOOF-g.

23. In Ooms, "A Sociologist's Perspective."

24. Neil Frude, "Marital Violence: An Interactional Perspective," in *Male Violence*, ed. J. Archer (London: Routledge Press, 1994), 153–159.

25. Julia Mansour, *Women Defendants to AVOs: What Is Their Experience of the Justice System?* (Women's Legal Services NSW, March 18, 2014).

26. Jane Wangmann, "'She said...' 'He said...': Cross Applications in NSW Apprehended Domestic Violence Order Proceedings" (PhD thesis, Faculty of Law, University of Sydney, 2009).

27. Kathleen J. Ferraro, *Neither Angels nor Demons: Women, Crime, and Victimization* (Boston: Northeastern University Press, 2006), 60.

28. Susan Miller, *Victims as Offenders* (New Brunswick, NJ: Rutgers University Press, 2005), 78.

29. "Campbell, Augustina" (pseudonym), "How Police Policies Allow Domestic Violence Victims to Be the Ones Arrested," post at brokeassstuart.com blog, https://broke assstuart.com/2016/08/08/how-police-policies-allow-domestic-violence-victims-to-be -the-ones-arrested.

30. Katherine S. van Wormer, "Women's Shelters and Domestic Violence Services Save the Lives of Men," *Psychology Today*, December 2010, https://www.psychologytoday .com/us/blog/crimes-violence/201012/women-s-shelters-and-domestic-violence-services -save-the-lives-men.

31. Michael Kimmel, "'Gender Symmetry' in Domestic Violence," *Violence Against Women* 8, no. 11 (2002).

8. STATE OF EMERGENCY

1. Julianna M. Nemeth, et al., "Provider Perceptions and Domestic Violence (DV) Survivor Experiences of Traumatic and Anoxic-Hypoxic Brain Injury: Implications for DV Advocacy Service Provision," *Journal of Aggression, Maltreatment & Trauma* 28, no. 6 (2019): 744–763.

2. U.S. crime reports, cited by the Centers for Disease Control, https://www.cdc.gov /violenceprevention/intimatepartnerviolence/fastfact.html.

3. Bureau of Justice Statistics, "Female Victims of Violence," BJS No. 228356 (September 2009), https://www.bjs.gov/content/pub/pdf/fvv.pdf.

4. ACLU, "DOJ Issues New Guidance for Police in Domestic Violence and Sexual Assault Cases," December 15, 2015, https://www.aclu.org/press-releases/doj-issues-new -guidance-police-domestic-violence-and-sexual-assault-cases.

5. National Coalition Against Domestic Violence, https://www.ncadv.org.

6. Safe Steps, *Safe Steps Family Violence Response Center: A Case for Support* (2017), https://www.safesteps.org.au/wp-content/uploads/2017/10/safe-steps-A-Case-for-Support-2017.pdf.

7. Safe Steps, *Annual Report, 2016–17.*

8. Safe Steps, *Annual Report, 2014–15.*

9. Heather Douglas, "Policing Domestic and Family Violence," *International Journal for Crime, Justice and Social Democracy* 8, no. 2 (2019): 31–49.

10. Douglas, "Policing Domestic and Family Violence," 41.

11. Details from the inquest into Kelly Thompson's death, conducted by the Victorian Coroner, April 21, 2016; Melissa Fyfe, "'I Fear He May Kill Me': How the System Failed Domestic Violence Victim Kelly Thompson," *Good Weekend,* December 4, 2015.

12. Inquest into Kelly Thompson's death, conducted by the Victorian Coroner, April 21, 2016, para. 280.

13. Fenella Souter, "How AVOs Are Failing Our Most Vulnerable Women," *Marie Claire,* July 31, 2014, https://nz.news.yahoo.com/how-avos-are-failing-our-most-vulnerable-women-24599330.html.

14. M. Segrave, D. Wilson, and K. Fitz-Gibbon, "Policing Intimate Partner Violence in Victoria (Australia): Examining Police Attitudes and the Potential of Specialisation," *Australian and New Zealand Journal of Criminology* (2016): 1–18.

15. Donna K. Coker et al., *Responses from the Field: Sexual Assault, Domestic Violence, and Policing,* University of Miami Legal Studies Research Paper No. 16-2 (October 1, 2015).

16. Marie Segrave, Dean Wilson, and Kate Fitz-Gibbon, "Policing Intimate Partner Violence in Victoria (Australia): Examining Police Attitudes and the Potential of Specialisation,"*Australian and New Zealand Journal of Criminology* (2016): 1–18.

17. Segrave, Wilson, and Fitz-Gibbon, "Policing Intimate Partner Violence in Victoria (Australia)," 7.

18. Segrave, Wilson, and Fitz-Gibbon, "Policing Intimate Partner Violence in Victoria (Australia)," 7.

19. Segrave, Wilson, and Fitz-Gibbon, "Policing Intimate Partner Violence in Victoria (Australia)," 7.

20. Segrave, Wilson, and Fitz-Gibbon, "Policing Intimate Partner Violence in Victoria (Australia)," 10.

21. Victoria Police, "Chief Commissioner Ken Lay Speaks at the Royal Women's Hospital White Ribbon Day Breakfast," November 23, 2012.

22. R. B. Felson, J. M. Ackerman, and C. A. Gallagher, "Police Intervention and the Repeat of Domestic Assault," *Criminology* 43, no. 3 (2005): 563–88.

23. Australian Domestic and Family Violence Death Review Network, *Data Report 2018* (May 2018), https://apo.org.au/node/174811.

24. Elizaveta Perova and Sarah Reynolds, "Women's Police Stations and Intimate Partner Violence: Evidence from Brazil," *Social Science & Medicine* 174 (December 2016): 188–96.

25. Kerry Carrington et al., *The Palgrave Handbook of Criminology and the Global South* (New York: Springer, 2018), 836.

26.   Christina Asquith, "Why Aren't U.S. Police Departments Recruiting More Women?" *The Atlantic*, August 30, 2016, https://www.theatlantic.com/politics/archive/2016/08 /police-departments-women-officers/497963.

27.   Domestic Violence Law Reform, *The Victim's Voice Survey: Victim's Experience of Domestic Violence and the Criminal Justice System* (Paladin, Sara Charlton Charitable Foundation and Women's Aid, 2014).

28.   Paul McGorrery and Marilyn McMahon, "It's Time 'Coercive Control' Was Made Illegal in Australia," *The Conversation*, April 30, 2019, http://theconversation.com /its-time-coercive-control-was-made-illegal-in-australia-114817.

9. THROUGH THE LOOKING GLASS

1.   Caroline Overington, "Child Custody: One Mother's Bitter Lesson in Sharing the Kids with Dad," *The Australian*, November 10, 2017.

2.   Helen Rhoades, Reg Graycar, and Margaret Harrison, "The Family Law Reform Act 1995: The First Three Years," *Australian Family Lawyer: The Journal of the Family Law Section of the Law Council of Australia* 15, no. 1 (2001): 1–8; H. Rhoades, "The Dangers of Shared Care Legislation: Why Australia Needs (Yet More) Family Law Reform," *Federal Law Review* 36, no. 3 (2008); R. Field et al., "Family Reports and Family Violence in Australian Family Law Proceedings: What Do We Know?," *Journal of Judicial Administration* 25, no. 4 (2016): 212–36; L. Laing, *No Way to Live: Women's Experiences of Negotiating the Family Law System in the Context of Domestic Violence* (New South Wales Health, University of Sydney, and Benevolent Society, 2010); D. Bagshaw et al., "Family Violence and Family Law in Australia: The Experiences and Views of Children and Adults from Families Who Separated Post-1995 and Post-2006," *Family Matters* 8 (2011): 49–61.

3.   *Congressional Record* 164, no. 158 (Tuesday, September 25, 2018), H8844–H8847, at H8844, https://www.congress.gov/crec/2018/09/25/modified/CREC-2018-09-25-pt1-PgH8844 .htm.

4.   Witness statement of Kelsey Lee Hegarty, Royal Commission into Family Violence, August 2015.

5.   Rae Kaspiew, "Separated Parents and the Family Law System: What Does the Evidence Say?," *Australia Institute of Family Studies* (2016), https://aifs.gov.au/cfca/2016/08/03 /separated-parents-and-family-law-system-what-does-evidence-say.

6.   Kirsty Forsdike et al., "Exploring Australian Psychiatrists' and Psychiatric Trainees' Knowledge, Attitudes and Preparedness in Responding to Adults Experiencing Domestic Violence," *Australasian Psychiatry* 27, no. 1 (February 2019): 64–68.

7.   Nico Trocmé et al., *Canadian Incidence Study of Reported Child Abuse and Neglect* (final report), Canadian Incidence Study of Reported Child Abuse and Neglect, National Clearinghouse on Family Violence (Ottawa: Health Canada, 2001).

8.   Nico Trocmé and Nicholas Bala, "False Allegations of Abuse and Neglect When Parents Separate," *Child Abuse & Neglect* 29 (2005): 1333–45.

9.   Trocmé and Bala, "False Allegations of Abuse," 1334.

10.   Harriet Alexander, "False Abuse Claims Are the New Court Weapon, Retiring Judge Says," *The Sydney Morning Herald*, July 6, 2013, https://www.smh.com.au/national/false-abuse -claims-are-the-new-court-weapon-retiring-judge-says-20130705-2phao.html.

11. *Encyclopaedia Brittanica* (online), s.v. "child abuse" (John Philip Jenkins, last updated February 27, 2020), https://www.britannica.com/topic/child-abuse.

12. Before the age of fifteen, 12 percent (956,600) of women had been sexually abused, compared to 4.5 percent (337,400) of men. Australian Bureau of Statistics, *4906.0—Personal Safety, Australia, 2005* (Canberra: ABS, 2006).

13. Richard A. Gardner, *True and False Accusations of Child Sex Abuse* (Cresskill, NJ: Creative Therapeutics, 1992).

14. Gardner, *True and False Accusations of Child Sex Abuse*, 594–95.

15. Gardner, *True and False Accusations of Child Sex Abuse*, 549.

16. Gardner, *True and False Accusations of Child Sex Abuse*, 576–77.

17. Gardner, *True and False Accusations of Child Sex Abuse*, 592–94.

18. William Bernet and Amy J. L. Baker, "Parental Alienation, DSM-5, and ICD-11: Response to Critics," *Journal of the American Academy of Psychiatry and the Law*, 41, no. 1 (March 2013): 98–104.

19. In 2008, Brisbane clinical psychologist William Wrigley was reprimanded by the Queensland Psychology Board for referencing PAS in evidence to the Family Court. Tony Koch, "Ruling Debunks Custody Diagnosis," *The Australian*, April 7, 2008.

20. Independent Children's Lawyer & Rowe and Anor [2014] Family Ct. App. 859, October 8, 2014.

21. Paragraphs 38 and 39, December 2014 judgment.

22. Joan S. Meier et al., *Child Custody Outcomes in Cases Involving Parental Alienation and Abuse Allegations* (GWU Law School Public Law Research Paper No. 2019-56/GWU Legal Studies Research Paper No. 2019-56), https://dx.doi.org/10.2139/ssrn.3448062.

23. S. Jeffries et al., "Good Evidence, Safe Outcomes in Parenting Matters Involving Domestic Violence? Understanding Family Report Writing Practice from the Perspective of Professionals Working in the Family Law System," *UNSW Law Journal* 39, no. 4 (2016): 1355.

24. "In Australia, Brown et al. (2003) reexamined the 100 cases of the Magellan Project (a quarter of them substantiated by a Child Protection Agency report) and found that allegations of abuse had been found to be false in only 11 cases. Mothers had made allegations twice as often as fathers (48 percent vs. 21 percent). While two-thirds of allegations by mothers (thirty-two cases of forty-eight) were substantiated, only one-third (seven cases of twenty-one) of allegations by fathers were substantiated. In only one case was the allegation made by the child and this case was substantiated. In most of the substantiated cases (thirty-two cases or 63 percent), the father was the perpetrator. Most of the other substantiated cases (16 or 31 percent) were other family members, but these did not include any mothers. The eleven cases where allegations were found to be false were fairly evenly divided between allegations by mothers (five) and allegations by fathers (six), but it was also noted that in most of these cases the alleging parent was receiving treatment for serious mental illness and/or had a history of being sexually abused as children themselves." Matthew Myers, "Toward a Safer and More Consistent Approach to Allegations of Child Sexual Abuse in Family Law Proceedings—Expert Panels and Guidelines," paper given at the World Congress on Family Law and Children's Rights, Sydney, March 2013.

25. E. F. Loftus and J. E. Pickrell, "The Formation of False Memories," *Psychiatric Annals* 25, no. 12 (1995), 720–25.

26.   Jess Hill, "In the Child's Best Interests," *Background Briefing*, ABC Radio National, June 14, 2015.

27.   Myers, "Toward a Safer and More Consistent Approach."

10. DADIRRI

1.   Sarah Deer, "Criminal Justice in Indian Country at the Berkeley Law Thelton E. Henderson Center for Social Justice Symposium, *Heeding Frickey's Call: Doing Justice in Indian Country* (Berkeley, CA, September 27–28, 2012) Conference Transcript," 37 *American Indian Law Review* (2013), 347–74, 376.

2.   Steven W. Perry, *American Indians and Crime 1992–2002* (U.S. Department of Justice, 2004) [hereinafter Perry (2004)]. See also Ronet Bachman et al., *Violence against American Indian and Alaska Native Women and the Criminal Justice Response: What Is Known* (August 2008), 3.

3.   Bachman et al., *Violence against American Indian and Alaska Native Women.*

4.   Angela Spinney, "FactCheck Q&A: Are Indigenous Women 34–80 Times More Likely than Average to Experience Violence?" *The Conversation*, July 4, 2016, http://the conversation.com/factcheck-qanda-are-indigenous-women-34-80-times-more-likely-than -average-to-experience-violence-61809.

5.   Our Watch, Australia's National Research Organization for Women's Safety (ANROWS), and VicHealth, *Change the Story: A Shared Framework for the Primary Prevention of Violence against Women and Their Children in Australia* (Melbourne: Our Watch, 2015).

6.   Quoted in Laura Murphy-Oates, "Vanished: Lost Voices of Our Sisters," *Dateline/The Feed* (no date), https://www.sbs.com.au/vanished.

7.   Lewis Gordon, "Social Justice Does Not Always Come from the Court Room: An Interview with Sarah Deer," APA Online blog (April 2, 2019), https://blog.apaonline.org/2019/04/02 /social-justice-does-not-always-come-from-the-court-room-an-interview-with-sarah-deer.

8.   André B. Rosay, "Violence against American Indian and Alaska Native Women and Men," June 1, 2016, https://nij.ojp.gov/topics/articles/violence-against-american-indian -and-alaska-native-women-and-men.

9.   Sarah Deer, *Heeding Frickey's Call*, 380.

10.   *Inquest into the Death of Sasha Loreen Napaljarri Green* [2018] NTLC 016, https://justice .nt.gov.au/__data/assets/pdf_file/0006/525417/A00592013-Sasha-Green.pdf.

11.   Martin Hodgson, "Ep 51: From Inside the Community," *Curtain: The Podcast*, March 29, 2018, https://curtainthepodcast.wordpress.com/2018/03.

12.   Quoted in Gary Fields, "On U.S. Indian Reservations, Criminals Slip through the Gaps," *Wall Street Journal*, June 12, 2007, https://www.wsj.com/articles/SB118161297090532116.

13.   Testimony offered during hearing before the Committee on Indian Affairs in the U.S. Senate, "Law Enforcement in Indian Country," June 21, 2007, https://archive.org/stream /gov.gpo.fdsys.CHRG-110shrg36303/CHRG-110shrg36303_djvu.txt.

14.   Quote provided by family lawyer George Newhouse.

15.   Office of the Attorney General, "Legislative Hearing on S. 2785, A Bill to Protect Native Children," March 16, 2020, https://www.pascuayaqui-nsn.gov/index.php/features /attorney-general.

16. Quoted in Tristan Ahtone, "Domestic Abusers Have Gone Unpunished in Native American Country—Until Now," Vice News, June 21, 2015, https://www.vice.com /en_us/article/mbnjxq/domestic-abusers-have-gone-unpunished-in-native-american -country-until-now.

17. "IAU interview Connor, 23 October 2014 (audio)," from Corruption and Crime Commission, *Report on the Response of WA Police to a Particular Incident of Domestic Violence on 19–20 March 2013* (April 21, 2016), paras. 56–59.

18. IAU interview, paras. 63–64.

19. IAU interview, para. 88.

20. IAU interview, para. 97.

21. IAU interview, para. 96.

22. IAU interview, para. 91.

23. IAU interview, paras. 106–8.

24. IAU interview, paras. 116–19.

25. IAU interview, paras. 116–19.

26. Mullaley Family media statement, June 8, 2016.

27. Mullaley Family media statement, June 8, 2016.

28. Natassia Chrysanthos, "'I Haven't Been Right Since': Mother of Murdered Baby Makes Discrimination Complaint," *The Sydney Morning Herald*, April 15, 2019, https://www.smh .com.au/national/i-haven-t-been-right-since-mother-of-murdered-baby-makes-discrimination -complaint-20190403-p51ah4.html.

29. Judy Atkinson, "Stinkin' Thinkin'" (1991), cited in Hannah McGlade, *Our Greatest Challenge: Aboriginal Children and Human Rights* (Canberra: Aboriginal Studies Press, 2012).

30. Judy Atkinson, *Trauma Trails: The Transgenerational Effects of Trauma in Indigenous Australia* (North Melbourne, Australia: Spinifex Press, 2003), 41.

31. Sarah Deer, *The Beginning and End of Rape* (Minneapolis: University of Minnesota Press, 2015), ch. 8 (ebook).

32. Mark St. Pierre, *Walking in the Sacred Manner: Healers, Dreamers, and Pipe Carriers* (New York: Simon & Schuster, 2012), 81.

33. Bonnie Clairmont, "Culturally Appropriate Responses for Native American Victims of Sexual Assault" (PowerPoint presentation), Tribal Law and Policy Institute, http://www .tribal-institute.org/download/NativeVictimsSexualAssault.pdf.

34. Liz Conor, *Skin Deep: Settler Impressions of Aboriginal Women* (Crawley, WA: UWA Publishing, 2016), ch. 2.

35. Conor, *Skin Deep*, ch. 2.

36. Zoe Holman, "*Skin Deep*: Reproducing Aboriginal Women in Colonial Australia, an Interview with Liz Conor," *openDemocracy*, February 2017, https://www.opendemocracy .net/en/5050/skin-deep-reproducing-aboriginal-women-in-colonial-australia.

37. Stefanie Wickstrom, "The Politics of Forbidden Liaisons: Civilization, Miscegenation, and Other Perversions," *Frontiers: A Journal of Women Studies* 26, no. 3 (2005): 168–198.

38. Donald L. Fixico, "When Native Americans Were Slaughtered in the Name of Civilization," History.com, March 2018, https://www.history.com/news/native-americans-genocide -united-states.

39. Richard Dodge, *The Plains of the Great West and Their Inhabitants*, quoted in Louise Barnett, *Touched by Fire: The Life, Death and Mythic Afterlife of George Armstrong* (Lincoln: University of Nebraska Press, 2006), 172.

40. Deer, *The Beginning and End of Rape*, ch. 2.

41. Deer, *The Beginning and End of Rape*, ch. 2.

42. Mary White Rowlandson, *A Narrative of the Captivity, Sufferings, and Removes, of Mrs. Mary Rowlandson: Who Was Taken Prisoner by the Indians, with Several Others; and Treated in the Most Barbarous and Cruel Manner by Those Vile Savages, —with Many Other Remarkable Events during Her Travels* (Leominster, MA: Printed [by Charles Prentiss] for Chapman Whitcomb, 1794), 91.

43. Liz Conor, personal interview.

44. Roxanne Dunbar-Ortiz and Dina Gilio-Whitaker, *"All the Real Indians Died Off," and 20 Other Myths about Native Americans* (Boston: Beacon Press, 2016), 39.

45. Andrea Smith, *Conquest: Sexual Violence and American Indian Genocide* (Durham, NC: Duke University Press, 2015), 23.

46. Phyllis Kaberry, *Aboriginal Woman Sacred and Profane* (London: Routledge, 2005).

47. A. P. Elkin, *Introduction to Kaberry*, quoted in Robert Manne, "The Lost Enchanted World," *The Monthly*, June 2007, https://www.themonthly.com.au/issue/2007/june/1283826310 /robert-manne/lost-enchanted-world.

48. Kaberry, *Aboriginal Woman*, 142–43.

49. *Encyclopedia of Women and Religion in North America: Women in North American Catholicism* (Bloomington: Indiana University Press, 2006), 1233.

50. Deer, *The Beginning and End of Rape*, ch. 2.

51. Theda Purdue, *Cherokee Women: Gender and Culture Change, 1700–1835* (Lincoln: University of Nebraska Press, 1998), 13.

52. Jan Noel, "The Powerful Influence of Iroquois Women," *Herizons* (2011), http://www .herizons.ca/node/566.

53. Evelyn Blackwood, "Sexuality and Gender in Certain Native American Tribes: The Case of Cross-Gender Females," *Signs: Journal of Women in Culture and Society* 10, no. 1 (Autumn 1984): 27–42.

54. William Roscoe, *Changing Ones, Third and Fourth Genders in Native North America* (New York: Palgrave Macmillan US, 1998), 78.

55. Kathleen Malley-Morrison and Denise Hines, *Family Violence in a Cultural Perspective: Defining, Understanding and Combating Abuse* (Thousand Oaks, CA: SAGE, 2004), 66.

56. Abigail Adams to John Adams, March 31, 1776, archived at Founders Online, https:// founders.archives.gov/documents/Adams/04-01-02-0241.

57. "The Constitution of the Iroquois Nations: The Great Binding Law Gayanashagowa," archived at http://www.vlib.us/amdocs/texts/iroquois-const.html.

58. Sally Roesch Wagner, "The Untold Story of the Iroquois Influence on Early Feminists," Feminist.com, https://www.feminist.com/resources/artspeech/genwom/iroquoisinfluence .html; Sally Roesch Wagner, *Handbook of American Women's History* (New York: Garland, 1990), 225.

59. Matilda Joslyn Gage, *Woman, Church, and State, 1893* (London: Persephone Press, 1980), 9–10.

60. Phyllis Kaberry, quoted in Jerry D. Moore, *Visions of Culture: An Annotated Reader* (Louisville, CO: Rowman & Littlefield, 2018), 255.

61. Atkinson, *Trauma Trails*, 36.

62. Marcia Langton, "Ending the Violence in Indigenous Communities," National Press Club Address (November 2016).

63. Quoted in Lisa Surridge, *Bleak Houses: Marital Violence in Victorian Fiction* (Athens: Ohio University Press, 2005), 5.

64. Neil Shaw, "The Devon Judge and His 'Rule of Thumb' on Beating Your Wife," Devon Live, November 3, 2017, https://www.devonlive.com/news/devon-news/devon-judge-rule-thumb-beating-725683.

65. Ruth H. Bloch, "The American Revolution, Wife Beating, and the Emergent Value of Privacy," *Early American Studies* 5, no. 2 (2007), 223–51.

66. Alana Piper and Ana Stevenson, eds., *Gender Violence in Australia: Historical Perspectives* (Melbourne: Monash University Publishing, 2019).

67. Frances Power Cobbe, "Wife-Torture in England," *Contemporary Review* (1878), in *Prose by Victorian Women: An Anthology*, ed. Andrea Broomfield and Sally Mitchell (Abingdon-on-Thames: Routledge, 2013).

68. Cobbe, "Wife-Torture in England," 310.

69. Cobbe, "Wife-Torture in England," 309.

70. Cobbe, "Wife-Torture in England," 296.

71. Cobbe, "Wife-Torture in England," 299.

72. Atkinson, *Trauma Trails*, 41.

73. Atkinson, *Trauma Trails*, 40.

74. W. E. H. Stanner, *The Dreaming and Other Essays* (Carlton, Australia: Black, 2011), 66.

75. Robert Hughes, *The Fatal Shore: The Epic of Australia's Founding* (New York: Vintage Books, 2012), 261.

76. Hughes, *The Fatal Shore*, 261.

77. Hughes, *The Fatal Shore*, 259.

78. "1641: Massachusetts Body of Liberties," from S. Whitmore, *Bibliographical Sketch of the Laws of Massachusetts Colony* (1889), 32–60.

79. Deer, *The Beginning and End of Rape*, ch. 5.

80. Deer, *The Beginning and End of Rape*, ch. 5.

81. Deer, *The Beginning and End of Rape*, ch. 8.

82. Jackie Huggins et al. "Letter to the Editors," *Women's Studies International Forum* 1, no. 5 (1991), 505–13.

83. Hannah McGlade, *Our Greatest Challenge: Aboriginal Children and Human Rights* (Canberra, Australia: Aboriginal Studies Press, 2012).

84. Amy Humphreys, *Representations of Aboriginal Women and Their Sexuality* (Brisbane: University of Queensland, 2008), 1.

85. Albert L. Hurtado, *Intimate Frontiers: Sex, Gender and Culture in Old California* (Albuquerque: University of New Mexico Press, 1999), 88.

86. Deer, *The Beginning and End of Rape*, ch. 3.

87. Larissa Behrendt, "Consent in a (Neo)Colonial Society: Aboriginal Women as Sexual and Legal 'Other'," *Australian Feminist Studies* 15, no. 33 (2000), 353–67.

88. Behrendt, "Consent in a (Neo)Colonial Society," 354.

89. Ann McGrath, *Illicit Love: Interracial Sex and Marriage in the United States and Australia* (Lincoln: University of Nebraska Press, 2015), xxiv.

90. Behrendt, "Consent in a (Neo)Colonial Society," 354.

91. Amy Nethery, "'A Modern-Day Concentration Camp': Using History to Make Sense of Australian Immigration Centres," in *Does History Matter?: Making and Debating Citizenship, Immigration and Refugee Policy in Australia and New Zealand*, ed. Klaus Neumann and Gwenda Tavan (Canberra: ANU E-Press, 2009), ch. 4.

92. Ruth A. Fink Latukefu, "Recollections of Brewarrina Aboriginal Mission," *Australian Aboriginal Studies* issue 1 (March 22, 2014).

93. Australian Human Rights Commission, *Lateral Violence in Aboriginal and Torres Strait Islander Communities—Social Justice Report 2011*, ch. 2, https://www.humanrights.gov.au/our-work /chapter-2-lateral-violence-aboriginal-and-torres-strait-islander-communities-social.

94. Michael A. Morrison and James Brewer Stewart, *Race and the Early Republic: Racial Consciousness and Nation-Building in the Early Republic* (Lanham, MD: Rowman & Littlefield, 2001), 164.

95. Inga Clendinnen, "Lecture 4: Inside the Contact Zone: Part 1." *The Boyer Lectures*, ABC Radio National, December 5, 1999.

96. Margaret Jacobs, *White Mother to a Dark Race: Settler Colonialism, Maternalism, and the Removal of Indigenous Children in the American West and Australia, 1880–1940* (Lincoln: University of Nebraska Press, 2009), 238.

97. Jim Kent, "Boarding School Memories Haunt Lakota Man," SDPB Radio, October 8, 2012, https://listen.sdpb.org/post/boarding-school-memories-haunt-lakota-man.

98. Hannah McGlade, *Our Greatest Challenge: Aboriginal Children and Human Rights* (Canberra, Australia: Aboriginal Studies Press, 2012).

99. Australian Human Rights Commission, *Bringing Them Home—Community Guide, 2007 Update* (2007), https://www.humanrights.gov.au/our-work/education/bringing -them-home-community-guide-2007-update.

100. Quoted in Jacqueline Goodman, *Global Perspectives on Gender and Work: Readings and Interpretations* (Lanham, MD: Rowman & Littlefield, 2000), 41.

101. Atkinson, *Trauma Trails*, 38.

102. Malley-Morrison and Hines, *Family Violence in a Cultural Perspective*, 64.

103. W. E. H. Stanner, *The Dreaming and Other Essays* (Melbourne, Australia: Black, 2011), 50.

104. Confidential evidence 689, New South Wales, ch. 11, in Human Rights and Equal Opportunity Commission, *Bringing Them Home: Report of the National Inquiry into the Separation of Aboriginal and Torres Strait Islander Children from Their Families* (Sydney: HREOC, 1997).

105. Inga Clendinnen, "Lecture 4: Inside the Contact Zone" (1999).

106. Judy Atkinson, "Violence against Young Women," paper presented at the 1994 Queensland Youth Forum "Making a Difference" (Brisbane: Queensland Government, 1994).

107. Rhianna Mitchell, "When Enough Is Enough," *The West Australian*, April 15, 2019, http://enewspaper2.smedia.com.au/wandaily/shared/ShowArticle.aspx?doc=WAN% 2F2019%2F04%2F15&entity=Ar00804&sk=9C6061A0.

108. Rhianna Mitchell, "The Remarkable Women of Yungngora Who Saved Their Town," *The West Australian*, April 14, 2019, https://thewest.com.au/news/indigenous-australians /the-remarkable-women-of-yungngora-who-saved-their-town-ng-b881166647z.

11. FIXING IT

1. Tom Dusevic, "In Hot Blood," SBS, November 22, 2016, https://www.sbs.com.au/topics /voices/feature/hot-blood.

2. Richard Denniss, "Money. Power. Freedom," speech to the Breakthrough conference, Victoria Women's Trust (2016).

3. Ross Homel, Peta McKay, and John Henstridge, "The Impact on Accidents of Random Breath Testing in New South Wales: 1982–1992," *Proceedings from the International Council on Alcohol, Drugs and Traffic Safety Conference* (1995), 849–55.

4. Lori Heise, "Gender-Based Abuse: The Global Epidemic," *Cadernos de Saúde Pública* 10, no. 1 (1994), S135–S145.

5. Lynn Marie Houston and William V. Lombardi, *Reading Joan Didion* (Santa Barbara, CA: ABC-CLIO, 2009).

6. "The National Plan to Reduce Violence against Women and Their Children 2010–2022," Department of Social Services, Australian Government, www.dss.gov.au/women/programs -services/reducing-violence/the-national-plan-to-reduce-violence-against-women-and-their -children-2010-2022.

7. For the ninth year in a row, Iceland was ranked number one on the *Global Gender Gap Report 2017* by the World Economic Forum.

8. Sigríður Dúna Kristmundsdóttir, "Defending Gender Part 2: The Best Place to Be a Woman," *SBS Dateline*, July 10, 2018.

9. Government of Western Australia, Department of Health, Smoking in Enclosed Public Places—the Tobacco Products Control Act 2006.

10. Merran Hitchick, "Australian Smokers to Pay More than $45 for a Packet of Cigarettes from 2020," *The Guardian*, May 3, 2016, https://www.theguardian.com/australia-news/2016 /may/03/smokers-to-pay-more-than-45-for-a-packet-of-cigarettes-from-2020.

11. M. M. Scollo and M. H. Winstanley, *Tobacco in Australia: Facts and Issues* (Melbourne: Cancer Council Victoria, 2018).

12. World Health Organization, "Smoking Prevalence, Total (Ages 15+)," Global Health Observatory Data Repository, 2016.

13. Big Mountain Data, "High Point 10–79," documentary [in production as of 2020].

14. COPS Office, *A Different Response to Intimate Partner Violence* (e-newsletter) 7, no. 9 (September 2014), https://cops.usdoj.gov/html/dispatch/09-2014/a_different _response_to_ipv.asp.

15. Daniel Duane, "Straight Outta Boston," *Mother Jones*, January/February 2006, https:// www.motherjones.com/politics/2006/01/straight-outta-boston.

16. John Tucker, "Can Police Prevent Domestic Violence Simply by Telling Offenders to Stop?" *Indy Week*, November 13, 2013, https://indyweek.com/news/northcarolina /can-police-prevent-domestic-violence-simply-telling-offenders-stop/.

17. "Using a Focused Deterrence Strategy with Intimate Partner Violence," *Community Policing Dispatch* 10, no. 10 (October 2017).

18. "Using a Focused Deterrence Strategy."

19. White House Office of the Press Secretary, *Government, Businesses and Organizations Announce $50 Million in Commitments to Support Women and Girls*, Fact Sheet, June 13, 2016.

20. Rachel Olding and Nick Ralston, "Bourke Tops List: More Dangerous than Any Other Country in the World," *The Sydney Morning Herald*, February 2, 2013.

21.   Alison Vivian and Eloise Schnierer, *Factors Affecting Crime Rates in Indigenous Communities in NSW: A Pilot Study in Bourke and Lightning Ridge* (Jumbunna Indigenous House of Learning, University of Technology Sydney, 2010).

22.   Vivian and Schnierer, *Factors Affecting Crime Rates.*

23.   Council of State Governments Justice Center, *Justice Reinvestment State Brief: Texas* (New York: Council of State Governments Justice Center, 2007).

24.   Greg Moore, *Operation Solidarity—Proactive Approach to Reducing Domestic Violence* (PowerPoint presentation, 2016).

25.   Moore, *Operation Solidarity.*

26.   Just Reinvest NSW, "New Evidence from Bourke," October 8, 2018, http://www.just reinvest.org.au/new-evidence-from-bourke.

27.   Maranguka Justice Reinvestment Project, *Impact Assessment, KPMG* (November 27, 2018).

28.   Maranguka Justice Reinvestment Project, *Impact Assessment.*

29.   Caitlyn Byrd, "In the Fifth Most Deadly State for Domestic Violence Deaths, a New South Carolina Program Sees First Flicker of Success," *Post and Courier*, January 21, 2017, https://www .postandcourier.com/news/in-the-fifth-most-deadly-state-for-domestic-violence-deaths -a-new-south-carolina-program/article_24d2329a-df60-11e6-83b4-d32bf089a0a7.html.

30.   Mike Calia, "Steve Bannon Warns: 'Anti-Patriarchy Movement' Is Going to Be Bigger than the Tea Party," CNBC, February 9, 2018, https://www.cnbc.com/2018/02/09/steve -bannon-womens-anger-is-going-to-be-bigger-than-the-tea-party.html.

Index

About the Author

Jess Hill is an investigative journalist who has been writing about domestic abuse since 2014. Prior to this, she was a producer for ABC Radio, a Middle East correspondent for *The Global Mail*, and an investigative journalist for *Background Briefing*. She was listed in *Foreign Policy*'s Top 100 Women to Follow on Twitter, and her reporting on domestic abuse has won two Walkley awards, an Amnesty International award, and three Our Watch awards.